# Visual information for everyday use

# Visual information for everyday use

## Design and research perspectives

EDITORS

HARM J. G. ZWAGA

THEO BOERSEMA

HENRIËTTE C. M. HOONHOUT

**UK**   Taylor & Francis Ltd, 1 Gunpowder Square, London EC4A 3DE
**USA**  Taylor & Francis Inc., 325 Chestnut Street, 8th Floor, Philadelphia, PA 19106

**British Library Cataloguing in Publication Data**
A catalogue record for this book is available from the British Library.
ISBN 0 7484 0670 0 (cased)

**Library of Congress Cataloging Publication Data are available**

Cover design by Bureau Mijksenaar
Typeset by Graphicraft Limited, Hong Kong
Printed in Great Britain by T. J. International Ltd, Padstow

Itaque architecti, qui sine litteris contenderant, ut manibus essent exercitati, non potuerunt efficere, ut haberent pro laboribus auctoritatem; qui autem ratiocinationibus et litteris solis confisi fuerunt, umbram non rem persecuti videntur. At qui utrumque perdidicerunt, uti omnibus armis ornati citius cum auctoritate, quod fuit propositum, sunt adsecuti.

Vitruvius, *De architectura*, Liber primus. In F. Granger (1970). *Vitruvius on Architecture* Cambridge, MA: Harvard University Press.

*Hence, architects who without scholarship pursued manual skill, did not win the authority corresponding to their labours, whereas those who merely trusted to logical reasoning and scholarship, seemed to chase a shadow, not substance. But those who had thoroughly studied both, like men equipped in full armour, attained their purpose sooner and with authority.*

Translation adapted by A. Hoonhout.

# Contents

# Foreword

When a proper history is written of the thinking and practices which cluster around information design – an awkward term for a still contested idea – due space should be given to two long conversations in Dutch forests, and to the books which emerged from them. *Visual Information for Everyday Use* is one of those books, and one of the things which it does is record the formal content of the second conversation: the Lunteren symposium on 'Public graphics' in 1994. The planners of the symposium, collaborating from their bases in Utrecht and Delft, had a simple idea: to 'bring together researchers and practitioners, to discuss approaches to public information across disciplines', and to establish 'public graphics' as a coherent field of study.

Fourteen years separate the books, and 16 the meetings: in the interval the landscape shifted politically, economically, culturally and technologically. *Visual Information for Everyday Use* charts many of the ways in which information design has been inscribed and practised on this changing terrain. To give just one minor index of change, in channels of discourse: the first meeting, at Het Vennenbos in 1978, eventually generated the book whose title, *Information Design*, echoed that of the print-on-paper journal which emerged soon after the conference; while a legacy of the second meeting was the stimulus to set up two e-mail discussion groups, 'InfoDesign' and 'InfoDesign-Cafe'.

I was lucky enough to be at the Lunteren symposium and have, elsewhere, set down a gathering of critical reflections upon it (*Information Design Journal*, **8**(1), 1995). But this book is more than a document of the symposium: I know something of the work involved in transforming a collection of 'conference pre-prints' – those often unstable, partially-formed, shooting scripts – into the formal shape of a book, a venture which now escapes the conversation's boundaries of time and place for a life of its own. Congratulations to the trio of editors!

What my own written retrospect did not do was try to capture the look and feel of the Lunteren meeting, so my account missed the personal inflections and styles, the excitements and tensions, the human buzz of face-to-faceness: that tangibly frictive stuff which can be grit in the oyster. All this points to more than differences between speech and writing; and perhaps only a fictional narrative could fill such an absence.

Four years on, I am confident enough to believe that there is a collectivity of interest which extends far beyond Lunteren and which embraces the theme of 'visual information for everyday use'. That collectivity is now re-convened by the writers and readers of this book. It points optimistically to what used to be called an 'invisible college', the spirit of which may be less reliably offered these days by the organizations and institutions in which many of us work. Engagement in a real, not virtual, community of interest is the promise of those conversations in the forest. And now, this book widens still further the field of participation.

PAUL STIFF
*Editor*, Information Design Journal
*The University of Reading*

# List of contributors

Austin S. Adams
*University of New South Wales, School of Psychology, Sydney 2052, NSW, Australia*

Simone P. Akerboom
*University of Leiden, Faculty of Social Sciences, Centre for Safety Research, PO Box 9555, 2300 RB Leiden, The Netherlands*

Paul Arthur
*Paul Arthur VisuCom Ltd, 30 St Andrew's Gardens, Toronto, Ontario M4W 2E1, Canada*

Angelique Boekelder
*University of Twente, Applied Linguistics, PO Box 217, 7500 AE Enschede, The Netherlands*

Theo Boersema
*Delft University of Technology, Faculty of Industrial Design Engineering, Jaffalaan 9, 2628 BX Delft, The Netherlands*

Christof Brugger
*International Institute for Information Design, Jörgerstrasse 22/2, A-1170 Wien, Austria*

Robert E. Dewar
*Western Ergonomics Inc., 3355 Upton Place NW, Calgary, Alberta T2N 4G9, Canada*

Barbara L. Glover
*North Carolina State University, Department of Psychology, Ergonomics Program, 640 Poe Hall, Campus Box 7801, NCSU, Raleigh, NC 2769-7801, USA*

Henriëtte C. M. Hoonhout
*Maastricht University, Psychology Department, PO Box 616, 6200 MD Maastricht, The Netherlands*

Karel M. Hurts
*Leiden University, Faculty of Social Sciences, Department of Theoretical and Experimental Psychology, PO Box 9555, 2300 RB Leiden, The Netherlands*

Yves Joannette
*Centre de recherche, Centre hospitalier Côte-des-Neiges, 4565 chemin de la Reine-Marie, Montreal, PQ, H3W 1W5, Canada*

Michael J. Kalsher
*North Carolina State University, Department of Psychology, Ergonomics Program, 640 Poe Hall, Campus Box 7801, NCSU, Raleigh, NC 2769-7801, USA*

Nirmal T. Kishnani
*Public Works Department, Ministry of National Development, 5 Maxwell Road, #16–00, Tower Block MND Complex, Singapore 0106*

Janice E. Leong
*Montague Design Pty Ltd, Office F6, 1 Barr Street, Balmain, NSW 2041, Australia*

Maureen MacKenzie-Taylor
*Communication Research Institute of Australia, PO Box 8, Hackett, ACT 2602, Australia*

Amy B. Magurno
*North Carolina State University, Department of Psychology, Ergonomics Program, 640 Poe Hall, Campus Box 7801, NCSU, Raleigh, NC 2769-7801, USA*

Nicolas Marchand
*Centre de recherche, Centre hospitalier Côte-des-Neiges, 4565 chemin de la Reine-Marie, Montreal, PQ, H3W 1W5, Canada*

Paul P. Mijksenaar
*Delft University of Technology, Faculty of Industrial Design Engineering, Jaffalaan 9, 2628 BX Delft, The Netherlands*

Wim Nijhuis
*Delft University of Technology, Faculty of Industrial Design Engineering, Jaffalaan 9, 2628 BX Delft, The Netherlands*

Michael J. O'Neill
*Herman Miller, Inc., Product Research, 375 W.48th St., Holland, Michigan 49423-5341, USA*

Wendy T. Olmstead
*Indiana Design Consortium Inc., PO Box 180, Lafayette, IN 47902, USA*

Romedi E. Passini
*Centre de recherche, Centre hospitalier Côte-des-Neiges, 4565 chemin de la Reine-Marie, Montreal, PQ, H3W 1W5, Canada*

Constant Rainville
*Centre de recherche, Centre hospitalier Côte-des-Neiges, 4565 chemin de la Reine-Marie, Montreal, PQ, H3W 1W5, Canada*

David Rogers
*Communication Research Institute of Australia, PO Box 8, Hackett, ACT 2602, Australia*

David Sless
*Communication Research Institute of Australia, PO Box 8, Hackett, ACT 2602, Australia*

Michaël F. Steehouder
*University of Twente, Applied Linguistics, PO Box 217, 7500 AE Enschede, The Netherlands*

Monica A. Trommelen
*University of Leiden, Faculty of Social Sciences, Centre for Safety Research, PO Box 9555, 2300 RB Leiden, The Netherlands*

Piet J. Venemans
*Eindhoven University, Faculty of Architecture, Building and Planning, PO Box 513, 5600 MB Eindhoven, The Netherlands*

Karel M. van der Waarde
*211 Boomlaarstraat – Box 2, 2500 Lier, Belgium*

Thomas L. Warren
*Oklahoma State University, English Department, Technical Writing Program, Morill 205, Stillwater, OK 74078-0135, USA*

Piet H. Westendorp
*Delft University of Technology, Faculty of Industrial Design Engineering, Jaffalaan 9, 2628 BX Delft, The Netherlands*

Michael S. Wogalter
*North Carolina State University, Department of Psychology, Ergonomics Program, 640 Poe Hall, Campus Box 7801, NCSU, Raleigh, NC 2769-7801, USA*

Patricia Wright
*School of Psychology, Cardiff University, PO Box 901, Cardiff
CF1 3YG, UK*

Harm J. G. Zwaga
*Utrecht University, Department of Psychonomics, Heidelberglaan 2,
3584 CS Utrecht, The Netherlands*

# By way of introduction: guidelines and design specifications in information design

HARM J. ZWAGA, THEO BOERSEMA and
HENRIËTTE HOONHOUT

## HISTORICAL PERSPECTIVE

In 1962 Conrad published a short article with the title 'The design of information'. In this article he mentioned an accident reported in the newspapers, where a boy froze to death because a search party was not organized – the boy's relatives knew he was missing, but did not know how to operate the public telephone at the end of their street to call for help. Conrad used this sad occurrence to highlight the fact that the widespread introduction of technology intended for the population at large implies that these systems, to serve their purpose, must also be fit for use by those of lower intelligence. Two examples of the kinds of systems Conrad mentioned are traffic and telephone systems. He predicted (rightly, we can now say) that these systems would grow and that with this growth they would acquire features that would make them more complicated to use. Still, everybody would be expected to use them correctly.

Conrad argued that these systems, notwithstanding their complexity, should be designed in such a way that everybody can use them quickly, easily and immediately without any special training or prolonged study. He argued that, during the design phase, the unavoidable user instruction and interface information should also receive sufficient attention, because they are part of the system and should be easy to understand as well. In Conrad's view the application of psychological knowledge as to how people process and understand instructions can contribute significantly to the design of usable instructions and other kinds of explanatory information.

In saying this, Conrad pointed to the fact that ergonomics, a discipline still in its infancy in 1962, should not only concentrate on the physical and perceptual human abilities and limitations, but it should also consider, in the same way, human information processing as part of its scope. He demonstrated the feasibility of this approach by showing how psychological knowledge about processing of text information could be used to develop better user instructions for the new telephone network which had been installed in the building where he worked. He related how he developed a user instruction for the task a user had to perform to transfer an outside call to another extension without going through the operator in the office, and he compared this instruction with the instruction provided by the manufacturer. He based the new instructions on an analysis of the task and a content analysis of the original instructions. The new set of instructions improved performance by 60 per cent, whereas just improving the cluttered layout of the original instructions increased performance by only 20 per cent.

A few years later, in 1965, Chapanis in a publication entitled 'Words, words, words' argued that ergonomists or human factors engineers are so focused on adapting machines to human capabilities and limitations that they ignore the fact that adding the right words to a tool or to the user interface of a machine may produce greater improvements than making changes to the machine itself. He stressed the point that machines had become too complex to be operated without written instructions, and that therefore the proper use of words in user instructions and interface labels should be a prime topic in human factors engineering. He went on to demonstrate this with examples of warnings and user instructions from different areas. Some of those warnings and instructions created confusion in the intended users. In all cases the cause of the confusion could be traced back either to the fact that the information conveyed by the messages did not match with what the end user could be expected to know, or to the wording of the messages, which was just too difficult to understand. Clearly, those who decided on the contents and wording of the messages (insiders) did not make a proper distinction between what they themselves knew about a situation or condition familiar to them and what others, the actual users, could be expected to know, nor did they allow for the level of education of the users.

Another major cause of confusion was the use of legally correct wording for (warning) texts. Chapanis remarked that, because of this, most are beyond the comprehension of the audience for which they are intended. As an example he quoted the following warning he found on a piece of electronic equipment:

> WARNING: The batteries in the AN/MSQ-55 could be a lethal source of electrical power under certain conditions.

On the equipment, next to the terminals, somebody had stuck a piece of paper with the words:

> LOOK OUT! THIS CAN KILL YOU!

As Chapanis pointed out, somebody had translated the message to meet the needs of the audience.

After demonstrating that the effectiveness of instructions, warnings, and interface labels plays a crucial role in guiding people's behaviour, he proposed 'a programme of research on learning'. In the outline of the programme he raised points such as 'user oriented approach to the design of documents', 'user evaluation before the introduction of a product' and 'designing instructions based on task analysis'. Chapanis stressed the point that, given the increasing complexity of machines and even of our very daily life, the proper use of words and pictures becomes crucial. He stated: 'Our modern day machines literally cannot be operated without them.'

Progress in the effective development of instructional texts, in any form, over a period of more than ten years following the publication of Chapanis' article was certainly not overwhelming. This can be concluded from an article published in 1977 by Broadbent, a leading figure, like Chapanis, in applied behavioural research. At that time Chapanis' and Conrad's ideas had not yet been widely accepted by ergonomists, although Broadbent could point to some relevant research that clearly followed the approach they advocated. In his article entitled 'Language and ergonomics', Broadbent still felt the need to make the point that instructional text or words played a crucial role in the operation of machines: 'It is a very clever man who can tell how to operate a public telephone simply by looking at it, without any instructions whatsoever.' What Broadbent wanted to stress here is that, in spite of the efforts of ergonomics to help create a usable product which could be operated without special training, the addition of some kind of instruction or explanation in text or graphics was unavoidable.

Broadbent demonstrated how the results of experiments could be used to produce more effective user instructions. His ultimate goal was to convince ergonomists that investigations into the understanding of sentences and instructions are just as feasible as collecting experimental evidence about the ease of handling of knobs and levers. He stressed that ergonomics should encompass language as an area that merits professional attention because instructions as to how to use a machine or any other interface would, with the increase of complexity of modern-world facilities, play an increasingly decisive role in the successful introduction of those products.

## THE APPLIED BEHAVIOURAL SCIENCE APPROACH TO DESIGN

Those researchers active in a field of applied behavioural science – in the context of this chapter mainly synonymous with perceptual and cognitive ergonomics – implicitly expect that designers concerned with the usability of their products will eagerly pick up the fruits of scientific investigations and use them in their designs. To the disappointment of ergonomists, however, designers do not read their ergonomics handbooks nor scientific journals with the latest research findings. Looking back at the developments over the last 35 years, one can conclude that for most of that time ergonomists did not understand what goes on in the design process. Implementing the right 'ergonomics' is just one of the many aspects a designer has to contend with, and ergonomics usually is not the designer's prime concern. To make it easier for designers to take note of the ergonomic findings, to be true to the fact that ergonomics is an applied science, ergonomists produced guidelines and rules. Many guideline documents have been published over the years. A recent one is *The Ergonomics of Workspaces and Machines: A Design Manual* (Corlett and Clark, 1995). All efforts have been in vain; designers generally ignore guidelines. It seems that ergonomists' efforts were wasted because they did not understand what designing was all about. In the next section is a discussion of why research, and the guidelines that have resulted from it, have to a large extent failed to entice designers to take ergonomics on board.

The publications by Conrad, Chapanis and Broadbent mentioned above will be used to introduce the points to be raised in this discussion. These publications are used for this purpose because they have already been described in detail, and because the experimental methods used in the investigations are representative of applied experimental research in general, not only in the 1960s and 1970s. Moreover, the three publications, and also the others mentioned in this section, are chosen as exemplars because they were written by highly respected researchers.

## Experimental results as design aids

The articles by Conrad, Chapanis and Broadbent have one striking aspect in common: graphic or industrial design as a discipline or a craft is never even mentioned by the authors. The actual designing of the products, in most cases printed text or labels attached to the interface of a machine, is either taken for granted or considered unimportant compared to the content of the messages.

Because it could have been that the instruction card provided by the manufacturer was difficult to read, Conrad 'designs' an improved instruction card using '... very clear type, larger than the original and a bigger line spacing'. These changes alone almost doubled the success rate. With the 'redesigned' instruction card, seven out of a group of 20 subjects could transfer a call compared to four out of 20 with the original instruction card. (As mentioned earlier, adapting the content of the instruction doubled performance again; from seven to 14 of 20.) Although Conrad does not show examples of the instruction cards – so it is not possible to judge how well he redesigned the card – one wonders if the improvement would not have been much bigger had a professional designer done the job.

Chapanis' publication shows supposedly literal representations of warnings. They are either all in capitals, or centre-justified, or left- and right-justified with short lines and large gaps between the words, or very narrow type, or combinations of these aspects. Chapanis demonstrated how the wording of these warnings could be improved, but failed to mention the possibility that a proper graphic design of the messages might also improve their usability. He was so completely focused on improving the messages by rewriting them that he faithfully showed his adapted messages in the original graphic design. In the examples where it applied, he did not even mention the fact that it would have been better not to use all capitals for a running text – a research finding already well known at that time. For Broadbent, too, the usability or comprehensibility of a text depends on its content and structure.

Compared to those aspects, the way a text is printed or otherwise produced is apparently irrelevant. At least he never, even indirectly, referred to this aspect. It is clear that most ergonomists, as well as other applied behavioural scientists, consider proper graphic design irrelevant, or they do not have the slightest idea that it can help to improve the usability of a message whether it is in words, or any other graphic form.

This is not to say that there has been no interest at all in the effectiveness of design characteristics of printed text, instructions, warnings, and other kinds of graphic material. In the period covered by the three publications mentioned (1962–1977) many studies have been published on legibility, readability or other usability aspects of printed text and other graphic products.

In general, these studies all use the same approach. A typical example (although numerous comparable studies have been published) is an investigation by Gregory and Poulton (1970) on the effect of right-justified and unjustified text on the readability and comprehensibility of reading material. Their results show that justification can make a difference, but that the effect depends much on line length and reading ability. They found the strongest effects, for both good and poor readers, when using lines with a length of 4.5 words. With lines of seven words the effect could still be seen in the performance of poor readers. The disadvantage of justification disappeared with lines of 12 words. The approach used in this study, which is common to practically all of these publications, is that a few characteristics of print are varied systematically while keeping other variables constant. This was and still is the accepted method in (behavioural) research. When applied properly, it allows conclusions with regard to the effect single variables have on performance, or to the effect of combinations of variables – the so-called interaction effects. When using this method, or experimental model, it is essential that only the selected variables are varied systematically and that all other variables which may affect performance are kept constant. If this is not the case, the interpretation of the results could be completely off the mark. All this works fairly well as long as the behavioural scientists stick to their own terrain, i.e., making changes to variables which determine cognitive demands, for instance understandability of instructions worded in passive and active sentences, or comprehensibility of positive and negative sentences. If, however, the experiments are conducted in an applied setting, care has to be taken that in defining the experimental conditions the knowledge and experience in the area of application is taken into account. One wonders how much typographic expertise was available to Gregory and Poulton (1970), because when they changed from lines of seven words to lines of 12 words, they also changed, without saying why, the point size from 9 to 11 points and the leading from 1 to 2 points. Typographers know that these changes can strongly affect the character and readability of a text block. One wonders whether the changes in performance found in this study resulted only from the changes in line length.

The investigations and experiments mentioned above as typical examples of the common ergonomics approach show in their manipulation of the (typographic) variables an insensitivity for or unfamiliarity with the accumulated experience and craftsmanship of the typographer or graphic designer. For a text this means taking into account, at least, the purpose of the text and whether or not components other than just plain text have to be printed. For graphic material this requires, among other things, good draughtsmanship, the balanced use of graphic options and good quality reproduction. All this means that the results of the kind of experiments referred to above have no credibility in the eyes of designers, because they do not do justice to the skilled use of different design options.

An early but significant study demonstrating that it is the balanced choice of design options that determines the usability of a design is one by Hartley *et al.* (1974). In 1972 the journal *Programmed Learning and Educational Technology* adopted a new typographic style. The most important changes were: from a two-column format to a single column with double width, reduction in type size from 11 to 10 points and increased interline space, and an increase in words per page by adding two lines per page. Hartley *et al.* (1974) determined the effects of this revised typographic format on reading speed, comprehension, scanning perform-ance and preference. They did not find any differences between the two formats.

The results contradict those of other studies, where performance differences are found for many single characteristics, such as single (wide) column and two-column formats, type size, etc. In the opinion of Hartley and his co-authors the testing of features of print in isolation is therefore not of much use. There is no such thing as 'the best' column width. The typographic features of printed matter should be chosen in relation to the requirements of the material to be printed. Line length (column width) can be relevant in the context of material consisting of sentences grouped in paragraphs, but is less important when there are also components such as tables, lists, diagrams and mathematical formulae. In these cases the constraints of a narrow column might be a disadvantage.

Hartley *et al.* (1974) concluded that the results of investigations and experiments on single design features are not applicable when the usability of that design is determined by the combined effect of many design determinants (e.g. line thickness, type size, illustrations, colours). This means that each product needs a coherent set of design specifications. Consequently, design requirements need to be specified taking into account the kind of information to be displayed, the purpose for which the graphic product will be used, the characteristics and aims of the intended users, and the effect design options have on each other when combined in one design.

## Guidelines as design aids

Designers rely predominantly on their professional training and acquired craftsman-ship when developing their designs. This was probably also the case in the period referred to above (the 1960s and 1970s). Yet, many of them certainly realized that ergonomics might be able to support them with useful information when making design decisions. This opinion was picked up eagerly and cultivated enthusiast-ically by ergonomists and other applied behavioural scientists, who promised to provide the essence of their knowledge in the form of design rules, guidelines and checklists. There are two reasons why they chose this way to make their knowledge available to designers. One was the requirement of the designers that they needed the information in an easily accessible way; they were not prepared to hunt actively for useful information that was 'perhaps hidden somewhere' in scientific journals and books. The other reason was that applied behavioural scientists and especially ergonomists were convinced that they could convert their knowledge into easy-to-follow guidelines and simple-to-apply rules. In fact, they felt that all their ergonomics research should eventually result in guidelines or even rules. In his publication cited earlier, Chapanis (1965) mentioned in a matter-of-fact way that guidelines for the format and other layout details of instructional material already existed, whereas guidelines which, in addition, said how to prepare and evaluate the content and understandability of printed material were still sadly missing. This was the general opinion amongst ergonomists in the 1960s and 1970s, and for many it still is.

As mentioned before, many documents and books with guidelines based on knowledge from the applied behavioural sciences have been compiled. They never became popular with their target audience (designers, engineers, etc.). This is not because the older guideline documents lacked accurate information, or suffered from a limited coverage of topics. Recent publications, which are more elaborate, are also ignored by their intended users, or are considered minimally useful. The users' main objection is that guideline are often too general, or even contradict each other. The conclusion has to be that guidelines based on applied behavioural research do not offer designers what they expect from them.

In the last ten years a number of investigations into the usability of guideline documents have been published (by applied behavioural scientists), all reaching roughly the same conclusions. Designers are not prepared to read academic literature, or to use experimental data. Often they are not even aware that this guideline information exists. However, Dillon (1994, Chapter 4), who discussed these studies in detail, also found in his survey conducted in Europe in 1993 that designers still seek further guidelines and usability standards. They also indicated that they were prepared to undergo some training in user-centred design methods. Dillon's investigations concerned the opinions of designers of electronic texts and documents, but it can be safely assumed that graphic and industrial designers feel the same needs. The rejection of the guidelines by these designers might even be stronger, as they can look back on many years of experience, in contrast to designers of electronic texts and documents, who have not been around as long. Designers are craftsmen and rely on training, acquired skills and experience. The result is that guidelines which tell them what is already established knowledge offer nothing new, whereas guidelines which go against sound practice are mistrusted. On the other hand, designers realize that the effectiveness of many of the products they are asked to develop is crucial. The consequences of a badly designed tax form can be enormous considering the costs to the government because of the unreliable information obtained and to the poor taxpayer who is taxed higher than needed. So, especially when making new products, designers see the need for good guidelines, because they cannot rely on their experience with previous, traditional products.

So why the contradiction: asking for guidelines only to reject them? Apparently ergonomists and designers each have a different understanding of the term guideline.

Dillon (1994, Chapter 4) concluded from the investigations he reviews in his book that designers want guidelines to be formulated in such a way that they can be used immediately in the design process. This means that, in the designer's view, a guideline should be presented as a design specification and not as a generalization of some aspect of human behaviour. This perception of a guideline is diametrically opposed to the way applied behavioural scientists see their guidelines. The guidelines they write can best be seen as attempts to integrate and summarize existing knowledge, experience and expert opinions with regard to generally defined task conditions (e.g. filling out a form, reading user instructions). Deliberately, the guidelines are stated in general terms, because in this way they not only reflect the knowledge and experience originating from many different sources, but they also serve the purpose of a guideline better, i.e., to be useful for a wide range of applications. So, the key to the disappointment of designers with the guidelines lies in the fact that designers expect very detailed and narrow guidelines or rules which they can use without more ado, whereas the scientists give general, broad guidelines. Additional knowledge of ergonomics or some other applied behavioural science discipline is required to be able to decide correctly how to apply guidelines to a specific case. This is in fact admitted by Corlett and Clark (1995) in the preface to their guidelines document where they say: 'References, and a bibliography for further reading are given, but the gradual development of an ergonomics viewpoint and expertise in ergonomics applications will be aided by the introduction into the design office of an ergonomics journal and association with an ergonomics society.'

## BRIDGING THE GAP BETWEEN GUIDELINES AND DESIGN SPECIFICATIONS

In 1996, at the end of a brilliant career of more than 40 years in human factors/ ergonomics, Chapanis published a book that reflects a mature and considered view of the practical application of ergonomics knowledge and of the task of an ergonomist during the development of a product. Compared to the attitude towards design he demonstrated early in his career, the book shows a complete change. Even in his foreword he mentions that close cooperation with design engineers has taught him that the aloof approach of ergonomics was unrealistic. It did not do justice (because of ignorance?) to the other aspects of the design process and did not consider at all the many sets of other requirements (costs, maintenance, material, durability, etc.). Traditional ergonomics produced its guidelines and expected designers/engineers to read them and figure out for themselves how to allow for them in their designs. He writes: 'The thing wrong with that approach is that, by and large, it does not work. Engineers, designers, and programmers don't read our textbooks, don't understand our guidelines and recommendations if they should happen to read them, and don't know how to design to satisfy our guidelines if they should happen to read them and try to follow them. There is no reason why they should. We should not expect designers to do jobs for which we have been trained, and they are not' (Chapanis, 1996, p. xi).

In Chapanis' view it is the task of an ergonomist to translate general guidelines and users' needs into product-specific specifications, i.e., statements of precise, specific requirements that a particular product – not a product in general – must meet to be usable.

Chapanis' book is probably the first book representative of a realistic approach to ergonomics that aims at applying ergonomics information and techniques in a usable form in the design of products. Since the beginning of the 1990s a number of articles have been published advocating this much more subservient role of ergonomics, just as Chapanis does. It is interesting to note that all authors combine a recognized academic status with many years of experience in the collaboration with designers. Prominent among them is Donald Norman, well known for his stimulating book *The Psychology of Everyday Things* (Norman, 1988), who was so bothered by the lack of reality in academic research that he left the academic world to put to the test his person-centred design philosophy in, as he says, 'the real world of business where many different practical constraints affect the final product' (Norman, 1993, p. xiii). Singleton (1994), in an article called 'From research to practice', talks about the different worlds of academic researcher and designer/practitioner. He sees a crucial role here for the ergonomics expert – not the researcher – as an intermediary. This can be a consultant in the company itself, an external consultant, or an academic with specific expertise. This intermediary knows both worlds and is able to reformulate experience gained in other design applications, or in research, in a form that is relevant for a particular design problem.

Both Singleton (1994) and Norman (1995) emphasized that it is necessary that designers publish about their design problems, the design process with its constraints, and the fact that value systems of research and product design differ significantly. Norman agrees that this will be hard to do, because in the practical world of the designer there is no reward in producing papers. The reward is a successful product. The aim of the researcher is a precise and elegant experiment, and the reward is a publication. Norman concludes that there is a lack of communication, because the researcher disappears in the research–publish cycle, with little concern for the real world outside the lab. Designers, but also ergonomics practitioners, are so absorbed by day-to-day problems, that they do not even consider reflecting on the experience gained in past projects.

In an article specifically intended for ergonomics researchers, Vicente *et al.* (1997) try to explain to them that this lack of communication exists because the researchers do not know about the problems designers face on a daily basis. They present a detailed discussion of the nature of the (ergonomics) problems designers have to cope with in the design process and the strategies they have developed to overcome them. Central concepts they use for their description of the designer's world are 'the wicked problem' and 'the science of muddling through'. Design problems are usually wicked problems. These are problems that are ill defined, unique, and have no 'right' or 'best' answer. With 'the science of muddling through' the authors refer to the use by designers of a combination of problem-solving strategies to solve design problems. This means that in actual practice the design process is iterative and non-linear, that new designs are usually based on previous designs, that decisions emerge of which it is difficult to trace when they were taken and by whom, that decisions are based on informal judgement founded on experience, and that the guiding principle is to arrive at satisfying, not optimizing, solutions. Only if ergonomics researchers understand that this is the world of the designer, can they support the end-users of ergonomics knowledge in their work domain.

It is clear that ergonomics guidelines developed without an understanding of the design world could never have been the tools or aids the designers expected. To make ergonomics information readily available for proper use in the design process an effective approach would be to provide the designers with what they need, i.e., ergonomics related product-specific design specifications. This topic will be considered after the connection between guidelines and design specifications has been discussed in the next section. Another approach to making ergonomics information available would be to train designers in ergonomics to the extent that they can interpret the guidelines and derive their own design specification. This last approach means that ergonomics should be part of the schooling of designers, or that training courses should be set up so that designers can acquaint themselves sufficiently with ergonomics as a technology. Teaching ergonomics to designers should be approached at the level of technology, not as an applied science, because it has to be incorporated in a craft. This means that apart from the necessary basic knowledge to support the notion of user-centred design requirements, the hands-on experience in the selection and use of methods and techniques are important topics in an ergonomics course. These are the tools for proper problem and task analysis and objective evaluation of design proposals. Although schooling designers in ergonomics is a crucial aspect in the relation between ergonomics and design, it will not be considered here any further because discussing a curriculum for such a course is outside the scope of this chapter. Before coming to the topic of application-specific design specifications, the next section presents a discussion of the relation between guidelines and design specifications.

## From guidelines to design specifications

Guidelines devised by ergonomists and other applied scientists are adequate to support and guide those same professionals when applying their knowledge in practice. However, when designers, without proper background knowledge and training, take the guidelines to be design specifications directly related to the choices they have to make when developing a product they often find the guidelines to be unworkable and hence useless.

However, the 'uselessness' of guidelines can vary. Guidelines based on physical or perceptual human abilities and limitations can indeed be written as design specifications and are therefore quite useful to designers. The truly 'useless' ones mostly have to do with the specifications a product should meet in order to match or compensate for human cognitive or task-performance abilities and limitations. Whether or not it is possible for ergonomists and others to meet the designers' needs by giving guidelines written as design specifications will depend on the extent to which the task or product being designed involves 'basic' or 'complex' tasks. Basic tasks comprise any use of the human senses (seeing, hearing, etc.), simple activities such as sitting and standing, and simple pattern movements. Complex tasks are combinations of all kinds of basic tasks, usually performed according to a plan. Tasks with a high level of complexity comprise intricate patterns of planned and purposeful behaviour, often with long-term aims. This means that in complex tasks, cognitive (sub)tasks such as decision making, problem solving, recalling and learning play an important role.

For basic tasks, detailed quantitative specifications can be given which always apply. For complex tasks this is not possible. For a printed text the design specifications determining the perceptual quality of the print, such as the minimum or optimal letter size or the contrast needed between letter and background, can all be specified in detail without any further information about the printed text. This detailed information can be provided in the context of requirements for basic tasks, because the task analysis is simple, and the effect of different variables on performance is known and described or even modelled. The requirements to perform a basic task are always the same; they are application independent.

What one has to do, however, to make the text easy to read, understandable and convincing cannot be detailed at the level of a design specification without knowing the purpose and content of the message (a warning, a user instruction), the kind of user the message is intended for (a trained technician, the public in general) and the conditions under which the text has to be used. If these particulars are not known, guidelines are generally worded and act as reminders for a domain specialist (e.g. an ergonomist) of the variables that should be considered in design. They often take the form of general conclusions derived from relevant research, for example:

Coding:
Whenever possible, coding of information should be avoided. If coding is used, the coding system should be simple to use and remember.

Because every complex task is a unique combination of tasks – basic tasks as well as cognitive tasks – the requirements that should be met to support a complex task will therefore be application specific. This means that specifications for the design of task support facilities such as user instructions, warnings and routing signs will also have to be application or product specific.

The product-specific design specification is the end result of a procedure. What is needed to complete such a procedure is somebody who understands the general guidelines – their origin and background – and who knows how to conduct a proper task analysis. Based on this task analysis and the constraints imposed by the user characteristics, the guidelines can be used in the real sense of the word, i.e., as guidance, to describe in detail the design specifications for a product. For a specific product, the coding guideline could result in the following design specifications:

Coding:
Use will be made of shape coding. There will be three coding levels represented by basic geometric shapes, preferably a triangle, a circle and a square. If other shapes are chosen, these shapes are suitable if 19 out of 20 respondents from a representative sample identify the shapes correctly in the test described in Appendix X of this document.

The specification now no longer refers to usability. It is specified in design related terms and, in this example, refers to a procedure to verify whether a design choice is acceptable.

To summarize: guidelines for the development of products allowing the optimum performance of basic tasks usually already exist in some form akin to design specifications. Guidelines for the development of usable products to support complex tasks, however, are usually worded too generally to make them useful. To transform them into product-specific design specifications a task analysis and a description of the user characteristics are needed. After these steps have been completed, the product-specific design specifications can be described in detail.

In the present context standards should be mentioned. Standards are certainly not an aid for designers who want to adapt their designs to human abilities and limitations. To a certain extent standards and guidelines are much alike. Standards are tools for domain experts to ensure that minimum criteria of usability are met. The aim of guidelines is to find the optimal solution. Standards do not indicate how the requirements can be incorporated into the design. Neither do guidelines. How to incorporate them into the design is left to the domain experts. However, what a good standard does specify is the way to verify, usually by a test procedure, that a design meets the minimum requirements set by the standard. In the case of guidelines, the design specifications, which are derived from those guidelines, allow the verification of the suitability of the design solution.

## Providing application-specific design specifications

As argued above, ergonomics training and expertise is a prerequisite for the proper transformation of general guidelines into product-specific design specifications. It would, of course, be an ideal situation if designers had the necessary knowledge and skills to do this themselves. Occasionally this might be the case, to a certain extent, with simple products, i.e., products to support simple tasks, or with a new product which is an improvement of an existing product. For products intended to support complex tasks, most designers have not mastered the necessary skills to perform a task analysis, to determine user requirements, and to derive from this information, with the help of ergonomics knowledge, the product-specific design specifications needed to 'build' usability into the product at a satisfying level. This means that an ergonomist has to be involved in the design process to collect the information needed to arrive at the design specifications for a satisfactory use of the product.

An ergonomist, who will always act as an intermediary between ergonomics information and the designer, can be involved in the design process at different levels of involvement. The most effective way is to have an ergonomics practitioner on the design team. This is what Chapanis (1996), Singleton (1994) and Norman (1995) assume to be the case. An important advantage of this level of involvement is that the regular interaction of designers and ergonomists not only is more effective, the collaboration is also more efficient because the contribution of the ergonomist can be timed better. Another advantage is that, depending on other constraints, an adequate selection can be made of techniques to generate the information needed to guide design decisions, e.g. evaluation of design alternatives using talk-through analysis if there is little time, or user trials with a rapid prototyping model if there is more time available or if the decision is really crucial.

Chapanis, Norman and Singleton who stressed a different approach to ergonomics practice, spoke from experience gained when involved in the development of large complex technical systems. Those systems take years to develop, and the question is not whether or not ergonomics input is needed, but what is the best way to facilitate it. When the product to be designed is an everyday affair, such as a user instruction for a hair dryer, rather than a process control system for a nuclear power station, it is much more difficult for a designer to convince the client that the help of other experts is needed to make a satisfying product. Because guidelines do not help, this is the point where a designer might decide to rely on his/her intuition, experience, take guidance from other designs, and assume that he/she is representative of the whole range of intended users of the product. Experience tells us that this approach is often far from successful. There are many examples where ergonomics input would certainly have resulted in a more satisfying product. Ergonomics input for many information design products such as timetables, forms, signage and warnings, which all have a well-defined function and purpose, can be given very early in the design process. This means that sensible design constraints are specified within which a designer has freedom of choice. With regular progress meetings to evaluate design proposals, the involvement of an ergonomist can be kept at a minimum and still be effective.

This approach to the involvement of ergonomists is not without its practical problems. As mentioned by Vicente *et al.* (1997), designing is not a process that moves in a predictable way from one stage to the next. It is the development of a unique product, and small changes can have far-reaching consequences. This means that an ergonomist must have some control over his/her own involvement and must be kept informed in order to be able to do so. If there is ergonomics input only at the start of a design process, it will often result in disappointment for the ergonomist due to the fact that his/her design specifications are not taken on because somebody has come up with a new design constraint, and nobody has bothered to ask for new design specifications. For the designer it will be disappointing, because the design specifications no longer apply, and intuition and experience have to take over again. For the client, the disappointment is that the product is not as satisfying as expected. Not having the ergonomist on the design team, but involving him/her as an outside consultant, requires a good understanding of what the task of the ergonomist is and how he/she should be involved in the design project.

## INFORMATION DESIGN

The discussion so far has been about how to provide a user with a usable product and how the input from ergonomics in the design process can help to achieve this aim. We started off with Conrad's discussion about the need for the well-considered design of information to guarantee the easy and effective use of technical systems for everyday use, Chapanis' concern about comprehensible warnings, and Broadbent's conviction that user instructions are an essential requirement in order to use complex equipment. The development of all these different kinds of text or graphics to support or aid the use of products or to guide behaviour is referred to as 'information design'.

## Information

The concept 'information' is related to meaning. Without going into a philosophical discussion about the meaning of meaning and its relation to information, let us accept that information is data organized in such a way that it can be used by people to serve their goals. The actual organization of the data evokes in the user a meaning. This organization can come into being because the user generates the interrelation between the perceived data, i.e., attaches a meaning to a set of data. The organization can also come into being because somebody else has processed and presented the data in such a way that it evokes in everybody else (ideally) the intended meaning, i.e., everybody comprehends the information.

An example of the organization of data by the perceiver is as follows: if you step on a dilapidated footbridge and you hear creaking noises, and you feel the boards bending beneath you, you process and interrelate both kinds of perceptual stimuli (data) and classify the bridge as a bridge that will not support your weight. An example of already organized data is a telephone directory. This 'data bank' is organized to serve a purpose: finding subscribers' telephone numbers. The information (the organized data) is presented in such a way that it is easy to perform the task: 'find a subscriber's number'. A directory can also be used to perform other tasks – although that may not be easy – such as finding the name of a subscriber listed under a given number. In this sense one can say that the data are 'pre-processed' to aid performing a particular task, but not processed to the extent that the information can only be used for that particular task. With additional processing by the user the pre-processed data can be used as a kind of half-finished product to generate other information as well. The aim of information design is the effective pre-processing of data.

## The information design product

The transfer of information (i.e., communication) can be effected in many ways. The aim, however, is always the same: we want a person to be aware of a specific 'meaning'. Because very few of us are mind-readers, humans use vehicles, or instruments, to transfer meaning or information from one mind to the other. Some of these vehicles we share with the animal world, such as growling or shouting to impress, or jumping up and down as a sign of happiness. As humans we have a more extended repertoire of body language. We can raise our eyebrows, wrinkle our forehead, and we can express ourselves with subtle differences in smiling and laughing. Our most powerful instrument to communicate of course is language. It is a powerful vehicle to transfer meaning, that has in its written form – a vehicle for a vehicle – enabled mankind to become what it is today with its culture and history.

Written language, as an instrument to transfer information, has been formalized and is largely defined by syntax and semantics, but not completely. Although the way of presenting written information is less open to individual expression than spoken language, the form in which the information is presented is important because it has its effect on the meaning evoking process. The way of presentation does not only affect information presented in written form, but also other graphic ways of representing concepts. Even the style used in the representation has its effects on the evoked meaning. These effects are mostly assumed to add connotative meaning, some meaning the perceiver is not consciously aware of.

Information is developed to let the perceivers know something about the external world; to let them comprehend something. Information developed to be used independently of the originator of the organization of the data has to be given some concrete form. This form is added to the information substance. Substance and form of the information and the user are therefore the determining factors in information design. When developing an information design product, the aim is to extend the boundaries set by instrumental constraints and user constraints as far as possible in the direction of the purpose of the information. This means that the driving force behind a design process (solving a wicked problem) is the possibility of a more satisfying solution than the one that at that moment in the development process is considered as attainable.

Because the solution of the design problem is determined by the interaction between the instrumental and user constraints, Flach and Dominguez (1995) prefer to speak of *use*-centred design. The success of a design depends on the coordination of the two sets of constraints: information with the appropriate means for action and the means for action with the appropriate information. Following the approach of Flach and Dominguez, it is evident that in the design process the user should not get preferential treatment, but neither should other design factors. The aim should be the integration of all design factors, including the human factor. This requires a management approach to design. A designer is a product development manager who coordinates the contribution of all the different experts and is the custodian of the budget and the time schedule. He/she is the focal point for contacts between the client and the design team. A good feeling for the company's 'political climate' and some negotiation skills are indispensable here. A very satisfying solution that goes against the company's tradition will not be acceptable to the client, but it might still be accepted when proposed with the right arguments and in the right way.

Before trying to describe what information design is, it is necessary to stress that it is neither graphic design in the sense of styling nor ergonomics. Both have to do with information design; they contribute to the final product, but are not the sole contributors. The aim of an information design project, and in fact of every design project, is to develop a viable product: a product that compares well with competing products, or serves a specific unique purpose. This means that a new product should satisfy at reasonable costs not only the needs of the user, but also those of the client/producer, and, when applicable, those of the distributor and retailer. Also the consequences of the introduction of the product for the environment may play a role in the development process. From the point of view of the user this relates to: appropriate pricing, easy availability, convenience of use, aesthetic appeal, and safety in disposal. Keeping all these points in mind and ignoring for the moment that in practice design processes are iterative and non-linear, one can say that information design is first the development of an effective organization of data to change this data into information, and then the development of an instrument (often a graphic product) to transfer the information in such a way that it adds to the user's knowledge base, or guides the user's task performance in an effective and convincing way.

## ABOUT THIS BOOK

This book is restricted to static public information products. Static refers here to the restriction that the use of the information artefacts is not interactive, thereby excluding all human–computer interaction applications. With public information we mean that the information is intended for people of all sections of the population, and that, as a rule, the information should be usable without special training. It is certainly true that the presentation of information by electronic means is increasing and is said to be overtaking the presentation of information by conventional means. It is a sobering thought, however, that we are still waiting for the paperless office, promised us some 20 years ago. In fact, there has been an explosive growth during those two decades in the production and use of print and other statically presented information products. This trend is often overlooked in our computer-dominated society. Paradoxically, the very thrust behind this growth is the frequent and diverse application of computers.

What we try to demonstrate with this book is that information design, especially the design of public information, has become an area in design that needs a special approach. An increasing number of designers admit that the complexity of current products, facilities and social structures intended to make life for everybody more comfortable can put excessive demands on people's cognitive abilities. There are too many members of the public at large with a less flexible mind who cannot cope with the 'conveniences of modern times'. Those designers who see a need for information design as a special area of attention are convinced that it is no longer justifiable to let design decisions for information products depend on the designer's intuition and traditional schooling alone. Objective information originating from applied behavioural research about users' needs and behaviour as well as new methods and techniques to evaluate design proposals on their usability have to be incorporated in the designer's approach to a design project. There are, however, considerably more designers who blame the users and not themselves when their information product – developed with the best intentions – falls short of expectations. These designers do not realize that the traditional design schooling fails to consider that two things have changed drastically in our society. One is that the range of users of current information artefacts is such that the designer's intuitive under-standing of the user's task is no longer sufficiently representative (neither intel-lectually nor socially) of the whole range of users. The other reason is that the complexity of the information products has increased to the extent that just con-centrating on an aesthetically pleasing end result will almost certainly produce a design that will fail as a task-support facility.

This book is for both groups of designers – those who are converted and those who are not. For those who agree that information design is an area needing special attention, the book shows the state of the art and might inspire and help them to develop even more effective information products. For those who think that informa-tion design is just the new hype in graphic design, the book shows that information design is more than caring for the externals of a design product alone, and that the aim should be a product that can be used successfully and satisfactorily by the intended user.

Applied behavioural scientists form the third group this book is aimed at. The book should convince them that only caring for the substance of an information design product or devising guidelines by generalizing from research findings is insufficient when asked to help design a viable product. The book should demon-strate to them that familiarity with the design process and understanding their role in the design process is a prerequisite to enable them to provide usable design support.

The book is organized along two lines: state-of-the-art overviews and practical applications, mostly case studies. Each of seven parts (Parts 2–8) is devoted to a main topic in information design. The first chapter in each of the parts is always a state-of-the-art chapter written by a leading expert on that topic. This chapter is followed by two or three smaller chapters describing case studies, demonstrating the use of area-specific methods and techniques described in the first chapter of the part. The topics of these seven parts are: User instructions; Warnings; Forms; Tables and graphs; Maps and plans; Wayfinding information; and Graphic symbols. These topics cover practically all forms of public information products made avail-able in 'hard copy'.

These seven parts are preceded by a general part (Part 1), consisting of two chapters, describing the fundamental methodological issues associated with the use of applied research in support of the development of an information product or with the product development process in general. These two chapters set the scene for the other chapters. They present applied behavioural science or cognitive ergo-nomics as just one of the contributors to the design process, and they promote the notion that the design process should be managed not only on a tactical level, but also on a strategic and policy level. This first part emphasizes the decisive role that usability testing in its different forms can have in design decisions – an emphasis that in turn is reflected in the other chapters.

## REFERENCES

BROADBENT, D. E. (1977) Language and ergonomics. *Applied Ergonomics* **8**, 15–18.

CHAPANIS, A. (1965) Words, words, words. *Human Factors* **7**, 1–17.

CHAPANIS, A. (1996) *Human Factors in Systems Engineering.* Chichester: Wiley.

CONRAD, R. (1962) The design of information. *Occupational Psychology* **36**, 159–162.

CORLETT, E. N. and CLARK, T. S. (1995) *The Ergonomics of Workplaces and Machines: A Design Manual.* London: Taylor & Francis.

DILLON, A. (1994) *Designing Usable Electronic Text: Ergonomic Aspects of Human Information Usage.* London: Taylor & Francis.

FLACH, J. M. and DOMINGUEZ, C. O. (1995) Use-centered design. Integrating the user, instrument, and goal. *Ergonomics in Design* **3**, 19–24.

GREGORY, M. and POULTON, E. C. (1970) Even versus uneven right-hand margins and the rate of comprehension in reading. *Ergonomics* **4**, 427–434.

HARTLEY, J., BURNHILL, P. and FRASER, S. (1974) Typographical problems of journal design. *Applied Ergonomics* **5**, 15–20.

NORMAN, A. D. (1988) *The Psychology of Everyday Things.* New York: Basic Books.

NORMAN, A. D. (1993) *Things That Make Us Smart: Defending Human Attributes in the Age of the Machine.* Reading, MA: Addisson-Wesley.

NORMAN, A. D. (1995) On the difference between research and practice. *Ergonomics in Design* **3**, 35–36.

SINGLETON, W. T. (1994) From research to practice. *Ergonomics in Design* **2**, 30–34.

VICENTE, K. J., BURNS, C. M. and PAWLAK, W. S. (1997) Muddling through wicked design problems. *Ergonomics in Design* **5**, 25–30.

# PART ONE

# Methods and Methodology

# CHAPTER ONE

# Usability testing in information design

AUSTIN ADAMS

## 1.1 INTRODUCTION

Much theoretical attention has been focused on the process of designing three-dimensional products, and of ensuring the ergonomic refinement of such products through appropriate steps in the design process. The view to be put forward in the following pages is that similar attention should be paid to the refinement of two-dimensional products – products that often contain writing and that are designed to communicate something. Both types of product are the result of a design process and there is no reason why questions should not be asked about the suitability of two-dimensional products to their purpose, just as we ask about the ergonomic suitability of three-dimensional ones. Yet, as consumers, we react quite differently to these two types of product.

When one of these three-dimensional products, a toaster for example, does not live up to expectations we complain, we demand our money back, we tell our neighbours, we do not buy from that manufacturer again, and the manufacturer is soon in trouble. Ergonomists and others may lament that we do this too seldom, but at least it is within our realm of understanding. Some of the more aggressive amongst us do it without hesitation, even with a modicum of glee.

But when a communication product is poorly designed we have a variety of reactions. We may sweat it out, trying to read between the lines, or we may ask someone nearby for a second opinion. Sometimes we throw the product – a manual, an instruction booklet, a brochure, a questionnaire – aside with a 'This is incomprehensible!' If the product is an impossible instruction manual we may then ask someone with prior experience of the three-dimensional product to which it refers to explain it to us. But whatever the information-design product we are most unlikely to take it back to the originator and complain. If we contact the originator at all it is probably to apologize for not understanding and to ask for assistance. The product may be incomprehensible, but there is always the nagging possibility that part of the problem is within ourselves, so we temper our complaint, and inertia takes over. Instead of taking the product back with a complaint, we put it aside or, if necessary, we get the required information some other way.

## 1.2   INFORMATION DESIGN AS PRODUCT DESIGN

Let us look briefly at what is supposed to happen during the design process, and in particular at how products are supposed to be refined during that process. Theories of the design process may have been devised with three-dimensional products in mind, but there is no reason not to apply these design processes to their two-dimensional relatives. The simplest and most general of such models may well be that of Popper (1979) (Figure 1.1).

Here a problem (P1) leads to a tentative solution (TS), that is subjected to processes of error elimination (EE) by means of repeated testing and modification, to result in a final solution (P2). The process does not end there, since the final solution will be found to involve further problems, and so on. The important aspect is that error elimination is required and that this error elimination can only occur through a process involving the comparison of observed performance characteristics against those expected.

A more detailed model (Figure 1.2) is described by Roozenburg and Eekels (1995). It begins with an analysis of the problem and stresses the development of criteria to be used in judging the success of a resulting design. The functioning of a potential solution is assessed in a simulation. The observed properties of this solution are used to infer the properties to be expected from the final solution, i.e., the actual product, still to be manufactured. The match between the expected properties, derived from the simulation, and those required from the product (the design criteria) determines the quality of the potential solution. The comparison between expected and required properties acts as a feedback loop in the design model.

Those who advocate such models may decry the fact that they are not observed in practice, but in the field of information design not even lip service is paid to the need to see the design process in terms of such models. Clients who pay for information design may feel that the careful development of criteria, and subsequent evaluation, is unnecessary, and designers may feel, perhaps without thinking about it very much, that they have sufficient intuitive understanding of the needs of the proposed users to be able to design for them without testing. But problems abound in the area of information design.

Perhaps the model shown in Figure 1.3 might assist in understanding the roots of some of the problems. The writer and the designer are shown working together in some manner using a mental model of the user and of the way in which the communication will be used. Within this mental model words, verbal structures, possibly illustrative pictures, and indeed a whole design concept are constructed.

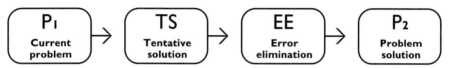

**Figure 1.1** An illustration of Popper's (1979) concept of problem solution through error elimination.

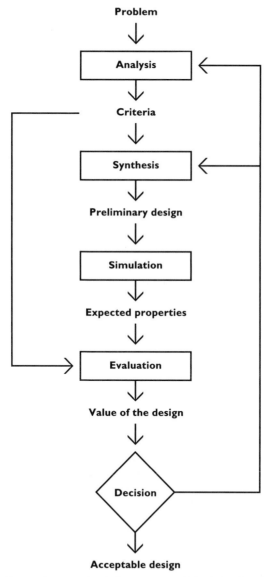

**Figure 1.2** The Roozenburg and Eekels (1995) model of the design process.

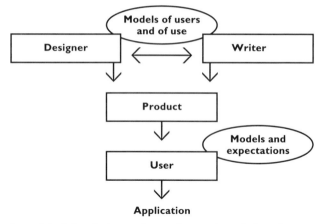

**Figure 1.3** A model of the design and use of a product designed to communicate.

When the user approaches the result, he or she brings a history of interaction with that type of communication product. The user will be of a certain social and cultural background, will have a certain education and ability level and will have a certain motivation regarding the use of the product. For example, if the user is familiar with a given type of product and wants to use a new version quickly it will be very unlikely that any fine print in the instructions accompanying the new version will be read. Thus, if design takes place in the context of a mismatch between the mental models of designer and user, the result is likely to be a dissatisfied user.

For example, consider a designer attempting to produce a symbol for the Olympics to indicate the presence of a money-changing facility. The designer's image may feature a pile of notes. Since the designer thought of this image in response to the need for something to symbolize a money-changing facility, the designer may well assume that the reverse process should occur when someone sees the symbol and attempts to interpret it. In reality, the immediate need of someone looking at the symbol might be to obtain money from a vending machine. The image of a pile of notes might fit quite well with that different need, thus leading the hapless viewer on a fruitless detour – all because the designer has not tested to determine whether the proposed design product is consistent with any alternative states of mind that are likely under the circumstances of use.

With even a simple design product, such as a symbol sign used in a defined context, there are often large mismatches between the designer's model and the user's model. Designers, and clients as well, who have thought through and developed the concepts involved in the communication, or who have otherwise learned to understand them, are no longer capable of putting themselves in the position of someone without that experience. The designer is like Adam or Eve in the garden of Eden – once the apple has been eaten there is no turning the clock back. The designer may try to approach the product as a naïve user would, but that is almost impossible as the critical knowledge cannot be eradicated. The only recourse is to question carefully appropriate potential users who have not been party to the design process.

The situation is like this with respect to the interpretation and use of artefacts generally, but with the products of information design it is easy to locate the source of any difficulty in the receiver rather than in the originator. To avoid such problems the only alternative is systematic usability testing of products against the reality of flesh-and-blood users.

### 1.2.1 Research versus testing

In the present discussion the word 'research' is reserved for that more general activity that is directed towards the accumulation of general principles. When specific answers to very specific questions are required the word 'testing' is more appropriate. Another reason for preferring the word 'testing' is that clients may be more likely to support it as being required to solve the immediate problem, whereas they might feel less inclined to support 'research' with its more general implications.

### 1.3 PERSUADING THE CLIENT OF THE NECESSITY FOR DESIGN-SUPPORT TESTING

Since this may often be difficult, a few words about it are necessary. If the designer raises the question of usability testing it will almost certainly come as a surprise to the client and may well be summarily dismissed unless an appropriate approach is carefully thought through. The right people must be approached carefully, but eventually the factor that will probably swing the tide will be the cost of getting the design wrong. What does it cost if:

- forms are incorrectly filled in;
- symbol signs are not comprehended;
- a financial prospectus is not clear;
- products are incorrectly used or not used at all because of poor instructions;
- repeat sales are lost through inappropriate product use because of poor instructions?

These points are not given just for their rhetorical value. If a client's financial advisers can be persuaded to provide appropriate details these costs will almost certainly turn out to be much higher than the marketing or customer relations department might imagine. Unfortunately, the department that can provide the relevant costing information will not usually be the one commissioning the information-design product.

Often the designer will be presented with already-completed copy. In such circumstances some discreet questions could be asked. How does the client know that the information is what is wanted, or that it will be understood as intended? Has anyone thought to ask users? Perhaps the design-process models given earlier, together with some of the testing methodologies discussed below, will bring to mind a strategy with respect to each project that will enable appropriate evaluation to be included where needed.

## 1.4   AN APPROACH TO EFFICIENT DESIGN-SUPPORT TESTING

Efficient usability testing involves choosing the most appropriate methods for the problem at hand. The purpose of testing is to provide design support and the emphasis should therefore be on obtaining the maximum design-related information for the testing effort. There is little point in offering a client an elaborate testing design that will be costly and will only answer a single question. Much more can usually be achieved. The following sections consider testing from the point of view of where it fits into the design process, and in each situation the need for efficiency is stressed.

### 1.4.1   Initial design and redesign will require different approaches

Where an information-design product is to be designed from scratch, the analysis process – the first box of Figure 1.2 – must be carefully considered. What does the client want to achieve and what assumptions will the user bring to the situation? A structure to the document must be determined, and this structure must conform to the user's expectations. Perhaps a very rough mock-up of the document that includes the major concepts can be produced, with the aim of testing the overall approach.

Where redesign of an existing information-design product is being carried out it may be possible to obtain very useful data from an analysis of the errors made by users of the existing product. Sless (Chapter 11) discusses this technique in the context of form design. If completed forms have been retained then archival information may be available concerning the number and types of errors that have been made in the past. With documents such as manuals or explanatory material there may be very useful information available from help desk staff or others who have been approached when the users of the original product have had problems. The information such people give may be anecdotal, but it can still be obtained and recorded systematically. It may be possible, for example, to go through the document carefully with each such person, recording their observations, and even their suggestions, about each part of the document.

Such an error analysis cannot of itself suggest appropriate redesign, but it can provide a basis for comparing the performance of a redesign. Furthermore, careful logical analysis of the errors will be able to suggest solutions that can be further tested as part of the redesign process. What is this 'testing', however, and how is it to be conducted?

### 1.4.2   Process testing may be more appropriate than outcome testing

In the context of educational evaluation, Scriven (1967) introduced the distinction between formative and summative evaluation. *Formative evaluation* is concerned with the processes by which an end is achieved; *summative evaluation* is concerned with the final event only. Often the terms *process testing* and *outcome testing* are used with the same distinction in mind, and they are the terms preferred here as they most clearly signify the distinction between the two approaches to the usability testing of documents. Sless (Chapter 11) uses the term *diagnostic testing* in the context of forms design to refer more generally to the process testing of such documents. Whatever the terms used, the important distinction is between testing the details of how a result is achieved as opposed to some kind of pass/fail testing of the result.

Unfortunately, when most behavioural scientists are asked to think about product evaluation they tend to think only of the evaluation of outcome or results. The traditional human-factors based approach is to set up several groups, each of which uses one of a number of alternative designs. Appropriate data on the use of the alternatives are recorded, and then statistical consideration is given to the question of whether or not one of those alternatives performed significantly better than another. There are a number of inefficiencies with this approach.

## Outcome testing usually needs large numbers of participants

If it is possible to give an estimate of the difference expected between the best and worst alternatives being considered then anyone with competence in statistics will be able to estimate the number of people required. However, it is very seldom possible to give such an estimate, with the result that a largish number of people is used – perhaps 20 or more in each group would be used as a rule of thumb.

## Outcome testing gives only outcome information

There are times when simple outcome testing is all that is required, such as when the best of a number of completed alternatives is to be chosen. However, the process of product redesign during product development will be greatly assisted by having more than the simple binary yes-or-no result provided by outcome testing. Information about how the product was misunderstood, or precisely what the user was thinking at the time of the misuse or misunderstanding, is needed to assist redesign. Thus more efficient testing, with an emphasis on obtaining critical process information, is required. An appropriate model is the usability testing commonly applied to computer programs. In relation to such testing Virzi (1992) has shown that about 80 per cent of usability problems are likely to be detected with four or five subjects and that the first few subjects will bring to light the most serious problems.

## Outcome testing assumes that finalized alternatives are available

The outcome approach assumes that there is available for evaluation a number of completed alternative designs. In the case of information design it may be relatively easy to make mock-ups. However, with information design the performance of the result depends not only on the specific words and expressions used, but also on details of layout, white space, and so on. In other words, there is little point in performing evaluation with only the text and not the layout. Thus, even with information-design products, standard outcome evaluation with completed alternatives may be expensive and inefficient.

## 1.5   DETAILS OF DESIGN-SUPPORT TESTING

A much more efficient approach is to consider each problem, or group of problems, as encountered and to perform efficient testing to answer the specific questions related to that design problem or problem area. This is process testing designed to evaluate the product-in-use. For this type of usability testing, conditions are set up to measure what happens during the use of the product. Although such testing is not difficult, careful preparation is necessary. Consideration must be given to the precise questions to be answered by the testing. Who will be used as subjects? How will the logistics be handled? How will results be recorded? These questions will now be considered in more detail.

### 1.5.1   The need for explicit performance criteria

Whenever a usability test is carried out there must be a criterion for what constitutes a pass of the test. Such criteria, particularly with document design, may be implicit, but somehow, somewhere, there must be some ideas about what constitutes an adequate document. If redesign is being carried out, then that redesign is presumably being undertaken because of some inadequacy in the original document. That inadequacy can itself give rise to the new performance criteria. Where a new design is involved, performance criteria originating from problems in use may not be available, but performance criteria of some kind will undoubtedly exist in some form in the minds of those commissioning the document.

Unfortunately, without prompting, performance criteria will seldom be discussed. There may even be some instances where the criteria may almost be invisible. For example, someone may have decided that a document is necessary for reasons of prestige only, and that its performance is irrelevant. However, even in these circumstances skilful questioning will elicit some kind of performance criteria. Attention can then be directly focused on these criteria and on how it will be decided whether they are met. It then follows without much further persuasion that some kind of testing is required. Reference to one of the models of the design process discussed earlier may be of assistance in making clear the need for explicit criteria.

Another reason for being clear about performance criteria is that unspoken performance criteria may differ substantially between individuals or groups involved in the design. Some, for example, may be happy with a document that gives general impressions and that requires access to help desk or sales personnel for detailed information, whereas others may be aiming to have a document that entirely removes the necessity for such contact. Thus, both as a guide to testing, and to ensure agreement about performance, there should be some discussion about required performance criteria. In particular, both client and designers must be clear about what constituted the criterion for satisfactory completion of the current brief.

Questions like these may assist in developing performance criteria:

- What is the stated purpose of the product?
- What other purposes might be important?
- Why, where and how is the product used?
- What stakeholders are there in the document, including non-users?
- What does each of these wish to achieve?

As the client assists in answering questions such as these, the need for ongoing testing during the design process will become self evident. Such discussions may make it easier for the client to accept that 'ongoing product testing as required' may be necessary.

### 1.5.2 Why is the testing being carried out?

There is little point in carrying out usability testing just because someone feels testing is necessary. Results in such an instance will seldom be found to meet expectations, and there will be recriminations when it is found that nothing useful has come of the testing. Initial testing might be required to determine the precise problems with an existing document. Such testing can be written specifically into the brief. However, once redesign has commenced it should be made clear that testing, for the purpose of evaluating alternative design solutions, will be carried out, and possibly cleared with the client beforehand.

Careful discussion of what question or questions are to be answered by the testing will help to make the usability testing efficient. For example, a discussion of which alternative wordings of a question or of an explanatory paragraph are to be tested may help clarify the purpose of that question or paragraph. Thus, the fact that testing is part of the design process may itself have the effect of clarifying ideas in the minds of both designers and client.

### 1.5.3 Who will be used as subjects, and how many will be needed?

It is important that agreement on this point be obtained with the client. There may be instances where almost anyone without prior experience of the product would do as a subject. However, from the client's point of view it may be important to provide face validity by using subjects chosen from among those who may be likely to use the product.

As mentioned earlier, research has shown that most problems with a product-in-use will be found with four or so subjects. Perhaps six to ten subjects may be needed to be certain. Where problems are known to exist, and only major problems are to be uncovered, then four subjects will almost certainly be sufficient to uncover those problems. Where an almost-final version is being tested it may be necessary to agree with the client (as a performance criterion) that testing will cease if no major problems are found with, say, ten subjects.

### 1.5.4   How will the logistics of testing be handled?

It will be necessary to set up an appropriate location, possibly in the client's premises, where subjects can be greeted and reassured that testing is for the purpose of evaluating the product, not themselves. There should be at least two staff to assist in testing. One should be with the subject, prompting with questions where necessary. Another should record results. Where the testing is of the general type, here are some examples of the questions that might be asked:

- As an introduction to the task:
  'Read this over and tell me what you're thinking while you're reading.'
- During a hesitation:
  'Tell me what you are expecting at this moment.'
- When the subject has finished reading something:
  'Can you tell me in your own words what it is saying?'
- A few days after reading an information-giving product:
  'Can you tell me what you remember of what you read the other day?'

As with the development of performance criteria, the process of discussing details of what questions will be asked and how they will be asked will force careful thought about the aims of the project, and that thought will itself assist the design process.

Finally, it is often useful to carry out audio- or videotaping of testing sessions as this makes it possible to go over the results again afterwards. It also provides a record that can be demonstrated to the client. Videotaping is expensive, and would only occasionally be appropriate, but some method of recording results should be used in order to enable the results to be openly discussed with the client should this be necessary.

### 1.5.5   The results

The final outcome of the testing session should be considered carefully. Is this to be a redesign of the product, or simply a list of suggestions for areas which cause user problems and which need improvement? Clearly the most satisfactory brief would be one which involves not only the testing but the continued refinement of the product to the point where it reaches whatever performance criterion has been agreed upon. It may, however, be that the client will only agree to one round of testing with suggested improvements. Careful thought will have to be given to these points during the initial negotiations, as much expensive time can be taken up when there is acrimony over whether or not a brief has been successfully concluded.

### 1.5.6 A note on focus groups

A brief word about focus-group testing is needed. To simplify it a little, the focus-group technique requires a group to assemble, under a leader or facilitator, to discuss various aspects of a product. The result is a qualitative statement summarizing opinion. For many in the area of product evaluation this is the only type of testing with which they are familiar, and the only type of testing that some clients will be prepared to fund without elaborate justification, simply because it is all that they, too, understand.

There is certainly a place within the marketing world for focus groups, but it is doubtful if this technique can be justified when details of information design are the topic of concern. In one example that will be discussed later a document giving instructions on using a new product was evaluated with a focus-group technique, and then later using formative evaluation in which quantitative behavioural data were obtained during product use. The focus-group results indicated that customers wanted to be told everything about the product in the document, but behavioural testing indicated that they did not look at the document until they needed it, at which point extraneous information greatly hindered its use.

Many focus-group techniques are possible, but in general the focus-group technique provides a summary judgement giving qualitative indications of participant reactions. As will be demonstrated later, it is not clear that when people use a product they will act in a way that is consistent with what they say about the product when they talk about it in a focus group.

### 1.6 SOME EXAMPLES OF DESIGN-SUPPORT TESTING

What follows are some examples of design-support testing in a variety of information-design areas. The first involves traditional outcome methods in a situation in which the development of the testing criteria was perhaps the most important step. This is followed by a discussion of the use of process-evaluation techniques in the development of an instructional document and then a hazard evaluation package.

### 1.6.1 Designing some railway warning signs

The first example deals with some railway warning signs where conspicuity was one of the problems. The main testing involved two outcome studies, one occurring after consideration of the results of the first. Further details are presented in Adams and Montague (1994). The important point about this example is that it involved careful analysis of the user's task so that the testing could closely reflect that real-world task.

When working on railway tracks in remote regions of Australia often four members of the work team are required to do nothing but wave flags to tell oncoming trains of the track work. Drivers are told the approximate location of the work but signals of some sort are required near the actual site. A plan was devised to replace the remote flagmen with signs, but how should the signs be designed to be clearly visible and also clearly distinguishable from each other? The original designs involved boards 400 mm wide × 1200 mm high with flags on top. One was to be positioned 2.5 km from the site. In case this board was not seen another was to be positioned 2 km from the site, then the third 'stop board' was to be 500 m from the site itself. However, the union involved was not happy with these signs and it was agreed that there should be a redesign and some testing.

The redesign began with some brainstorming to generate conspicuous elements that would nevertheless be distinguishable from each other and that would also result in an easily remembered sequence from the first board to the second and then to the final stop board.

In testing these signs the major difficulty was to determine an appropriate measure that adequately reflected the real-world task. The boards were to stand out at a distance, so conspicuity was clearly involved. But there was also the question of discriminability, since the boards were to be distinguishable from each other and from anything else that might be similar. How should these properties be measured?

One method, discussed by Cole and Jenkins (1980), would be to flash the items briefly on a screen, say for 200 milliseconds, and ask observers to report what they see. The more conspicuous items should be reported more often. However, this method would need many subjects. A more efficient method that would appear to the client to be more closely related to the real-world task was required. One was devised based on the real-life task. Normally a train driver watching the track first sees that there is a sign ahead, then identifies a particular sign. A more conspicuous sign would therefore be one that leads him to say 'I see something there' from a greater distance. More discriminable signs would be ones that the driver could distinguish, that is identify correctly, from a greater distance. The method chosen to evaluate these questions was to use laboratory mock-ups involving a photograph of a rail-track scene on which test signs could be mounted so that they looked just like sign boards at the side of the rail track. Subjects walked towards each photograph until relevant questions could be answered.

The first question was the conspicuity question, 'Is there something there?' When the first of the new boards was compared with the first of the original design, both were shown to be visible from approximately the same distance. Informal questioning of subjects during this testing suggested that the flags on the boards did not contribute to conspicuity. Since the flags would be a problem in the field, a conspicuity test comparing a board with flags against one without was carried out. Results showed only a slight advantage to the one with flags and this advantage was judged to be outweighed by the inconvenience of the flags. The second question related to discriminability and the relevant question was 'What is present?' Results showed that the new design could be seen at approximately 1.43 times the distance at which the old design could be seen, making it clearly the preferable alternative. Thus the testing not only clarified the performance advantage of the new design, but provided concrete results which made it much easier for the person who designed the original boards to accept the change with grace.

An important question in this research related to the degree of reality required in the testing situation. Was the laboratory mock-up involving photographs adequate? Since all the testing involved comparing alternatives it was agreed that the very much more expensive field testing was not justified. It was agreed that the proposed laboratory testing would provide adequate measures of the relative performance of the alternatives being considered.

## Conclusion

The testing had two major outcomes, one of which was social in nature – the testing made it easier for the new design to be accepted as it provided objective evidence in favour of the new design rather than opinion. The other outcome, that was not expected, was that the flags placed atop the original designs added little to either conspicuity or discriminability. There was much arguing about the fact that in reality the flags would wave in the breeze. However, flagmen often simply hold their flag up rather half-heartedly without movement. Also, the flags could wrap around the pole and thus become much less visible.

Another effect of testing such as this is that the process of deciding what testing should be done assists the design team in clarifying the questions to be asked and hence in determining the evaluation criteria required in the design-process models. Answering questions about what to measure forces consideration of what is really important. Such was definitely the case in the present example. Testing such as this is then design-support testing in a number of ways. In terms of resources, the testing took two professionals, with assistance, some three days to arrange and carry out.

As a final note, it is surprising how much money clients are prepared to pay for qualitative testing of items such as logos. Yet they are reluctant to spend any money at all on testing related to objective communication. Perhaps this example, and the next also, have convinced at least some clients that usability testing can be cost-effective.

### 1.6.2   Designing a simple instruction card

The next example illustrates the testing and retesting emphasized in the model of Figure 1.2. It involved the redesign of written instructions to accompany a new product, a facility allowing credit card users to charge a phone call to their normal credit card using any telephone. The facility is offered by the financial institution which issues the credit card. Customers who take this product are given an additional four-digit 'Telecode' which they must use to identify themselves.

**Making local, long distance and
international calls in Australia.**

**Touchtone dialling method.**

1. Dial ⟨1811⟩ or, where this number is not
   accessible (eg some hotels and private
   payphones), dial ⟨008 05⟩ followed
   immediately by ⟨1811⟩.

2. Wait for the voice message.

3. Enter your ⟨—— card number⟩ then press ⟨#⟩.

4. Enter your ⟨Telecode⟩ then press ⟨#⟩.

5. Enter the number you wish to call then
   press ⟨#⟩.

**Remember** to press ⟨#⟩ after each complete
number. If you make a mistake press the ⟨*⟩
button. For recorded assistance, say ⟨help⟩.

**Voice recognition method.**

1. Dial ⟨1811⟩ or, where this number is not
   accessible (eg some hotels and private
   payphones), dial ⟨008 05⟩ followed
   immediately by ⟨1811⟩.

2. Wait for the voice message.

**Figure 1.4**   The relevant section of a card giving instructions for using a credit card
to pay for telephone calls from a normal telephone.

In the present case there was an original design that was known to be causing
users some difficulty in that there was evidence that many who tried the service
gave up without success. Thus there was error information related to the original
design. The information regarding how to operate the service was on a card about
$8 \times 16$ cm that folded in three to become credit-card sized and suitable for carrying
in a wallet. The offending section, shown in Figure 1.4, referred to the use of the
facility within the country.

The important concepts that this card was required to tell the user about were these:

- There is an access code that you must dial first. In some hotels and private
  payphones this access code is different.
- There is a voice message that welcomes you and gives some instructions.
- At the appropriate time you must enter three things, ending each by pressing the
  hash key. These are your credit card number, your Telecode, and the number
  you wish to call.
- If you make a mistake you can press the star key and repeat the entire number,
  that is, the entire credit card number, Telecode, or number to be called. You can
  also say the word 'Help' to obtain additional instructions.

- There is another way of entering the required information that can be used on any phone, but it is the only method applicable if you have an older pulse or decadic telephone line. This involves speaking each digit, one at a time, after a beep. (More details about this method were given on a later page of the card.)

Not mentioned on the card shown above is the fact that if you have a pulse or decadic phone line, and you also have a newer telephone with a key labelled 'Mode' or 'Tone', you can press this key after dialling the access code and then proceed using key entry. Also not mentioned is the fact that for normal key entry you can begin to enter as soon as the welcome voice begins. You do not have to wait for any beep. Both these two points were to be included in the new instructions.

The brief was that the voice cues, at least initially, were not to be changed. Initial testing of the card was to be by giving naïve users fictitious numbers and asking them to make a phone call. But what information would be tested?

Some focus-group testing had indicated that users wanted all the background information. The focus group results suggested that users wanted to know about the difference between pulse and tone lines and that they wanted to know about the voice entry method. The initial brief was therefore to try to educate users to understand the difference between pulse and tone lines. We thought it would be easy to ask the user to dial either zero, or perhaps their access code. If they heard clicks while doing this it would indicate a pulse line, whereas if they heard tones then that would indicate a tone line.

Instructions were made up telling the user to listen while they entered their access code. As designers of these instructions we knew that we were asking the user to listen to the sounds made concurrently with dialling, that is, the sound of the dialling itself. However, we found that users dialled, often without listening, then raised the handset to their ear to listen for the clicks or the tone. It was very frustrating! Why would these users not understand? Of course, if the phone push-buttons are in the handset itself it is almost impossible to listen while dialling anyway. Clearly this method, which seemed such a good idea, would not work.

All that was needed was trials by a few naïve users to make two things clear. Firstly, that listening while dialling is impossible, and secondly, that any preliminary instructions about type of phone line will not be read. Users want to make their call, not find out about what type of line they have! At least that was how it seemed, as most skipped over any preliminary explanation and started dialling the access number. Few users knew there were different types of phone lines, and never before in their experience had the type of line affected the way they made a call, so they felt they could safely ignore the preliminaries. It also became clear that as soon as the welcoming voice began users paid attention to the message and ignored the written instructions.

It was decided not to attempt to teach users about types of phone lines but to lead all users through the key entry method and revert to voice recognition only if they had difficulty. After nine different testing sessions testing various combinations of wordings, the instructions shown in Figure 1.5 were chosen.

| Have ready  • your [credit] card number<br>            • your [code] number<br>            • the number to call | **Keypad entry reminders**<br>• To finish each number press **#** (hash)<br>• If you make a mistake press **✶** |
|---|---|

**Dial 1811**
From some hotels and payphones
you will need to dial 008 05 1811

**Press the MODE or TONE button
as you hear the 'welcome' message**
If there is no button just continue

**Follow the recorded instructions**
Press **#** to finish each number

On some phones you may find
that keypad entry doesn't work.
You will be asked to use an easy
voice entry method instead.

**Unsure? Say 'HELP' at any stage**

• **Fast track**
You can use [this system] faster
by starting to dial as soon as
the recording message begins.

**Voice entry reminders**
• To finish each number say 'STOP'
• If you make a mistake
or if a digit is said back
to you incorrectly, say 'CANCEL'

**Follow-on calls**
You can make two follow-on calls
without re-entering your card details.
Just wait on the line for instructions.

**Figure 1.5**    The text of the instructions after nine testing iterations.

This project illustrated well the need for iterative testing noted in the design-process models. After nine discrete versions, each tested with four to ten or so subjects, a proposed solution was agreed upon with the client.

### 1.6.3   Designing an industrial hazard self-evaluation booklet

Another recent project has been the design of a booklet to assist businesses, particularly small ones, assess workplace hazards. The idea was to help them do this, and hence satisfy proposed laws, without their having to resort to expensive consultants. As work on this project has only just begun, the following discussion will stress the range of methods that might be used in relevant evaluations.

The booklet begins with some explanations and it suggests that a small team carry out the required steps. First it is necessary to discover all the possible hazards, and these include not only plant and possibly chemical hazards, but also procedural hazards such as those associated with manual handling. Then there is a process for deciding how important each of these hazards is, and finally a plan must be decided on for some kind of action with respect to each.

As to each hazard, two things must be decided: the likelihood of injury, and its possible severity. One proposal was to use a grid with columns for severity and rows for likelihood. When high severity combines with high likelihood there will be a number 1 in the square to indicate that this hazard should have a high priority for action, and so on.

There are many other questions about the design of this document, for example:

- Document length. Is it better to give full explanations in a longish document or to have a short document that will result in major hazards being identified and action taken? That is, how is efficacy to be measured, and does the length of the document affect that efficacy?

- Finding hazards. The document includes a prompt list to assist amateurs to find hazards. How should this be set out and does it genuinely assist amateurs to find most of the hazards professionals would find? Can the document's instructions assist in improving the amateur's success rate?

- Rating the hazards. Will the ratings given by amateurs relate reasonably well to those professionals would give? How do details of the priority assessment grid affect the ratings?

Traditional outcome-oriented testing techniques require that alternative documents be set up, given to different users and the results assessed. In the present situation it may be necessary to do this to some extent, but some of these questions can be answered more efficiently by process-oriented testing. By arranging for a research assistant to meet with the people who would be using the document, feedback can be obtained about how much of the document the users read before beginning the hazard evaluation task. Another way would be to sit with the users afterwards and either ask them how much of the document they read, or possibly go through the document, page by page, briefly asking them what parts of each page they found useful. The assistant should mark up the document as the readers go through, or the proceedings could be tape recorded. Immediately after the interview the assistant should write suitable summary notes. In some instances, although probably not in this one, video recordings of the process can be useful.

### The need for writers and designers to work together

An important point to make with respect to this project, and any others like it, is that care must be taken to introduce appropriate design elements into the document to be tested. If the point of any testing is to determine whether particular phrases or concepts are understood then the layout of the testing material will probably not affect the results, although there has been little research on this point. However, if the object of the testing is the use of a document as a whole, for example how much of it is read, details of the document's layout will normally play a crucial part. It is therefore of the utmost importance that the document be tested with such details in place. Writers and behavioural scientists together may be able to test the comprehension of wording, but they cannot go further without the collaboration of designers. Perhaps that is why very little appropriate testing is carried out – it can only occur when writers and designers are part of an integrated team.

### 1.7 CONCLUSION

Designing good information-giving material is a difficult task, but it is one that can be assisted greatly by appropriate usability testing. Users of information products still largely blame themselves when faced with poor design, so we have not yet reached the point where there is a consumer-led requirement for proven adequacy in information design. Nevertheless, poor information design can cost clients money, and it is often quite easy to show this. Thus the push for research-based design must come from designers. On the other hand, designers must realize that the originators of an information-design product are almost never in a position to judge the impact the product will have on naïve users. Hence testing with naïve users is necessary.

It may help us to determine our approach to usability testing if we bear in mind a model of the design process and of why, when, and how testing fits into that process. If we are clear about these things it will help us to convince clients of the need for usability testing. The approach to design-support testing advocated here is that careful thought should be given to gaining the most benefit from the available resources. This will seldom be through large-scale outcome-oriented testing, but will most often be achieved by taking a process-oriented approach in which small testing projects are undertaken at appropriate points in design development. Then, instead of a product that we merely think will do its job, we will be able to deliver a product that we know will perform as it should. We will know how it should perform and we will have shown that it lives up to expectations.

## ACKNOWLEDGEMENTS

The author wishes to thank Mary Montague, the staff of Montague Design, and the late Jim Montague for their collaboration with the research projects mentioned in this chapter and for their ideas and comments.

## REFERENCES

ADAMS, A. S. and MONTAGUE, M. (1994) Efficient testing of conspicuity and discrimination in warning signs. *Information Design Journal* **7**, 203–210.

COLE, B. L. and JENKINS, S. E. (1980) The nature and measurement of conspicuity. *Proceedings of the Australian Road Research Board Conference* **10**, 99–107.

POPPER, K. R. (1979) *Objective Knowledge*. Oxford: Clarendon Press.

ROOZENBURG, N. F. M. and EEKELS, J. (1995) *Product Design: Fundamentals and Methods*. Chichester: Wiley.

SCRIVEN, M. (1967) The methodology of evaluation. In: TYLER, R. W. and GAGNÉ, R. M. (Eds), *Perspectives of Curriculum Evaluation*. Chicago: Rand-McNally.

VIRZI, R. A. (1992) Refining the test phase of usability evaluation: how many subjects is enough? *Human Factors* **34**, 457–468.

# CHAPTER TWO

# Cooperation between graphic designers and applied behavioural researchers

WIM NIJHUIS and THEO BOERSEMA

## 2.1 THE FEASIBILITY OF COOPERATION

Our society has become very complex and grows even more complex at a high pace. As one of the consequences, the solution of many problems requires knowledge from different disciplines. In most disciplines there is a tremendous amount of knowledge and insight available but effective solutions to complex problems can only be reached when information from various disciplines is adequately integrated. This integration depends on successful cooperation of specialists, whereas clear and usable guidance for cooperation is still scarce.

This chapter tries to fill this gap for the cooperation between a graphic designer and an applied behavioural researcher. It focuses on situations where the designer needs specific knowledge about product users and their behaviour that the designer cannot readily acquire or generate on his/her own strength and therefore seeks the assistance of a researcher. The line of reasoning starts from the notion that conflicts will arise easily when two or more people are involved in a creational process. One of the causes for conflict is a misunderstanding of each other's problems and the methods to solve them. This chapter begins with a methodological discussion demonstrating that in the case of design and applied research this misunderstanding can be avoided because there are decisive similarities between the two activities. Subsequently, the design and research activities are considered as subsystems of a design project. An indication is given as to how project management can be used to steer a design project to its ultimate goal: a new, graphic, product.

## 2.1.1   Design compared with applied research

The general question of how to incorporate research activities effectively into a design project cannot be answered by considering daily design activities. At this operational level there are innumerable procedures to create different solutions for all types of design problems. The approach taken here is to examine design, and later on also applied research, not at the operational level but at the strategic and tactical levels. The hierarchy of strategy, tactic and operation is common in the disciplines of systems analysis and management (e.g. Miser and Quade, 1988). Strategies are chosen at the level of policy, the most general level of management procedures.

The activity of design is aimed at filling a need by creating a new product or enhancing an existing one. In the literature on design and design methodology, many general models of design can be found. After evaluating a large number of these models, Roozenburg and Eekels (1995) defined design as a cycle (Figure 2.1a) with analysis, synthesis, simulation and evaluation as its main steps. After the evaluation a decision is made on how to proceed. Such a decision can be to accept the design solution or to try and improve the result by iterating a number of steps of the design cycle. Graphic design, as a special type of design, is concerned with a specific type of product and therefore has its own particular difficulties and procedures. However, at a more abstract level graphic design fits in the design cycle model.

Design, or product development, can be regarded as a form of problem solving. As a consequence, problem-related data play an essential role in every design project. This information is used to define the problem, to generate solutions, to draw up criteria, and to test the solutions in order to decide whether they solve the problem. Usually, designers collect the data they need themselves using various sources, such as literature, brochures of competing products, people involved (e.g. manufacturer, retailer, user), comparable products and relevant situations. Sometimes, however, the information needed is not available and has to be derived from applied empirical research. When this is the case, calling in a researcher can be necessary.

As with design, research, and also applied research, can be defined as a problem-solving activity. A researcher strives for knowledge that fills a gap. Despite this analogy between design and research, the cooperation between a designer and a researcher can be hampered for instance by different behavioural codes, professional jargon, differences in dealing with aspects of time and costs, deviating opinions about the validity or usefulness of results. A designer aims for a viable product within practical constraints, whereas a researcher, even in the field of applied research, typically seeks new knowledge that can be generalized to a variety of situations and conditions. The worlds of design and research can seem miles apart but the interests of the users who need a new product are served best by effective cooperation. Below it is argued that a clear understanding of strategic models of both design and applied research can serve as a starting point for mutual understanding between representatives of the two disciplines.

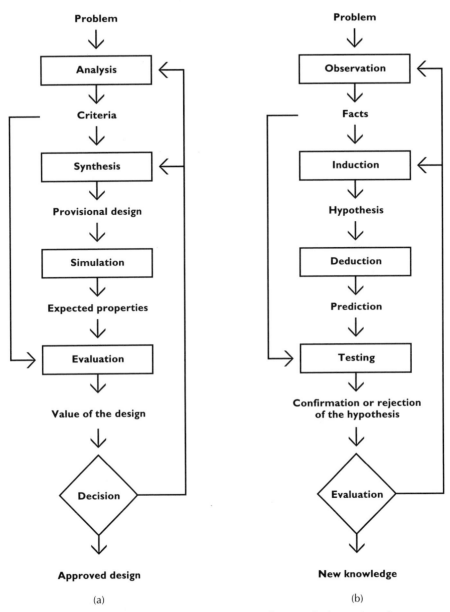

**Figure 2.1**   Basic cycle of design (a) and empirical research (b) as given by Roozenburg and Eekels (1995).

## 2.1.2  Strategic models of design and applied research

A strategy is a finalistic normative model, which means that it does not describe reality as it is but how it should become eventually. This description fits both design, in which a new product is sought, and research, which aims at adding to existing knowledge. A strategic model is appropriate when two or more intelligent subsystems (persons, groups) interact on the basis of incomplete information about each other (Lievegoed, 1991). Designers and researchers who are not fully informed about each other is the rule rather than the exception. Interaction of subsystems with incomplete information about each other has proven to be a complicated relation. Mostly, the interaction amounts to a clever form of negotiation (Lievegoed, 1991). Negotiation can end in two ultimate situations: joint consultation, based on a common aim and with open sharing of relevant information, or conflict, if aims preclude each other and information is withheld.

For negotiation to develop into joint consultation it is a prerequisite that the researcher understands the strategic level of a design process and the designer understands the strategic approach of research. Mutual understanding is best supported by showing designers and researchers that their professions have more in common than they probably assume. For this purpose, congruent strategic models of design and research are developed in the rest of this section.

Before strategic models of design and research can be discussed, the building and use of models in practice need to be explored. Models help to understand reality, they reduce objects and situations to their quintessence, and increase insight into the main connections (Bailey, 1983). An unavoidable side-effect of these benefits is the loss of detail due to simplification of elements, relations, and their time-bounded status. Models are also restricted because they are developed to serve a special purpose in a specific situation to help the originators understand certain aspects of reality. A lack of accuracy, consistency or equality in abstraction of elements and relations may not affect adversely the use of the model by the originators themselves. However, from the moment such a model is published and is used by others under other conditions and for other purposes, the weaker aspects of a model may seriously limit its usefulness. This should be kept in mind during the search for similarities between design and research with the use of available models.

As mentioned earlier, Roozenburg and Eekels (1995) presented a strategic model of design: the design cycle (Figure 2.1a). In addition, they analysed De Groot's (1969) widely recognized methodological view on empirical behavioural research. De Groot describes this research as a cycle consisting of observation, induction, deduction, testing and evaluation. In an attempt to compare the strategies of design and research, Roozenburg and Eekels (1995) developed a model of De Groot's (1969) description of empirical research (Figure 2.1b). They constructed this model to be congruent with their model of design (Figure 2.1a) and contrasted the corresponding elements of both cycles: analysis with observation, synthesis with induction, simulation with deduction, evaluation with testing, and decision with evaluation. There appeared to be no convincing similarity in the third, fourth and fifth step. Therefore, Roozenburg and Eekels (1995) concluded that the cycles of design and research are principally different and that the two professions each require their own methodology.

However, there are at least two possibilities to develop strategic models for design and research that are congruent and can be expected to adequately reflect analogous processes in the two professions. Firstly, in the research cycle induction and deduction are two forms of reasoning. By taking these two steps together the strategic model of research can be reformulated as: observation, reasoning, testing and evaluation. Secondly, the design cycle can be made more similar to the research cycle of Figure 2.1b by splitting the synthesis into two steps: functional design and material design (e.g. Hubka, 1982; Pahl and Beitz, 1984; Verein Deutscher Ingenieure, 1993). The strategic model of design thus becomes: analysis, functional design, material design, simulation, evaluation and decision. These two possible changes are in fact tactical rearrangements, which are, not surprisingly, necessary because the present purpose of the models does not coincide with the intentions of their originators. De Groot (1969) highlights the important step of reasoning by choosing a higher level of resolution. Roozenburg and Eekels (1995) were familiar with models that itemize the synthesis step but they aimed in particular for the most compact and basic model.

In Figure 2.2 a compromise is chosen between the two possible rearrangements just mentioned. The number of steps in the design cycle is not changed but in the synthesis two substeps are introduced, which emphasizes the complexity of this step. In the research cycle, induction and deduction are taken together in one step, reasoning. In addition to this compromise, the models in Figure 2.2 are adapted on a few minor points. A discussion of these points is beyond the scope of this chapter. It suffices to state that the aim of these changes is to make the models optimally instrumental in comparing the activities of designers and researchers.

### 2.1.3   Conclusion

Effective teamwork, or joint consultation, of a designer and a researcher requires an understanding of each other's discipline. It was argued that in this respect knowledge of models of design and applied research at the strategic level can be useful. Figure 2.2 shows congruent strategic models of design and applied research. In the next section, the similarities and differences between the processes covered by the models are discussed.

## 2.2   SIMILARITIES AND DIFFERENCES BETWEEN THE STRATEGIC MODELS OF DESIGN AND APPLIED RESEARCH

### 2.2.1   Problem

Both models of Figure 2.2 start with a problem but these problems are not of the same nature. The design problem is the lack of an acceptable product; the applied

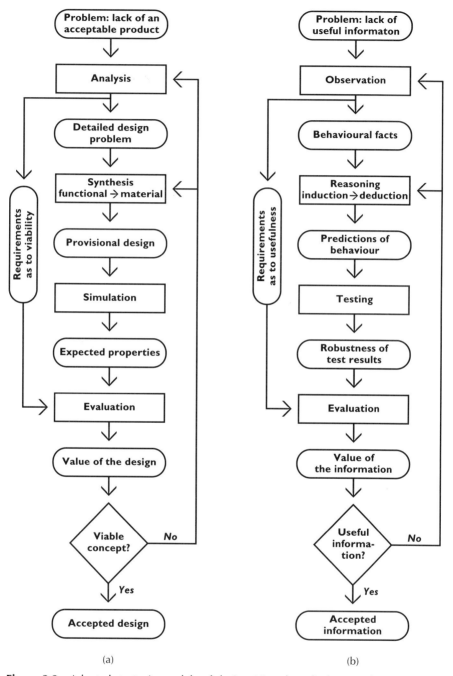

**Figure 2.2**   Adapted strategic models of design (a) and applied research
(b) Meaning of the shapes: rectangle, procedure; rectangle with rounded corners,
result; diamond, decision-making process; arrow, relation and chronological order.

research problem is the lack of sufficient information about behavioural aspects in relation to the product. It is important to note that the research problem is derived from the design problem. The research problem does not exist until the designer realizes that there is a need for product-specific behavioural information. This dependency is common to all types of applied research and constitutes the difference between applied and fundamental research. Some observations about the design problem will now be presented.

A design problem is usually not 'owned' by the designer but by a client of the designer. A skilled designer does not accept every design problem. The decision of a designer to accept it or not depends on the answers to the following questions:

- Is the problem really a design problem, or do good solutions already exist?
- If it is a real design problem, can it be solved within the constraints of knowledge, money and time?
- If the way out is not quite clear, are there any alternatives, and is it possible to generate, in time, specific knowledge during the design process?

If the answers to these questions are satisfactory, i.e., if the estimated chance of success is high enough to start a design process, then the designer can decide to accept the assignment.

A behavioural information problem and, consequently, the need to make contact with an applied behavioural researcher can emerge during the preliminary examination of the design problem. At this early stage it may be necessary that a researcher makes an inventory of existing relevant knowledge. Information problems can, of course, also arise at later stages of a design process, but the more experienced and professional the designer is, the sooner a researcher will be involved.

Before accepting a research problem the researcher needs answers to questions that are similar to those of the designer:

- Is applied research needed to solve the problem, or is there already enough relevant information about the topic?
- If it is an applied research problem, can it be solved within the constraints of available knowledge, money and time?
- If the way out is not quite clear, are there alternatives to help the designer when, in the worst case, the research fails to produce useful results?

An extra difficulty in answering these questions is the indirect relation between the researcher and the client. The researcher depends on the designer's interpretation of the design problem. Therefore, the researcher has a high interest in a correctly defined design problem.

However, the availability of an explicit and well-defined design problem cannot be taken for granted. The principal problem here is that design problems are ill-defined by nature (e.g. Archer, 1979; Cross, 1989), but daily practice suggests that many designers do not even examine the design problem as thoroughly as they could. What they seem to love most is the development of possible solutions, and therefore they often want to start the design cycle at the synthesis phase. This means that the project lacks a strategic approach: the question of what reality should be like at the end of the project receives insufficient attention. Designers indulge too easily in their own creativity. They also know that this attitude gives them a certain flair, which is sometimes seen as a feature of quality. However, it has been shown (Nijhuis, 1995) that bad product designs have more to do with a lack of good problem definition and data collection than with a lack of originality and creativity of the designer. Analogous to designers, researchers are not always very interested in the nature of their (research) problem. Much applied research is devised without its aim being sufficiently clear. In other words: a strategic approach, specifying the aim, is lacking here also.

For cooperation to be successful the designer and the applied researcher should share a basic strategic interest. If this is absent, cooperation is already threatened at the point of departure: the problem definition. Although joint consultation is still possible, conflicts will easily develop.

The discussion above of the design and research problem has shown that they are different, but also that there are major similarities between the questions designers and applied researchers should answer. These similarities are the basis for successful cooperation.

## 2.2.2  Analysis and observation

Once a – properly formulated – problem has been accepted, the design and research strategies start with, respectively, analysis and observation. To determine in which aspects these two tactics differ and/or correspond, it is necessary to go to a higher level of resolution, i.e., to switch from tactic to operation. An outline of operational activities of designers and applied behavioural researchers is presented below.

What do designers do when they analyse a design problem? Basically, a designer considers the situation as it is now and thinks about how it should be, taking into account requirements that the new product should meet. When formulated in general terms, these requirements are always the same: ease of use, in combination with, for instance, cheap and easy manufacturing; a handy way of distribution; and the possibility to remove and dismantle the product without environmental trouble. These requirements may seem simple; they just need some quantification, and then the designer should be able to start and create a new product that meets the requirements and solves the design problem. The quantification of these requirements, however, can be a first and delicate obstacle on the way to a new product. Difficulties arise because, in many cases, the requirements are rather subjective, depend on the state of the art in the disciplines involved, and are sometimes conflicting with one another. All together, this can seriously endanger the synthesis process. Despite these difficulties, the set of requirements should be well balanced to give the synthesis a chance of success. At the end of the analysis, a designer should have reached the following intermediate results:

- a detailed design problem: an adequate description of the design problem as a whole and its main parts;

- provisional procedures for the synthesis, based on an understanding of the alternative ways to arrive at feasible solutions;

- requirements concerning the viability of the new product: a list of criteria to steer the design process.

So much for the task of the designer during the phase of analysis. Now, what does a researcher do at the operational level during the observation phase, and how does this compare to the activities of a designer? According to De Groot (1969) a researcher collects facts and ideas and categorizes and abstracts these in relation to certain criteria. Researchers often use implicit assumptions to steer the process of searching for facts and ideas. The observation should yield three intermediate results:

- facts and ideas about behaviour, relevant to the use of the product;

- provisional hypotheses, of which the researcher expects that they can be formulated more formally during the reasoning phase;

- requirements concerning the usefulness of the knowledge that is needed.

The better the research problem is defined, the more useful the results of the observation will be, and the easier it will be to achieve these results.

It is concluded that at the tactical level of analysis and observation the general descriptions of the activities of a designer and an applied researcher are highly similar: both collect, select, record, and, especially, analyse data within a certain context in preparation for the next phase.

### 2.2.3   Synthesis and reasoning

The description of a design problem or an applied research problem, however well-defined, never leads directly to its solution. The essence of a design problem is the need to develop a product that fulfils a certain function. The intended result of the synthesis is a provisional design of the product. Usually, it is impossible to create an optimal design in one single go, due to too many degrees of freedom and uncertainties at the start of the synthesis. For this situation Hubka (1982) recommends that the designer creates, successively, functional, potential and materialized solutions. A functional solution defines the working principle and functional structure of the product. A materialized solution in addition, completely describes the product's forms and materials. A potential solution lies between a functional and a materialized solution: geometry and materials are defined roughly up to a level that allows fruitful discussion with people involved. The feasibility of a solution depends on its expected performance in the processes of producing, selling, using, and removing. Sometimes preferences as to working principles, forms, and materials can be established as early as in the phase of problem definition. In many cases, however, final decisions cannot be made until the end of the synthesis by evaluating materialized solutions.

An applied behavioural researcher can provide information for the evaluation of all three types of solutions. Figure 2.3 (from Marinissen, 1993) shows an attempt, by an experienced designer, to model the link between research on the use of a product and the level of concreteness of the product design, from sketches to a prototype. Marinissen (1993) developed this model by combining the design cycle of Figure 2.1a with a number of research activities concerning the use of the new product. Compared with the design cycle, the tactical phases of analysis and synthesis are replaced by a number of operations, in the squares of Figure 2.3. The results of the operations are positioned between the squares. The tactical phases of simulation, evaluation and decision are apparently left out. Simulation and evaluation seem to be condensed into one operational step, observation, which is placed in a parallel. Observation here is not to be confused with the tactic observation of the research model of Figure 2.2. The parallel suggests that the activity observation can be executed separately, for instance by a researcher. The strong point of the model is that it can be of assistance in discussions about the relation between the development of solutions and the observation of their use. On the other hand, the model is somewhat oversimplified and may become a threat to effective cooperation if the designer and the researcher do not realize that the situation in real life is usually more complex.

An important feature of the model of Figure 2.3 is the policy to develop solutions in concentric, or iterative, steps from functional structures up to a materialized solution. Policy, as mentioned before, is the top level of the hierarchy: policy, strategy, tactic, operation. The essence of the concentric approach of the design process is that the designer, explicitly or implicitly, passes through the design cycle more than once. A model of a concentric-cyclic design process is shown in Figure 2.4. Per cycle the design result becomes more concrete, and its use and other aspects can be examined from a rough up to a very detailed level. As a consequence, the information needed to proceed with the design process can be collected increasingly more purposefully. An additional advantage of a concentric-cyclic design process is the possibility to reformulate the design problem step by step in a more concrete and quantified way. Researchers, when aware of the concentric design approach, are better able to tune the content of their contribution and its level of detail to the design process.

Before going deeper into the question of cooperation, an analysis is needed of what happens during the creative process of reasoning by a researcher. Reasoning consists of two mental processes: induction and deduction. Induction implies that the researcher formulates hypotheses, relevant to the use of the product and based on the behavioural facts and ideas collected during the observation. De Groot (1969) describes hypotheses as assumptions about connections between phenomena in reality from which verifiable predictions can be derived. The specification by the researcher of these predictions is called deduction. The process of deduction also includes empirical or experimental particularization of terms, for instance specifying an operational definition. Predictions have to be explicit and precise to make their verification possible. If little knowledge relevant to the research problem is

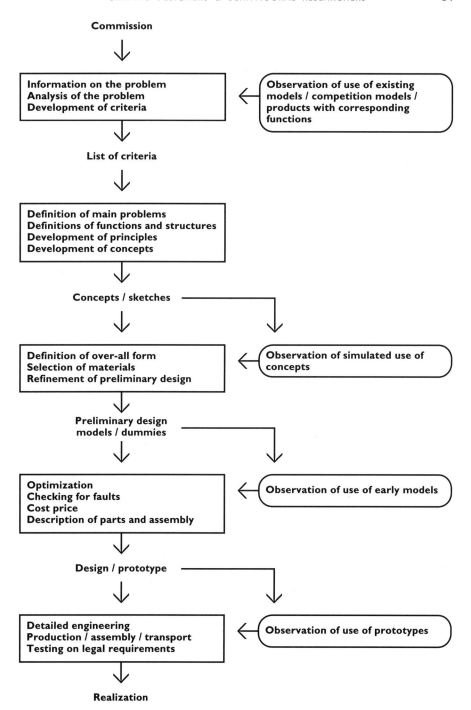

**Figure 2.3**   Relation between the phases in a design project and options for different kinds of user tests (from Marinissen, 1993, with permission from The Ergonomics Society of Australia).

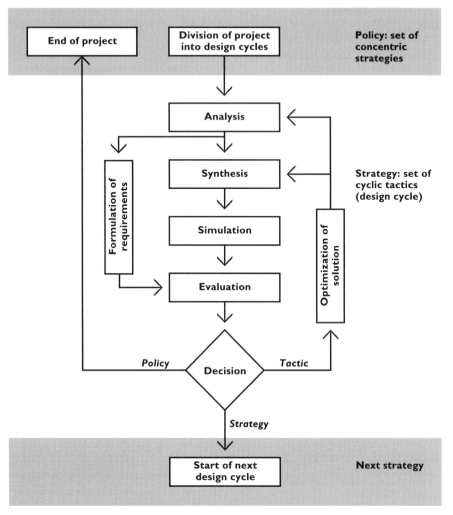

**Figure 2.4**  Model of a concentric-cyclic design process. At the end of each design cycle there are three options: to try and enhance the quality of the solution (a tactical decision), to start the next design cycle (a strategic decision), or to end the project because an adequate solution is achieved or seems unfeasible (a policy decision).

available, it can be difficult to arrive at verifiable predictions in one step. Analogous to the design process, a concentric process may then be the appropriate approach.

The creative phase in both disciplines is a tense one. The chances of success of the phases of synthesis as well as reasoning depend strongly on the availability of general knowledge and the degree to which this knowledge can be interpreted in relation to the design or research problem at hand. As a consequence, the creative phases can only be controlled to a certain extent, and success cannot be enforced. If this is known to the designer as well as to the researcher, they can balance the relevance of specific new information to the design process and the research needed to generate this information. As a result, the research problem can be adapted to meet the new aims.

Cooperation between designer and researcher during the synthesis should be close. When the designer regularly presents the evolving design solutions to the researcher, the researcher can better control the process of reasoning and tune it more precisely to the knowledge needed. It should be noted again here that the contact between designer and researcher is lacking completely in Figure 2.2. This is a great simplification of reality. There should be even more contact than suggested in Figure 2.3. The type of model shown in Figures 2.2 and 2.3, however, is not suitable to show a large number of operational activities. This requires planning models, like for instance the network technique, the discussion of which is beyond the scope of this chapter.

In conclusion: both synthesis and reasoning are creative processes, the success of which depends heavily on the amount of knowledge available. If it proves difficult to arrive in one single step at a promising design solution or verifiable predictions about people's behaviour, both the designer and the researcher should switch over to a concentric approach. At the operational level there are, admittedly, very few similarities between the processes of synthesis and reasoning, but at the tactical level there does not seem to be much difference.

### 2.2.4 Simulation and testing

The purpose of the simulation phase of design is to establish the properties and the performance of the new product. The crucial point here is that this has to be done before the product has been actually produced or used. This means that the designer has to imagine the product's functioning, using her or his own and others' experience, general information, and the results of specific tests and experiments. In other words, the numerous assumptions made during the synthesis of the provisional product have to be tested now for their correctness. In this respect the designer does not differ much from the researcher who has formulated one or more predictions that have to be checked during the testing phase. The results of the test or experiment should show whether a prediction is correct, and whether the hypothesis is supported or not.

To simulate the new product's functioning, some kind of model of the product has to be constructed. The typical approach of designers is to make sketches or a three-dimensional dummy. There are, however, other types of model that may be more adequate. Based on the kind of similarity between the original and the model, Roozenburg and Eekels (1995) distinguish four types of model: structure models, iconic models, analogue models, and mathematical models. In practice, models often fall under more than one type. When an applied behavioural researcher is involved in the design project to verify assumptions and predictions about the behaviour of the product's users, it is crucial that the researcher and the designer thoroughly discuss the choice of an adequate type of model. The efficiency and effectiveness of the tests depend on this choice.

The success of involving an applied researcher during the simulation phase of a design project can be threatened in a number of ways. Firstly, some designers have an aversion to leaving the simulation, and thus part of the evaluation, to someone else. They expect trouble and more work. Secondly, in a typical design project not much time is left for the simulation; most of it has been used up during the synthesis. A third threat is that in most cases the generalizability of the test results is restricted. The natural attitude of researchers is to seek rather general knowledge, whereas a design project requires specific experiments, the results of which are mostly not highly generalizable. However, when a designer and a researcher cooperate with conviction during the simulation, and especially when the researcher was already involved from the start of the project, the researcher can develop adequate tests that steer the design process effectively. Under these circumstances, the initiative in the design project can even switch from the designer to the researcher in the simulation phase.

It is concluded that the tasks of a designer and an applied researcher during the simulation and testing phases have much in common. In these phases, both put their earlier assumptions to the test.

### 2.2.5  Evaluation of design and knowledge

The simulation of the product's functioning should have yielded an impression about the properties of the new product. Using this impression and the requirements that resulted from the analysis, the designer now has to decide about the viability of the new product. This judgement can be difficult to make, because a product design seldom meets all requirements. This implies that decisions have to be made about the relative importance of the requirements. Therefore, the evaluation of a new product as a whole is often rather subjective. Because of this subjectivity, it is important that the evaluation is conducted in a structured manner, and that the way one has arrived at the conclusions is recorded. Only then is it possible to revert, when necessary, to this evaluation process during a following concentric cycle.

The applied researcher, on the other hand, has to evaluate the knowledge obtained as to its usefulness for the design process. The evaluation should be based on the requirements agreed upon previously in a discussion by the designer and the researcher. Nevertheless, this evaluation, too, will almost inevitably have an interpretative character. One should be on guard against the tendency of researchers to overestimate the importance of their test results, which cover only part of the evaluation of the new product. Such overestimation may endanger a viable integral solution to the design problem.

### 2.2.6  Decision on viability and usefulness

The designer has to develop a viable product, which means that the product can compete successfully with comparable products. In order to do so, the new product should satisfy a need at reasonable costs to the producer, the distributor, the user and the environment. If it is decided that the product design meets these conditions, the design project is accomplished, and production can start.

The results of research are useful for a design project if they contribute to the realization of a certain aspect of the product design. The information resulting from the investigations of the researcher is just as useful when it demonstrates the inadequacy of a proposed solution, even if, as a consequence, the whole design project fails to yield a successful new product. However, if a researcher shows, objectively, that a product design is not feasible, a well-balanced functional and emotional relationship between the designer and the researcher is needed to prevent a professional discussion from turning into a personal conflict.

### 2.2.7   Conclusion

In this section, design and applied research were compared step by step. In contradiction with the view of Roozenburg and Eekels (1995) it was argued that there is a close analogy between the processes of product design and applied behavioural research. Not only is it possible to construct congruent strategic models of the two disciplines (Figure 2.2), but it is also shown that the corresponding tactics are remarkably similar. Differences exist only at the operational level, where specific skills and methods are used to achieve intermediate results. The basis for cooperation between a designer and an applied researcher should be a joint interest in final and intermediate results, the acceptance of each other's specific methods of working, and the use of strategic models of design and applied research. In the next section the focus is shifted to the practical management of a design project.

### 2.3   BASIC MANAGEMENT METHODS TO COORDINATE DESIGN AND APPLIED RESEARCH ACTIVITIES

An understanding of the strategic and tactical similarities and the operational differences between design and applied behavioural research is a necessary condition for cooperation between representatives of the two disciplines. The strategic models of Figure 2.2 are not a sufficient basis, however, for the daily practice of a design project. In this section, it is shown how a systems approach of management (Johnson *et al.*, 1963) can be used to develop the strategic models into a network of effectively ordered operational activities of both designer and applied researcher and how this management approach can be used to steer these activities, and their results, to the final goal: a new product.

Why is it necessary to talk about management when two professionals, who know their own discipline and are familiar with the other, are working together? The reason for this is that the disciplines of design and research themselves are not about those everyday circumstances that inevitably affect the execution of activities in practice. Despite these influences, a predefined goal has to be reached at a certain moment, and this means that steering to the goal is vital. In cybernetic terms (e.g.

Klir, 1987), the goal-implementing system, here design or research, can only be kept on track with a goal-steering system, here project management.

The systems approach of management includes four basic functions: organizing, planning, communication, and steering. Moreover, four aspects of a project are distinguished: contents (the aim of the project), procedure (the activities necessary to achieve the aim), means (people as well as materials), and budget (time and money). The systems approach of management is considered in more detail below.

### 2.3.1  Organizing and planning a design project

The term design project has been used loosely until now but should be defined more formally before the functions of organizing and planning can be discussed. According to Johnson *et al.* (1963), a project is a temporary gathering of men and means, directed to realize a particular aim within certain constraints as to time and costs. Thus, a design project is a project aimed at creating a new product. The definition of a project makes explicit the relation between management, activities and goals. By considering the cooperation between a designer and an applied researcher as a project, according to the formal definition above, the scope of the discussion broadens from the aspects of contents and procedure, covered in the previous sections, to the aspects of means and budget.

Most design projects are set up in, what is called in systems analysis terms (e.g. Miser and Quade, 1988), a bottom-up style. This means that activities are listed and grouped, based on experiences in previous projects. Mostly, the simulation and evaluation phases (Figure 2.2) are only roughly described, and steering occurs late and often after the event. Such a way of working, no matter how common, is an ideal breeding ground for conflicts; time and money can run out unnoticed, and a sound basis for decisions about the project's progress is lacking.

A more effective way to organize a design project in which a designer and an applied researcher are to cooperate, is to start from the strategic models of design and applied research developed above, to use a concentric approach of both design and research, implying a planned evaluation of intermediate results, and to set up a management system to control the execution of all activities and their results. This policy is called a top-down approach. Top-down organizing and planning of a project does not preclude or prohibit jumps or inversions of activities, which deviate from the original plan, to occur during the execution of the project. However, when the goals are clear, and when an approach of working from general to specific in well-defined cycles is agreed upon at the start of the project, deviations from a plan can be handled without endangering the whole project.

The main advantage of working top-down in organizing and planning a project is a smaller chance of conflicts arising during the execution. These conflicts were already solved during the organization of the project, or the project did not start because the conflicts could not be settled. Conflicts are more easily avoided if there are clear frameworks of intermediate and final goals and, in addition, procedures to achieve these goals that are accepted by all people involved (e.g. Kerzner, 1995). In most projects, some conflicts will remain, for instance because these were not considered as important at the start of the project. Insight into various types of conflict may help to cope with them. Pondy (1967) describes three basic types: competition for scarce resources, drives for autonomy, and divergence of intermediate goals. In a design project in which a designer and an applied researcher cooperate, all three types can arise: the designer is not prepared to spend much time and money to obtain extra information, or there is a fear to loose control over a part of the process, or the designer and the researcher disagree about aims to be reached. Blake and Mouton (1964) describe techniques to use when conflicts occur. According to them, a confrontation with each other's procedures and the readiness to reach compromises by bargaining will result in positive effects in the end, whereas smoothing of a difference of opinion, forcing through an option, and withdrawal from a discordant situation are short-term solutions that do not remove the core of the conflict.

To cooperate in a project successfully, a designer and an applied researcher should have at least some notion of the advantages of the top-down approach. This provides a basis to reach an agreement about the project's content (the intermediate and final aims) and the procedures to be followed. However, for the planning of a project to become complete, means and budget should also be considered. Changes in the procedures or even the content of the project may become necessary once details about people, materials, equipment, time and money are worked out. These particular points can be negotiated specifically as soon as a general framework is known. Once planning has been done, the organization of the project is fixed, and people and other means can be reserved. By doing so, a first and important step is made to avoid conflicts and to facilitate effective cooperation.

### 2.3.2 Communication as a condition to steer a project effectively

A plan is a simplified model of future events. Reality is usually more complex and less predictable than the model suggests. This means that no plan passes off as it was devised, and steering during the execution of a plan is therefore essential. Consequently, aims, tasks, means and budget have to be adjusted on a regular basis. This is also a threat to cooperation because adjusting priorities may cause conflicts. Conflicts can be avoided by clear communication about the set-up as well as the execution of the project. Proper record keeping is a means to assure the right course of the project. Its importance is underestimated, however, and it is often given a low priority or even ignored. As a result, agreements on completion dates, for instance, become indistinct, and the 'day-to-day tyranny' stipulates the progress of things.

Cooperation should not only be based on mutual understanding of each other's work but also on respect for the other party. Giving adequate information about progress at the right moment, i.e., as defined in the project's planning, is a way of showing respect. Adequate communication not only concerns the content of the project, i.e., the new product, but also the procedures, the means and the budgets. Information about the last three aspects may seem of secondary importance, because

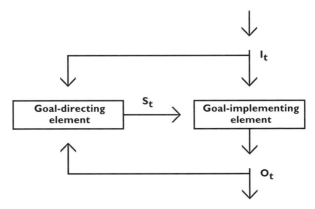

**Figure 2.5**  Full-information paradigm for process control. I, input; O, output; S, steering; t, time.

they are not really part of the specialisms of the designer and the applied researcher. However, this kind of information is essential to the cooperation between the two disciplines, simply because all four aspects (contents, procedure, means and budget) are basic entities of a project. When a project is properly planned, it becomes evident that these four aspects are strongly interrelated.

The gist of the foregoing is that without communication there will be no cooperation. Adequate communication is, however, no guarantee that a project's goal is actually achieved. Information as used in design projects is time-related, because situations and opinions change during the course of the project. In the literature on process control the full-information paradigm is described (e.g. Klir, 1987). This model (Figure 2.5) can be used to steer a design process in a dynamic way. In the model, feedforward and feedback information is used to steer a goal-implementing process, here design. In both the design and the research processes of Figure 2.2 the requirements are the steering medium. If it is accepted that both the input of each tactical phase and these requirements are time-dependent, and that answers to design and research questions evolve from conceivable options into practical solutions, it can be understood that steering a project is really a skill on its own. Each decision to adjust the design or research process is also time-related and depends on the insights of the moment. The effects of each adjustment should be observed carefully, because wrong steering decisions may harm the project. To evaluate the effects, information is needed as to contents, procedure, means and budget, which were already shown to be essential for the planning of a project.

Even good communication between a designer and an applied researcher cooperating in a project cannot always prevent the development of latent conflicts, but it helps to solve conflicts as soon as they become overt, before they start having a growing negative influence on the project's progress (Pondy, 1967). Consequently, communication is an important basic function of management, which means that the designer and the applied researcher have to accept that there is more to be discussed than information about the new product itself to give cooperation a chance.

### 2.3.3   Conclusion

From a methodological perspective it is possible to initiate cooperation between a designer and an applied researcher based only on the aspects of contents (i.e., the goal) and procedure, as discussed in Section 2.2. In the present section it was argued, however, that more is needed to make this cooperation a success. Generally speaking, the effectiveness of the cooperation can be improved by defining well-considered tactical results, and its efficiency can be improved by selecting operational methods that are adequate in relation to these tactical results and also have an acceptable profit to costs ratio. For the sake of the usefulness of the approach in daily practice it was suggested earlier that two additional steps have to be made: firstly, drawing up a plan for design and research activities based on methodological considerations and, secondly, combining these activities with management activities. The end result is a finalistic model at the operational level, comprising tactical and strategic results to be achieved by the designer and the applied researcher at fixed moments in time. The model should also contain a number of measures to control the execution of the project plan.

When applied to a small project, the approach described above may seem over-kill, but that is only the case when the strategic and tactical steps are elaborated in too small a detail. Analysis of any completed project will show that all management functions and aspects have been present to a certain extent. A new project can be set up in a systematic way based on an understanding of the systems approach and the experiences of the participants in previous projects. When the top-down approach advocated here has become daily routine, it will help to speed up the planning process of a project.

### 2.4   FINAL REMARKS

Cooperation can be conceived as working together by two or more parties towards a specific goal by realizing intermediate and final results with an acceptable number of conflicts during the execution of the tasks to be completed. From a methodological perspective it was recommended earlier to avoid conflicts by working top-down, that is using well-defined and coherent structures as subsystems of a total approach. In summary, this total approach of the cooperation between a designer and an applied researcher can be characterized as: design management attuned to research management, both based on principles of general project management, with extra attention to the control of conflicts.

In the previous sections of this chapter, the total approach was, for the sake of the argument, constructed bottom-up. The chapter started off with discussions about design and applied research, then management ideas were added, and finally it was concluded that cooperation means working efficiently under an acceptable amount of stress due to conflicts. The chapter could have been written top-down just as well: starting with conflict management and ending with the specific characteristics of design and applied research. However, such a top-down argument would not have been very convincing to both designers and applied researchers who are unfamiliar with controlling conflicts from a management perspective. In daily life, people are used to discovering things by starting bottom-up from known items and then creating new things or ideas. By looking backwards the top-down view can be developed by systematically structuring results and processes and grouping actions at higher levels of abstraction.

Formulated in a top-down manner, the recommended way of cooperating is to combine basic management functions with methods of conflict management and mix this combination with strategic approaches of design and applied research. Defined like this, the approach to cooperation advocated in this chapter is a general policy. With regard to the question of how to elaborate this policy into operational activities of a designer and an applied researcher, a number of general remarks were made in the previous sections of this chapter.

As mentioned before, cooperation is easily threatened by conflicts between people involved in a project. Therefore, the management of conflicts is an essential element. Cooperation does not concern specific tasks as such – they should be executed adequately of course – but has to do with interest in the relationship between each activity and the goals of the project. This means integration of activities at higher levels of abstraction. There are, however, many professionally trained people, perhaps guided by earlier experiences, who seclude themselves from ideas about integration. Lack of knowledge is not the main obstacle on the road to good cooperation, but the unwillingness to enter a field full of unknown conflicts outside one's own discipline. An effective attitude towards cooperation can be encouraged by explaining the need for clear commitments within well-defined frameworks. The top-down approach described in this chapter can help to achieve that.

Cooperation requires smooth conditions, to be created in addition to the professional work. This takes time, costs money and, as a consequence, seems to be conflicting with the basic activities of design and applied research. This conflict is to be solved first in order to create the momentum to maintain the cooperation during the execution of the project. Conflicts should be solved by confrontation and the willingness to accept compromises. If this can be achieved, a project in which a designer and an applied researcher cooperate, has a good chance of success.

## REFERENCES

ARCHER, L. B. (1979) Whatever became of design methodology? *Design Studies* **1**, 17–18.
BAILEY, K. D. (1983) Relationships among conceptual, abstracted, and concrete systems. *Behavioral Science* **28**, 219–232.
BLAKE, R. R. and MOUTON, J. S. (1964) *The Managerial Grid: Key Orientations for Achieving Production Through People.* Houston: Golf.
CROSS, N. (1989) *Engineering Design Methods.* Chichester: Wiley.
DE GROOT, A. D. (1969) *Methodology: Foundations of Inference and Research in the Behavioural Sciences.* The Hague: Mouton.
HUBKA, V. (1982) *Principles of Design Engineering.* London: Butterworth.

JOHNSON, R. A., KAST, F. E. and ROSENZWEIG, J. E. (1963) *The Theory and Management of Systems*. New York: McGraw-Hill.

KERZNER, H. (1995) *Project Management: A Systems Approach to Planning, Scheduling, and Controlling* (5th edn). New York: Van Nostrand Reinhold.

KLIR, G. J. (1987) The role of methodological paradigms in systems design. In: NADLER, G. (Ed.), *Proceedings of the 1987 International Congress on Planning and Design Theory: Plenary and Interdisciplinary Lectures*, pp. 5–10. New York: The American Society of Mechanical Engineers.

LIEVEGOED, B. (1991) *Managing the Developing Organisation: Tapping the Spirit of Europe*. Oxford: Blackwell.

MARINISSEN, A. H. (1993) Information on product use in the design process. In: POLLOCK, C. M. and STRAKER, L. M. (Eds), *Ergonomics in a Changing World: Proceedings of the 29th Annual Conference of the Ergonomics Society of Australia*, pp. 78–85. Downer: Ergonomics Society of Australia.

MISER, H. J. and QUADE, E. S. (Eds) (1988) *Handbook of Systems Analysis: Craft Issues and Procedural Choices*. Chichester: Wiley.

NIJHUIS, W. (1995) 'Integrated planning of design projects', internal report, Faculty of Industrial Design Engineering, Delft University of Technology.

PAHL, G. and BEITZ, W. (1984) *Engineering Design*. London: The Design Council.

PONDY, L. R. (1967) Organizational conflict: concepts and models. *Administrative Science Quarterly* **12**, 296–320.

ROOZENBURG, N. F. M. and EEKELS, J. (1995) *Product Design: Fundamentals and Methods*, Chichester: Wiley.

VEREIN DEUTSCHER INGENIEURE (1993) *Methodik zum Entwickeln und Konstruieren technischer Systeme und Produkte*. VDI 2221. Berlin: Beuth.

# PART TWO

# User Instructions

# CHAPTER THREE

# Printed instructions: can research make a difference?

PATRICIA WRIGHT

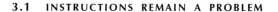

## 3.1 INSTRUCTIONS REMAIN A PROBLEM

Confusion and clutter are failures of design not attributes of information.

(Tufte, 1990, p. 53)

### 3.1.1 The costs

Instructions are part of daily life. We all operate machines, use community services (e.g. transport, leisure or communication facilities) and have health care requirements. Failure to understand or carry out instructions can have serious consequences. Machines operated incorrectly may be unsafe. Quality of life is reduced when help and support available is not known. Misuse of medicines and nutritional products damages consumers' health. Services people do not adopt, because they do not understand how to access them, increase costs to service providers. It also wastes consumers' money and loses manufacturers further sales. For example, Waller (1993) commented on an attempt to microwave his supper, 'By following the instructions carefully I recently managed to fuse a ready-meal to its container and render it inedible'. Unfortunate consequences arise from recipients not understanding, and so not acting appropriately, on information in solicitors' letters (Adler, 1993). International legislation can make things worse. For people concerned about what they eat, or with special dietary requirements, the nutritional information listed with ingredients is an implicit instruction advising 'Eat me' or 'Don't eat me'. Black and Rayner (1992) found many people did not interpret this material to make appropriate decisions when ingredients were provided in the numerical form required by the

European Economic Community (Commission of the European Communities, 1990). Most people do not know if 0.3 grams of sodium per 100 grams is above or below average. Black and Rayner examined alternative label designs, asking people, 'Do you think this food would be a wise choice for a healthy diet?' Errors fell from 35 per cent to 12 per cent when numbers were supplemented with verbal and graphic information. So design can clearly make a difference, and research can provide evidence to quantify this difference.

### 3.1.2   Coping with diverse readerships

Printed instructions address an audience having a wide range of visual and reading abilities, including those for whom the language of the instructions is not their first language. Differences in domain knowledge and problem-solving skills influence how people interpret and comply with instructions. So it is not surprising that instructions may sometimes fail to communicate; but it is surprising that writers have difficulty recognizing these troublespots (Lentz, 1995). When reviewing written advice given to the elderly, Epstein (1981) concluded, 'The people who produce the leaflets are all more or less convinced that they have turned out a good product. The four experts on information design whom we consulted were of a different opinion.'

Pressures from international commerce may favour pictures for solving problems of language translation, as with airline safety instructions. However, customers of a Japanese photocopier company have asked for English keywords in addition to the icons on the machine, because many of the icons were not understood (Howard *et al.*, 1991). Research on computer interfaces suggests that combining words and icons can be better than either alone (e.g. Guestello *et al.*, 1989). Words were more successful than symbols for conveying instructions on bank-teller machines (Stern, 1984), but much depends upon the details of the icons, the words, the tasks and the readers. Researchers do not always make clear the boundary conditions within which their findings will apply.

### 3.1.3   Beyond language improvements

Because poor instructions can be disastrous, one might expect the quality of instructions to improve steadily. The evidence is mixed. Instructions for using consumer products still cause problems, yet machine manufacturers increasingly recognize the value of ergonomic constraints preventing machines being mis-assembled or misused. The videotape recorder illustrates how instructions can be avoided. Many people have difficulties setting their video recorders to tape a future programme (Thimbleby, 1991). Manufacturers have responded with a technological solution. Newspapers publish code numbers alongside daily listings of television programmes. People with appropriate equipment need only key in these numbers and the machine decodes them into a specification of the programme and channel to record. Ways of by-passing difficult instructions extend beyond complex technology. Some soft drinks need to be shaken gently before opening. If shaken too much, the contents fizz out. Putting the ring-pull on the base of the can encourages people to turn the can over to open it, thereby providing the required amount of shaking (Waller, 1994). No written instructions are needed. Forms designers are often encouraged to ask themselves, 'Is your question really necessary?' Instruction writers can ask whether readers' behaviour can be engineered by means other than print. They may start by querying the need for particular content. This is what Jansen and Steehouder (1984) did when they found the main obstacle preventing people in Holland from understanding a public leaflet was its content not appearance. Language simplification is sometimes opposed on the grounds that it detracts from more productive options, such as simplifying an administrative system (Penman, 1993). Certainly instructions are not a safe or reliable way of compensating for poor product design or system complexity.

Some organizations have improved their printed communications with the public; but for these improvements to be maintained organizations need to establish adequate design procedures (Duffy, 1981). 'Training and education alone will not solve the problem of effective ongoing documentation unless other institutional factors make their contribution. For example, if company documentation standards do not enhance and support good, effective documentation efforts, no book or training seminar can help' (Brockman, 1990, p. 26). The legal profession is evidence of this. In 1918 the House of Lords in the UK recognized that punctuation was a rational and helpful part of written English. Yet this insight continues to be ignored by legal writers. In contrast, the risk of legal liability encourages pharmaceutical companies to include more information about medicines and clearer instructions on leaflets accompanying medicines sold over the counter. But visual and linguistic clarity will not guarantee successful communication if the concepts in the minds of readers and writers differ. When instructions say, 'Take one tablet three times a day at meal times' the writer usually means 'Not on an empty stomach' but readers may think this refers to approximate clock times, especially if they never eat breakfast. So writers need to appreciate that their readers' misinterpretation has implications for the content of the information. But is it all down to the writers? Does research have any part to play in improving the quality of printed instructions?

### 3.1.4  A shift in research focus

Thirty years ago it was recognized that written instructions were a neglected research area (Chapanis, 1965). Twenty years later written information was seen to play an increasing part in working life (Chapanis, 1988). This information extended beyond words and paper to include information on computer screens. Researchers also shifted their focus away from print. Conference and journal publications of the Ergonomics Society contain a small and declining number of studies of printed information (Wright, 1986). Yet printed instructions remain ubiquitous throughout contemporary life, both at home and at work. 'It is rare today to find an apparatus which is not also explained in multi-lingual and pictorial instructions' (Gombrich, 1990, p. 45). Whether you want to wash your cushion covers or transfer your phone calls to another office for the afternoon, you will probably need to consult printed instructions (cf. Norman, 1988, p. 18). Fortunately many information design principles for computer screens also apply to print. Nevertheless print affords a different range of design options and so can enable, and may require, different design solutions to communication problems. Twyman (1982) provided an elegant taxonomy of the design space for visual graphic language, but this has yet to be powerfully exploited in research on printed instructions. One of the difficulties, as van der Waarde shows in Chapter 5, can be capturing the adequacy of the relation between text and illustrations. The usefulness of other taxonomies is currently being explored (see Westendorp, Chapter 6), but the link between the structure and function of instructions is sensitive to many contextual factors as we will see below.

Research has established that the design of instructions can change the way people read them. One study of machine instructions concluded, 'Differences between instructions appeared to affect not just the speed and accuracy with which they were used but the way in which they were used as well. The detailed analysis of the errors indicated that the style of presentation of the instructions determined the strategy people adopted for using them and hence the kind of information sought from the detail of the diagrams' (Szlichcinski, 1984, p. 464). This implies that research can shed light both on how people read, and on the design features that will encourage and support specific kinds of reading.

## 3.2  INFLUENCES ON DESIGN DECISIONS

### 3.2.1  Considering all the options

It is tempting, but not safe, to assume that all educated adults can write good instructions. When adults were asked to direct a stranger across town, many people described the route they would take, although this was a twisty route through the city centre that was extremely difficult to direct people along (Wright et al., 1995). In contrast, when people selected among pre-drawn routes, they picked one that was easier to follow. This suggests they better appreciated the design options when reading than when writing. Very few people included sketch maps with their directions, although they drew adequate route sketches when asked to; moreover, they selected the sketch rather than the verbal description, when choosing among alternatives. So these amateur instruction-givers seem to have overlooked the option of including a sketch. Do professionals ever make similar mistakes? Van der Waarde (Chapter 5) reports that pictorial elements are relatively rare in patient package inserts. Time pressures, plus cost and other resource limitations could easily reduce the range of design options considered at the outset. So this may remain a risk even for professional designers.

Steehouder and Jansen (1987) showed the inadequacy of relying on 'public relations officers or freelance journalists' to produce public information leaflets. Writing clear instructions is a specialized communication skill that needs to be learned. It may help technical writers make the case for greater allocation of resources and organizational support, if they can use research findings to establish that specialized skills are needed for their job and that these do not come pre-packed with the laser printer.

In large companies, product instructions are often written by technical authors whose status within the organization can be 'pretty low on the corporate totem pole'. They are not well paid nor held in great esteem. If a technical writer wants to get ahead, he or she tries to move as quickly as possible into management (Dobrin, 1983, p. 246). Yet technical writing is cognitively very complex because it integrates expertise from many different areas: verbal skills and the rhetoric of communication; typographic design and page layout; illustration; administration of the document development process; and often the management of a writing team (Wright, 1987). There are probably many reasons for organizations undervaluing the expertise of their writers. Good design as a product is often invisible, in the sense that readers have no appreciation of the problems that were solved and no realization that the information could have been presented in other ways. 'But while the technology has moved on at a great rate, ways of managing the business of internal and external communication via the printed word are often as amateurish and messy as they used to be. Indeed technology has compounded the mess' (Orna, 1994, p. 14). Steinberg (1980) pointed out that we may all believe we know a great deal about written communication, but many of us know different things and some of these beliefs are contradictory. Different professional groups (domain experts, graphic designers, professional editors) noticed different things when commenting on the graphics in science texts (Benson, 1994). Yet no professional group spotted all the trouble spots that hindered readers. Lentz (1995) has reported similar findings with leaflets promoting safe alcohol consumption. Therefore, relying on the expert opinion of professionals does not guarantee success. Usability testing will be needed.

### 3.2.2  Juggling constraints and trade-offs

Professional writers, either as outside consultants or as members of the client organization, may need to juggle numerous constraints. Instructions for a pay phone had to include not only the necessary telephone instructions but also the logo denoting the client's corporate identity, the international standards for emergency symbols, the logos of six credit card companies, the phone number of a helpline, and five national flags (Waller and Lewis, 1992). All this information had to be printed on vandal-proof, fire-resistant material and fit within a designated space. Coping with so many constraints can leave little incentive to consider usability issues as well.

Designers are under pressures from both peers and clients to create products having 'quality'. This is a slippery concept (Wright, 1994). On the one hand it refers to features traditionally seen as denoting high standards of production and presentation. These traditions may be yesterday's news because as professions develop so do views of what is right, or safe, or feasible; and these views may ignore usability. Shifting the focus from 'quality' to 'usability' raises new questions such as whether the instructions can or will be used. Unless both questions have affirmative answers, money is wasted printing the instructions. Unfortunately, clients may not be the users of the instructions and may have other criteria to satisfy. In large organizations bulk purchase is often the rule. Machines such as photocopiers are bought by purchasing departments which take decisions based on tenders. These tenders emphasize costs and functionality. So the purchase decision can be made without usability ever being considered (Norman, 1988, p. 157). There is a need to get these decision-makers to appreciate the hidden costs of machines that are difficult to use. Research findings may help to make these costs salient.

### 3.2.3   Readers' information needs

Even when writing usable instructions is the goal, a lack of knowledge about the audience and their information needs can result in product-oriented rather than user-oriented design (Schriver, 1989, 1992, 1997). Product orientation shows itself in the nomenclature used in instructions. Not only strange technical jargon, although that can be encountered all too easily, but even familiar words can fail to communicate because they mismatch the terminology that readers would spontaneously adopt. For example, a new phone system in my office was installed in February 1994. It lets people set a password on their handset to prevent others using the phone in their absence. Printed instructions for doing this are accessed through a booklet's table of contents under the word 'lock'. This is a familiar enough word that readers understand; but they do not search for 'lock' when wanting to set or change their password. Product-oriented design can also be seen in the decisions about the sequence in which information is given. The printed sequence needs to correspond to that which most users would expect (for a critique of the instructions for our previous office phone system see Norman, 1988, pp. 19–21).

How can writers know the way their readers will respond? Numerous difficulties face those who turn to academic journals, whether designers, students or researchers. An on-line search can be frustrating because many keywords for written instructions have other dominant meanings in the research literature. For example, 'instructions' retrieves data on training, 'directions' finds studies concerned with future trends, the research located by 'information' deals with information technology. So locating research on printed instructions is not trivial. Once found, the papers will be scattered through many different journals. Few libraries take them all. After a paper has been obtained, there remains a translation problem because the domain content, the readers studied, and the reading situation will all differ from those facing the writer. Judging whether these findings can be safely generalized to the current design task requires assistance. It has long been known that a design solution that works well in one context may not be appropriate in another, even when domain and audience remain the same (Wright and Reid, 1973). A detailed appreciation of the cognitive demands that the instructions make in particular contexts and for specific audiences is always needed. Research publications are too piece-meal to help writers attain this. Perhaps the contacts formed at interdisciplinary conferences offer a faster means of locating the information needed. Through dis-cussions with these contacts, writers may discover that the information they really want is something rather different.

Another way writers can find out about readers is user testing, a procedure widely adopted by those designing computer interfaces (e.g. Hornby *et al.*, 1992; Nielsen, 1993) and endorsed by many contributors to this volume (e.g. Adams, Chapter 1; Sless, Chapter 11). Several methodologies exist, varying in whether the designer participates in the users' world or users become directly involved in design activities. In the latter approach, known as participative design, different techniques contribute at different stages of design (for an overview see Kuhn and Muller, 1993). Nevertheless, knowing what to measure, and how, requires skill because the precise details of test implementation can be crucial (Schumacher and Waller, 1985). People may demonstrate that they understand every word of the instructions when reading them aloud, but may systematically skip certain steps when carrying them out (Marcel and Barnard, 1979). Questionnaires have pitfalls (Foddy, 1993). People's response to specific design features increases when these are drawn to their attention (Keller-Cohen *et al.*, 1990). General questions such as, 'Do you think any changes should be made?', produce fewer answers than specific questions, 'Do you think there should be more space here?' (Fox, 1981). User-testing locates trouble spots in instructions; eradicating these requires understand-ing their cause. This means appreciating how people read and respond to instructions. Can researchers provide the necessary insights, and if so how can these be appro-priately conveyed?

### 3.2.4  Summarizing research findings

Psychologists have studied reading in many contexts, including its development in children and its breakdown following brain injury; but they have their own agenda. Their priority is to understand the mental processes that underlie reading, and to represent this understanding in an explicit and testable model. In order to keep the complexity manageable, each model addresses selective facets of reading. There exist models of discourse understanding (e.g. Van Dijk and Kintsch, 1983), models of textual search (e.g. Guthrie, 1988) and models of the memory processes involved in reading (Baddeley, 1990). However, when people follow instructions they engage in many of these mental activities. Only a few psychological models explicitly con-sider the integration of these disparate processes (e.g. Barnard, 1987), and applying the individual models to the design of printed instructions is difficult. Szlichcinski (1984) proposed that instruction-using behaviour is similar to other forms of prob-lem solving. There is much truth in this. Unfortunately the links between problem solving and the design of instructions have not been worked through. People want-ing to apply research findings may prefer the evidence to be expressed in something other than theoretical models.

Guidelines that distil the wisdom of experts in the field have a long and honour-able tradition. Indeed the compendium of advice by Hart (1893) continued to have tremendous influence on decisions about typographic style throughout the next century (Walker, 1993). Requests for guidelines abound and researchers respond (e.g. Hartley, 1981; Saunders, 1982). A 117-item checklist summarizes recom-mendations on writing instructions for consumer products (Cooper and Page, 1989). Guidelines seem to make research findings accessible but in order to be safely and effectively applied they require expertise in the relevant domain, for they seldom have the status of universal truths, and sometimes may even seem to conflict (see the discussion of word order in Section 3.3.4 below). Writers need to know the risks from contravening the guidance. If the print is smaller than that recommended will people just be slower, or will they bring their eyes too close to danger zones trying to read the warning notice that says, 'Do not get too close', or will many people be prevented from accessing the material at all? Creating usable instructions involves calculating such consequences. Writing involves trade-offs and comprom-ise. Calling guidelines a checklist pays lip service to this problem but scarcely assists in its solution. Lists of research findings may be helpful, but they are not enough. Writers need to know how readers will respond in a very particular com-bination of circumstances, such as when trying to use a pay phone in a foreign country. User testing may help, but the 'invent–test–revise' cycle could benefit from input at the 'invent' stage that gives insights into how readers will behave. The following framework seeks to make such a contribution.

### 3.3   THE WAY PEOPLE READ INSTRUCTIONS

### 3.3.1   A three-category framework

Just as motorists need to acquire a feel for what other road users may do, so may a perspective for appreciating what readers are doing and why suffice. An exist-ing framework for how adults read computer documentation (Wright, 1983) can be applied to printed instructions. Because it does not yield insights that are counter-intuitive, it is tempting to think that all 'good designers' would write instructions consistent with the features suggested by the framework. It remains an empirical ques-tion whether this framework is only of value to inexperienced designers, or whether the design activity involves juggling so many factors that the framework offers a useful memory aid and cross checking device even for experienced designers.

The original framework subdivided readers' activities into three categories:

- searching for relevant information;
- understanding and remembering what was read;
- applying the knowledge gained from reading.

Each of these categories has relevance to printed instructions and no linear process is implied by the subdivision. For example, people may be correctly following an instruction when they realize that these particular steps are not relevant to their current goal. So they carry out further search looking for a different procedure. In order to illustrate the design implications of this framework let us consider each of these categories in turn.

### 3.3.2 How people locate instructions

In daily life, people do not follow all the instructions that they encounter, only those relating to goals that they currently have. If their goals can be attained or their questions answered without reading anything, then that is usually the preferred option (Keller-Cohen *et al.*, 1990). As Sless (Chapter 11) noted in the context of form-filling, people adopt the principle of 'least reading effort'. An obvious design implication is that factors deterring readers should be minimized. Yet instructions, whether in a printed leaflet or stuck onto a machine or printed on the product packaging, are often embedded in marketing information, general warnings or legal disclaimers. Making instructions harder to find increases the chances that readers will not bother.

Sometimes the reason that people do not look is because they believe that there is nothing that they need to know – e.g. you just plug it in and switch it on (Wright *et al.*, 1982). So instruction writers need to start with the questions that are uppermost in readers' minds. If people approach a coin-operated machine asking, 'Where do I put money in?' then the first instruction needs to address this. Trying to get people to start somewhere else can be wasted effort.

The activity of searching is itself a complex mental process with at least four constituents, no matter whether the instructions are verbal or pictorial. Searchers must first decide what to look for, then how to search for it. After this they carry out and monitor the search activity. Finally they locate the information being sought and the search is over. Design factors can influence all these activities.

People often prefer asking someone rather than trying to find the answer in a printed leaflet because asking the right person can change your query (e.g. you ask, 'Where do I switch it on?' and they reply, 'Have you plugged it in?'). Readers may need to understand the range of machine or system functions in order to select their search target. Appliances as diverse as washing machines and computers are often operated within only a narrow range of their functionality (Wurman, 1989). Through sequencing procedural information, writers can draw readers' attention to the need to revise their search target. Requiring people to remove their credit card before dispensing a ticket is an example of this kind of constraint (Erdmann and Neal, 1971). So issues of content and presentation become closely enmeshed when viewed from the perspective of what people do when following instructions. This is an important difference from how decisions about content and presentation may appear when viewed from the standpoint of product requirements.

### Legibility and attention

Readers who are searching will skim through instructions, so these need to be highly legible. There has been much research on legibility, and Black (1990) reviews the

issues relating to desktop publishing. Hard and fast rules are not appropriate because legibility requirements relate to the context of use. Warnings need to be
legible at a safe distance and placed where they will be noticed. Verhoef (1986)
reported that 50 per cent of people failed to notice an 'Out of order' sign on a
machine because it was not in people's line of vision. Related problems can be
found in printed leaflets where informative headings and subheadings can assist
readers who are skimming. In longer leaflets, page headings that indicate the content of the page are much more helpful than repetition of the manufacturer's name.
These are ways in which instruction writers can help readers who are searching for
information.

### Problems ending the search

Searchers monitor their progress, asking themselves questions such as, 'Have I
done this?', 'Should I now look there?' and 'What else might it be called?' They
may stop searching too soon. Several users of a train ticket machine bought unnecessarily expensive tickets by selecting an ordinary return instead of the cheaper
evening fare appropriate at the time of purchase (Verhoef, 1988). Similar problems
can arise when details about freezer storage durations are grouped by storage length
(Barnard and Marcel, 1984). If each group has several pictures representing different kinds of foods, readers might interpret the first animal as denoting the category
meat, and not notice that the meat they are storing belongs in another category. A
design solution is to present meat as a heading and list varieties of meat underneath
this, so drawing people's attention to the need to discriminate among various kinds
of meat. Similarly if a phone system enables five kinds of call transfer, searchers
will expect these to be grouped together in the instruction booklet, and may give up
the search if they do not find the one they are looking for on a page where several
others are described. Searchers may also continue past the relevant information if it
does not closely match their search target. The mismatch can be one of terminology
(e.g. people looking for the 'Way out' of a building may immediately recognize
'Exit' but not 'Entrance', still less 'Main hall').

   Once instructions have been found they need to be understood. Combining
words and icons can increase the noticeability of instructions or warnings, and also
help readers understand and remember them (Young and Wogalter, 1990). Like the
activity of searching, the category of 'understanding' refers to a cluster of psychological processes that can be separately supported by design decisions.

### 3.3.3   How people understand and remember instructions

### Context and language

Instructions can be understood at many levels. In some situations a shallow understanding, rote retention, and hasty application may suffice. For example, a graphic
showing the orientation for inserting a ticket in a slot is likely to be read, acted
upon, and forgotten. Understanding is influenced by both the context in which

instructions are given and the way they are expressed. When manufacturers include additional claims on a package, in order to promote sales, this can affect readers' understanding of health information such as nutritional content (Black and Rayner, 1992). Negative information can cause problems in many contexts; File and Jew (1973) found that people recalled 20 per cent more from affirmative instructions (such as, 'Extinguish cigarettes' or 'Remove shoes') than they did from the equivalent prohibitions ('Do not keep shoes on'). Barnard and Marcel (1984) in their study of pictorial instructions pointed out that negative instructions (e.g. 'Do not perform the next action until . . .') were more successful if readers were explicitly told to wait, otherwise many people skipped from action to action, as if asking themselves only, 'What do I do next?' So contextual and linguistic factors can combine, even when there are no written words in the instructions.

## Understanding depends on expectations

Readers often have expectations about the procedures to be followed (Wright *et al.*, 1982). These expectations take the form of a description of the goal of the activity (e.g. obtaining a drink from a vending machine) together with 'empty slots' to be filled by details of the actions to be taken (e.g. the slots may be 'inserting money', 'selecting item' but the detailed steps that fill these slots will vary across machines). This kind of mental structure has been called a schema (Schank and Abelson, 1977). Typically people read instructions with the aim of filling the slots in their current mental schema. For familiar devices people may already have established schemas. For novel devices or unfamiliar procedures, giving people a schema can make the instructions easier to follow (Kieras and Bovair, 1984; Dixon, 1987a, 1987b).

Through a decade of painstaking and careful research Dixon has applied this schema approach in his work on written instructions (Dixon, 1982; Dixon *et al.*, 1993). He has shown that instructions are followed more accurately when they start by giving the reader a description of the task goal (Dixon, 1987b). For example, he measured how long people spent reading instructions that specified drawing simple geometric shapes to make a meaningful picture. These instructions mentioned what the picture would be either at the beginning or at the end. Reading was faster when the picture was named at the beginning ('This will be a picture of a coat hanger. Draw a wide triangle and put a C on top') rather than at the end ('Draw a wide triangle and put a C on top. This will be a picture of a coat hanger'). People were also more accurate when the picture was mentioned first. Mistakes occurred because people guessed how the components might fit together before they were told, and they did not always modify their guesses later. Giving people schemas to help them interpret what they read may be particularly important for older readers (approximately 66 years), who were found to spend longer reading and remembered less when a schema was not provided (Byrd, 1993).

Either words or pictures can provide readers with schemas (Glenberg and Langston, 1992). So too can analogies. Hayes and Henk (1986) compared analogies and illustrations for instructions on how to tie knots. Analogies helped performance two weeks later but the illustrations were helpful both immediately and later. But analogy can be a false friend because readers do not always restrict their inferences to the points of similarity intended by the writer. Examples may have similar problems, yet they offer another way of helping readers bridge the gap between the generality of the instructions and the specific actions they must take. This may be useful when schemas having several dependencies within them need to be learned. However, the inclusion of examples can change people's reading strategy. Lefevre and Dixon (1986) introduced contradictions between the main text and the examples and waited for readers to comment on the discrepancies. Many people followed the example without noticing any incompatibilities. So writers may need to assess, perhaps by usability testing, whether their use of examples is enhancing or detracting from the attention that readers give to the main text.

## Using temporary memory

People's expectations about procedures come from information in their long term memory systems. There are other memory systems, often referred to collectively as 'Working memory' (Baddeley, 1990). These memory processes are used when people intend to remember information only temporarily, for example while setting heat level and cooking time on a microwave, and they too can be supported by the design of instructions. Research has shown that for short, meaningful information people seldom remember the text verbatim, rather they infer the gist and remember that (Fillenbaum, 1966; Johnson-Laird and Stevenson, 1970). Such gist memory is very prone to errors arising from prior knowledge and expectations (see above). If writers discover what assumptions their readers will make (e.g. through usability testing) they can explicitly correct assumptions that may lead to mistakes.

Many people have access to a mental 'blackboard' which they can use to remember things for a short time. The information on this blackboard need not be words. People are more likely to use non-verbal forms when instructions are given pictorially or when the items mentioned in the procedure are linked by spatial terms (e.g. above, beside). Johnson-Laird (1983) has discussed the importance of mental models in influencing the way people reason about the world. There have been no detailed extensions of this work to the design of instructions, but it is known that intervening actions can disrupt this form of temporary memory so it is not suitable for lengthy sequences.

When a seemingly arbitrary sequence of steps must be performed, people may say these over to themselves while carrying them out. Remembering with this form of temporary memory is supported by visually grouping information into small chunks. Using this kind of internal speech, people are more likely to make mistakes on the steps just after the middle of a sequence than on the steps at the beginning or the end. Indeed, when mistakes are uncommon research suggests that they are most likely to be transpositions of two adjacent steps rather than the omission of one of them. Instruction writers can use space or typography to break long procedures into shorter sequences and so reduce such mistakes (Boekelder and Steehouder, Chapter 4).

### 3.3.4 How people carry out instructions

*Creating action plans*

Finding and understanding instructions are essential preliminaries, but people's beliefs and attitudes may lead them to disregard an instruction at a later stage (Wogalter, Chapter 7). For readers willing to comply with the instructions, their next step is to devise an action plan and carry it out. Typically action plans are hierarchies of goals, each being expanded by readers into a series of steps to attain the goal. Action plans can differ from mental models or schemas created when understanding the instructions because they incorporate details specific to the reader's immediate circumstances. For example, goals involving coins necessitate plans for retrieving the coins from purse or pocket. The greater the similarity between the action plan and any mental model already formed, the easier readers will find it to follow instructions.

Combining text and illustration can help people follow a sequence of instructions (Morrell and Park, 1993) but much depends on the illustrations. Lowe (1993) provides a useful summary of how diagrams can fail as communication devices, e.g. if readers are uncertain about the viewpoint. In large flow-charts, the visual structure may become so convoluted that it cannot be easily grasped by readers. However, when the actions to be taken are hedged with conditions, it may be difficult for writers to give a coherent overview, and here flow-charts may help people work out what should be done as the next step.

Verbal instructions can generate difficulties either from terminology or word order. Terminology influences understanding when it is unfamiliar, but plays havoc with the implementation of an action plan when it is misconstrued by readers or the text is incorrect – as when the instructions refer to a yellow button but the machine only has green buttons. Close coordination between writers and product designers can reduce such mistakes.

The writer's choice of word order can slow comprehension but can have a much bigger impact on the ease of creating action plans. In English, the word order reflects a subject–predicate distinction, but the order needed in an action plan may be different. Short instructions are not a problem, e.g. 'Push the button'. When writers need to explain which button is meant, or describe where the button is, the instructions lengthen, e.g. 'Push the button under the flap on the right hand side'. This sounds reasonable English, nevertheless the action plan created by readers has the sequence:

- locate the right hand side,
- find the flap,
- lift the flap,
- find the button,
- push the button.

This planned sequence of actions reverses the order in which the steps were mentioned in the instructions. We have some ongoing research suggesting that for procedures involving few steps, people are faster when instructions maintain the subject–predicate order, perhaps because the processes of understanding rather than planning dominate performance. However, as the number of steps increases so does the advantage of having the order of mention match the order of the action plan. One reason for this is that people separately tag the order of mention and the chronological order of the actions (Clark and Clark, 1968). So errors can arise when these tags become lost or mixed, and this is more likely with longer sequences.

The order in which information is mentioned in instructions is critical whenever people are unfamiliar with the task (Dixon *et al.*, 1988). Newcomers benefit from having instructions state the action to be performed explicitly and mention it early in the instructional sequence. Details of any antecedents or consequences of the action are better placed after the action itself. These order effects occur with pictorial as well as with verbal instructions (Marcel and Barnard, 1979). The problems of segmenting pictorial instructions have been discussed by Gombrich (1990). Even for instructions involving explicit contingencies, such as 'unless', readers find it easier if the contingent information is given after the action. People spend less time reading, 'Press the button unless the number is odd' than 'Unless the number is odd press the button' (Wright and Hull, 1986; Dixon, 1987a).

When attaining a specific goal involves numerous steps, memory processes are again important. Memory is influenced by familiarity as well as quantity, so there need not be many steps in a novel procedure before memory problems arise. Writers can help in these circumstances by visually chunking the material, to dissuade readers from trying to remember too much at once (Boekelder and Steehouder, Chapter 4). Writers can also provide cues (such as numbering) that help readers keep track of how far they have got through the sequence (Frase and Schwartz, 1979). Several studies have demonstrated the value of making the graphic layout of information on the page reflect the meaningful units within the text (e.g. Martin, 1989; Cumming, 1990).

Carrying out an action plan in a specific context can involve problem solving. For example, readers may have a well-formed plan to put their credit card in a slot, but when examining the machine they may need to decide which slot gives the parking ticket and which takes credit cards. Often labelling on the machine could help, which again shows the value of writers and product designers working together during product development.

## Feedback about actions

Unless readers get feedback while carrying out instructions, Norman (1988) suggests two kinds of communication gulf may occur. The first is a gulf of execution when the machine does not enable the intended action. This can happen if the content of the instructions is wrong – a mistake which reflects both the lack of communication between product developers and instruction writers, and also the failure to test the instructions before printing them. Norman's second gulf is the gulf of evaluation, when readers are unable to assess their progress. People find it very frustrating to perform a series of actions only to discover at the end that these have not been successful. Readers need to be reassured about their interpretation of the instructions as they implement their action plans. The technique of walking through instructions, doing literally what they say and only that, is often enough to uncover both chasms (Schumacher and Waller, 1985). Providing readers with feedback may require a liaison between information designers and product or system designers. Sometimes 'intelligent' agents can detect when people are making mistakes and draw their attention to the fact, e.g. the reminder to drivers that they have left the car lights on. Such technological solutions apply more easily to machine instructions than to service or health care instructions, but some organizations have discovered the value of including reminders on the return envelope listing all the items that should be enclosed, or steps that should have been completed before the form is sent back.

An important part of an action plan is the self-testing and repair of mistakes by readers (Guthrie *et al.*, 1991). When people realize they have made a mistake they may ask, 'What do I do now?' So instructions need to include explanations of how to recover from common errors. Usability testing has a vital part to play in revealing these errors. In addition, a cognitive focus, such as that outlined above, suggests the most likely kinds of errors: transposition errors caused by short term memory processes; interpretation errors caused by prior knowledge; misunderstandings arising from linguistic processes; and referential errors caused by action plans. Only when these 'reading' difficulties are appreciated can appropriate support for readers be devised.

The framework outlined here still leaves considerable scope for design expertise and flair. For those preferring firmer guidance, it may leave too much underspecified. By emphasizing the range of mental activities encompassed in the phrase 'following instructions' it shows why guidelines are inadequate and why trade-offs arise between supporting readers' understanding and helping them generate action plans. The purpose of the framework is to help writers shift their focus from the textual details, to include readers' behaviour in the task domain and with the printed material, when making decisions about how to communicate instructions.

## 3.4   MISUNDERSTANDINGS ABOUT RESEARCH

### 3.4.1   Psychological research might be too narrow

Dillon (1994) suggests that many of the problems inherent in electronic text design spring from the lack of a design relevant description of the reading process. Studies of readers do not yield 'plug and play' solutions because psychologists seldom explore much of the design space. Although Dixon's work gives valuable insights into how people follow instructions, it does not generate a 'best buy' for writers. It focused on verbal instructions, whereas if directing someone to draw a particular shape it would be simpler to give them a picture to copy. The research objectives did not require examining all possible ways of giving the instructions. Indeed the design space is too vast to be mindlessly explored; there are too many combinations of tasks, design options and reading strategies (cf. Barnard, 1987). Some researchers have done large scale parameter plotting studies. Hartley and Trueman (1985) reported 17 investigations of headings that varied in location and linguistic style within a four-page leaflet. Yet even such a thorough study cannot predict whether the findings will generalize to other topics or audiences. Indeed, the magnitude of the differences in time to read or act upon instructions may be so small that they seem of no practical significance in the real world. Yet if small time differences in the laboratory reflect differences in cognitive demands, these may become errors and have serious consequences in real life. So design improvements observed when highly motivated volunteers work in conditions of quiet with few distractions, can become much larger differences in the bustle of the real world where only part of the reader's attention is given to the instructions.

Problems of generalization arise in many research areas. The problem is particularly acute where theory is weak. Medicine has developed techniques for systematically reviewing research evidence (Chalmers and Altman, 1995). Instead of considering the design space, cognitive psychologists build models to account for behaviour in specific contexts. That does not necessarily help designers. The framework of readers' behaviour outlined above is seeking a middle ground between the precise but narrow scope of the modellers and the gaps left by the parameter plotters.

### 3.4.2  The ecological validity of research

Research volunteers read because they are asked to and are paid for compliance; but writers want to know how people would read information that really mattered. Black and Rayner (1992) found improvements in nutrition labels were most effective for those who cared little about healthy eating; people who did care already had strategies for coping with the poorer information. Psychologists test their models using performance measures rather than preference data. People may prefer a design other than that used most accurately (e.g. Keller-Cohen *et al.*, 1990) and may be more willing to read the preferred instructions. Writers have to assess for any specific instructions how to make the trade-off in the support they give readers for looking at, understanding, and following instructions.

The textual materials used in experimental studies can also raise questions about ecological validity. Sometimes researchers deliberately devise novel machines, or invent new procedures in order to reduce the effects of readers' prior knowledge. However, writers are interested in readers' expectancies and presuppositions. People forgetting a dose of medication can choose to ignore this or take extra medicine later. The safer option is to ignore the omission, but unless writers know people will act safely they will want to include this in the instructions. The framework outlined above would not flag this specific misunderstanding, but by explicitly drawing attention to the action plans people create, and the importance of feedback, it would have alerted writers to the need to consider common action slips.

### 3.4.3 The link between usability testing and research

We know that instructions can fail because writers are not involved during the process of product design. If product developers have met writers holding different opinions, they may consider their own views to be just as good. One way of countering this is for writers to cite empirical evidence supporting their advice. Usability testing offers such support, but is difficult to have early in the product development cycle. Moreover, relying on usability testing may lead to refinement of what is in principle the wrong solution, rewording the instructions instead of circumventing them through product enhancements (Wright, 1995). Usability testing flags the existence of trouble spots. Knowing how to remove these problems requires other expertise. The framework outlined above provides ways of thinking about the causes of readers' problems. It also signposts danger zones within the design space. The essence of this suggestion is that it is more useful for writers to know what to avoid than to be told what to do. Design compromise is safe as long as it avoids readers entering danger zones such as search failures, misunderstandings or faulty action plans. This perspective has implications for the design of usability studies themselves.

### 3.4.4 Designer–researcher dialogue

Information has greatly increased its importance as a consumable commodity. Elsewhere I have explored the metaphor of how the 'information eaters' might be adequately fed (Wright, 1978). That exploration suggested a need for 'greater co-operation between those studying the digestibility of information [psychologists], those training people to eat more wisely [educationists], and those who select and blend the ingredients of written communications [writers and information designers].' Why is this not happening? Much of the answer lies with the professional agendas of each community.

There are dialogues between information designers and researchers taking place. For example, they occur within the sphere of human–computer interaction, where the economic costs of thousands of telephone enquiries from confused customers are very visible to management. It is unclear how a fruitful exchange of views might be extended to other professional groups. Is asynchronous interaction appropriate, through journals or newsletters? These forms of interchange are slow; not so the electronic information highway. Perhaps face to face meetings are needed to remove barriers between professions, barriers of perspective, priorities and terminology. If so, are more interdisciplinary conferences needed? Both synchronous and asynchronous exchange have existed for over a decade without removing the professional constraints that keep the communities apart because neither group gains peer approval through this interdisciplinary activity. So the time spent is costly. Writers find it helpful to meet with colleagues who understand the problems of client briefs and pragmatic constraints; researchers present their findings to peers for evaluation. A prerequisite for successful dialogue is that it has professional value to both sides. The research community could accept the challenges to their theoretical formulations posed by the need to account for why particular communication solutions succeed or fail. Instruction writers might find it supplements their craft knowledge concerning the suitability of design alternatives if they can shift perspective from writer to reader (Stiff, 1996), and if there are signposts in the cognitive quicksands and quagmires where communications become bogged down.

Concern about the design of instructions continues because even now many are difficult to follow, and the hidden costs to industry and the community are not widely appreciated. Developments such as desktop publishing make matters worse because amateurs seldom have the range of skills needed for designing usable instructions, although this is not always recognized by management. Readers may blame themselves for misunderstanding, rather than identifying poor design as the culprit. Even writers, who know that through their design choices they can change readers' behaviour, may find themselves hamstrung by organizational attitudes and power structures. Empirical data offer ammunition in the fight to change attitudes within organizations. Research on reading instructions provides evidence that this involves much more than just perceiving the words or pictures. Legibility is necessary but not sufficient. There are many kinds of support that readers need from writers. Research underscores the 'Why' and the 'How' of that support, leaving the 'When' and the 'What' to the writer.

## REFERENCES

ADLER, M. (1993) Why do lawyers talk funny? *Information Design Jornal* 7, 175–176.

BADDELEY, A. D. (1990) *Human Memory: Theory and Practice*, Hillsdale, NJ: Lawrence Erlbaum Associates.

BARNARD, P. J. (1987) Cognitive resources and the learning of human–computer dialogues. In: CARROLL, J. M. (Ed.), *Interfacing Thought: Cognitive Aspects of Human–Computer Interaction*, pp. 112–158. London: MIT Press.

BARNARD, P. and MARCEL, T. (1984) Representation and understanding in the use of symbols and pictograms. In: EASTERBY, R. S. and ZWAGA, H. J. G. (Eds), *Information Design*, pp. 37–75. Chichester: Wiley and Sons.

BENSON, P. (1994) Problems in picturing text, PhD thesis submitted in the Psychology Department at Carnegie-Mellon University.

BLACK, A. (1990) *Typefaces for Desktop Publishing: A User Guide*. London: Architecture Design and Technology Press.

BLACK, A. and RAYNER, M. (1992) *Just Read the Label: Understanding Nutrition Information in Numeric, Verbal and Graphic Formats*. London: Her Majesty's Stationery Office.

BROCKMAN, R. J. (1990) *Writing Better Computer User Documentation*. New York, NY: Wiley and Sons.

BYRD, M. (1993) The effects of age on the ability to read and remember textual material describing how to perform skilled procedures. *Journal of Gerontology* 12, 83–99.

CHALMERS, I. and ALTMAN, D. G. (1995) *Systematic Reviews*. London: BMJ Publishing Group.

CHAPANIS, A. (1965) Words, words, words. *Human Factors* 7, 1–17.

CHAPANIS, A. (1988) 'Words, words, words' revisited. *International Review of Ergonomics* **2**, 1–30.

CLARK, H. H. and CLARK, E. V. (1968) Semantic distinctions and memory for complex sentences. *Quarterly Journal of Experimental Psychology* **20**, 129–138.

COMMISSION OF THE EUROPEAN COMMUNITIES (1990) Council Directive of 24 September 1990 on nutrition labelling for foodstuffs, 90/496/EEC.

COOPER, S. and PAGE, M. (1989) *Instructions for Consumer Products*. London: Her Majesty's Stationery Office.

CUMMING, G. (1990) Liturgical typography: a plea for sense-lining. *Information Design Journal* **6**, 89–99.

DILLON, A. (1994) *Designing Usable Electronic Text: Ergonomic Aspects of Human Information Usage*. London: Taylor and Francis.

DIXON, P. (1982) Plans and written directions for complex tasks. *Journal of Verbal Learning and Verbal Behavior* **21**, 70–84.

DIXON, P. (1987a) The structure of mental plans for following directions. *Journal of Experimental Psychology: Learning, Memory and Cognition* **13**, 18–26.

DIXON, P. (1987b) The processing of organizational and component step information in written directions. *Journal of Memory and Language* **26**, 24–35.

DIXON, P., FARIES, J. and GABRYS, G. (1988) The role of explicit action statements in understanding and using written directions. *Journal of Memory and Language* **27**, 649–667.

DIXON, P., HARRISON, K. and TAYLOR, D. (1993) Effects of sentence form on the construction of mental plans from procedural discourse. *Canadian Journal of Experimental Psychology* **47**, 375–400.

DOBRIN, D. N. (1983) What's technical about technical writing? In: ANDERSON, P. V., BROCKMAN, J. and MILLER, C. R. (Eds), *New Essays in Technical and Scientific Communication: Research, Theory and Practice*, pp. 227–250. Farmingdale, NY: Baywood Publishing Co. Inc.

DUFFY, T. M. (1981) Organizing and utilizing document design options. *Information Design Journal* **2**, 256–266.

EPSTEIN, J. (1981) Informing the elderly. *Information Design Journal* **2**, 215–235.

ERDMANN, R. L. and NEAL, A. S. (1971) Laboratory vs. field experimentation in human factors: an evaluation of an experimental self-service airline ticket vendor. *Human Factors* **13**, 521–531.

FILE, S. E. and JEW, A. (1973) Syntax and the recall of instructions in a realistic situation. *British Journal of Psychology* **64**, 65–70.

FILLENBAUM, S. (1966) Memory for gist: some relevant variables. *Language and Speech* **9**, 217–227.

FODDY, W. (1993) *Constructing Questions for Interviews and Questionnaires*. Cambridge, UK: Cambridge University Press.

FOX, J. J. (1981) Design of a record form for a clinical trial. *Clinical Research Reviews* **1**, 157–161.

FRASE, L. T. and SCHWARTZ, B. J. (1979) Typographical cues that facilitate comprehension. *Journal of Educational Psychology* **71**, 197–206.

GLENBERG, A. M. and LANGSTON, W. E. (1992) Comprehension of illustrated text: pictures help to build mental models. *Journal of Memory and Language* **31**, 129–151.

GOMBRICH, E. (1990) Pictorial instructions. In: BARLOW, H., BLAKEMORE, C. and WESTON-SMITH, M. (Eds), *Images and Understanding*, pp. 26–45. Cambridge, UK: Cambridge University Press.

GUESTELLO, S. J., TRAUT, M. and KORIENEK, G. (1989) Verbal versus pictorial representations of objects in a human–computer interface. *International Journal of Man-Machine Studies* **31**, 99–120.

GUTHRIE, J. T. (1988) Locating information in documents: a cognitive model. *Reading Research Quarterly* **23**, 178–199.

GUTHRIE, J. T., BENNETT, S. and WEBER, S. (1991) Processing procedural documents: a cognitive model for following written directions. *Educational Psychology Review* **3**, 249–265.

HART, H. (1893) *Rules for Compositors and Readers at the Clarendon Press, Oxford* (39th edn). Oxford: Oxford University Press.

HARTLEY, J. (1981) Eighty ways of improving instructional text. *IEEE Transactions on Professional Communication* **24**, 17–27.

HARTLEY, J. and TRUEMAN, M. (1985) A research strategy for text designers: the role of headings. *Instructional Science* **14**, 99–155.

HAYES, D. A. and HENK, W. A. (1986) Understanding and remembering complex prose augmented by analogic and pictorial illustration. *Journal of Reading Behavior* **18**, 63–78.

HORNBY, P., CLEGG, C. W., ROBSON, J. I. and MacLAREN, C. R. (1992) Human and organizational issues in information systems development. *Behaviour and Information Technology* **11**, 160–174.

HOWARD, C., O'BOYLE, M. W., EASTMAN, V., ANDRE, T. and MOTOYAMA, T. (1991) The relative effectiveness of symbols and words to convey photocopier functions. *Applied Ergonomics* **22**, 218–224.

JANSEN, C. and STEEHOUDER, M. (1984) Improving the text of a public leaflet. *Information Design Journal* **4**, 10–18.

JOHNSON-LAIRD, P. N. (1983) *Mental Models*. Cambridge: Cambridge University Press.

JOHNSON-LAIRD, P. N. and STEVENSON, R. (1970) Memory for syntax. *Nature* **227**, 412.

KELLER-COHEN, D., MEADER, B. I. and MANN, D. W. (1990) Redesigning a telephone bill. *Information Design Journal* **6**, 45–66.

KIERAS, D. E. and BOVAIR, S. (1984) The role of a mental model in learning to operate a device. *Cognitive Science* **8**, 255–273.

KUHN, S. and MULLER, M. J. (Eds) (1993) Participatory design. *Communications of the ACM* **36**, 24ff.

LEFEVRE, J. and DIXON, P. (1986) Do written instructions need examples? *Cognition and Instruction* **3**, 1–30.

LENTZ, L. (1995) 'Who can tell us what quality a document has?', paper presented at Forum '95 in Dortmund, Germany, November.

LOWE, R. (1993) *Successful Instructional Diagrams*. London: Kogan Page.

MARCEL, A. J. and BARNARD, P. J. (1979) Paragraphs of pictographs: the use of non-verbal instructions for equipment. In: KOLERS, P., WROLSTAD, M. E. and BOUMA, H. (Eds), *Processing of Visible Langage*. New York: Plenum Press.

MARTIN, M. (1989) The visual hierarchy of documents. In: *Proceedings of 36th International Technical Communication Conference*, Vc-32-5. Washington, DC: Society for Technical Communication.

MORRELL, R. W. and PARK, D. C. (1993) The effects of age, illustrations and task variables on the performance of procedural assembly tasks. *Psychology and Aging* **8**, 389–399.

NIELSEN, J. (1993) *Usability Engineering*. London: Academic Press.

NORMAN, D. A. (1988) *The Psychology of Everyday Things*. New York, NY: Basic Books.

ORNA, L. (1994) Managing information products. *IDeAs* **12**, 14–15.

PENMAN, R. (1993) Unspeakable acts and other deeds: a critique of plain legal language. *Information Design Journal* **7**, 121–131.

SAUNDERS, A. (1982) Writing effective assembly procedures. *IEEE Transactions on Professional Communication* **25**, 20–21.

SCHANK, R. C. and ABELSON, R. (1977) *Scripts, Plans, Goals, and Understanding.* Hillsdale, NJ: Lawrence Erlbaum Associates.

SCHRIVER, K. A. (1989) Evaluating text quality: the continuum from text-focused to reader-focused methods. *IEEE Transactions on Professional Communication* **32**, 238–255.

SCHRIVER, K. A. (1992) Teaching writers to anticipate readers' needs: what can document designers learn from usability testing? In: PANDER MAAT, H. and STEEHOUDER, M. (Eds), *Studies of Functional Text Quality*, pp. 141–157. Amsterdam: Rodopi.

SCHRIVER, K. A. (1997) *Dynamics in Document Design.* New York, NY: Wiley.

SCHUMACHER, G. M. and WALLER, R. (1985) Testing design alternatives: a comparison of procedures. In: DUFFY, T. M. and WALLER, R. (Eds), *Designing Usable Texts.* Orlando, FL: Academic Press.

STEEHOUDER, M. and JANSEN, C. (1987) From bureaucratic language to instructional texts: how to design an effective problem-solving tool for citizens. *Information Design Journal* **5**, 129–139.

STEINBERG, E. R. (1980) A garden of opportunities and a thicket of dangers. In: GREGG, L. W. and STEINBERG, E. R. (Eds), *Cognitive Processes in Writing*, pp. 155–167. Hillsdale, NJ: Lawrence Erlbaum Associates.

STERN, K. R. (1984) An evaluation of written, graphic and voice messages in proceduralised instructions. *Proceedings of 28th Annual Meeting of Human Factors Society*, pp. 314–318. Santa Monica, CA: Human Factors Society.

STIFF, P. (1996) The end of the line: a survey of unjustified typography. *Information Design Journal* **8**, 125–152.

SZLICHCINSKI, C. (1984) Factors affecting the comprehension of pictorial instructions. In: EASTERBY, R. S. and ZWAGA, H. J. G. (Eds), *Information Design*, pp. 449–466. Chichester: Wiley and Sons.

THIMBLEBY, H. (1991) Can humans think? The Ergonomics Society Lecture. *Ergonomics* **34**, 1269–1287.

TUFTE, E. R. (1990) *Envisioning Information.* Cheshire, CT: Graphics Press.

TWYMAN, M. (1982) The graphic presentation of language. *Information Design Journal* **3**, 2–22.

VAN DIJK, T. A. and KINTSCH, W. (1983) *Strategies of Discourse Comprehension.* New York, NY: Academic Press.

VERHOEF, L. W. M. (1986) Using a ticket vending machine: a perceptual model. In: OBORNE, D. J. (Ed.), *Contemporary Ergonomics*, pp. 173–177. London: Taylor & Francis.

VERHOEF, L. W. M. (1988) Decision making of vending machine users. *Applied Ergonomics* **19**, 103–109.

WALKER, S. (1993) Happy birthday Hart's rules. *Information Design Journal* **7**, 177–178.

WALLER, R. (1993) Information overload. *IDeAs* **10**, 5.

WALLER, R. (1994) Not in content, but (in form)ation. *IDeAs* **11**, 6.

WALLER, R. and LEWIS, D. (1992) Payphone user-guides: an information-design archetype. *Communicator* **3**, 12–13.

WRIGHT, P. (1978) Feeding the informaion eaters: suggestions for integrating pure and applied research on language comprehension. *Instructional Science* **7**, 249–312.

WRIGHT, P. (1983) Manual dexterity: a user-oriented approach to computer documentation. In: JANDA, A. (Ed.), *Proceedings of CHI '83 Conference on Human Factors in Computing Systems*, pp. 11–18. Boston, MA: CHI.

WRIGHT, P. (1986) Phenomena, function and design: does information make a difference? In: OBORNE, D. J. (Ed.), *Contemporary Ergonomics*, pp. 1–18. London: Taylor & Francis.

WRIGHT, P. (1987) Writing technical information. *Review of Research in Education* **14**, 327–385.

WRIGHT, P. (1994) Quality or usability? Quality writing provokes quality reading. In: STEEHOUDER, M., JANSEN, C., VAN DER POORT, P. and VERHEIJEN, R. (Eds), *Quality in Documentation*, pp. 1–38. Amsterdam: Editions Rodopi.

WRIGHT, P. (1995) Evaluation, design and research: empirical contributions to the beginnings and ends of design procedures. *Information Design Journal* **8**, 82–85.

WRIGHT, P. and HULL, A. J. (1986) Answering questions about negative conditionals. *Journal of Memory and Language* **25**, 691–709.

WRIGHT, P. and REID, F. (1973) Written information: some alternatives to prose for expressing the outcomes of complex contingencies. *Journal of Applied Psychology* **57**, 160–166.

WRIGHT, P., CREIGHTON, P. and THRELFALL, S. M. (1982) Some factors determining when instructions will be read. *Ergonomics* **25**, 225–237.

WRIGHT, P., LICKORISH, A., HULL, A. J. and UMMELEN, N. (1995) Graphics in written directions appreciated by readers but not writers. *Applied Cognitive Psychology* **9**, 41–59.

WURMAN, S. (1989) *Information Anxiety: What To Do When Information Doesn't Tell You What You Need to Know.* New York, NY: Bantam Books.

YOUNG, S. L. and WOGALTER, M. S. (1990) Comprehension and memory of instruction manual warnings: conspicuous print and pictorial icons. *Human Factors* **32**, 637–649.

# CHAPTER FOUR

# Switching from instructions to equipment: the effect of graphic design

ANGELIQUE BOEKELDER and MICHAËL STEEHOUDER

## 4.1 INTRODUCTION

What kind of research do text designers need? Much of the practical research in text design can be characterized as testing – the aim is to verify whether a given document is effective or not. Effectiveness may be defined in terms of acceptability, persuasiveness, usability or otherwise. Testing is of direct relevance for the actual practice, but, of course, test results cannot usually be generalized.

At the opposite side of the spectrum we find the pure academic research which aims to find and validate theories, for instance theories of reading and understanding texts (e.g. Singer, 1990) or theories of procedure acquisition (Anderson, 1983; Bovair and Kieras, 1991). However, such theories are usually very difficult to relate to actual design decisions.

We believe that practice is served best by research into 'functional relationships' between design issues and reading behaviour. We want to know how the behaviour of the reader can be influenced in a way which we assume to be effective or recommendable. For instance, we may try to focus the reader's attention on specific elements of the text, or facilitate the reader's skipping of certain elements if they are not relevant to the specific needs of the situation. Research can help to identify the behaviour of the readers and to determine design issues that influence their choices.

## 4.2  THE EXPERIMENT

In the experiment reported in this chapter, we focus on one strategic decision readers have to make while they are working with equipment using written instructions. Essential in using instructions is the interaction between the text on the one hand and the operations to be carried out with the equipment on the other. We assume that three basic reader tasks are involved:

- Selecting the information relevant to the task (including searching, skipping irrelevant information, adjusting reading intensity to the relative importance of the information; cf. Wright, 1989).

- Inferring a 'mental action plan': translating the information from the text into a procedure which enables the readers to accomplish their goal.

- Switching from the text to the equipment (and vice versa); the reader has to decide when to stop reading and start acting, and when to interrupt acting in order to continue to read again.

The issue of switching has been raised in a study by Jansen and Steehouder (1992) which examined the problems people face when filling out government forms. Most forms are accompanied by explanations and instructions as to how to answer the questions. The study showed that many errors occurred because form-fillers stopped reading the instructions too soon or too late. When they stopped too soon, they missed essential information; when they stopped too late, they had read irrelevant information which confused them and led to errors.

Switching behaviour might also be important to user instructions for technical equipment. Since people tend *not* to read *all* of the instructions before they start 'working' (cf. Carroll, 1990; Steehouder and Jansen, 1992), it seems important that they switch from document to equipment at the most suitable moment. Generally, this will be immediately after reading a single step.

In the experiment it was investigated to what extent graphic separation of information in an instruction influences switching behaviour of readers. In the experiment the separation consisted of simply ruling off 'units' of information, in such a way that it looks like every unit is put in a separate box. Of course, other methods of separation might have similar effects, such as spacing or using different background colours or patterns for each unit.

### 4.2.1  Hypothesis

When a series of steps is presented with graphic boundaries (e.g. lines) between the steps, these boundaries will influence the moment at which the reader will switch from text to equipment to carry out a required action (e.g. press buttons).

**Figure 4.1**   Simulated thermostat interface on computer screen.

### 4.2.2   Participants

Fifty-eight undergraduate students (37 males and 21 females) participated in the experiment. Their age varied between 17 and 30 years. They were all students at the University of Twente, The Netherlands.

### 4.2.3   Materials

A programmable thermostat of a central heating system was simulated on a personal computer (Figure 4.1). The buttons of the simulated thermostat could be pressed using the mouse of the computer. This enabled the users to alter, for example, the time or the temperature on the display of the simulated thermostat. On the original thermostat the function of each of the buttons was clearly indicated. However, because we did not want the subjects to take advantage of these inscriptions, we substituted them by (meaningless) numbers.

The principle of the thermostat is that at certain times of the day (determined by the user) the temperature in the house automatically rises or falls. For example, if one gets up at 7 o'clock, the thermostat can be programmed in such a way that the temperature will be 19°C at 7:00. If one normally leaves the house at 8 o'clock to go to work, the thermostat can be programmed in such a way that the temperature falls to 12°C at 8:00. In this way, four periods per day can be programmed. In the instructions these periods were called: 'get up', 'leave the house', 'come home' and 'sleep'. It is possible to configure three different programmes for weekdays, Saturday and Sunday.

The original instructions were adapted to create three versions of the instructions which were used in the experiment:

- An instruction in prose format (Figure 4.2; from now on referred to as the *prose* condition).
- An instruction divided into units, each reflecting one step of the procedure; steps were separated by ruling them off; a step consisted of the condition(s) for

| |
|---|
| Press button 2. On the display you will see 13:00 MO (Monday). |
| Press button 4 repeatedly until the correct day is displayed. |
| Press button 9 or button 10. With button 9 the time increases, with button 10 the time falls. Keep the button pressed until the right time is displayed. |
| Press button 2 again. You have now programmed the day and the time. |

**Figure 4.2**    Fragment of the instruction in prose format.

| |
|---|
| Press button 2. On the display you will see 13:00 MO (Monday). |
| Press button 4. Press this button repeatedly until the correct day is displayed. |
| Press button 9 or button 10. With button 9 the time increases, with button 10 the time falls. Keep the button pressed until the right time is displayed. |
| Press button 2 again. You have now programmed the day and the time. |

**Figure 4.3**    Fragment of the instruction in diagrammatical format where all information about one step is presented in one box.

| |
|---|
| Press button 2. |
| On the display you will see 13:00 MO (Monday). |
| Press button 4. Press this button repeatedly until the correct day is displayed. |
| Press button 9 or button 10. With button 9 the time increases, with button 10 the time falls. |
| Keep button 9 pressed until the right time is displayed. Press button 2 again. You have now programmed the day and the time. |

**Figure 4.4**    Fragment of the instruction in diagrammatical format where not all information about one step is presented in one box.

the action, the action itself, and the result(s) of the action (Figure 4.3; from now on referred to as the *stepwise* condition).

■ An instruction in which units were again separated by lines, but now the units did not cover one single step; instead, seven units contained only part of the information about a single step while the rest of the information was included in the next unit, and nine units contained information about more than one step (Figure 4.4; from now on referred to as the *inconsistent* condition).

To illustrate the inconsistent condition, Figure 4.4 shows that information about the *effect* of the action in the first unit ('pressing button 2') is mentioned in the next unit. Note the difference with the stepwise condition (Figure 4.3) where all information about pressing button 2 is presented in one unit. Another form of inconsistency is shown in the last unit of Figure 4.4, where two actions are mentioned within one unit.

All three instructions consisted almost entirely of simple sentences, each containing just one type of information: action information ('press button 7'), background information about the buttons ('button 9 to move the time forward, button 10 to move the time backward') or information to check ('on the display you see 13:00 MO'; 'you have now set the time and temperature'). To avoid the text becoming too predictable and artificial, we had to make some exceptions to this principle, for instance in the sentence 'press this button repeatedly until the correct day is displayed' which contains action information ('press this button') as well as information to check ('until the right day is displayed'). In total, the instructions contained seven procedures, which together consisted of 59 sentences. The sentences were the same for the three versions. The instructions were presented in a booklet, with an assignment printed at the top of each page, followed by the corresponding procedure.

### 4.2.4   Experimental procedure

The subjects were randomly assigned to the three conditions: prose (18 subjects), stepwise (20 subjects) and inconsistent (20 subjects). They were asked to complete the seven tasks using the instructions, while reading aloud the assignments as well as the instructions. The subjects had to carry out the assignments in the given order. They were not allowed to look up information in the preceding pages of the booklet. Each subject was videoed and key selections were recorded into logfiles.

### 4.2.5   Data analysis

The video recordings were used to register for each subject what he/she did after each sentence. The events were categorized as:

- reading on;
- checking;
- pressing buttons;
- something else (e.g. the subject skipped the sentence and did not read it at all).

We expect that subjects will press one or more buttons after having read one step of the instruction. In the prose version, the readers have to decide for themselves where the information about one step ends (and so, where they should switch). The other versions *suggest* that the information about one step ends where a line is inserted. That line indicates the moment the subject has to switch to the equipment. In order to relate the activities of the subjects to the presence or absence of lines, we counted the events after each of the 59 sentences of the instruction. Scores were analysed using analysis of variance.

**Table 4.1**   Effects of line placement on switching from text to equipment
(= pressing buttons on the equipment)

|  | How often was reading a sentence followed by pressing a button? | | |
|  | Prose | Stepwise | Inconsistent |
|---|---|---|---|
| Sentences followed by a line only in the stepwise condition (n = 6) | 2.1 | 4.1 | 0.5 |
| Sentences followed by a line only in the inconsistent condition (n = 8) | 3.7 | 1.8 | 6.2 |

### 4.2.6   Results

To determine whether lines controlled the switching behaviour of our subjects, we focused on two groups of sentences in the instruction.

The first group consisted of six sentences followed by a line in the stepwise condition, but *not* followed by a line in the inconsistent condition. In the stepwise condition these lines marked exactly the boundaries between the steps, which were the places where readers would normally be expected to switch. There were no lines at these places in the inconsistent condition.

The second group consisted of eight sentences followed by a line in the inconsistent condition, but *not* followed by a line in the stepwise condition. In the inconsistent condition these lines occurred at places *within* one step of the instruction, a place where the subjects were *not* expected to switch.

Table 4.1 shows the mean number of occasions the subjects pressed a button, for the first group of sentences where lines were missing in the inconsistent condition as well as for the second group of sentences with redundant lines.

A one-way analysis of variance showed that in the first group of sentences the mean number of times subjects pressed a button differs for prose, stepwise condition, and inconsistent condition ($F = 24.71$, df = 2, $p < 0.01$).

Post hoc comparisons showed that for this group of sentences, all three formats differed significantly from each other. This result indicates that after a sentence followed by a line, subjects switched more often than after a sentence not followed by a line.

There were also differences in the second group of sentences ($F = 40.59$, df = 2, $p < 0.01$). Post hoc comparisons showed that for Group 2 also all three formats differed significantly from each other. These data indicate that if there is a line at a point where readers are normally not expected to switch, as in the inconsistent condition, subjects switched more often at that point, compared to subjects in the stepwise condition (where no lines were drawn at that point in the instructions).

## 4.3 CONCLUSION

Based on the results, we can conclude that ruling off sentences in instructions influences the switching behaviour of people.

- If boxes contained more than one action (buttons to press), subjects tended to postpone actions until they had read the entire box, which resulted in a greater proportion of 'pressing two or more buttons'.

- If instructions contained lines marking the boundaries between two steps (stepwise condition), subjects tended to switch at that point more often than if such lines were absent (prose and inconsistent condition).

- If instructions contained lines within one step, where readers are not expected to switch (inconsistent condition), subjects tended to switch nevertheless more often than when such lines were absent (prose and stepwise condition).

The conclusions need to be verified. The participants were forced to work more or less step-by-step, and to read the instructions carefully and aloud. Research indicates, however, that usually instructions are not read very carefully (e.g. Wright, 1989; Carroll, 1990; Steehouder and Jansen, 1992). It would be interesting to investigate whether switching behaviour can also be controlled by lines in more realistic circumstances.

In this experiment very simple instructions were used for a relatively simple piece of equipment. The instructions were not branched, and there was no additional information such as examples, illustrations, footnotes, etc. Further research will be needed to investigate whether the effect found in the experiments also holds for more complex instructions.

### REFERENCES

ANDERSON, J. R. (1983) *The Architecture of Cognition*. Cambridge, MA: Harvard University Press.

BOVAIR, S. and KIERAS, D. E. (1991) Towards a model of acquiring procedures from text. In: BARR, R., KAMIL, M. L., MOSENTHAL, P. B. and PEARSON, P. D. (Eds), *Handbook of Reading Research: Vol. 2*, pp. 206–229. New York: Longman.

CARROLL, L. M. (1990) *The Nurnberg Funnel: Designing Minimalist Instruction for Practical Computer Skill*. Cambridge, MA: MIT Press.

JANSEN, C. J. M. and STEEHOUDER, M. F. (1992) Forms as a source of communication problems. *Journal of Technical Writing and Communication* **22**, 179–194.

SINGER, M. (1990) *Psychology of Language: An Introduction to Sentence and Discourse Processes*. Hillsdale: Erlbaum.

STEEHOUDER, M. F. and JANSEN, C. J. M. (1992) Optimizing the quality of forms. In: PANDER MAAT, H. and STEEHOUDER, M. F. (Eds), *Studies in Functional Text Quality*, pp. 159–172. Amsterdam: Editions Rodopi.

WRIGHT, P. (1989) The need for theories of NOT reading: some psychological aspects of the human–computer interface. In: ELSENDOORN, B. and BOUMA, H. (Eds), *Working Models of Human Perception*, pp. 319–340. London: Academic Press.

# CHAPTER FIVE

# The graphic presentation of patient package inserts

KAREL VAN DER WAARDE

## 5.1 PATIENT PACKAGE INSERTS

Patient package inserts provide patients with information about a specific medicine. These inserts are developed and produced by the pharmaceutical industry, and are included in medicine packages. European regulations stipulate that every medicine must be accompanied by such an insert from January 1994 onwards (Directive 92/27/EEC, 1992). Approximately 40 000 different inserts have had to be produced.

There are two main reasons for supplying inserts to patients (Donnelly, 1991). The first is to increase the effective use of medicines. The supply of printed information could increase the patients' knowledge about their medicines (about the treatment, the instructions, and side-effects), and it could change attitudes of patients (improve satisfaction with a medicine, and influence a risk–benefit assessment). The provision of information could also increase appropriate medicine-taking behaviour (compliance), and increase the number of reactions from patients (reporting of side-effects, and questions asked). The second reason for supplying inserts is that the patient has a right to be informed.

Patients have three main purposes for reading inserts (Vander Stichele *et al.*, 1991). In the first place, patients seem to be interested in information about safety related matters, such as side-effects, and risks involved. Patients need this information to make decisions on whether to use a medicine or not. Secondly, patients consult an insert to find out how to administer a medicine. And thirdly, patients read inserts to find out about the indications of a medicine. This last information can reassure patients by confirming that the appropriate medicine has been prescribed. It also tells patients which effects could be anticipated and whether these effects are positive or should be cause for concern. Patient package inserts have been extensively investigated by medical, pharmaceutical and linguistic researchers (see for example Bogaert *et al.*, 1989; Mann, 1991). Several investigations have shown that at least 75 per cent of patients say they read inserts (Gibbs *et al.*, 1989; Rupf, 1991).

The EU directive states that inserts should include the following seven information sections:

- Identification of a medicine (names, active ingredients, and the name of the manufacturer).

- Therapeutic indications.

- Information necessary before taking a medicine (contraindications, precautions, interactions and special warnings).

- Instructions for use (dosage, method and route of administration, and the duration of the treatment).

- Description of undesirable effects.

- Information about expiry date and storage instructions.

- Date of the most recent revision of the insert.

The choice of this list of sections is mainly based on common sense and some research results (see for example Joossens, 1989, 1993). The list still contains some historical remnants, which can be traced back to 1968, when the first patient-oriented warnings had to appear on medicine packages.

Although this list of information sections seems to provide a solid starting point for the development of inserts, there are many unresolved issues. For example, the discussion of what an undesirable effect actually entails and the way in which this should be worded is still ongoing. The situation regarding liability and copyright issues is also still unclear. However, despite these difficulties, it seems clear that the development of inserts is worth the effort simply because patients are happier with inserts than without them (Vander Stichele and Bogaert, 1989).

It should be clear that providing patient package inserts is only a small part of the process of supplying patients with information about their medicines. Most information is supplied orally by general practitioners or medical specialists during the consultation, or by pharmacists who dispense the medicines. Inserts are usually the only printed information available to patients, and they can only be read after a medicine has been acquired. It is therefore important to make these inserts as effective as possible.

One of the factors which influence the effectiveness of the use of inserts is the visual or graphic presentation. The graphic presentation of current patient package inserts seems to suggest, however, that they are considered to be of little importance. Not much has improved since Walter Modell wrote in 1967 that most inserts are 'printed in Lilliputian type on Bible paper, are hard to handle and very difficult to read' (Modell, 1967, p. 776).

## 5.2 A FRAMEWORK FOR THE DESCRIPTION OF GRAPHIC PRESENTATION

In order to discuss graphic presentation, it seems essential to distinguish between insert development and insert use. During development, complex medical information is transformed and presented in a single insert. The relation between the intended information content and the graphic presentation can be called 'concordance'. This process is reversed when inserts are used. A user looks at an insert and can extract information from it. The relation between the graphic presentation and insert use can be called 'suitability'.

In order to describe the concordance and the suitability of graphic presentation in inserts, it is essential to apply some sort of descriptive framework (for a brief discussion of several descriptive frameworks see Van der Waarde, 1993). Structured documents, such as inserts, are often described as a collection of objects. A description could initially try to describe the smallest (atomic) objects which might have an influence on insert use. This description of the smallest objects can be expanded to include a description of relations between these objects. A third level of description could encompass characteristics related to a complete document. The description which follows focuses on each of these three levels. The complete framework is illustrated in Figure 5.1.

### 5.2.1 Level 1 – graphic components

The first type of graphic component is the *verbal* component. A possible definition of verbal components is that they are all meaningful marks which can be pronounced. Common topics are the use of serif or sanserif typefaces, the justification mode, the dimensions of type (x-height, line space and capital height), the line length, the type weight, and the use of upper and lower case characters (see for example Luna, 1992). This is the most common type of graphic component in patient package inserts.

The second type of component is the *pictorial* component. A pictorial component is a graphic mark, or group of marks which relates, however distantly, to the appearance or structure of a real or imagined object (Twyman, 1985). Several taxonomies for this type of component have been developed (for example Goldsmith, 1984). The majority of illustrations in inserts show how a medicine should be administered. However, pictorial components rarely occur in inserts.

The third type of graphic component is the *schematic* component. Schematic components are separable graphic marks which cannot be categorized as either verbal or pictorial. Examples of schematic components are rules, bullets, arrows and background colours. Schematic components can only be used in combination with other types of graphic components. The most common schematic component in inserts is a single line border around verbal components.

The fourth type is the *composite* component. A composite component is a configuration of graphic marks which cannot be further separated, but can consist of any combination of verbal, pictorial and schematic components. Examples of

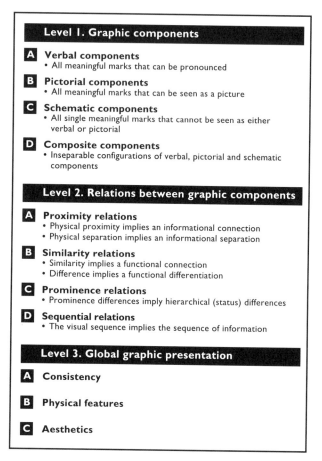

**Figure 5.1**  Framework for the description of graphic presentation.

composite components are diagrams, charts, tables and annotated illustrations (see for example Weidenmann, 1994). Composite components are very rarely used in inserts.

The distinction between these four types of graphic components is not an absolute division. For example, some pictograms can be classified as pictorial, or as schematic, or as composite components. However, these four types of components are sufficient for an initial description of the smallest graphic objects in inserts.

### 5.2.2   Level 2 – relations between components

The first relation, *proximity*, refers to the distance between graphic components. Graphic components which are positioned close together suggest that there is a strong relation between information elements; components which are positioned further apart are less related. This type of relation is frequently described as the grouping of information, or the use of space (see for example Hartley, 1994). Figure 5.1

illustrates this relation. In this figure the first level consists of four groups. Each group consists of a reversed capital letter, a bold text, and a roman text. Only the distance between these elements determines this grouping arrangement.

The second relation between graphic components is the *similarity* of graphic components. A visual similarity is an indication of a functional kinship: components which look similar have a similar hierarchical status. Graphic components which look different present information elements with a different status. In Figure 5.1 the reversed headings are purposefully made to look similar, thereby indicating that the information is on the same hierarchical level (for a discussion of the similarity principle see Medin *et al.*, 1993).

The third relation can be described as the *prominence* relation. The prominence differences between graphic components is an indication of the amount of difference in hierarchical status between information elements. The larger the contrast between graphic components, the larger the difference in status of information (Dobson, 1979). In Figure 5.1 the difference in prominence between the bold and the roman version of the typeface indicates the amount of difference in status of these elements.

The fourth relation is the *sequential* relation. The sequence of the graphic components indicates the succession of the information elements. In printed information, this sequence is to a large extent determined by the reading direction (Winn, 1993). In Figure 5.1 the information elements follow each other vertically downwards.

These four relations are interrelated: changing one will affect the others. It is thereby necessary to take into account that the sequence of the information sections in inserts is determined by the EU directive.

### 5.2.3   Level 3 – the global graphic presentation

At least three characteristics of the global graphic presentation of an insert have to be considered. These characteristics are important because they provide the reader with a first impression of the information content of an insert.

A first characteristic is the *consistency* of the application of graphic variables in a document. A consistent use of graphic components and relations between components throughout an insert can make the information structure easier to grasp.

A second characteristic is the *physical features* of a document. For example, the dimensions of the document, the paper quality, printing inks, shine-through and reflection can be described.

The last characteristic related to the overall graphic presentation is the *aesthetic aspects* of inserts. These aspects are probably the most difficult ones to describe, but they are mentioned most often in relation to graphic presentation.

### 5.3   DESCRIBING THE GRAPHIC PRESENTATION OF INSERTS

The purpose of the development of a graphic presentation is to construct an insert which is maximally effective. The most effective graphic presentation is achieved when as many readers as possible can be accommodated by a single insert. The suggested framework may be helpful in two ways.

Firstly, the framework provides an approach for organizing discussions (e.g. between clients and designers) which try to establish whether a specific graphic presentation is the most appropriate in representing information about medicines in inserts (concordance). A systematic approach may make the integration of general design guidelines and experimental evidence possible. Looking at the most recent inserts, there seem to be three shifts:

- The amount of verbal components is reduced in favour of the other three types of components.

- The relations between graphic components are exploited to visualize relations between information elements.

- The general factors are considered in order to provoke a more favourable impression.

Secondly, the framework could be used to investigate the influence of graphic presentation on insert use. Each component, relation between components, and overall characteristic can be modified to improve the effectiveness of graphic presentation (suitability). Empirical studies and usability tests need to be undertaken to establish the influence of graphic presentation on the effectiveness of inserts.

### REFERENCES

BOGAERT, M., VANDER STICHELE, R., KAUFMAN, J. M. and LEFEBVRE, R. (Eds) (1989) *Patient Package Insert as a Source of Drug Information*. Amsterdam: Elsevier Science Publishers.

DIRECTIVE 92/27/EEC (1992) Council Directive 92/27/EEC of 31 March 1992 on the labelling of medicinal products for human use and on package leaflets. *Official Journal of the European Communities* **L113**, 30-4-1992, 8–12.

DOBSON, M. W. (1979) Visual information processing during cartographic communication. *The Cartographic Journal* **16**, 14–20.

DONNELLY, M. C. (1991) Background to patient information in the European Community. In: MANN, R. D. (Ed.), *Patient Information in Medicine*, pp. 5–12. Carnforth: Parthenon.

GIBBS, S., WATERS, W. F. and GEORGE, C. F. (1989) The benefits of prescription information leaflets (1). *British Journal of Clinical Pharmacology* **27**, 723–739.

GOLDSMITH, E. (1984) *Research into Illustration*. Cambridge: Cambridge University Press.

HARTLEY, J. (1994) *Designing Instructional Text* (3rd edn). London: Kogan Page.

JOOSSENS, L. (1989) Why patient package inserts: a consumer view. In: BOGAERT, M., VANDER STICHELE, R., KAUFMAN, J. M. and LEFEBVRE, R. (Eds). *Patient Package Insert as a Source of Drug Information*, pp. 19–25. Amsterdam: Elsevier Science Publishers.

JOOSSENS, L. (1993) *La lisibilité de l'étiquetage et des notices des médicaments*. Bruxelles: Centre de Recherche et d'Information des Organisations de Consommateurs.

LUNA, P. (1992) *Understanding Type for Desktop Publishing*. London: Blueprint.

MANN, R. D. (Ed.) (1991) *Patient Information in Medicine*. Carnforth: Parthenon.

MEDIN, D. L., GOLDSTONE, R. L. and GENTNER, D. (1993) Respects for similarity. *Psychological Review* **100**, 254–278.

MODELL, W. (1967) How to stuff a stuffer and cook a wolf. *Clinical Pharmacology and Therapeutics* **8**, 775–781.

RUPF, R. E. (1991) 'Evaluation of patient oriented drug information: package leaflets as viewed by the patient and their impact on outpatients' behaviour during treatment', PhD thesis. Basel: University of Basel, Faculty of Philosophy and Natural Sciences.

TWYMAN, M. (1985) Using pictorial language: a discussion of the dimensions of the problem. In: DUFFY, T. and WALLER, R. (Eds), *Designing Usable Texts*, pp. 245–314. Orlando, FL: Academic Press.

VANDER STICHELE, R. and BOGAERT, M. G. (1989) Patient package inserts: the Belgian experience with a mandatory program. *Drug Information Journal* **23**, 673–677.

VANDER STICHELE, R., VAN HAECHT, C. H., BRAEM, M. D. and BOGAERT, M. G. (1991) Attitude of the public toward technical package inserts for medication information in Belgium. *Drug Information and Clinical Pharmacy; The Annals of Pharmacotherapy* **25**, 1002–1006.

VAN DER WAARDE, K. (1993) 'An investigation into the suitability of the graphic presentation of patient package inserts', PhD thesis. Reading: Reading University, Department of Typography & Graphic Communication.

WEIDENMANN, B. (1994) Codes of instructional pictures. In: SCHNOTZ, W. and KULHAVY, R. W. (Eds), *Comprehension of Graphics*, pp. 29–42. Amsterdam: Elsevier Science Publishers.

WINN, W. (1993) Perception principles. In: FLEMING, M. and LEVIE, W. H. (Eds), *Instructional Message Design, Principles from the Behavioral and Cognitive Sciences*, pp. 55–126. Englewood Cliffs, NJ: Educational Technology Publications.

# CHAPTER SIX

# Text, pictures or flowcharts for specific types of information

PIET WESTENDORP

## 6.1 INTRODUCTION

In a relatively short period of time, electronic products have become very versatile and very difficult to use. The ongoing rapid development of microprocessors, memory chips and other microelectronic elements will make more and more features possible in the near future. Therefore, the instructions will be longer and longer.

User manuals have not only become more voluminous, but more varied, too. Designers of user manuals nowadays can choose from a variety of alternatives to prose text. They may use schematic forms like tables or flowcharts (logical pictures) or choose from a variety of (representational) pictures. This may be done to avoid translations, but often the motivation seems to be based on the misconception that a picture is always worth a thousand words. This may sometimes be true and sometimes not. The important thing is to find out exactly when a (representational or logical) picture is the most effective medium and when text is more effective in communicating instructions for use. From the users' point of view this 'when' means 'for what task'; from the designers'/writers' point of view this means 'for what type of information'. Therefore, it is worthwhile investigating which medium is most effective for which type of information.

## 6.2 RESEARCH

A considerable amount of research has been conducted to establish the usefulness of pictures in text (e.g. Levie and Lentz, 1982). Much of this research was directed at the effectiveness of pictures in school books and other texts. Many contrastive tests have been performed in which either pictures were added to text or text was added to pictures.

This type of research has met with increasing criticism. Stone (1980) noted that the materials used in tests where the effectiveness of text was contrasted with that of pictures were rarely described in terms of their relevant characteristics. In a review of meta-analyses and other studies, Clark (1983) found no learning benefits to be gained from employing any specific medium to deliver instructions. Schumacher and Waller (1985) found that in most of the tests both content and form of the material had been chosen subjectively. Wright (1988) wondered what purpose could be served by comparing a good example of x with a bad example of y. Sims-Knight (1992) concludes that most of the research is atheoretical and that often the answers are complex – what is true for one kind of visual is not true for another.

Bieger and Glock (1984/85) presented a possible remedy for some of these problems. They developed a taxonomy of categories of information to classify the content of instructive picture–text materials in a way that would permit generalizability to other materials. This taxonomy consists of nine types of information: inventory, descriptive, operational, spatial, contextual (which provides the theme or organization for other information that may precede or follow; it informs about the general outcome of following certain procedures), covariant (which specifies a relationship between two or more pieces of information that vary together, like cause and effect, problem and solution, action and result), temporal, qualifying, and emphatic. Bieger and Glock further hypothesized that of these nine categories of information types only four were essential for effective use of picture–text materials: inventory, operational, spatial and contextual. These hypotheses were confirmed in experiments.

On the basis of this taxonomy Bieger and Glock (1986) compared instructions for assembly tasks in yet another series of experiments, varying pictures and text for specified categories of information. They found that textual presentation of spatial information produced fewer errors, whereas pictorial presentation of spatial information reduced performance times drastically. Pictorial presentation of contextual information substantially reduced assembly times and slightly reduced the number of assembly errors. Bieger and Glock found no differences between pictorial and textual depiction of operational information.

Anoskey and Catrambone (1992) compared the Bieger and Glock taxonomy with those developed by Booher (1975), Wickens et al. (1983), and Feiner and McKeown (1990). This comparison shows that the Bieger and Glock taxonomy is the most detailed one and that the Feiner and McKeown taxonomy can be mapped with the Bieger and Glock taxonomy. Anoskey and Catrambone conclude that the strong correspondence between the two most detailed taxonomies supports their use as a classification scheme.

A major problem for application of the Bieger and Glock taxonomy is the decision at which level the material should be analysed. Bieger and Glock analysed the texts on a word and sentence level for all categories except contextual and pictures on the level of each picture as a whole. We decided to categorize on paragraph and complete picture level. We determined the primary goal of each paragraph or illustration and used that as the criterion to decide into what category the information should be classified. We did not find any problems in reaching agreement about the classification.

## 6.3   TEST

Comparing the efficiency of text and logical (abstract, e.g. flowcharts) or representational (realistic) pictures is to a certain degree atheoretical because content and form of text and pictures are usually chosen subjectively. Applying the Bieger and Glock (1984/85) taxonomy does help to describe the content of the materials used in terms of their relevant characteristics, but the design of text and pictures still has to be chosen somewhat subjectively. In this test we used a telephone system, because for this kind of equipment, and for the kind of tasks involved, the drawings are usually two-dimensional, whereas for instructions involving the assembly of a product, three-dimensional drawings are often the obvious choice (e.g. to indicate orientation, location or composition of elements). In three-dimensional drawings many choices have to be made that may have a severe impact on efficiency (perspective or axonometric, exploded view, cutaway or ghost view, point of view, etc.). For the kind of equipment for which only the front view with keys and a display is important for operation (most modern electronic products), simple two-dimensional drawings are the obvious choice. Now discussion of the form will be restricted to the style elements, e.g. the thickness of the lines and how realistic the drawings of fingers should be.

On the basis of the taxonomy six variations of a user manual for a telephone system were designed and in tests compared with the original – text-based – user manual, varying text, representational and logical pictures (flowcharts) for operational, contextual and covariant information.

The specified types of information in the original user manual (Version 1) were presented in flowcharts or representational pictures or were left out (Table 6.1). Versions 2 and 3 were included because Bieger and Glock found that contextual

**Table 6.1**   Seven variations of a user manual for a telephone system

| Version | Information type and medium |
| --- | --- |
| 1 | Original user manual |
| 2 | Contextual information in a flowchart |
| 3 | No contextual information |
| 4 | Operational information in pictures |
| 5 | Operational information in a flowchart |
| 6 | Covariant information in a flowchart |
| 7 | No covariant information |

information was vital for proper comprehension of the instructions; Versions 4 and 5 were included because Bieger and Glock found no significant difference between textual and pictorial depiction of the operational information; and Versions 6 and 7 were included because Bieger and Glock found this information to be unimportant.

Text was always in the simple present, imperative style. Flowcharts were designed according to the ISO 5807 (ISO 1985) standard. Pictures were simple realistic two-dimensional drawings of buttons, displays, etc. The size of the manuals varied from 30 to 35 pages.

These variations of the user manual were compared in tests. Seventy subjects (ten for each version; all students, male and female equally distributed over the versions) were asked to perform the same five tasks and performance times were recorded. Each task had to be successfully completed before a subject was allowed to go on to the next task. Help would be offered after two minutes, but this appeared not to be necessary. One of the seven versions of the manual was provided. We supposed that it would be impossible to do the tasks without using the manual and although we did not ask subjects to read the manual, they all used it.

### 6.4   RESULTS

For each version ten subjects were asked to perform five tasks, but in Versions 3 and 4 only nine subjects actually performed the tasks. $t$ Tests were conducted to analyse the results for the various versions. For each subject the total time (in seconds) to complete the five tasks was computed; then, for each version the total time of the ten subjects was used to calculate the mean (Figure 6.1). $t$ Tests were conducted to analyse the scores for the seven versions. Detailed results are presented in Westendorp (1994).

In this test, leaving out certain types of information (covariant, contextual) in instructions, or presenting specific types of information in different media (text, pictures, flowcharts) did lead to significant differences in performance (one-way ANOVA: $F = 13.39$, df $= 6$, $p < 0.001$).

The versions with the contextual information in flowcharts (Version 2) and without contextual information (Version 3) proved to be significantly more efficient than the version with the contextual information in text (Version 1) ($t = 7.79$, df $= 18$, $p < 0.001$; and $t = 7.22$, df $= 17$, $p < 0.001$ respectively).

The version with the contextual information in flowcharts appeared only to have been used by one subject for one task. Therefore Version 2 could – to a certain degree – also be considered as a version without contextual information. So, in contrast to Bieger and Glock, we found contextual information to be superfluous. It seems that users do not need to know an a priori explanation of what exactly will be the result of their actions. Discovering afterwards what exactly was meant is probably more efficient.

Presenting operational information in pictures (Version 4) is significantly more efficient ($t = 3.03$, $p < 0.008$) than presenting this information in text (Version 1), but the variance between subjects is high (Levene's test for equality of variances:

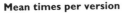

**Mean times per version**

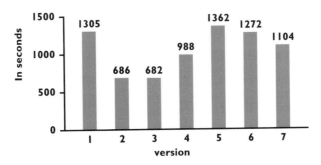

| | Original user manual |
|---|---|
| 2 | Contextual information in flowcharts |
| 3 | No contextual information |
| 4 | Operational information in pictures |
| 5 | Operational information in flowcharts |
| 6 | Covariant information in flowcharts |
| 7 | No covariant information |

**Figure 6.1** Mean times to complete the tasks.

$F = 0.047$, $p < 0.830$). Some subjects did the tests quite quickly, but others performed much slower using pictorial operational information. Bieger and Glock found little effect of the mode of presentation of operational information on performance.

Presenting operational information in a flowchart mode appeared to be counter-productive: Version 5 was the least efficient. This is remarkable since all subjects were students of a university of technology and had some experience with reading (and designing!) flowcharts. Perhaps flowcharts are more useful for complex tasks with many decisions to be made. In this test, with its rather simple tasks, texts proved more efficient.

The original manual (Version 1 in the text) contained quite a lot of covariant information. Comparing this version and Version 6, also with covariant information, with Version 7, which was without covariant information, showed that Version 1 was significantly less efficient than Version 7 ($t = 2.21$, df = 18, $p < 0.04$). Version 6 was less efficient compared to Version 7, but the difference was not significant ($t = 1.14$, df = 18, $p < 0.176$). It may be somewhat premature to conclude that covariant information is better left out for these kinds of tasks: in our test the subjects needed the covariant information only for one of the five tasks. Here the version without covariant information was much more efficient than the versions with covariant information (subjects using Version 7 performed this task 38 per cent faster than those using Version 6, and 32 per cent faster than those using Version 1). In our tests covariant information was usually the feedback of the machine. It seemed that users did not feel the need to have some kind of confirmation in the manual of the feedback of the machine. Either the sound or the information on the display was enough. This may be because the reactions of telephones are generally known and understood. It may be different in situations where the user is left in uncertainty by the feedback of the machine.

## 6.5   CONCLUSIONS

In this test, flowcharts appeared not to be an efficient mode of presentation. The versions with operational and covariant information in flowcharts (Versions 5 and 6) were less efficient than the versions with this type of information in text or representational pictures. The differences with Version 1 are not significant, but Version 5 with the operational information in flowcharts is the least efficient of all versions. If flowcharts are applied in instructions, it is usually mainly for the operational information.

Leaving out specific types of information seems to be quite efficient for user manuals. Leaving out contextual information is more efficient than including it and the same holds true for covariant information. This may give support to the ideas Carroll (1990) has expressed about the minimal manual. The findings reported here may also help to specify the guidelines for a minimal manual.

## REFERENCES

ANOSKEY, A. M. and CATRAMBONE, R. (1992) Text and graphics in instructional design. In: TOMEK, S. (Ed.), *Computer Assisted Learning, 4th International ICCAL Conference*, Wolfsville, Canada, pp.74–86. Berlin, Springer.

BIEGER, G. R. and GLOCK, M. D. (1984/85) The information content of picture–text instructions. *Journal of Experimental Education* **53**, 68–76.

BIEGER, G. R. and GLOCK, M. D. (1986) Comprehending spatial and contextual information in picture–text instructions. *Journal of Experimental Education* **54**, 181–188.

BOOHER, H. R. (1975) Relative comprehensibility of pictorial information and printed words in proceduralized instructions. *Human Factors* **17**, 266–277.

CARROLL, J. M. (1990) *The Nurnburg Funnel; Designing Minimalist Instructions for Practical Computer Skills*. Cambridge, MA: MIT Press.

CLARK, R. E. (1983) Reconsidering research on learning from media. *Review of Educational Research* **53**, 445–459.

FEINER, S. K. and MCKEOWN, K. R. (1990) Generating coordinated multimedia explanations. In: *Proceedings of the 6th IEEE Conference on Artificial Intelligence Applications*, pp. 290–303.

ISO (1985) *Information Processing, Documentation Symbols, Conventions for Data, Program Network Charts, System Resources Charts, ISO Standard 5807*. Geneva: International Organization for Standardization.

LEVIE, W. H. and LENTZ, R. (1982) Effects of text illustrations: a review of research. *Educational Communication and Technology Journal* **30**, 195–232.

SCHUMACHER, G. M. and WALLER, R. (1985) Testing design alternatives: a comprehension of procedures. In: DUFFY, T. and WALLER, R. (Eds) *Designing Usable Texts*, pp. 377–403. Orlando: Academic Press.

SIMS-KNIGHT, J. E. (1992) To picture or not to picture: how to decide? *Visible Language* **26**, 325–388.

STONE, E. (1980) 'Reading text with pictures', paper presented at the annual meeting of the American Educational Research Association, Boston.

WESTENDORP, P. H. (1994) 'Tekst, beeld of stroomdiagram voor technische instructies? Toepassing van de taxonomie van Bieger and Glock op de gebruiksaanwijzing van de Lacis telefoon', internal report, Delft University of Technology.

WICKENS, C. D., SANDRY, D. and VIDULICH, M. (1983) Compatibility and resource competition between modalities of input, central processing and output: testing a model of complex task performance. *Human Factors* **25**, 227–248.

WRIGHT, P. (1988) Issues of content and presentation in document design. In: HELANDER, M. (Ed.), *Handbook of Human Computer Interaction*, pp. 629–652. Amsterdam: Elsevier Science Publishers.

# PART THREE

# Warnings

# CHAPTER SEVEN

# Factors influencing the effectiveness of warnings

MICHAEL S. WOGALTER

## 7.1 INTRODUCTION

The basic goal of safety programmes and hazard analysis is to prevent personal injury and property damage. Warnings, the topic of this chapter, are one of several methods that can be used to defend against harmful outcomes. Warnings may be delivered by signs, on labels, in product manuals, and in other ways described later. The two principal purposes of warnings are to communicate information about potential hazards effectively and to reduce unsafe behaviour that might otherwise occur without their presence. However, warnings are not the best injury-prevention strategy to use (by themselves), particularly if other more effective methods can be employed instead of, or in addition to, warnings.

Several other hazard prevention methods are generally preferred over warnings if they can be properly incorporated into a product/task/environment system. Four hazard prevention methods, in their order of preference, are indicated. The first and best defence against injury is to remove or design out the hazard so that users are not exposed to the danger. Substituting a safe chemical for one known to cause injury is one example of hazard removal. Another way to remove a hazard is to ban a dangerous product from being sold, or if the product has already been purchased, to issue a recall to make a retrofit design change or to exchange the product for a better-designed one.

However, for some equipment, products, environments and jobs, there is no practical way to remove all of the potential hazards and still have a functional product. One example of this is the common power lawnmower which inherently has mechanical, heat, chemical and/or electrical hazards. When hazards cannot be removed, the next best defence against accidents and injury is to guard against them, or in other words, to place some kind of barrier between people and the hazard. For example, many current lawnmowers have a 'dead man' switch that automatically shuts down the blade when the handle is released. This is a procedural guard. Also, many lawnmowers have a shield that drags on the ground behind the mower to prevent debris from flying out in the operator's direction. This is an equipment guard.

Whereas potential accidents can frequently be avoided through proper design and guarding, there are still many kinds of products/tasks/environments for which the hazards cannot be eliminated by these methods. In such cases, the third line of defence against hazards is to educate and train individuals who may use or come in contact with the hazard. Proper training can ensure that employees and users know about the hazards and ways to avoid them (Racicot and Wogalter, 1995). However, there are many situations where formal education and training may not be possible or practical. This is true for consumer products, where manufacturers have limited control over the behaviour of users of their product. In such cases, hazard control is often accomplished through warnings.

Warnings are similar in several ways to the other hazard-control methods. The most obvious connection is with educational/training programmes in which the intention is to communicate knowledge about the hazards and how to avoid them. In addition, warnings can also be considered a type of guard that lacks the usual solid physical barrier often associated with guards. It is a kind of informational guard. Warnings can also serve in combination with the other methods as an additional (redundant) control strategy, as a reminder to persons who already 'know' about the hazard, and to prevent product misuse. By themselves, warnings are the least preferable method to control against accidents and injury, mainly because they are the least reliable. There are many points at which they might fail. People may not see or attend to them, may not understand them, may not produce the appropriate attitudes and beliefs and/or may not motivate people to comply with them. Therefore, they should be considered as a last line of defence and not as a replacement for good design, guarding and education/training. The other methods, particularly the first and second – designing out and guarding against the hazard – are better methods of hazard control.

Thus, warnings are necessary when other hazard-control methods cannot be effectively employed. Given this state of affairs and the fact that warnings are not totally reliable, the principle question is: How can warnings be designed to maximize their effectiveness? The remainder of this chapter addresses this question.

Research has suggested that warnings should contain certain elements:

- a signal word such as 'Danger' and 'Caution' that enables people to recognize that the message is a warning, that a hazard is present, as well as providing information on the hazard level (with 'Danger' signalling more serious and probable injury than 'Caution');
- a description of the hazard, e.g. in the case of a no diving sign, a statement such as 'Shallow water' provides information about the specific danger involved;

- a description of the consequences that could occur if the person fails to obey the warning's directions, e.g. 'You can be permanently paralysed';
- the directions or instructions, i.e., the specific actions that should or should not be done, e.g. 'No diving'.

These four basic elements of warnings are probably a minimum standard. This chapter will discuss factors that go beyond these components. In addition, despite what has just been stated not all warnings need to have all four of the above mentioned components. These are special cases. How one might go about determining the necessary characteristics of warnings will be described later when testing is discussed. However, at this juncture two examples will be mentioned to illustrate the point. One is a sign for wet floors. The consequences statement 'You may slip and fall' is already well known by everyone and so it does not add anything new to what people already know. Another example is the common 'Stop' sign. Here there is nothing more than one word telling the instruction of what to do (plus a distinctive eight-sided shape and red colour). Other statements are not necessary because everyone knows them. Except for these and a limited number of other cases, warnings should generally have all of the four above mentioned components to give people an appreciation of the hazards and to enable them to make informed decisions. Warnings should be designed to match the abilities of the persons to whom they are directed (Laughery and Brelsford, 1991). The warning designer must be careful not to assume that people know as much about the hazard as they do (Laughery, 1993). What may seem obvious to some people, may not be obvious to others. More will be said about the information transmission mission of warnings later.

Beyond providing information, a second major purpose of warnings is to change behaviour. The intent is to redirect people away from unsafe acts that they might otherwise do without the warning. The behavioural purpose of warnings is probably more important than the informational purpose, because ultimately it is more vital to have people avoid the hazard than it is for them to know about it and still get hurt. For example, it is more desirable to ensure that children avoid a hazard than it is for them to understand its nature. Nevertheless, both the informational and behavioural purposes of warnings are important. In recent years, a growing body of research has revealed many factors that influence both aspects.

## 7.2 A HUMAN INFORMATION PROCESSING MODEL OF WARNING EFFECTS

Much of the research on warnings can be organized into coherent units using a theoretical model derived from cognitive psychology. This approach divides people's mental processes into a sequence of stages. Figure 7.1 shows a fairly simple human information processing model. This scheme is not only useful in organizing the factors that influence the effectiveness of warnings, but also can be used to explain why a warning message might fail to achieve the previously mentioned goals of

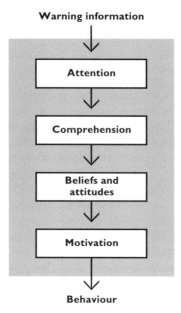

**Figure 7.1**   A human information processing model showing a sequence of stages leading to compliance behaviour.

informing people about the hazard and promoting safe behaviour. As the model shows, before behavioural change can occur (the last stage), processing of the warning must successfully pass through several earlier stages.

Initially the warning must capture attention; that is, it must be noticed. Then, the message contained in the warning must be comprehended. The warning must also agree with the person's attitudes and beliefs. Further, the message must motivate the user to comply with the directed behaviours. The fact that this model proceeds in a temporal sequence implies that there are potential 'bottlenecks' that could prevent the process from being completed. If the warning is not noticed in the first place, the information in the warning will not pass on to any subsequent stages, and of course, behaviour will not be changed. Even though a warning may capture attention, it may not be effective if the message is not understood by the user. Merely examining and reading the warning does not necessarily mean people comprehend it. People must understand all of the words and the grammar, and properly interpret any accompanying symbols and pictorials. But even if the warning is noticed and understood, the process will go no further if the warning does not adequately influence the person's beliefs and attitudes in the appropriate direction, which can be quite difficult to do if the warning is communicating information that is in opposition to the person's existing beliefs and attitudes. Finally, even if the processing of the warning is successful up to this point, the warning will not be behaviourally effective if it does not motivate or energize the user to perform the appropriate safe actions.

Thus, the stages are potential bottlenecks, which could cause processing to stop, preventing it from going further and modifying behaviour. The following sections describe the factors that influence warning effectiveness at each stage of the model.

## 7.3 EFFECTIVENESS FACTORS AT EACH STAGE

Most warnings are transmitted visually (e.g. signs and labels) but may also be transmitted by the other sensory modalities (e.g. auditorily via tones and speech, olfactory via odours, and kinesthetically via vibration). This chapter will focus on the visual modality.

### 7.3.1 Attention

Most environments are cluttered, so in order for warnings to be seen they must possess characteristics that facilitate their standing out from the background (Wogalter et al., 1993c). In other words, they should be conspicuous or salient relative to their context (Wogalter et al., 1987; Young and Wogalter, 1990; Sanders and McCormick, 1993).

Warnings should be of high contrast relative to the background (dark ink on light background, or vice versa) (Barlow and Wogalter, 1993; Sanders and McCormick, 1993). They should have large, legible bold-faced alphanumeric characters. The specific sizes of the printed letters should be based on visual angle which is a function of the actual feature size and the distance from the viewer (at least 5 to 10 degrees of arc on the retina and greater is preferred). Other variables important for adequate size include the characteristics of the target population (discussed below), whether or not movement is involved (and how fast and in what direction), and the illumination conditions, among others (Sanders and McCormick, 1993).

Another factor is placement. A general principle is that warnings should be located close to the hazard, both physically and in time (Wogalter et al., 1987; Frantz and Rhoades, 1993; Wogalter et al., 1995a). A warning describing the potential for a hydrogen gas explosion placed on a car battery or attached to booster cables is much more likely to be noticed at the proper time than a warning in the car owner's manual.

The inclusion of certain kinds of information in the warning can also increase its ability to gain attention. These features include: a signal word (e.g. 'Danger', 'Caution') (Chapanis, 1994; Wogalter and Silver, 1990, 1995) that is paired with a signal icon (a triangle enclosing an exclamation point) (Laughery et al., 1993a; Wogalter et al., 1994a), and a graphic pictorial (e.g. Jaynes and Boles, 1990; Laughery et al., 1993a). The colours red, orange and yellow are commonly used in warnings to indicate different levels of hazard (from greater to lesser, respectively) (Bresnahan and Bryk, 1975; Collins, 1983; Chapanis, 1994; Kalsher et al., 1995; Wogalter et al., 1995b); however, the choice of colour should also depend on the environment in which the warning is placed (Young, 1991). A red warning in an environment that is also largely red will not stand out.

There are several kinds of situations where the amount and type of information that can be placed on a warning is constrained. A common reason is limited space (e.g. on the label of a small container), but such constraint may also be due to warning distance and speed of movement (such as in traffic signs). Several alternatives can be considered. One is to include all the necessary information in the warning regardless of the resulting size. Another alternative is to leave out information. This may be acceptable if there is a more complete and readily accessible warning elsewhere (e.g. an accompanying manual). Some research has shown that a well-located brief persuasive safety sticker can be effective in getting users to read a set of longer, more detailed warnings in the accompanying instruction manual (Wogalter et al., 1995a). Another solution is to increase the size of a product label or sign so that there is more surface area upon which to print more information or use larger type or both (Barlow and Wogalter, 1991; Wogalter et al., 1993b; Wogalter and Young, 1994; Kalsher et al., 1996).

Warnings should have properties that allow them to be seen in degraded conditions such as low illumination, smoke, or fog (e.g. Lerner and Collins, 1983). In addition, warnings should be adequately lit (by directed or back-lighting) and/or have good reflectance so that they are visible under reduced-light conditions (Sanders and McCormick, 1993).

Another important concern in developing noticeable warnings is the characteristics of the target population. Some of the target persons may have reduced sensory capabilities. If individuals with vision or hearing impairments (e.g. older adults) are expected to be part of the target audience (which is often the case), their capabilities and limitations should be taken into account when designing the warning, as for example by making the signs or labels larger (Laughery and Brelsford, 1991). To increase the likelihood that safety information will be conveyed to individuals who have sensory deficits, it is particularly important that the warning be composed of the conspicuity features discussed above. Another strategy is to present the warning information redundantly in two or more modalities (e.g. visually and auditorily) when practical and/or possible (Wogalter and Young, 1991; Wogalter et al., 1993c). Redundant presentation also has the advantage of capturing the attention of target persons occupied with other tasks that monopolize one modality but not the other.

An important issue with respect to attention getting is habituation. Over time, a warning will attract less attention. However, a warning with many conspicuity features will habituate at a slower rate than a warning without them. There are also other ways to counter habituation. The main one is stimulus change which is achievable by modifying the visual characteristics of an existing warning every so often so that it looks different. New ways to counter habituation have been provided by recent technology such as the ability to electronically control warning exposure so that presentation occurs when needed (e.g. with motion sensors). Sophisticated detection and control systems can enable sign personalization (e.g. using the targeted individual's name) and variable presentation schedules (cf. partial reinforcement) (Wogalter et al., 1994b; Racicot and Wogalter, 1995).

Another way to counter habituation, as well as to capture attention more generally, is to use interactive warnings. Users physically interact in some way with the warning while performing a task (such as moving the warning in order to use a piece of equipment). Theoretically, interactive warnings serve to break into the habitual performance of a familiar task (i.e., interrupting a well-learned behavioural script), causing the individual to attend to the warning (Lehto and Papastavrou, 1993). Over time even interactive warnings will habituate, but the process is slowed down (Frantz and Rhoades, 1993; Duffy *et al.*, 1995; Wogalter *et al.*, 1995b; Conzola and Wogalter, 1996; but also see Hunn and Dingus, 1992).

Related to the habituation issue is standardization (Vigilante and Wogalter, 1996). Recently, there has been an increased push for the development of design standards for warnings. There are positive aspects for standardization (e.g. people will know that the sign or label is a warning when they see it). However, the downside is that standardization may promote similarity in appearance which in turn is likely to facilitate habituation-type problems. That is, having a standard look conflicts with habituation countermeasures. If all warnings have a similar style, then changes made only to the content may go unnoticed. People may think that they already know the information because it looks similar to what they have seen previously. Clearly, standardization entails trade-offs regarding attention; this is an issue that needs to be addressed in research.

Lastly, in order to ensure that the warning gains attention, it is important that it is tested with a representative sample of the target population. Evaluation may take many forms such as:

- collecting numerical ratings or rankings of various potential warning designs;
- evaluating legibility for different designs presented at varied distances and under degraded conditions;
- measuring reaction time to displays with and without a warning;
- assessing memory to the signs (which if they remember them indicates that they must have looked at them);
- recording looking behaviour (e.g. direction and duration of gaze).

The best evaluations are those that most closely replicate the conditions and tasks of the risk situation. Thus, measurement of looking behaviour in the actual environment with a hidden video camera is a more valid assessment than questionnaire ratings.

### 7.3.2 Comprehension

If the warning captures attention, then the next important processing stage that must be completed is comprehension. Understandable warnings are necessary to give individuals an adequate appreciation of the hazard so that they can make informed judgements.

One common – but frequently erroneous – assumption by persons who have control over the design or selection of warnings is that everyone in the target audience understands the hazard as well as he or she does. This assumption should be avoided because those in control of the design or selection of warnings are usually not representative of the target audience. Target audiences often have a wide range of mental and physical characteristics. What seems 'common sense' to some persons may not be 'common sense' to others (Laughery, 1993).

Safety communications should *not* be written at the average or median-level percentile person because this will exclude approximately 50 per cent of the people below that point. Rather warnings should be written so that they are understandable for the lowest level of the target audience that can practically be reached (Laughery and Brelsford, 1991).

What are some reasonable assumptions that we can make? If the at-risk target audience includes people who do not have strong language skills (including children, the less educated, and those lacking robust knowledge of the language in which the warning is written), then generally it can be assumed that they will not understand complex verbal messages. In general, if there are two or more terms or statements that mean the same thing, then the best one (with all other aspects being equal) will be comprised of short, frequently-used (common) terms.

In addition, there are some other convenient methods to determine (albeit only approximately) the understandability of textual messages. Various readability formulae are available that are based on frequency-of-use counts, word and sentence length, etc. (though some of the formulae need to be adapted for shorter length, non-punctuated text; see Silver *et al.*, 1991). Moreover, there are teacher workbooks which contain terms that are appropriate for different ages (Silver and Wogalter, 1991). Another rough method is to have a sample of the target audience give numerical understandability ratings for various exemplary messages. However, these methods are only an approximation of what is possibly adequate. They can serve to eliminate poorly written messages, but they do not indicate whether people will actually understand them. Actual testing of the material using a representative sample of the target population (as will be described in more detail later) is the best method of determining whether people understand the message.

Another important comprehension factor is explicitness. Explicit messages contain specific information detailing what the hazard is, giving definitive instructions on what to do or how to avoid the hazard, and giving the consequences of not complying (Laughery *et al.*, 1993b; see also Trommelen and Akerboom, Chapter 9). Warnings that state 'Use in a well-ventilated area' or 'May be hazardous to health' do not convey much useful information because they are too vague. More specific messages like 'Use in a room with forced air or with at least two open windows' or 'Can cause lung cancer which almost always leads to death' are preferred because they tell what the necessary conditions are for use, what the particular problem is, and the potential outcome. Trommelen and Akerboom (Chapter 9) found that explicit warnings for child-care products were not only preferred and the instructions remembered better by participants, but also the products were perceived as more hazardous and the potential injuries more severe than products without explicit warnings.

Pictorials can be another useful way to increase understanding of the hazards. Pictorials are covered more extensively in other chapters in this book, but some brief mention here is appropriate because they can be an important component of warnings. Pictorials can illustrate the hazard, the instructions and/or the potential consequences. Well-designed pictorials have the ability to communicate large amounts of information at a glance and can be useful in reaching persons who cannot read a printed verbal message, either because of vision problems (e.g. with older adults) or because they do not possess good verbal skills or knowledge of the language being used in the warning (e.g. foreign visitors, illiterates, the less educated, children) (Lerner and Collins, 1980; Collins, 1983; Zwaga and Easterby, 1984; Boersema and Zwaga, 1989; Laux *et al.*, 1989).

Sometimes pictorials are contained within a circle surround (indicating a permitted or recommended situation) and sometimes with a slash through it or an X (indicating prohibition of the depicted situation). In various warning systems, other surround shapes have been designated certain meanings (e.g. octagon, triangle, rectangle, etc.). However, with a few exceptions such as the octagonal stop sign or the triangular yield sign, it is not clear that people know (or even learn over time) what the shapes mean without training. This may be due to the fact that surround shapes are inconsistently used across various systems.

The best way, and perhaps the only way, to determine whether the warning will be comprehended is to test it on a representative sample of the target audience to determine whether they understand it (Lerner and Collins, 1980; Wogalter *et al.*, 1987). Such sampling was performed by Dewar and Arthur (see Chapter 8). They developed and evaluated a set of multi-panel pictorials for a variety of hazards near hydroelectric stations. They sampled individuals from various target populations including illiterates, older people, natives, etc. Their tests revealed that most of the pictorial messages were well understood by the individuals tested. Dewar and Arthur's good sampling of individuals likely to be near the hydroelectric station strengthens the contention that the pictorials will be beneficial in communicating the intended messages in the field.

The testing can involve different methods. The best is an open-ended response test (as used by Dewar and Arthur, see Chapter 8) where participants are shown a verbal warning or pictorial and asked what it means to them. The difficulty of this method lies mainly in grading the responses after data collection is completed. Often people do not clearly express what they mean so scoring is partially based on interpretation. Responses can be scored using various criteria from strict to lenient (see, for example, Young and Wogalter, 1990, for a description) and/or judged as completely or partially correct, etc. Two independent judges should evaluate the responses (without knowledge of conditions if it is an experiment) using agreed-upon criteria to provide a measure of reliability.

Other common testing techniques involve multiple choice or matching tests where the correct responses are mixed together with incorrect (distractor) responses. These methods are less desirable than the open-ended method because the results are strongly dependent on the distractor alternatives that are provided. Moreover, these tests are less realistic in the sense that they do not reflect the kinds of retrieval operations that people perform with real-world warnings (i.e., we do not normally choose from distractor answers in trying to understand a warning). Other tests include rankings and ratings, but these tests only tell which of the group of alternative versions may be better; they do not provide strong evidence on whether the message is truly understandable under realistic conditions.

If the testing shows that a substantial number of people do not understand the message, or worse, misunderstand it (i.e., a critical confusion), then this suggests that the warning should be redesigned and retested. One example illustration of misunderstanding is the phrase 'low birth weight' that appears in some cigarette warnings in the USA. This message is intended to admonish pregnant women not to smoke because their babies might be born prematurely, etc. However, some women have interpreted the phrase to mean that smoking can help keep their weight down in the late stages of pregnancy. Had this phrase been tested with a representative sample of women of child-bearing age, before it was put on packages, this misinterpretation would likely have been noted, and another less ambiguous phrase used instead. Testing can also be used to collect data on how a warning can be improved if a new or redesigned warning should be necessary.

As mentioned earlier, well-designed pictorials can potentially communicate large amounts of information at a glance. However, it is also true that poorly designed pictorials may communicate nothing (other than perhaps that a warning is present) or worse, the wrong message (Lerner and Collins, 1980; Laux et al., 1989). So, like verbal messages, pictorials can be misinterpreted. Consider a pictorial that accompanied the verbal warnings for Acutane (Roche Dermatologics, Nutley, NJ), a drug for severe acne that also causes severe birth defects in babies of women taking the drug just before or during pregnancy. The pictorial shows a side-view, outline shape of a pregnant woman within a circle-slash surround. The intended meaning is that women should not take the drug if they are pregnant, or if they are not pregnant, to take precautions against getting pregnant. However, some women have incorrectly interpreted the pictorial to mean that the chemical might help them to avoid getting pregnant. Again, early testing using a representative sample of the target audience (women of child-bearing age) would have provided information about this misinterpretation. Also, input from test participants can be used to generate ideas for new designs (if the testing reveals that one is needed). Of course, the new designs should be tested to ensure that they are understandable (Wolff and Wogalter, 1993; Magurno et al., 1994). The process may require several rounds of iterative test and design that should continue until an adequate level of comprehension is achieved (see Dewar and Arthur, Chapter 8).

### 7.3.3   Beliefs and attitudes

Given that a warning has been attended to and understood, then the next major stage concerns beliefs and attitudes. Beliefs refer to an individual's knowledge of a topic that they accept as true (regardless of its actual veracity). Beliefs are used to form opinions, expectations and judgements. Attitudes are similar except there is more emotional involvement. Given their similarity, beliefs and attitudes are grouped into one stage for the purposes of the current model. This was an arbitrary decision as beliefs could have been grouped with the previous stage and attitudes as a separate emotional component.

This processing stage has not garnered as much research as the two earlier stages, but beliefs and attitudes can strongly influence whether a warning will be effective. Among the factors that affect warning processing at this stage are familiarity and perceived hazard–risk.

It is important to note that beliefs and attitudes can also affect processing at earlier stages. For example, individuals who believe something is safe may not look for a warning, and even if they notice it they may not examine it further. This effect reveals that the flow of information through the model's stages is not linear. Indeed it is likely that all stages of processing feed back onto each other (in a loop fashion). The idea that later stages affect earlier stages was alluded to in the discussion of the effect of habituation at the attention stage where repeated exposure produces knowledge which has a negative effect on noticeability.

Similarly, people who frequently use the same product or perform the same task will tend to believe that there is less risk than perhaps they should. This familiarity effect has been noted in numerous research studies (e.g. Godfrey et al., 1983; Wogalter et al., 1991, 1995a) that indicate that people more familiar with a product / equipment or task are less likely to read a warning. Of course, familiarity does not invariably result in unsafe behaviour. Indeed, familiarity frequently produces safer behaviour, because more is known about the situation. Nevertheless, such beliefs are likely to make it difficult to get people to read warnings for a similar, but more dangerous product than they are accustomed to (Godfrey and Laughery, 1984). In such cases, stalwart intervention steps such as making the product appear dramatically different from the old product and/or interactive warnings might help to break into people's set beliefs and attitudes.

Another important factor associated with beliefs and attitudes is hazard–risk perception. Persons who do not perceive something is hazardous will be less likely to notice or read a warning. Even if they read it, they may not comply if they are not convinced of the hazard. Hazard–risk perception is closely related to familiarity. As people become more familiar with something they generally perceive it to be less hazardous. However, research (e.g. Wogalter et al., 1991, 1993a) suggests that the hazard–risk perception is more closely tied to precautionary intent than familiarity.

Even more intimately tied to hazard–risk perception are people's beliefs in how severely they might be injured. In fact, research (e.g. Wogalter et al., 1991, 1993a) suggests that people's notions of how hazardous a product is, is almost entirely based on how seriously they think they could be injured. At the same time, people apparently do not readily consider the likelihood or probability of those injuries in making hazard–risk judgements (Wogalter and Barlow, 1990; Young et al., 1990, 1992). More will be said about injury severity in the next processing stage, which concerns motivation.

Lastly, if a warning message is in opposition with existing beliefs and attitudes, then it is likely that it will be ignored. The basis of the discrepant beliefs may be due to several factors such as familiarity and hazard–risk perception. In such cases, it is necessary that the message be sufficiently persuasive to change beliefs and attitudes. Doing this in practice is very difficult because people may not look for or read a warning in the first place (due to existing beliefs and attitudes, for example). This problem is noted in a study by Wogalter *et al.* (Chapter 10) assessing compliance to a car battery jumper cable warning. The hazard associated with jump starting a car is explosion from a spark igniting hydrogen gas released by the batteries. To avoid this hazard there is a sequence of cable connections that avoids having a spark produced near the battery (by making the last connection to a ground, e.g. a metal portion of the engine). However, most people believe (erroneously) that the batteries should be connected pole-to-pole (positive to positive and negative to negative). Enhanced warnings increased the number of people doing the cabling accurately, but without such enhancements or no warning, virtually everyone did it wrong. Thus, it becomes critical that the warnings possess attention-getting features and comprehension characteristics so that there is some chance of relaying a persuasive argument to convince the individual to comply. Considerable social psychology research has dealt with persuasion (Chaiken and Eagley, 1976), but additional work on warnings is needed (McGuire, 1980; Wogalter *et al.*, 1989). Persuasion is also linked to the next stage, motivation.

### 7.3.4  Motivation

A warning that is noticed, understood, and that successfully fits with the individual's beliefs and attitudes also needs to motivate people to comply with its directives. One of the critical determinants of compliance motivation is the concept of 'cost' which can be distinguished in two ways: cost of compliance and cost of non-compliance.

People are usually motivated to comply with warnings because of the associated potential negative consequences (costs) of not complying, including physical injury to themselves and others, property damage, or monetary loss. In industrial or public settings (or other controlled situations), cost of non-compliance can refer to fines or penalties levied by supervisors or government agencies for unsafe behaviours.

The cost associated with compliance can also be a strong motivator. Compliance usually requires some action in response to the warning message involving time, effort and/or money. If people perceive the cost of complying to be greater than the expected benefits of not complying, then they are less likely to comply. The following studies illustrate how motivation can be affected by cost. In one field experiment (Wogalter *et al.*, 1987), people's behaviour was observed responding to a warning posted on a broken door. The warning either directed people to use an adjacent door (low cost) or a different set of doors roughly 60 metres away (high cost). The results showed that most people obeyed the warning in the low cost condition (94 per cent), but it was totally ignored when cost was high (0 per cent).

This finding was supported in another study, in which people performed a mock chemistry task (Wogalter et al., 1989) in which a warning directed participants to wear a mask and gloves. The mask and gloves were either located on the table where they performed the task (low cost) or the items were located in an adjacent room (high cost). When located nearby, 73 per cent of the people used the protective equipment. However, when located more distantly, less than 17 per cent used them. These studies demonstrate that as cost of compliance increases, the effectiveness of a warning decreases. Sometimes the expenditure of even a minimal amount of effort can dissuade a person from complying with a warning.

Costs of compliance can be minimized in several ways. In a hazardous workplace compliance costs can be reduced by providing at no expense the required safety equipment, reducing effort needed to use this equipment (Wogalter et al., 1987, 1989), and ensuring the equipment is comfortable (Casali and Lam, 1986).

Whereas cost of compliance may decrease warning effectiveness, its effects can be facilitated by increasing the cost of non-compliance. The negative outcomes described in a consequences statement can convey the cost of non-compliance. To maximize its effect, the consequence statement should use explicit language telling users exactly (specifically) what can result if they do not comply (Laughery et al., 1993b). In addition to providing a better understanding of the nature of the hazard, explicit consequences give users an appreciation of the potential injury severity that might result. Perceived injury severity is a major factor in motivating people's precautionary intentions (Wogalter and Barlow, 1990; Wogalter et al., 1991; Young et al., 1990, 1992). Being explicit about severe injury motivates people as they generally want to avoid such outcomes.

In opposition to the notion of giving explicit severe consequences, is the suggestion from the marketing literature that warnings that promote too much fear arousal will be less effective than warnings that promote a more moderate level of fear arousal. This has been called the 'boomerang' effect because it implies that a strong warning (e.g. one that conveys disastrous consequences) will turn people off, causing them to ignore the warning. However, if the consequences are permanent paralysis, severe burns from a caustic substance, or death, should this not be expressed in the warning even though the information may provoke relatively high arousal? As stated earlier, it is important to give people a fair account of the nature of the hazard and potential consequences of not complying; therefore, toning down or leaving out critical information in order to reduce fear arousal would seem inappropriate. In fact, high fear arousal is probably an important motivating force for warning compliance.

Another motivator of warning compliance is social influence. Research (Wogalter et al., 1989) shows that if people see other people comply with the warning, they will be more likely to comply themselves. Likewise, if they see someone else not comply, they are less likely to comply. Social influence is an external factor with respect to warnings (as opposed to an internal factor such as its design). There are other important external factors. Time pressure frequently causes stress which restricts people's processing and could result in a failure to notice a warning (Magurno and Wogalter, 1994). The effects of these non-design factors illustrate the need for a systems approach that considers influential environmental and personal factors present in the risk situation.

## 7.4 SUMMARY AND ADDITIONAL COMMENT

This chapter has given a broad overview of some of the most important issues in the design and implementation of warnings. As discussed at the outset, warnings are but one method of hazard control. There are other, usually more effective methods (e.g. design out the hazard, ban the product or outlaw the situation, guard against the hazard) to protect against accidents and injuries.

The overview indicates that:

■ warnings should be designed so that they will be noticed and examined;

■ the information presented should be understandable by their intended population;

■ the message should have persuasive elements to change incongruent attitudes and beliefs;

■ the warning should motivate people to comply.

The first two stages are very important and have received the most attention in the warning research literature. Both are necessary but not sufficient conditions for warning effectiveness. The last two stages, attitudes/beliefs and motivation, are as important as the other two but are much less researched.

How do you know whether the warning has the right combination of desirable features to support high levels of compliance? Many of the factors discussed in this chapter can be designed into a warning without a great deal of decision making, but others will be more difficult because trade-offs must be made. One potential conflict is the principle of explicitness which says that the warning should give specific information regarding the hazard and consequences. This rule will, in some situations, conflict with other warnings design principles, for example, adequate print size. This is a problem when the explicit wording is lengthy while at the same time there is limited surface area to print the information and/or persons must be able to read the material at an adequate distance. Therefore, there is a decision to be made regarding print size versus explicitness. Another related trade-off is between brevity and explicitness. In making compromises, how does one know the best solution? Answers come from testing the warning to confirm (or disconfirm) whether the trade-offs are successful.

Testing can be carried out in several ways, from subjective ratings to actual behavioural compliance and can be directed at specific intermediate stages of information processing. Thus, the model can help to reveal the location of the problem (i.e., bottleneck). With this information, adjustments can eliminate the obstacle. Several rounds of iterative testing might be necessary until an adequate warning is developed that successfully passes through all of the stages.

Two additional points should be noted. One is that measurement of warning effectiveness should continue after the warning is in place. As already discussed, over time the warnings will become less effective due in part to habituation, but also because people and situations change over time. Also, after the warning is in use, there may be opportunities to collect data that could not otherwise be obtained in short-duration studies.

The other point concerns time. Because some products and equipment have very long expected lifespans, it is important to make sure that the materials comprising the warning (e.g. pigments, glue, etc.) are sufficiently durable to last as long as or longer than the product's anticipated life. Also, operator manuals that accompany most products when purchased new are frequently not transferred to subsequent owners (Rhoades *et al.*, 1991; Wogalter and Baneth, 1994). Given that second-hand owners need to know about product safety, maintenance, repair etc., it is important that they have access to this information. One way to facilitate availability is to permanently attach a label to the product with the manufacturer's complete address and telephone number so that people can request a replacement manual (Wogalter and Baneth, 1994).

Lastly, by considering the warning factors described in this chapter, hazard communications can be developed that can increase people's knowledge about hazards, but even more importantly, they can be used to reduce unsafe behaviour and decrease accidents and injury.

## ACKNOWLEDGEMENTS

The author wishes to thank Stephen L. Young for his thoughtful input at the developing stages of this chapter.

## REFERENCES

BARLOW, T. and WOGALTER, M. S. (1991) Increasing the surface area on small product containers to facilitate communication of label information and warnings. In: *Proceedings of the Interface 91*, pp. 88–93, Santa Monica, CA: Human Factors Society.

BARLOW, T. and WOGALTER, M. S. (1993) Alcoholic beverage warnings in magazine and television advertisements. *Journal of Consumer Research* **20**, 147–156.

BOERSEMA, T. and ZWAGA, H. J. G. (1989) Selecting comprehensible warning symbols for swimming pool slides. In: *Proceedings of the Human Factors Society 33rd Annual Meeting*, pp. 994–998. Santa Monica, CA: Human Factors Society.

BRESNAHAN, T. F. and BRYK, J. (1975) The hazard association values of accident-prevention signs. *Professional Safety* January, 17–25.

CASALI, J. G. and LAM, S. T. (1986) Over-the-ear industrial hearing protectors: an assessment of comfort issues. In: *Proceedings of the Human Factors Society 30th Annual Meeting*, pp. 1428–1432. Santa Monica, CA: Human Factors Society.

CHAIKEN, S. and EAGLEY, A. H. (1976) Communication modality as a determinant of message persuasiveness and message comprehensibility. *Journal of Personality and Social Psychology* **34**, 605–614.

CHAPANIS, A. (1994) Hazards associated with three signal words and four colours on warning signs. *Ergonomics* **37**, 265–275.

COLLINS, B. L. (1983) Evaluation of mine-safety symbols. In: *Proceedings of the Human Factors Society 27th Annual Meeting*, pp. 947–949. Santa Monica, CA: Human Factors Society.

CONZOLA, V. C. and WOGALTER, M. S. (1996) Compliance and recall of operator manual instructions: the use of supplemental voice and print directives and warnings. In: MITAL, A., KRUEGER, H., KUMAR, S., MENOZZIE, M. and FERNANDEZ, J. E. (Eds), *Advances in Occupational Ergonomics and Safety I*. Amsterdam: IOS Press.

DUFFY, R. R., KALSHER, M. J. and WOGALTER, M. S. (1995) Interactive warning: an experimental examination of effectiveness. *International Journal of Industrial Ergonomics* **15**, 159–166.

FRANTZ, J. P. and RHOADES, T. P. (1993) A task analytic approach to the temporal placement of product warnings. *Human Factors* **35**, 719–730.

GODFREY, S. S. and LAUGHERY, K. R. (1984) The biasing effects of product familiarity on consumers' awareness of hazard. In: *Proceedings of the Human Factors Society 28th Annual Meeting*, pp. 388–392. Santa Monica, CA: Human Factors Society.

GODFREY, S. S., ALLENDER, L., LAUGHERY, K. R. and SMITH, V. L. (1983) Warning messages: will the consumer bother to look? In: *Proceedings of the Human Factors Society 27th Annual Meeting*, pp. 950–954. Santa Monica, CA: Human Factors Society.

HUNN, B. P. and DINGUS, T. A. (1992) Interactivity, information and compliance cost in a consumer product warning scenario. *Accident Analysis and Prevention* **24**, 497–505.

JAYNES, L. S. and BOLES, D. B. (1990) The effects of symbols on warning compliance. In: *Proceedings of the Human Factors Society 34th Annual Meeting*, pp. 984–987. Santa Monica, CA: Human Factors Society.

KALSHER, M. J., WOGALTER, M. S. and RACICOT, B. M. (1996) Pharmaceutical container labels: enhancing preference perceptions with alternative designs and pictorials. *International Journal of Industrial Ergonomics*, **18**, 83–90.

KALSHER, M. J., WOGALTER, M. S., BREWSTER, B. and SPUNAR, M. E. (1995) Hazard level perceptions of current and proposed warning sign and label panels. In: *Proceedings of the Human Factors and Ergonomics Society 38th Annual Meeting*, pp. 351–355. Santa Monica, CA: Human Factors and Ergonomics Society.

LAUGHERY, K. R. (1993) Everybody knows: or do they? *Ergonomics in Design* July, 8–13.

LAUGHERY, K. R. and BRELSFORD, J. W. (1991) Receiver characteristics in safety communications. In: *Proceedings of the Human Factors Society 35th Annual Meeting*, pp. 1068–1072. Santa Monica, CA: Human Factors Society.

LAUGHERY, K. R., VAUBEL, K. P., YOUNG, S. L., BRELSFORD, J. W. and ROWE, A. L. (1993b) Explicitness of consequence information in warnings. *Safety Science* **16**, 597–613.

LAUGHERY, K. R., YOUNG, S. L., VAUBEL, K. P. and BRELSFORD, J. W. (1993a) The noticeability of warnings on alcoholic beverage containers. *Journal of Public Policy and Marketing* **12**, 38–56.

LAUX, L. F., MAYER, D. L. and THOMPSON, N. B. (1989) Usefulness of symbols and pictorials to communicate hazard information. In: *Proceedings of the Interface 89*, pp. 79–83. Santa Monica, CA: Human Factors Society.

LEHTO, M. R. and PAPASTAVROU, J. D. (1993) Models of the warning process: important implications towards effectiveness. *Safety Science* **16**, 569–595.

LERNER, N. D. and COLLINS, B. L. (1980) *The Assessment of Safety Symbol Understandability by Different Testing Methods*. PB81–185647. Washington, DC: National Bureau of Standards.

LERNER, N. D. and COLLINS, B. L. (1983) Symbol sign understandability when visibility is poor. In: *Proceedings of the Human Factors Society 27th Annual Meeting*, pp. 944–946. Santa Monica, CA: Human Factors Society.

MAGURNO, A. B. and WOGALTER, M. S. (1994) Behavioral compliance with warnings: effects of stress and placement. In: *Proceedings of the Human Factors and Ergonomics Society 38th Annual Meeting*, pp. 826–830. Santa Monica, CA: Human Factors and Ergonomics Society.

MAGURNO, A., WOGALTER, M. S., KOHAKE, J. and WOLFF, J. S. (1994) Iterative test and development of pharmaceutical pictorials. In: *Proceedings of the 12th Triennial Congress of the International Ergonomics Association*, Vol. 4, pp. 360–362.

McGUIRE, W. J. (1980) The communication–persuasion model and health-risk labeling. In: MORRIS, L. A., MAZIS, M. B. and BAROFSKY, I. (Eds), *Product Labeling and Health Risks: Banbury Report 6*. Coldspring Harbor, NY: Coldspring Harbor Laboratory.

RACICOT, B. M. and WOGALTER, M. S. (1995) Effects of a video warning sign and social modeling on behavioral compliance. *Accident Analysis and Prevention* **27**, 57–64.

RHOADES, T. P., FRANTZ, J. P. and HOPP, K. M. (1991) Manufacturers' product information: is it transferred to the second owner of a product? In: *Proceedings of the Interface 91*, pp. 100–104. Santa Monica, CA: Human Factors Society.

SANDERS, M. S. and McCORMICK, E. J. (1993) *Human Factors in Engineering and Design* (7th edn). New York: McGraw-Hill.

SILVER, N. C. and WOGALTER, M. S. (1991) Strength and understanding of signal words by elementary and middle school students. In: *Proceedings of the Human Factors Society 35th Annual Meeting*, pp. 580–594. Santa Monica, CA: Human Factors Society.

SILVER, N. C., LEONARD, D. C., PONSI, K. A. and WOGALTER, M. S. (1991) Warnings and purchase intentions for pest-control products. *Forensic Reports* **4**, 17–33.

VIGILANTE, W. J. JR and WOGALTER, M. S. (1996) The ordering of safety warnings in product manuals. In: MITAL, A., KRUEGER, H., KUMAR, S., MENOZZIE, M. and FERNANDEZ, J. E. (Eds), *Advances in Occupational Ergonomics and Safety I*. Amsterdam: IOS Press.

WOGALTER, M. S. and BANETH, R. C. (1994) Availability of owner's manuals for 'second-hand' consumer products. In: *Proceedings of the Human Factors and Ergonomics Society 38th Annual Meeting*, pp. 447–450. Santa Monica, CA: Human Factors and Ergonomics Society.

WOGALTER, M. S. and BARLOW, T. (1990) Injury likelihood and severity in warnings. In: *Proceedings of the Human Factors Society 34th Annual Meeting*, pp. 580–583. Santa Monica, CA: Human Factors Society.

WOGALTER, M. S. and SILVER, N. C. (1990) Arousal strength of signal words. *Forensic Reports* **3**, 407–420.

WOGALTER, M. S. and SILVER, N. C. (1995) Warning signal words: connoted strength and understandability by children, elders, and non-native English speakers. *Ergonomics* **38**, 2188–2206.

WOGALTER, M. S. and YOUNG, S. L. (1991) Behavioural compliance to voice and print warnings. *Ergonomics* **34**, 79–89.

WOGALTER, M. S. and YOUNG, S. L. (1994) Enhancing warning compliance through alternative product label designs. *Applied Ergonomics* **24**, 53–57.

WOGALTER, M. S., GODFREY, S. S., FONTENELLE, G. A., DESAULNIERS, D. R., ROTHSTEIN, P. R. and LAUGHERY, K. R. (1987) Effectiveness of warnings. *Human Factors* **29**, 599–612.

WOGALTER, M. S., ALLISON, S. T. and McKENNA, N. A. (1989) Effects of cost and social influence on warning compliance. *Human Factors* **31**, 133–140.

WOGALTER, M. S., BRELSFORD, J. W., DESAULNIERS, D. R. and LAUGHERY, K. R. (1991) Consumer product warnings: the role of hazard perception. *Journal of Safety Research* **22**, 71–82.

WOGALTER, M. S., BREMS, D. J. and MARTIN, E. G. (1993a) Risk perception of common consumer products: judgments of accident frequency and precautionary intent. *Journal of Safety Research* **24**, 97–106.

WOGALTER, M. S., FORBES, R. M. and BARLOW, T. (1993b) Alternative product label designs: increasing the surface area and print size. In: *Proceedings of the Interface 93*, pp. 181–186. Santa Monica, CA: Human Factors Society.

WOGALTER, M. S., KALSHER, M. J. and RACICOT, B. M. (1993c) Behavioral compliance with warnings: effects of voice, context, and location. *Safety Science* **16**, 637–654.

WOGALTER, M. S., JARRARD, S. W. and SIMPSON, S. W. (1994a) Influence of signal words on perceived level of product hazard. *Human Factors* **36**, 547–556.

WOGALTER, M. S., RACICOT, B. M., KALSHER, M. J. and SIMPSON, S. N. (1994b) The role of perceived relevance in behavioral compliance in personalized warning signs. *International Journal of Industrial Ergonomics* **14**, 233–242.

WOGALTER, M. S., BARLOW, T. and MURPHY, S. (1995a) Compliance to owner's manual warnings: influence of familiarity and the task-relevant placement of a supplemental directive. *Ergonomics* **38**, 1081–1091.

WOGALTER, M. S., MAGURNO, A. B., CARTER, A. W., SWINDELL, J. A., VIGILANTE, W. J. and DAURITY, J. G. (1995b) Hazard association values of warning sign header components. In: *Proceedings of the Human Factors Society 39th Annual Meeting*, pp. 979–983. Santa Monica, CA: Human Factors and Ergonomics Society.

WOLFF, J. S. and WOGALTER, M. S. (1993) Test and development of pharmaceutical pictorials. In: *Proceedings of the Interface 93*, pp. 187–192. Santa Monica, CA: Human Factors Society.

YOUNG, S. L. (1991) Increasing the noticeability of warnings: effects of pictorial, color, signal icon and border. In: *Proceedings of the Human Factors Society 35th Annual Meeting*, pp. 580–584. Santa Monica, CA: Human Factors Society.

YOUNG, S. L. and WOGALTER, M. S. (1990) Effects of conspicuous print and pictorial icons on comprehension and memory of instruction manual warnings. *Human Factors* **32**, 637–649.

YOUNG, S. L., BRELSFORD, J. W. and WOGALTER, M. S. (1990) Judgments of hazard, risk, and danger: do they differ? In: *Proceedings of the Human Factors Society 34th Annual Meeting*, pp. 503–507. Santa Monica, CA: Human Factors Society.

YOUNG, S. L., WOGALTER, M. S. and BRELSFORD, J. W. (1992) Relative contribution of likelihood and severity of injury to risk perceptions. In: *Proceedings of the Human Factors Society 36th Annual Meeting*, pp. 1014–1018. Santa Monica, CA: Human Factors Society.

ZWAGA, H. J. G. and EASTERBY, R. S. (1984) Developing effective symbols for public information. In: EASTERBY, R. S. and ZWAGA, H. J. G. (Eds), *Information Design: The Design and Evaluation of Signs and Printed Material*, chap. 15, pp. 277–297. New York: Wiley.

# CHAPTER EIGHT

# Warning of water safety hazards with sequential pictographs

ROBERT DEWAR and PAUL ARTHUR

## 8.1 INTRODUCTION

Warning messages must attract attention and be readily understood by all who are exposed to the hazard. They should also convey the nature and seriousness of the hazard and the consequences of failure to heed the warning. The use of illustrations and pictographs can be helpful, but care must be taken to ensure that they are easily understood. Research has shown that many warning pictographs are poorly understood (Dewar *et al.*, 1994). Some have even been thought to mean the opposite to their intended meaning.

Word messages for warnings have often been found to be ineffective, even when words such as 'Notice', 'Attention' and 'Careful' are used (Silver and Wogalter, 1991). Research on the effectiveness of pictographs and graphics to convey warnings has produced mixed results. They are not always easy to understand and do not necessarily lead to compliance. However, they are 'readable' at a much greater distance than words. In addition, the use of a combination of pictorials and words has been found to be more effective than either alone. For example, Jaynes and Boles (1990) measured the percentage of students in a chemistry laboratory who noticed, read, recalled, and complied with warning messages presented with words, pictographs or the two combined. The combination was more effective than either alone in terms of compliance and the messages being noticed. Young and Wogalter (1988) showed that the presence of icons with word warning messages in an instructional manual facilitated memory for the messages.

Sequential art, another way of identifying comic strip techniques, has been used to convey instructions for assembling furniture, operating machines, etc. Multiple pictures are used to indicate the sequence of actions. This approach may also be

useful to convey the nature of hazards and the consequences of inappropriate behaviour, especially with complex messages. This approach was used in the present
study.

This research involved the development and evaluation of a visual warning
system to indicate hazards on or near water in the vicinity of hydroelectric generating stations. Many of the messages were considered too complex to be conveyed
clearly with a single pictograph. In addition, it was deemed important to indicate
both the nature of the hazard and the consequences of failure to heed the warning.


## 8.2  SURVEY 1

### 8.2.1  Method

A questionnaire survey was conducted to evaluate the comprehension of 12 hazard
warning messages (using sequential pictographs) among a wide variety of subjects.

### Subjects

Several groups of subjects were tested in order to obtain as wide a variety of
respondents as possible, in terms of age, education, literacy and participation in the
relevant recreational activities near hydro stations. A total of 429 people participated, including volunteers from the following sources: senior citizens, English as a
Second Language (ESL) students, illiterate adults, university students, members of
canoeing and fishing clubs, firemen, teenagers, and natives.

### Stimulus material

Twelve black and white sequential pictographic warning messages depicting a
variety of water safety hazards were evaluated using a questionnaire which included a depiction of each of 12 messages in a three-panel sequence of pictographs
without words, as well as with words. An example of these pictographs is shown in
Figure 8.1.

### Procedure

Most participants were tested in groups, except for approximately one-third of the
low literacy adults, who were tested individually. Three groups for whom the
questionnaire was self-administered were given the survey and asked to return it
within a specified time to the contact person in their organization. The subjects'
task was to write out the meanings (one under each) of the 12 graphic warning
messages shown (in one of six random orders) without words. Following this, they
then saw these graphic warnings with accompanying word messages beneath, and
were asked to indicate on five-point rating scales (1 = very easy; 5 = very hard)
how easy it was to understand the versions with and without words.

**Figure 8.1** Original and redesigned versions of 'No fishing, rising water' sequential pictographs. Intended meaning: 'Fishing here is dangerous. Waters can rise rapidly anytime. You may lose your balance and be swept away in the current'.

The responses to the comprehension questions were scored as either correct, partially correct (had the right idea and would take the appropriate action) or wrong (including 'don't know' responses and no answers). For the purpose of data interpretation, the first two types of answers were considered correct. Approximately one-third of the questionnaires completed by each group of subjects were scored by two researchers and the scoring was then finalized so that the level of agreement on scoring was 95 per cent. Thereafter, the questionnaires were scored by one person.

### 8.2.2 Results

Table 8.1 indicates the percentage of subjects giving each response to each message without words. Also in this table are the ratings for the messages with and without words, based on the five-point rating scale.

The findings indicate that seven of the pictographic messages were well understood without words (based on the assumption that fewer than 25 per cent wrong responses is acceptable), whereas four – those referring to rising water levels and undertow – were especially difficult. Responses to the rising water pictographs often reflected the idea of rough water or storms.

The overall level of understanding of the messages tested was approximately 75 per cent, with 39 per cent of the responses being completely correct. An examination of group differences shows that the level of understanding of the messages was greatest among the two recreation groups associated with outdoor activities on water, the fishers and canoeists, whereas those having greatest difficulty were the seniors and low literacy adults.

The ratings of the graphic messages with and without words (Table 8.1) showed a strong preference for the former. *t* Test comparisons showed that all differences between the mean ratings of the versions with and without words were statistically

**Table 8.1**  Percentage comprehension scores and comprehension ratings for first survey (N = 429)

| Message | Percentage | | | Average rating | |
| --- | --- | --- | --- | --- | --- |
| | C | PC | W | With words | Without words |
| Fish behind fence | 31 | 52 | 17 | 1.35 | 2.20 |
| No fishing, slippery rocks | 64 | 22 | 14 | 1.22 | 1.88 |
| No fishing, rising water | 30 | 38 | 32 | 1.32 | 2.54 |
| No ice fishing | 9 | 78 | 13 | 1.30 | 2.29 |
| No boating, rising water | 10 | 27 | 63 | 1.59 | 3.87 |
| No boating, undertow | 11 | 25 | 64 | 1.48 | 3.21 |
| No diving | 77 | 17 | 6 | 1.13 | 1.42 |
| No swimming, undertow | 25 | 41 | 34 | 1.41 | 2.85 |
| No snowmobiling | 46 | 41 | 13 | 1.26 | 1.85 |
| Unaccompanied child | 69 | 5 | 26 | 1.37 | 2.56 |
| Missing child | 72 | 7 | 21 | 1.36 | 2.57 |
| No skating | 22 | 70 | 8 | 1.29 | 2.10 |

C = correct; PC = partially correct; W = wrong.
1 = very easy; 5 = very hard.
p < 0.001 for all comparisons.

significant (p < 0.001). The greatest differences in ratings were for the messages relating to rising water and undertow, which is consistent with the comprehension results.

### 8.3  SURVEY 2

#### 8.3.1  Method

A second survey was conducted to determine comprehension of seven revised versions of the messages used in Survey 1.

*Subjects*

In the follow-up survey 229 subjects from four of the same sources (but different people) as in the first survey – illiterate adults, ESL students, teenagers, and natives – were tested.

*Stimuli*

Revised versions of seven of the messages from the first survey were examined. Two versions of four of the new graphics were tested. One version included, in the

**Table 8.2** Percentage comprehension scores, comparing signs in the two surveys

| Message | C | | PC | | W | |
|---|---|---|---|---|---|---|
| | 1 | 2 | 1 | 2 | 1 | 2 |
| Fishing behind fence | 28 | 37 | 48 | 42 | 23 | 21 |
| No fishing, rising water | 23 | 41 | 47 | 40 | 30 | 19 |
| No ice fishing | 4 | 19 | 83 | 72 | 23 | 9 |
| No boating, rising water | 6 | 23 | 31 | 44 | 63 | 33 |
| No boating, undertow | 11 | 36 | 31 | 41 | 58 | 23 |
| No snowmobiling | 35 | 33 | 49 | 48 | 16 | 19 |
| Missing child | 63 | 63 | 0 | 0 | 37 | 37 |

C = correct; PC = partially correct; W = wrong.
1 = first survey; 2 = second survey.

first panel, a general warning pictograph (exclamation mark within a triangle), as used to convey a general warning, for example, on highway signs in Europe (see Figure 8.1).

*Procedure*

The procedures for soliciting and testing subjects and for scoring the data for the second survey were the same as in Survey 1.

### 8.3.2   Results

Table 8.2 indicates the percentage of subjects giving each response to each revised message and to the same messages in the first survey. The latter data include only comparable groups of subjects (illiterate adults, ESL students, teenagers, and natives). Five of the messages were well understood, while two – one referring to rising water levels and the other to missing children – still presented difficulties.

A comparison was made of the results of the two surveys using data for the same types of subjects. The resulting comparison involved 177 participants from the first, and 229 from the second survey. Table 8.2 shows that there were dramatic improvements in understanding of two messages which were very poorly understood initially ('No boating, rising water' and 'No boating, undertow'), as well as substantial improvement in two others ('No fishing, rising water' and 'No ice fishing'). A series of chi-square tests indicated that the differences between the first and second survey results were highly significant statistically ($p < 0.001$) for these four messages. The remaining three messages showed no change. The presence of a general warning pictograph (!) in the first panel in four of the graphics made no consistent difference to the level of understanding of these messages.

## 8.4    DISCUSSION

The greatest difficulty was encountered for the messages about danger from rising water and from undertow. In many responses to these items there was no clear understanding of the reason for the hazard. One difficulty here is that the situation appears safe, as there is no visible evidence of potential rising water or undertow; two hazards which may occur suddenly and at unpredictable times. Based on the results of the first survey, it is apparent that four of the pictographs needed to be revised to depict the nature of the hazard more effectively.

The majority of participants in the second survey were substantially challenged by this task. One can consider that 'experimental illiteracy' was imposed on the subjects, in that the complete lack of words in the messages meant that past experience with the written language was of no help in understanding these warning messages. In addition, the novelty of the graphics and their contents presented a further challenge to their comprehension. The ESL group was composed of about 50 per cent Asian people and 25 per cent from Eastern Europe, while the remainder were from the Caribbean and the Middle East. Most of these subjects had about two months' exposure to the English language. Winter activities such as snowmobiling and ice fishing would be unknown to most of them. The low literacy subjects were functionally illiterate, in many cases due to limitations in intellectual functioning.

Results of the evaluation of the redesigned warning messages have generally been positive, with greater levels of understanding being found for four of the messages. Two messages, however, are still difficult for many people to understand.

## 8.5    CONCLUSION

This project has demonstrated how sequential art techniques can be developed and used effectively to convey warning messages to a variety of people, including illiterate adults, young people, and those with limited use of written language. Whereas nearly all of the 12 warning messages, in either their original or redesigned form, were well understood, it is evident that two of the warnings cannot easily be conveyed in this manner. This finding, along with the much higher ratings of effectiveness for pictographic messages accompanied by words, supports our view (which is supported also by other researchers) that the combination of pictographs and words will be the most effective way to communicate the complex warning messages that are required in the vicinity of hydroelectric stations. These messages are currently, throughout most of the world, communicated with words alone.

## ACKNOWLEDGEMENTS

We wish to express our thanks to the Canadian Electrical Association for funding this project, and to Mr Randy Raban, the project manager of Manitoba Hydro, for his advice and encouragement throughout this project.

## REFERENCES

DEWAR, R. E., KLINE, D. W. and SWANSON, H. A. (1994) Age differences in comprehension of traffic sign symbols. *Transportation Research Record* **1456**, 1–10.

JAYNES, L. S. and BOLES, D. B. (1990) The effect of symbols on warning compliance. In: *Proceedings of the 34th Annual Meeting of the Human Factors Society*, pp. 894–897. Santa Monica, CA: Human Factors Society.

SILVER, N. C. and WOGALTER, M. S. (1991) Strength and understanding of signal words by elementary and middle school students. In: *Proceedings of the 35th Annual Meeting of the Human Factors Society*, pp. 590–594. Santa Monica, CA: Human Factors Society.

YOUNG, S. L. and WOGALTER, M. S. (1988) Memory of instructional manual warnings: effects of pictorial icons and conspicuous print. In: *Proceedings of the 32nd Annual Meeting of the Human Factors Society*, pp. 905–909. Santa Monica, CA: Human Factors Society.

# CHAPTER NINE

# Explicit warnings for child-care products

MONICA TROMMELEN and SIMONE P. AKERBOOM

## 9.1 INTRODUCTION

Effective safety information should result in safe behaviour. Consumers' respons-
iveness to safety information is strongly affected by perceived hazardousness (Donner
and Brelsford, 1988; Friedmann, 1988; Otsubo, 1988; Young *et al.*, 1990; Wogalter
*et al.*, 1991). Unfortunately, the perceived hazardousness for child-care products is
low (Trommelen, 1994a). One of the factors that influences perceived hazardousness is the explicitness of warnings. Sherer and Rogers (1984) found that a more
detailed and specific description of an event had a positive effect on severity ratings
of possible injuries and on recall of the information. In addition, effects were also
found on perceived hazardousness (Laughery and Stanush, 1989), and on the intent
to act cautiously with a product (Laughery and Brelsford, 1991).

Thus, to be effective, warnings should be explicit and inform consumers on:

- what to do and what to avoid in order to use the product safely;
- the nature of the product-related hazard;
- the possible consequences in terms of injuries (see ANSI, 1991; Wogalter *et al.*,
  1987; Goldhaber and deTurck, 1988).

The quality of safety information provided with child-care products in The Netherlands has been found to be poor (Hagenaar and Trommelen, 1992); in particular the
consequences of unsafe behaviour in terms of injuries are hardly ever mentioned.

Regarding consumers' preference, inconsistent results have been found. Vaubel
(1990) found that for common consumer products non-explicit warnings were preferred to explicit ones. However, a later study by Vaubel and Brelsford (1991) showed
that for fictitious products, consumers overwhelmingly preferred explicit warnings

to non-explicit warnings. This indicates that consumers cope with uncertainty about potential harm by arming themselves with more detailed information.

The study discussed in this chapter investigated the effectiveness of explicitness in warnings provided with child-care products, and was based on the following research questions:

- Does explicitness of warnings influence: the perceived hazardousness of child-care products, the perceived likelihood of injury with child-care products, the perceived severity of possible injuries, the precautionary intent to use child-care products in a safe manner, and/or recall performance?
- Do people prefer explicit information?

To the authors' knowledge, no research has been done in this area before, despite the fact that accidents with these products may be serious.

## 9.2   METHOD

### 9.2.1   Subjects

Ninety students from Leiden University participated in the experiment; their average age was 22 years and there were 57 females and 28 males (for five respondents gender was not recorded). None of the participants had children of their own, but half of them had experience with children, because they babysit regularly. Thus, half of the respondents were unfamiliar with the products investigated, and the other half may have used the products. All of the respondents can be considered as potential future purchasers of child-care products.

### 9.2.2   Material

Six child-care products were selected from the database of the 1989 Dutch Home and Leisure Accident Surveillance System (PORS) of the Dutch Consumer Safety Institute (CSI, 1990). To determine whether the subjective hazard relates to objective accident frequencies, three child-care products with a relatively high and three products with a relatively low accident frequency were chosen (see Table 9.1).

**Table 9.1**   Products with high and low accident frequencies selected from PORS

| High accident frequency | Low accident frequency |
| --- | --- |
| Changing table (39) | Car seat (2) |
| High chair (19) | Baby carrier (1) |
| Bicycle seat (17) | Cradle (1) |

The accident frequencies for 1989 are in parentheses (CSI, 1990).

A questionnaire asked for every child-care product the following:

1   How hazardous is a ( . . . ) in your opinion?

2   How likely is it that a child or adult will get hurt by (using) the ( . . . )?

3   How severe would the injury be if a child or adult got hurt?

4   How cautious would you be when using a ( . . . )?

5   Write down three warnings you think should be given with this ( . . . ), and name the reasons for giving these warnings.

6   Please reproduce the three warnings you have just read about this ( . . . ) as literally and completely as possible.

7   Which of the warning formats do you prefer?

The first four questions used a five-point scale, with a rating of 1 indicating low and 5 indicating high level on the dimension. To quantify the amount of warning information and to analyse the results of the reproduction and production tasks (Questions 5 and 6), warnings were coded into simple propositions (Kintch, 1974).

### 9.2.3  Procedure

Subjects received the material of only four of the six products investigated. The following four conditions were used:

- without warnings (no-warning control condition);
- with instruction warnings (short-warning condition);
- with instruction + hazard warnings (extended-warning condition);
- with instruction + hazard + consequence warnings (explicit-warning condition).

For each product the material consisted of a line drawing. For the last three conditions the line drawing was accompanied by three warnings that admonished different product-related hazards (in Dutch). The warnings were either formulated in a non-explicit, an extended, or an explicit manner. An example warning for a high chair is given below.

> Keep objects like hot pans and sharp knives away from your child (*instruction*). Your child might try to touch them (*hazard*) and may suffer burns or cuts (*consequence*).

First, subjects received a product in the no-warning condition. The no-warning condition was always shown first because otherwise the warnings of the other conditions could bias the perception of the product in the no-warning condition and could influence the production task. Immediately after that subjects answered Questions 1 to 4. Then, subjects were asked to write down three warnings they themselves would supply with the product and explain why (Question 5). After the production task, subjects received line drawings of three other products, one with short, one with extended, and one with explicit warnings, in a random order. They had to read the warnings and complete Questions 1 to 4 of the questionnaire.

Subjects were then asked to reproduce the warnings as literally and completely as possible (Question 6). Finally, subjects were asked to indicate which of the warning types they preferred, as well as how much experience they had with children.

### 9.3   RESULTS

### 9.3.1   Rating scales

The mean scores of the 90 respondents on the first four questions were averaged over the six child-care products. Warning condition had a significant positive effect on perceived hazardousness, perceived severity of injury and precautionary intent (Friedman ANOVA by ranks, respectively $\chi_r^2$ corrected for ties = 16.283, df = 3, p < 0.005; $\chi_r^2$ = 30.188, df = 3, p < 0.005; $\chi_r^2$ = 8.827, df = 3, p < 0.05). Additional multiple comparisons (p ≤ 0.05) revealed that products with no warnings were perceived as less hazardous and the injuries as less severe than products with extended or explicit warnings (means: 2.1 vs. 2.5 and 2.6; means: 2.4 vs. 3.3 and 3.6). Subjects reported they would be less cautious with products when no warnings were provided than they would be with products provided with explicit warnings (means: 3.3 vs. 3.7). Products with short warnings were also perceived as less hazardous, and possible injuries as less severe when compared with products with explicit warnings (means: 2.2 vs. 2.6; means: 3.1 vs. 3.6).

In the no-warning condition subjects perceived products with high accident frequencies as significantly (Mann–Whitney U tests) more hazardous than products with low accident frequencies (means: 2.3 vs. 1.9, U = 171, p < 0.05). Furthermore, they perceived it as more likely that injuries could occur for products with high accident frequencies than for products with low accident frequencies (2.3 vs. 1.9, U = 161, p < 0.05). Severity of injury and precautionary intent did not differ significantly between products with high and low accident frequencies (means: 2.4 vs. 2.3; means: 3.5 vs. 3.1).

### 9.3.2   Reproduction and production of warnings

With the increase of to-be-remembered propositions, the percentage correct recall decreased. Subjects reproduced 72 per cent of the short warnings, 70 per cent of the extended warnings, and 61 per cent of the explicit warnings. However, the opposite pattern was obtained for the instruction part of the warning. In the short-warning condition 72 per cent of this part was reproduced, whereas a significantly larger part (83 per cent) was reproduced in both the extended and explicit-warning condition.

For the explicit-warning condition, the instruction is best remembered (83 per cent), followed by the hazard (54 per cent), and the consequence (46 per cent). The same pattern was obtained for the production task: 92 per cent of the subjects mentioned some kind of instruction, 60 per cent mentioned the hazard, and 26 per cent mentioned the consequences of unsafe use.

### 9.3.3 Preference of warning type

The short warning was preferred by 4 per cent, the extended warning by 39 per cent, and the explicit warning by 51 per cent of the subjects (6 per cent missing).

## 9.4 CONCLUSIONS

Results of the present study are consistent with previous studies and provide empirical evidence for the positive effect of explicitness in warnings on hazard perception. Subjects perceived the child-care products with both extended and with explicit warnings as more hazardous and possible injuries as more severe than products without warnings. The same differences in perception were found between explicit and short warnings. The explicit warnings also induced higher precautionary intent than no warnings. In addition, explicit warnings were preferred by half of the respondents. Thus, although the differences between the extended and explicit warnings never reached statistical significance, we would advise that explicit warnings be used for child-care products.

The child-care products investigated in this study were divided into two groups: one with a relatively high, and one with a relatively low accident frequency. In the no-warning condition, products with high accident frequencies were indeed perceived as more hazardous and more likely to lead to injuries than products with low accident frequencies. Thus, the subjective hazardousness seems to be in accordance with the objective accident frequencies. However, severity rate and precautionary intent did not differ between the two groups.

Explicitness has a stronger effect on the hazard perception of low accident frequency products than of high accident frequency products. However, it should be noted that explicit warnings on products with high accident frequencies may be beneficial in cases where these products are – erroneously – perceived as relatively harmless.

Explicitness in warnings resulted in a better recall of the instruction part, despite the fact that subjects had to process more information, which generally has a negative influence on recall. This positive effect on recall might be explained in terms of elaboration. Instructions embedded in a sentence with additional information cause a richer representation in memory and more cues for retrieval.

The instruction part was more frequently produced and reproduced than the hazard and consequence parts. Apparently people do not often think of hazards and the consequences of unsafe behaviour themselves, which suggests that they should be mentioned in a warning.

This study is part of a larger project of prenormative research for the European Committee for Standardization. At their request (CEN/TC 252/PG 6/WG 5), a warning grammar, with which warning sentences can be formulated, has been developed (Trommelen, 1994b). In addition, a basic set of explicit warnings against the most frequent and severe hazards (Trommelen, 1994b), and a number of warning symbols have been developed for child-care products (Akerboom *et al.*, 1995).

Before warnings can be prescribed in European Standards for child-care products, they have to be tested. Future research will focus on testing the standardized explicit warning sentences for child-care products in a number of European countries. When the results of the testing are satisfactory, the warnings will be incorporated in European standards for child-care products.

## REFERENCES

AKERBOOM, S. P., MIJKSENAAR, P., TROMMELEN, M., VISSER, J. and ZWAGA, H. J. G. (1995) *Products for Children: Development and Evaluation of Symbols for Warnings.* Amsterdam: Consumer Safety Institute.

AMERICAN NATIONAL STANDARDS INSTITUTE (ANSI) (1991) *American National Standard Specification for Accident Prevention Signs, Z535.* New York: ANSI.

CONSUMER SAFETY INSTITUTE (CSI) (1990) *Jaaroverzicht Privé Ongevallen Registratie Systeem, PORS 1989* [Annual Survey of the Dutch Home and Leisure Accident Surveillance System]. Amsterdam: CSI.

DONNER, K. A. and BRELSFORD, J. W. (1988) Cuing hazard information for consumer products. In: *Proceedings of the Human Factors Society 32nd Annual Meeting*, pp. 532–535. Santa Monica, CA: Human Factors Society.

FRIEDMANN, K. (1988) The effect of adding symbols to written warning labels on user behavior and recall. *Human Factors* **30**, 507–515.

GOLDHABER, G. M. and DETURCK, M. A. (1988) A dimensional analysis of signal words. *Forensic Reports* **1**, 193–206.

HAGENAAR, R. and TROMMELEN, M. (1992) *A Study on Hazard and Safety Information Accompanying Children's Products.* Leiden: Leiden University, Centre for Safety Research.

KINTCH, W. (1974) *The Representation of Meaning in Memory.* Hillsdale, NJ: Lawrence Erlbaum Associates.

LAUGHERY, K. R. and BRELSFORD, J. W. (1991) Receiver characteristics in safety communications. In: *Proceedings of the Human Factors Society 35th Annual Meeting*, pp. 1068–1072. Santa Monica, CA: Human Factors Society.

LAUGHERY, K. R. and STANUSH, J. A. (1989) Effects of warning explicitness on product perception. In: *Proceedings of the Human Factors Society 31st Annual Meeting*, pp. 431–435. Santa Monica, CA: Human Factors Society.

OTSUBO, S. M. (1988) A behavioral study of warning labels for consumer products: perceived danger and use of pictographs. In: *Proceedings of the Human Factors Society 32nd Annual Meeting*, pp. 536–540. Santa Monica, CA: Human Factors Society.

SHERER, M. and ROGERS, R. W. (1984) The role of vivid information in fear appeals and attitude change. *Journal of Research in Personality* **18**, 321–334.

TROMMELEN, M. (1994a) Perceived hazardousness of child-care products and the effectiveness of safety information. *International Journal for Consumer Safety* **1**, 81–91.

TROMMELEN, M. (1994b) *Products for Children: Standardisation of Warnings.* Amsterdam: Consumer Safety Institute.

VAUBEL, K. P. (1990) Effects of warning explicitness on consumer product purchase intentions. In: *Proceedings of the Human Factors Society 34th Annual Meeting*, pp. 580–583. Santa Monica, CA: Human Factors Society.

VAUBEL, K. P. and BRELSFORD, J. W. JR (1991) Product evaluations and injury assessments as related to preferences for explicitness in warnings. In: *Proceedings of the Human*

*Factors Society 35th Annual Meeting*, pp. 1048–1052. Santa Monica, CA: Human Factors Society.

WOGALTER, M. S., BRELSFORD, J. W., DESAULNIERS, D. R. and LAUGHERY, K. R. (1991) Consumer product warnings: the role of hazard perception. *Journal of Safety Research* **22**, 71–82.

WOGALTER, M. S., GODFREY, S. S., FONTELLE, G. A., DESAULNIERS, D. R., ROTHSTEIN, P. R. and LAUGHERY, K. R. (1987) Effectiveness of warnings. *Human Factors* **29**, 599–612.

YOUNG, S. L., BRELSFORD, J. W. JR and WOGALTER, M. S. (1990) Judgements of hazard, risk, and danger: do they differ? In: *Proceedings of the Human Factors Society 34th Annual Meeting*, pp. 503–507. Santa Monica, CA: Human Factors Society.

# CHAPTER TEN

# Connecting jumper cables: the effectiveness of pictorial warnings

MICHAEL S. WOGALTER, MICHAEL J. KALSHER,
BARBARA L. GLOVER and AMY B. MAGURNO

## 10.1 INTRODUCTION

Each year, people are injured improperly jump starting their vehicle. They connect booster cables by incorrectly attaching them to the four battery terminals (i.e., positive to positive and negative to negative). These occurrences suggest the correct procedure is not commonly known (De Puy, 1990). The correct connection involves making the last connection for the car with the dead battery to an earth away from the battery. This procedure avoids having a spark ignite hydrogen gas from the battery, possibly causing an explosion and release of sulphuric acid.

Previous research has shown that warnings can be effective in influencing behaviour. Factors such as the inclusion of colour (Kline et al., 1993) and pictorials (Jaynes and Boles, 1990) have increased compliance behaviour compared to their absence. However, their positive effects are not unequivocal (Duffy et al., 1993; Wogalter et al., 1993). In addition, a tag-type warning has been shown to facilitate compliance (Wogalter and Young, 1994). In the present study, two experiments were conducted to investigate the effectiveness of coloured tag-type warnings pictorially illustrating proper battery cable connection.

## 10.2 EXPERIMENT 1

Participants diagrammed the procedure for jump starting two vehicles using booster cables while a warning tag was present or absent. Participants also completed a questionnaire about their car battery knowledge.

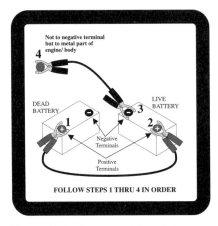 

**Figure 10.1**    The two sides of the tag warning used in Experiments 1 and 2. (In Experiment 1, this warning was printed with black letters on an orange background. In Experiment 2, the enhanced tag warning was identical in content except the background was of a bright saturated red and yellow colour.)

### 10.2.1    Method

Sixty-five North Carolina State University undergraduates participated. A two-sided orange tag warning with black print was developed using information from the Battery Council International (Chicago). One side of the tag illustrated the proper connection procedure. The other side of the tag listed, pictorially and verbally, the hazards of improper connection. The physical dimensions of the tag were $9.5 \times 8.3$ cm. Figure 10.1 shows both sides of the tag.

Participants were shown a drawing which depicted an overhead view of two automobiles with the engine compartments exposed. One was labelled 'dead battery car' and the other 'live battery car'. They were asked to draw in, with red and black felt-tip pens, the cables and the connection points, and also to number the sequence. In the warning present condition, participants examined the tag before drawing connections. In the warning absent group, no tag was provided. When participants completed the diagram, they filled out a questionnaire assessing: knowledge about the hazards/dangers associated with car batteries, their experience and ownership of jumper cables, and their preference of several possible placements of the warning (on the jumper cables, on the battery, in the engine compartment, in the owner's manual, on the inside of the glove box door, and on the sun visor) on a Likert-type scale from 1 (definitely do not prefer) to 7 (very much prefer).

### 10.2.2    Results

Diagram accuracy was scored with two criteria, strict and lenient. With strict scoring (correct connections, colour and order), participants exposed to the tag warning diagrammed the battery connections more accurately (26.5 per cent) than did participants who were not exposed to the warning (0 per cent) ($\chi^2_{(1, N=65)} = 9.52$, p < 0.01). With lenient scoring (correct connections and correct order), participants exposed to the tag warning were more accurate (41.2 per cent) than participants not exposed to the warning (6.5 per cent) ($\chi^2_{(1, N=65)} = 10.54$, p < 0.01).

With strict scoring (at least four hazards mentioned), participants exposed to the warning had greater hazard recall (32.4 per cent) than those not exposed to the warning (3.2 per cent) ($\chi^2_{(1, N=65)} = 9.14$, p < 0.01). With lenient scoring (at least three hazards mentioned), there was no significant difference between conditions.

With strict scoring (at least four precautions mentioned), participants had greater precaution recall (14.7 per cent) than those not exposed to the warning (0.0 per cent) ($\chi^2_{(1, N=65)} = 4.94$, p < 0.05). With lenient scoring (at least three precautions), participants exposed to the warning had greater precaution recall (79.4 per cent) than those not exposed to the warning (41.9 per cent) ($\chi^2_{(1, N=65)} = 9.62$, p < 0.01).

The preferred location for the battery booster warnings/instructions was analysed with a 2 (tag versus no tag condition) × 6 (location) mixed-model analysis of variance (with the last factor repeated). The analysis showed only a main effect of location ($F_{(5, 315)} = 40.52$, p < 0.0001). Comparisons using the Newman–Keuls test showed that placement on the cables ($M = 5.92$) and on the battery ($M = 5.65$) did not differ and both were significantly preferred over all other locations (p < 0.05). The owner's manual ($M = 4.51$) was no different than the engine compartment ($M = 4.01$), but both were significantly preferred over the glove box ($M = 3.19$) or the sun visor ($M = 2.99$), which did not differ.

No other questionnaire item differed by warning presence/absence condition. A total of 68 per cent correctly identified the presence of acid in batteries and 91 per cent associated red and black markings with positive/hot and negative/earth, respectively.

## 10.3   EXPERIMENT 2

In Experiment 2 the presence versus absence of a warning was also examined, but here a behavioural compliance measure in an incidental exposure paradigm was used. In addition, the effectiveness of a manufacturer's current tag warning was compared with an enhanced (multicolour) tag warning.

### 10.3.1   Method

Twenty-four undergraduates from Rensselaer Polytechnic Institute participated. Participants were told that they would be tested on their knowledge of basic automobile maintenance facts and procedures. All procedures were carried out in an automotive shop, on two adjacently parked cars. The batteries in both vehicles were removed and replaced with realistic-appearing non-functional battery shells to eliminate any potential for injury. Several 'filler' tasks (determining tyre air pressure and engine oil, brake fluid and radiator coolant levels) were included to disguise the study's true purpose.

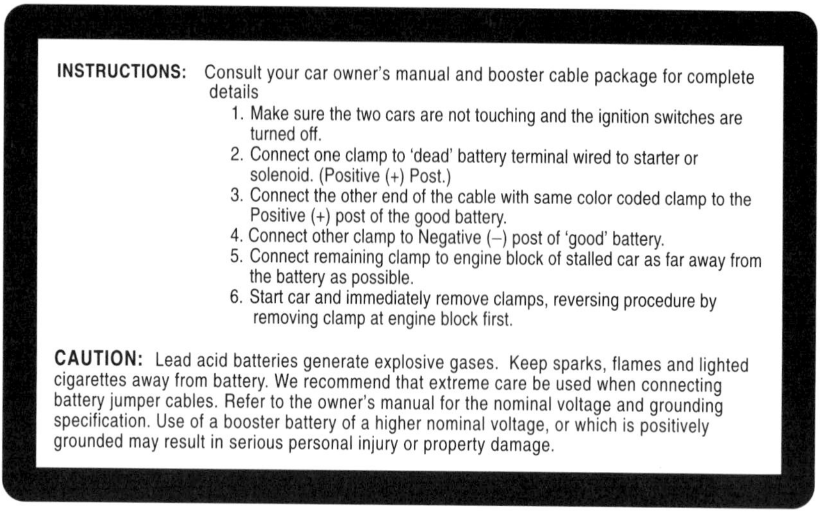

**INSTRUCTIONS:** Consult your car owner's manual and booster cable package for complete
details
1. Make sure the two cars are not touching and the ignition switches are
   turned off.
2. Connect one clamp to 'dead' battery terminal wired to starter or
   solenoid. (Positive (+) Post.)
3. Connect the other end of the cable with same color coded clamp to the
   Positive (+) post of the good battery.
4. Connect other clamp to Negative (–) post of 'good' battery.
5. Connect remaining clamp to engine block of stalled car as far away from
   the battery as possible.
6. Start car and immediately remove clamps, reversing procedure by
   removing clamp at engine block first.

**CAUTION:** Lead acid batteries generate explosive gases. Keep sparks, flames and lighted
cigarettes away from battery. We recommend that extreme care be used when connecting
battery jumper cables. Refer to the owner's manual for the nominal voltage and grounding
specification. Use of a booster battery of a higher nominal voltage, or which is positively
grounded may result in serious personal injury or property damage.

**Figure 10.2**   The original manufacturer's tag warning. The other side was printed in
Spanish.

All necessary tools to perform these tasks (e.g. tyre gauge, hygrometer and
towels) were provided nearby. In the main task of interest, the participant was to
jump start the car with the dead battery using the booster cables provided. There
were three booster cable sets, differing according to the warning conditions. Each
participant received one of these sets. Booster cables in the control condition had no
instructions or warnings. In the unenhanced tag condition, the cables were equipped
with an original manufacturer's tag label, measuring $10.8 \times 5.7$ cm, with printed
verbal instructions and warnings on one side in English and on the reverse side in
Spanish. Figure 10.2 shows this label.

The enhanced warning resembled that used in Experiment 1, except that bright
saturated yellow and red colours were added to the print and background, and that the
tag was laminated. The enhanced tag dimensions were $9.5 \times 8.3$ cm. Both tag warnings
were attached approximately 10 cm from the clamps at one end of the cables.

The sequence of steps performed by each participant was recorded. After this
task, participants completed a questionnaire to assess whether they had seen and
could recall the contents of the warning.

### 10.3.2   Results

Four of the eight participants in the enhanced tag condition accurately connected
the booster cables to the two cars. However, none of the participants in the two
other conditions correctly made the battery connections. The effect was significant
$(\chi^2_{(2, N=24)} = 9.60, p < 0.01)$. The pattern for seeing and recalling the warning content,
as assessed by the questionnaire, mirrored the compliance results.

## 10.4 DISCUSSION

The results of these two experiments illustrate several points. The first is that people do not know the correct, safe way to connect car battery booster cables. The reason for this is probably that people have viewed other individuals successfully, but incorrectly, jump start cars by connecting the corresponding poles of both batteries – an error that could lead to an explosion. Indeed, participants in Experiment 1 indicated that they had viewed other people jump start cars an average of 11 times. Most of the time, this method will successfully start a vehicle without an explosion, which reinforces the potentially dangerous behaviour. Another factor is that many people probably do not know what an electrical earth is or where inside the engine compartment a usable earth connection might be made. Also, painted surfaces, increased use of plastic and rubber components in newer automobiles, as well as build-up of grease and dirt on metal parts makes locating a proper earth connection difficult.

The second point is that the mere presence of a warning does not guarantee proper safe behaviour. The original manufacturer's warning produced no proper connections. The enhanced warning was evidently better in overcoming the participants' mistaken belief on how car batteries should be connected.

The third point is that, while we were able to facilitate proper connection with the enhanced tag warnings, the percentages of correct connection were not as high as desired. Performance might be increased by enhancing the warning even further and perhaps by placing several (redundant) warnings at relevant locations (e.g. both on the battery and on the cables).

Perhaps the best way to accomplish the goal of safer jump starting is to redesign some of the involved components. For example, the cables themselves could be explicitly labelled on one end 'to be used for the *live* car battery' and the other end 'to be used for the *dead* car battery'. In addition, one of the clamps of the dead battery cable could be designed to appear different from the other clamps to make users aware that it should not be connected to the negative terminal of the dead battery. Similarly, an interactive warning design (e.g. Duffy *et al.*, 1993) that requires users to manipulate the warning physically might be useful in alerting users to read the label information. Finally, a particular place in the engine compartment could be designated (and well labelled) as the 'earth' for use in jump starts.

Careful consideration of vehicle components and cable design, in conjunction with the use of a well-designed set of warnings, could increase the frequency of correct battery connections and decrease injuries.

### REFERENCES

DE PUY, D. (1990) Be aware of costly mistakes. *Modern Tire Dealer* 12.

DUFFY, R. R., KALSHER, M. J. and WOGALTER, M. S. (1993) The effectiveness of an interactive warning in a realistic product-use situation. In: *Proceedings of the Human Factors and Ergonomics Society 37th Annual Meeting*, pp. 935–939. Santa Monica, CA: Human Factors and Ergonomics Society.

JAYNES, L. S. and BOLES, D. B. (1990) The effects of symbols on warning compliance. In: *Proceedings of the Human Factors Society 34th Annual Meeting*, pp. 984–987. Santa Monica, CA: Human Factors Society.

KLINE, P. B., BRAUN, C. C., PETERSON, N. and SILVER, N. C. (1993) The impact of colour on warnings research. In: *Proceedings of the Human Factors and Ergonomics Society 37th Annual Meeting*, pp. 940–943. Santa Monica, CA: Human Factors and Ergonomics Society.

WOGALTER, M. S. and YOUNG, S. L. (1994) Enhancing warning compliance through alternative product label designs. *Applied Ergonomics* **24**, 53–57.

WOGALTER, M. S., KALSHER, M. J. and RACICOT, B. M. (1993) Behavioral compliance with warnings: effects of voice, context, and location. *Safety Science* **16**, 637–654.

# Forms

CHAPTER ELEVEN

# Designing and evaluating forms in large organizations

DAVID SLESS

## 11.1 INTRODUCTION

No research takes place in a vacuum, and research on forms is no exception: it breathes in the air of consumerism and its reformist ideology. Consumerism emerged as a political force in the developed world in the post-war period. One expression of this rising tide of consumerism was the growth of the 'Plain English' movement, seeking to reform bureaucratic and business writing practices that disadvantaged consumers and citizens. An example is a publication such as *Plain English* (Roberts, 1988).

The resulting business and government initiatives provided many opportunities for researchers and designers to collaborate in developing forms and advancing our understanding of form design and forms completion behaviour.

By the early 1980s there was a substantial body of research, case histories, and accumulated practical wisdom (Siegel, 1979; Cutts and Maher, 1981; Holland and Redish, 1981; Rose, 1981; Miller, 1984; Waller, 1984; Wright, 1984).

Many of these earlier studies – with the exception of the work by Miller and Waller – were based on the application of theory and methods from human information processing and ergonomics – the systems view (e.g. Singleton, 1989). This approach led to a number of important contributions but left unaddressed the social and political aspects of designing forms within large organizations. Ben Shneiderman, commenting on designing user interfaces within large organizations observed from his own experience:

> The social and political environment surrounding the implementation of a complex information system is not amenable to study by controlled experimentation . . . The experienced project leader knows that organizational politics and the preferences of

individuals may be more important than the technical issues in governing the success
of an interactive system.                                    (Shneiderman, 1987, p. 393)

Forms are one of the most important interactive systems used by organizations,
whether as paper forms, predating the advent of computers, or as data entry screens
within information systems. As this chapter will show, forms are deeply susceptible
to the political relations within organizations. Therefore, to say, as some do, that a
design might have worked but for the politics is to miss the point. If one is to
design forms within a large organization one must factor these powerful relations
*into* the design process, not treat them as external. However, to do so one needs a
theoretical framework that deals with concepts outside ergonomics and information
processing. These include concepts of conversation, meaning, inferred readers and
authors, position, genres, politeness, contempt, respect, power, control, subversion
and resistance. One needs to use categories such as stakeholders, citizens, clients
and consumers and be able to work through the subtle differences in relationships
between people and institutions that are implied by these categories.

In order to do so, it is useful to approach the problem of forms design from the
perspective of a constructionist theory of communication (Sless, 1986; Penman,
1993). This theory proceeds from the assumption that we *construct* our social
reality in and through our communicative activity – through conversation. Hence,
the conversation that takes place in a form – the question and answer sequence –
enables both the form-filler and the organization to construct the relationship
between them. From this view, forms are central in explaining the relationship
between large organizations and individuals, between producers and consumers, or
citizens and the state (Sless, 1988). This view also allows us to look beyond the
reformist agenda in which forms design is conventionally located and take in some
of the more problematic issues of power, ideology and the status of the individual
in our society.

## 11.2  FORMS DESIGN: A MULTI-SKILLED COMMUNICATION CRAFT

Forms design is an information design craft, not a science. The critical differences
between a craft and a science is one of purpose and tradition. Information design is
first and foremost concerned with solving practical problems within and through a
specific cultural and historical context. To that end, information designers draw on
the full range of skills, knowledge and processes available to them, some of which
predate scientific knowledge by many thousands of years. Scientists can only draw
on the stock of replicable research findings and generalizations in their field (Sless,
1992).

The task of forms design is to create effectively the means by which the conversation between individuals and organizations can take place. Most importantly,
from a methodological point of view, the basic unit of analysis in this framework is
the relationship between a form and its user, not the form or its user in isolation

from each other. Moreover, this is not the user as information processor but the user as a fully active social being taking part in a conversation from a particular position and with particular interests. This is a central proposition, the significance of which will become apparent as we proceed.

## 11.3   FORM-FILLING BEHAVIOUR AND EVALUATION OF FORMS

We now know a great deal about form-filling behaviour – the conversation between individuals and forms. But when the work reported in this chapter began, little was known of these conversations. As Frohlich (1986) observed in his ground-breaking study of these conversations: 'Research workers have tended to view forms as static documents, paying more attention to the manifest content of form material than to the selective use of that material by form-fillers' (p. 43).

This static view of forms was in part the result of the kinds of post hoc methods that had been used to evaluate forms, relying on form-fillers' recollections of form completion rather than observing form-fillers actually completing the form. The sequences of events – the dynamic struggle to make sense of and complete a form – are lost in these post hoc methods.

Frohlich, in contrast, observed people actually completing a form. The form he used was one developed for the Department of Health and Social Security (DHSS) in the UK and previously reported on by Waller (1984). Frohlich, like Holland and Redish (1981), recognized that a form was a type of conversation: '. . . form-filling . . . suggests a carry-over of familiar skills and expectations typical of natural conversation . . . [The type of conversation] is that of an interview or interrogation, with the form-filler in the role of respondent' (Frohlich, 1986, p. 57).

From his observations, Frohlich suggested conversational principles that applied to form-filling, such as, 'I work through the questions in the order they appear on the form', 'I miss out questions that do not seem to apply to me', and the Principle of Least Reading Effort: 'I only read what seems to be necessary to maintain form-filling progress' (there are seven principles altogether).

Some of the principles show clearly how form-fillers try to cope when the conversation breaks down, which it does frequently. Breakdown becomes apparent in the large number of errors found on completed forms. Barnard et al. (1979) reported on this, and in work on major government and insurance forms, error rates as high as 100 per cent have been found; that is, at least one completion error on every form. In one published case history a mean error rate of seven per form was reported (Fisher and Sless, 1990).

Completion errors on forms can be of four basic types: omission, commission, mistakes, and transcription (Sless, 1985a). Errors of omission occur when form-fillers miss information by failing to complete a particular section of the form; errors of commission occur when form-fillers add information that was not asked for; mistakes arise when the information given is incorrect; and errors of transcription occur when data from another document are transcribed incorrectly. However, knowing what type of errors have occurred on a form does not tell us *why* they have occurred. Experience confirms Frohlich's finding that to find out why the errors occurred one must observe the form being completed. It is in the dynamics of the transaction between form-filler and form that one is able to see the patterns of behaviour which lead to errors.

From this type of direct observation it is clear that the Principle of Least Reading Effort accounts for a substantial proportion of the errors. Frohlich estimated that form-fillers read less than 50 per cent of relevant explanations and instructions on the forms he observed.

This was first observed on a massive scale in a project which began in 1984 to overhaul the major Australian Taxation Office (ATO) public form, Tax Form 'S'. Taxpayers made many errors on the form because they did not follow instructions. The first attempt to overhaul the form had tried to solve the problem by 'translating' instructions into plain English. This failed. As the researchers commented:

> On the criteria of delivering better quality information . . . neither [plain English] form is any more than a marginal advance over the old form. Our qualitative assessment . . . is that there are only marginally fewer errors and omissions in the information supplied by taxpayers on the test forms than was the case when the old form was tested.
>
> (Lenehan *et al.*, 1985)

Observations showed that form-fillers applied the Principle of Least Reading Effort to all forms whether in gobbledegook or plain English, skipping headings, instructions and explanations that they deemed inappropriate.

If the form was to be improved, form-filling behaviour had to be altered, that is, the conversation between form and form-filler had to be restructured. This was done by introducing what was later called the *directed form*. The seeds of this solution lay in Waller's work on the DHSS form (1984), where it was partially, and sometimes unsuccessfully, applied, as Frohlich's observations showed.

Rather than leaving the choice of questions to answer up to the form-filler, the directed form developed for the ATO *required* the form-filler to answer *each question*. The difference can be seen clearly in Figure 11.1.

Figure 11.1a shows how the question was asked in the 'plain English' version, whereas Figure 11.1b shows how the same question was asked in the directed form used for all taxpayers in 1986.

Before the 1986 form, a vast amount of both qualitative and quantitative data were collected on taxpayer behaviour. This included a pilot study in Western Australia in 1985 with over a quarter of a million taxpayers, probably one of the largest pilot studies ever! The data from this pilot study confirmed Frohlich's findings, and further showed that among the most likely instructions to be missed were the preliminary instructions, those supposed to be read before filling in the form, because form-fillers perceive the task as primarily one of form-filling, not reading. Nothing seemed to induce taxpayers to read any of this preliminary content; the went straight to the answer space and started filling out the form. The effect of this

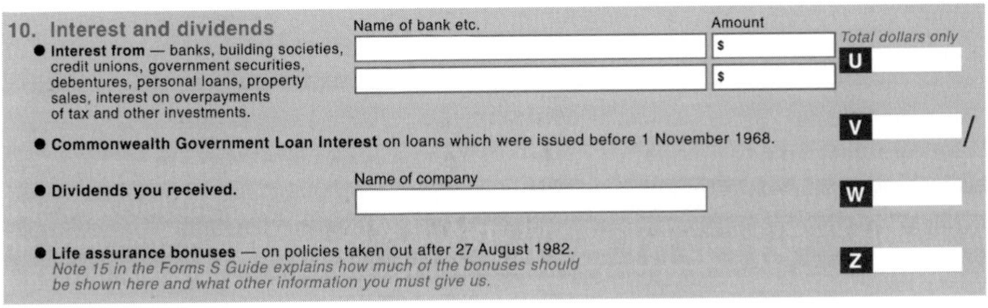

**10. Interest and dividends**

Name of bank etc.                                    Amount

- **Interest from** — banks, building societies, credit unions, government securities, debentures, personal loans, property sales, interest on overpayments of tax and other investments.

  $ _____    Total dollars only    **U**

  $ _____

- **Commonwealth Government Loan Interest** on loans which were issued before 1 November 1968.    **V** _____ /

- **Dividends you received.**

  Name of company _____    **W** _____

- **Life assurance bonuses** — on policies taken out after 27 August 1982.    **Z** _____
  *Note 15 in the Forms S Guide explains how much of the bonuses should be shown here and what other information you must give us.*

(a)

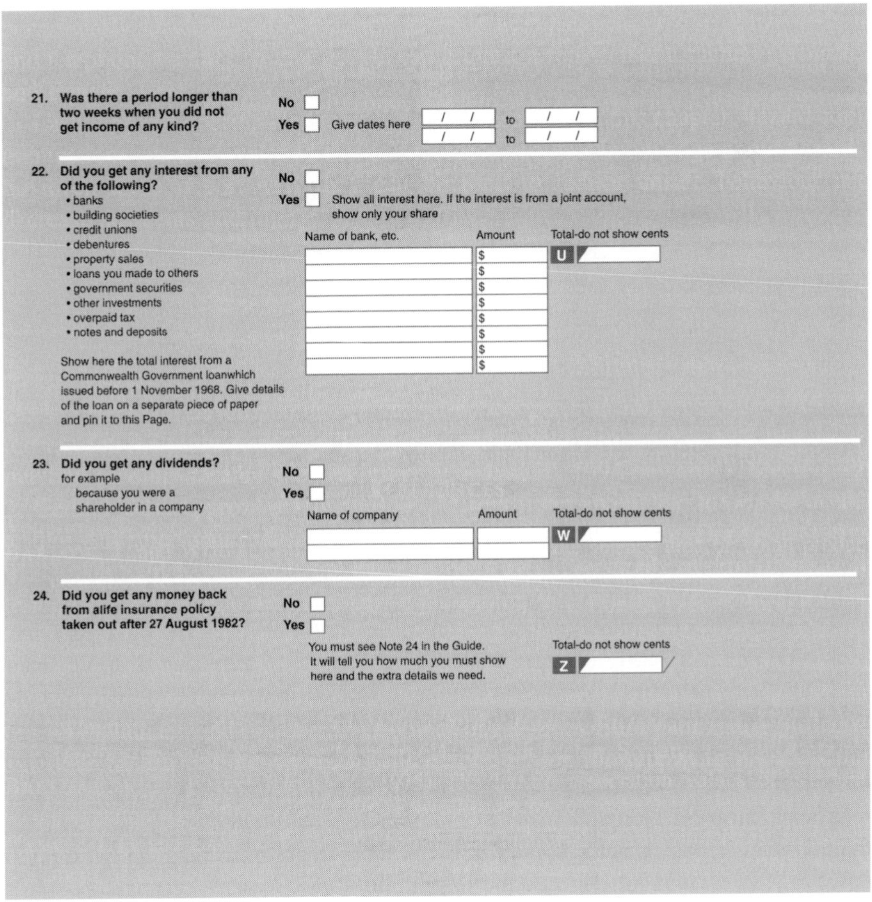

21. Was there a period longer than two weeks when you did not get income of any kind?

    No ☐
    Yes ☐    Give dates here  / / to / /
                               / / to / /

22. Did you get any interest from any of the following?
    - banks
    - building societies
    - credit unions
    - debentures
    - property sales
    - loans you made to others
    - government securities
    - other investments
    - overpaid tax
    - notes and deposits

    Show here the total interest from a Commonwealth Government loan which issued before 1 November 1968. Give details of the loan on a separate piece of paper and pin it to this Page.

    No ☐
    Yes ☐    Show all interest here. If the interest is from a joint account, show only your share

    Name of bank, etc.        Amount        Total-do not show cents
                              $            **U** _____
                              $
                              $
                              $
                              $
                              $
                              $
                              $

23. Did you get any dividends?
    for example
        because you were a
        shareholder in a company

    No ☐
    Yes ☐

    Name of company        Amount        Total-do not show cents
                                          **W** _____

24. Did you get any money back from a life insurance policy taken out after 27 August 1982?

    No ☐
    Yes ☐

    You must see Note 24 in the Guide. It will tell you how much you must show here and the extra details we need.

    Total-do not show cents
    **Z** _____

(b)

**Figure 11.1**  Difference between undirected (a) and directed (b) forms collecting the same data.

**Table 11.1**  Number of words in preliminary instructions in successive versions of a tax form

| | |
|---|---|
| 'Plain English' | 321 |
| West Australia | 107 |
| National release | 44 |

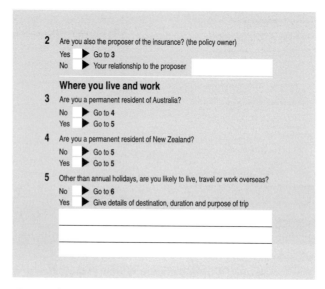

**Figure 11.2**  Design showing routeing devices and section headings.

finding on the form's design is dramatically illustrated in the progressive reduction of the number of words in the preliminary instructions from the 'plain English' version, via the WA pilot version, to the final version released to all taxpayers (Table 11.1).

The data from the pilot study also confirmed the benefits of the directed form. This type of form subtly changes form-filling behaviour from one of topic scanning, applying the principle of least reading effort – where the form-fillers decide which questions to answer on the basis of a minimal reading of captions or headings – to one in which the form-fillers could fill in the form only by making a series of decisions based on reading the questions. This is a qualitative change which requires a different approach: instead of skimming over a question and deciding for themselves whether or not it applies to them, form-fillers must read the question in order to answer 'Yes' or 'No'. So the imposition of the 'Yes/No' changed people's reading of questions, but not their reading of instructions.

In the directed form, headings are subordinated to question numbers which reinforce the sequential nature of the task. This also enables the use of strong routeing devices throughout the form. Figure 11.2 shows an example of a more recent design showing the routeing device.

Experiments and refinements with this type of design continued through a number of forms. The results are impressive, with the number of forms needing repair sometimes dropping from 100 per cent down to 11 per cent. In one case the total number of errors was reduced by 97.2 per cent (Fisher and Sless, 1990) where of the total number of questions answered, only 2.8 per cent were incorrect. But it is important to point out that this dramatic reduction was not accomplished with forms used by ordinary citizens or consumers, but with forms completed by professional insurance agents who knew the field they were working in.

The research also showed that by using a variety of conversational devices it was possible to translate a great many instructions into 'Yes/No' questions. Unfortunately, this can result in a very long form, collecting valueless 'data'. Moreover, there will always be a residual set of instructions that cannot be translated into questions.

How then can we change form-filling behaviour so that instructions as well as questions are read? Earlier research, involving other types of graphic tasks, had shown that user errors could be dramatically reduced if the changes were made to the user's task, rather than to the graphic material itself (Sless, 1981, pp. 150–157).

Thus the forms' design team began to explore other solutions that radically changed form-fillers' instruction-reading tasks. The objective was to get people to perform two quite separate tasks: to read instructions and to provide information. The solution – the experimental tax form shown in Figure 11.3 – was a type of form in which all instructions and captions were removed from the form and placed on a separate document so that there is no way the form-filler can complete this type of form *without* referring to the instructions.

This design has many advantages and is enormously liberating typographically. One of the most difficult challenges facing forms designers is to integrate text and answer spaces in a way that is coherent, yet they have quite different requirements. Separating these functions into two documents greatly simplifies the design and editing.

There was some concern, when the form was first developed, that people would have difficulty tracking between the two documents, but in fact it was not a problem at all: people had no difficulty. They used the answer space to track back to the instructions. Most importantly, there was a radical change in form-filling behaviour: not just an *improvement* in reading of instructions, but a *total* reading of instructions. Instead of people reading just a little bit and then trying to answer the question, they were reading all the instructions, before going to the answer space. If one takes full account of form-fillers' limited capacities, and discounts errors that arise from design features that ignore these limitations, approximately 2 per cent of answers remain incorrect for unexplained reasons. This is an extremely low error rate, if compared with error rates on conventional forms (Morehead and Sless, 1988).

The ATO adopted the basic principle of this design, calling it the Tax Pack. Unfortunately, the ATO implementation ignores so many skill limitations of ordinary form-fillers that they have lost any advantage they might have gained in terms of reduced error rates. For example, many form-fillers, particularly those with poor educational backgrounds, have difficulty with computations. The Tax Pack, by imposing the full administrative burden on the taxpayer, requires taxpayers to make many

**21.** Did you get any of the following?
  • Age pension
  • Invalid pension
  • Widows pension
  • Single parent's pension
  • any other pension or benefit from the Australian
    government which is not shown on a group certificate.

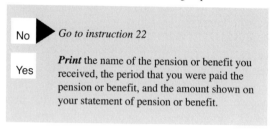

**21.**

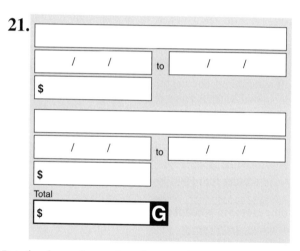

**Figure 11.3** Details of question and explanation booklet, followed by details of answer space.

calculations. There is yet to be a good implementation of this type of design. We suspect many organizations have been inhibited from doing so because of the greatly disliked Tax Pack. Just the appearance of something similar to the Tax Pack is enough to put people off!

Nonetheless, the original type of directed form is now widely used in large public and private Australian institutions, including government departments, statistical and research organizations, motoring organizations, insurance companies, banks, legal aid services, workers compensation schemes, and grant awarding bodies.

Many of these have been highly successful in reducing error rates and improving productivity, but only where they have been developed using a systematic methodology.

## 11.4   FORMS DESIGN METHODS — GENERALIZED PROCEDURE

Forms design methods are an example of a more generalized information design methodology. We can see this clearly in the type of diagram Wright (1984) adapted from Felker (1980) to describe the forms design process. Similar diagrams are used in symbol design (Foster, 1990). This is not surprising since both are concerned with managing a conversation.

However, in the light of experience with many forms design projects, and with a recognition of the central role that organizational politics plays in forms design, these methods have been greatly elaborated and refined (Fisher and Sless, 1990).

All these methods derive from the more generalized field of design methods, as developed in such areas as product engineering, systems and architectural design (Jones, 1980).

The essence of the method consists of:

- defining objectives;
- developing prototypes;
- testing and modifying prototypes repeatedly until optimum performance is reached consistent with the objectives;
- implementing the design.

Despite its generality, this method or approach is still very rarely used in forms design, which is one reason why so many badly designed forms find their way into use.

Here is a list of the sequence of stages that constitute good forms design approach.

1   Identify the dominant voices in the organization's conversations.

2   Decide what information needs to be collected or given.

3   Find out who are the users of the form.

4   Find out about the context in which the information is to be collected or given.

5   Develop a prototype of the form.

6   Test the form with users to see if it works.

7   Modify the form in the light of the testing.

8   Repeat testing and modification at least three times.

9   Introduce the form on a small pilot scale.

10   Modify the form on the basis of the results from the pilot.

11   Introduce the form.

12   Monitor the form in use, measuring against known benchmarks.

Obviously a great deal could be said about each of these stages, and in later sections I will deal with some of these in detail. But it is worth making two general observations. Firstly, for long and complex forms, these stages can take a long time. Six months would be a typical time span from beginning to end. Secondly, Stage 1 above only identifies who the stakeholders are but not the detailed negotiations with stakeholders, which have to go on throughout the development of the form, and which are critical to the eventual success of the project. I will discuss these in more detail later.

## 11.4.1  Testing and benchmarking

Testing and benchmarking play a central role in good forms design as can be seen in the approach described above, and there have been many reviews of potential testing methods (Wright, 1979; Holland and Redish, 1981; Sless, 1985a).

Even though no large-scale comparative evaluation of methods has been published, nor any meta-analysis of the type undertaken in other areas (e.g. Nielsen and Levy, 1994), a sufficient body of experience has been accumulated to suggest that some testing and benchmarking methods may be better than others in large organizations where there is often a shortage of resources and skills to undertake the work. In such environments, testing methods have to be robust, easy to apply, and highly predictive of the outcome. The range has been narrowed down to two methods: error analysis and diagnostic testing.

## 11.4.2  Error analysis

An error analysis consists of counting and tabulating the number and type of errors that have occurred on a sample of forms. Error analysis is the most important quantitative measure of a form's performance. It is the basic quantitative benchmark against which the performance of one form can be compared with another, and some of the less obvious but major costs in using forms can be estimated. Good design can reduce the incidence of errors on forms. But one cannot begin to improve the design of a form if one does not know how well or how badly the form has performed in the past. An error analysis will say something about what has happened, but not why.

There are always more errors made in completing forms than are visible through an error analysis. For this reason error analysis should never be used as the only source of information of a form's performance. But when used in conjunction with diagnostic testing, error analysis can be very powerful.

## 11.4.3  Diagnostic testing

A diagnostic test is an investigation of a form in use. It allows one to see first hand the way in which people use forms. Interviews give unreliable information on what people remember about forms; analysing errors tells one something about what went wrong, but not *why*. Observation allows one to get closer to the question of why a particular behaviour occurred. We need to know why a particular behaviour occurred before we redesign or modify a form.

Previous research (Sless, 1979) and practical experience in the field have shown that to develop successful designs at least three cycles of testing and modification are required. With complex forms the number of cycles could be much higher. At least three cycles of testing and modification are needed, because firstly, changing a form to eliminate one fault may introduce a new one, and secondly, it is impossible to pick up all the faults in one round of testing and modification. The best one can hope for is that one can correct all the faults in two rounds of modification, with the third test confirming the performance of the form.

## 11.5   FORM DESIGN GUIDELINES

Miller (1984) captured the essence of good forms design when he observed that:

> The appearance of the form should not only be inviting, but should enhance the importance of what information the user is to supply. That is its reason for existence. Many forms seem to have contempt for the user's data . . . The quality of the paper, typography, printing can appear to belittle the importance of the users' effort in filling it out, and of the transaction in which the form's content is an essential part. The quality of these factors is more than a subtle indicator, to users, of the originator's attitude towards them and to the importance of the transaction.                    (p. 536)

Miller clearly points the way when he suggests that we must stop creating forms that show contempt for the form-filler's data. We must replace contempt with respect. Guidelines can not only be used to deal with the technical issues of good forms design, they can also emphasize the user's point of view and thereby lend a certain dignity to a humble task, to make the ordinary act of completing a form important and valuable. We have written many sets of guidelines for forms designers with Miller's words in mind.

But are such texts useful? Anecdotal evidence suggests that texts are seldom used. Moreover, guidelines can quickly ossify and become rules. For example, we developed a set of guidelines for one organization based around a graphics software package that allowed only a limited number of fonts and font sizes. That software package now has much more flexible font control, to allow a more sensitive and appropriate use of typography. Unfortunately, six years on, the organization still regards its original guidelines as the 'gold standard', and is highly critical of anything that does not conform to it.

Balanced against the risk of ossification is the need to retain corporate memories of skills and procedures. Many contemporary organizations have got rid of people with information design skills, often without realizing their value to the organization. A set of guidelines, despite the many limitations of such documents, is sometimes the only remaining repository of knowledge on which future staff can draw. However we choose to make our knowledge and skill available, whether through guidelines or through software systems, making available our accumulated practical wisdom and research findings is an important part of improving forms design practice.

## 11.5.1   Language, context and design issues

Language on forms is highly contextual which means that no set of guidelines on the use of language can fully anticipate the specificity of particular contexts. We have to observe the language in use to judge whether or not it is appropriate.

This is another way of saying that the basic unit of analysis is the relationship between a form and its user, not the form or its user isolated from each other, and not the language of the form on its own. This is why we emphasize one overarching principle: always test the form diagnostically, and be prepared to change wording as a result of testing.

Wright and Barnard (1975) provided a summary of general reading principles, as they apply to documents in general. Useful though it is, it gives little insight into the dynamics of reading on forms where principles of good conversation management seem more important than principles that apply to continuous text. Sequence, turn taking, and voice become the focus, rather than words. Rogers (Chapter 13) elaborates that point.

The graphic issues of forms are no less contextual than language. But with a combination of appropriate functional units, typographic specifications, and grids it is possible to provide the form designer with an appropriate vocabulary in typography and graphics.

There are clearly too many technical details to mention in this chapter, but I would like to mention one small innovation that in my view captures the essence of Miller's concern for form-fillers: it is the use of the floating white box against a tinted background, used in many of the illustrations in this chapter.

This is now a common feature of many forms. When used appropriately these simple graphic features dignify the form-fillers' task with importance – they make the task performed by the form-filler the most prominent on the form. As the testing on Tax Form 'S' showed, this feature enables the form-fillers to estimate how much work is involved in completing the form and allows them to check their answers easily when the form is completed. These features also dignify the task for people processing the form – often themselves the victims of a form's poor design – by making the form's data more readily identifiable and legible.

## 11.5.2   Electronic design systems

Features like the floating white box were not an innovation of the electronic design systems of the last decade, but they are the type of feature that has benefited greatly from this technology, and they serve to illustrate what this new technology has meant for forms design. In 1983, a form with floating boxes took the South Australian Government Printer ten days from presentation of a marked-up design to production of a proof. The cost of typesetting alone for each page was about $300. In 1985, using a Macintosh, the same form was created directly, with no intermediate typesetting or mask cutting. We then printed a laser proof copy in a matter of seconds. The cost of the equipment and the time taken to master it was fully amortized after creating 50 pages.

The great leap forward was not just the rapid and cheap production of final artwork. More importantly, it enabled us to generate prototype forms rapidly and then iteratively test and modify them. I had anticipated the need for this type of methodology in some earlier research (Sless, 1979) but it was not until the advent of the Apple Macintosh that we had a cheap way of putting this methodology into practice.

This technology has had a profound effect on our design methods and in our way of thinking about the design process. It has enabled us to integrate traditional design and writing crafts with powerful analytical tools and the more recent crafts of testing. For me this has been the fulfilment of a dream. In the early 1980s when it was nothing more than a hope, I wrote:

> The new information age will require many information designers. They will have to be capable of taking information users into account as part of their professional activity. This will require a redefinition of their job, an acknowledgment of their own limitations and an informed and sensitive awareness of the needs of the information user. The last of these can only be achieved by forming better theories about users, developing methods of design research that are not dependent on outside expertise, and acquiring an informed sense of the history of information design, combining all these to create new conventions to meet new communication needs and technologies.
>
> (Sless, 1985b, p. 2)

We have now gone some way towards developing the integrated methods which will enable us to develop guidelines and train the next generation of information designers. But we need to look beyond these aspects of the design process to get a full picture of this emerging craft. We need to turn our attention to performance and to the politics of design beyond that.

### 11.5.3  Standards of performance

What kinds of standards of performance should we expect from our emerging craft? It is clear that the traditional visual standards of aesthetic judgement employed by graphic designers are no longer a sufficient basis for judging information design. We cannot simply look at a form and say it is well-designed on the basis of its appearance alone. We must judge a design by its performance, by what people can and want to do with it. A well-designed form should be appealing and inviting to the form-filler, it should also be easy to use.

In this shift to form design one can see the force of the methodological point that the basic unit to form design of analysis is the relationship between a form and its user. When we set standards of performance for forms we are setting standards for managing conversations, not for printed or electronic artefacts.

The most obvious measures of a form's performance are error rates and the cost of repairing them. But although error rates offer an easy numerical way of judging a form's performance, the meaning of the numbers can vary considerably and comparisons of error rates between different forms may be meaningless. For example, when a form is filled in by a client at a counter with the help of a clerk, many errors can be corrected as part of the conversation between the client and the clerk, and never find their way onto the form. Such conversations can mask design faults. Therefore, when making a judgement about error rates, we must always look at the conversation through which the form lives, rather than at marks on paper. Forms that live through different conversations may not be comparable.

But if these measures are done on a routine basis, they can be used to get a sense of changing performance in a quick and simple way. We have found that a form's functional life can be remarkably short, sometimes less than six months. This is not at all surprising if one thinks of a form as a conversation. Conversations, by their nature, are changing all the time. In ordinary discourse they are constantly modified to keep pace with the changed relations and circumstances. Forms' functionality deteriorates because the conversations of which they are a part change, but the forms themselves do not.

One useful measure is the time someone takes to complete a form. For example, in our diagnostic testing on two comparably complex forms – Tax Form 'S' and the Austudy form – we observed that it took people about 30 minutes to complete each form. In both cases, after about 20 minutes form-fillers started to show signs of tiredness and lack of concentration. Error rates in the latter third of both these forms tended to be higher than other parts of the form. We do not know whether this rise in errors was due to form-filler fatigue or the fact that some of the questions in this latter third were particularly complex, but we suspect there to be some correlation between the number of questions on the form and the error rates we measured.

Time taken for completion is also a useful measure because it tells us something about the burden we are placing on the form-filler. This is a hugely neglected area where real costs are often hidden. Often organizations will take account of their own internal costs but fail to take account of the costs borne by the form-filler. In Australia, for example, most of the cost of processing tax returns is borne by the public. The Tax Pack has become a monster. Far from being a vehicle of enlightened government, it has become the means by which the Australian Taxation Office (ATO) has externalized its administration, placing the burden of tax assessment on the citizen. Our own estimates suggest that for every cent spent by the ATO on tax collection, citizens are spending up to nine cents extra in complying with the taxation law, much of this extra being taken up by professional fees to accountants. Well over 60 per cent of salary and wage earners refuse to use the Tax Pack and get a professional to complete their tax returns for them.

Frequently used but totally misleading figures on forms' performance are printing costs or document size. In the USA, where there has been a 'paperwork reduction' policy, some have interpreted this to mean a reduction in the size of the pieces of paper rather than a reduction in the work associated with processing the forms. Printing and paper bills may go down, but the work, which is by far the largest cost, does not.

Improved forms using the methods described above – apart from our directed data sheet – are usually longer and can easily occupy twice as many pages as their

**Table 11.2** Improvements in processing time for new forms (seven pages long), versus old forms (two pages long), both collecting the same data

| Data sets | Average diference (seconds) |
|---|---|
| First set | −87.6 |
| Second set | −60.2 |
| Third set | −37.6 |
| Fourth set | −19.8 |
| Fifth set | +31.4 |

unimproved counterparts while asking the same number of questions. But they are less costly to repair and no more costly to process. In fact, our data suggest that they may be faster to process. Table 11.2 gives some comparative figures of the time taken to process an old design of a motor vehicle insurance form of two A4 pages, and a new design asking for the same data in seven pages (Penman, 1990).

Staff members keyed in five sets of data on the old form and the same five data sets on the new form.

The negative sign indicates the new form took longer to process than the old form. The positive sign indicates the new form was processed faster. With each data set processed, staff became progressively faster on the new form and by round five the new form was being processed faster than the current form. These figures are consistent with our findings in other projects where the data have remained confidential.

This type of measurement, despite its numerical quality, is not neutral. We took these measurements in order to demonstrate an argument. There is nothing clean or scientific about such measures, they are part of the ongoing debates within any organization about costs and benefits, improvements in productivity and profitability, and changes in relations with clients and customers. They are part of the politics of design. And it is therefore fitting that I now turn in the final section of this chapter to the political issues of forms design.

## 11.6  MANAGING THE DESIGN PROCESS

### 11.6.1  Forms in an organizational context

Forms are the unloved beasts of burden in the information society; they fetch and carry the raw material – information – on which organizations depend. Without forms most organizations would grind to a halt. They are the principle means by which the state and businesses conduct their relationships with people, whether as citizens or consumers. Forms are the core of that relationship. The fact that forms are badly designed tells us directly about the quality of that relationship. It is messy, unfair, and, in the main, serves the interests of the state or business, not the citizen or consumer.

We are fortunate to live at a time when equity and efficiency seem to go hand-in-hand. It has not always been so, and it may not be so for long. I say this not to undermine our collective efforts with cynicism; there is important work to be done in giving the prosaic aspects of our lives dignity and respect, as Miller suggested. I say this to supply an insight into the fragile political climate that sustains our efforts, a climate we must be prepared to fight for. We need to be advocates as well as researchers and designers.

I would not wish to understate or minimize the challenge. Forms are integral to organizational procedures and are subject to multiple control by a large number of interests. Without understanding this organizational context and developing strategies for dealing with it, most attempts to improve forms will fail.

## 11.6.2   Negotiations, dominating voices and politics

In successful forms design projects, about 50 per cent of the project time is devoted to politics and negotiation with dominant voices in an organization.

Imagine six or more people, each with a totally different interest and a belief that their interest is more important than anyone else's, separately engaging you in a conversation about one subject. There is a very good chance that they will each give a different account of their conversation with you. How would you bring all these conversations together? This in essence is the problem one faces with designing forms in an organization. Forms are a part of a type of conversation. But each interest within an organization sees that conversation in a different way.

We have found it particularly useful when dealing with this organizational context to use the Logic of Positions (Sless, 1986). Put simply, the logic enables us to deal with the fact that what one sees or does not see of any communicative phenomenon depends on one's position within the communicative landscape, and on one's relationship with that communicative phenomenon. Just as each person in a landscape can see some things but not others, depending on where they are standing, so, by analogy, in communicative environments we all engage in conversations from our own point of view and with our own interests in mind. We see the texts we write and read from our own unique position in the communicative environment.

But although we cannot see the communicative environment from somebody else's position, we try to imagine their communicative activity. For example, administrators may not be able to see the forms they create from the form-filler's point of view. But they create an image of that form-filler – what I call an *inferred reader* – to fill that hidden part of the landscape (Sless, 1986). These shadowy images – inferred readers and authors – inhabit all our communicative experience in a powerful way. Often they are inseparable from our opinions about a particular text. If one listens carefully to conversations one will quickly learn to spot these shadowy figures. Below is a typical example from a senior lawyer in a bank:

> You cannot afford to separate the two ideas in that paragraph with a full stop. It would encourage people to ignore the second clause, which tends to qualify the first. It might just possibly lead to misunderstanding.

> (Westpac Banking Corporation, 1987, p. 5)

Clearly the lawyer is not offering us a legal opinion. He is offering us an opinion about an inferred reader, one not based on any detailed knowledge about human reading behaviour. This is part of what we have to deal with when designing forms or any other texts in an organizational context.

The first task then in managing the design process is to identify all the separate voices in the conversation, and the inferences they make about other users of the form, and, as in ordinary conversations, some people will be dominant.

Typically in large contemporary organizations the dominant voices represent the dominant interests within the organization. In an insurance company, for instance, these will be underwriters, lawyers, agents, investment managers, marketing managers, administrators, and information system managers. Each will come with a variety of inferred readers; they will each tell you how other stakeholders use the forms; and they will all give you different accounts of how the company's customers use the forms. To make matters worse, their inferred readers, about which they hold strong opinions, can change in unpredictable ways. And because it is not part of their professional knowledge, they can be extremely undisciplined, erratic, and contradictory in their opinions. What they tell you will in part depend on your position, or rather what they think your position is. You are not a neutral observer. You are, like them, in the landscape and a participant in the conversation.

This then is the reality of design in a large organization. But it is not entirely depressing. Because the inferred readers of dominant voices are changeable, you can have a powerful effect in shaping them, by providing the dominant voices with a glimpse of the one thing they do not have: direct experience with actual form-fillers. You can bring them back selected news and evidence from the front line, as it were – at the interface between the organization and its public. This can be very potent, particularly if the evidence is good. Error rates are very useful in this regard. Many organizations of our time claim to be 'customer driven'. Therefore, news from the driving seat is of more than ordinary interest.

It is important to remember that dominant voices do not have to agree with each other. They only have to agree that the design meets their needs. If the negotiations with dominant voices are handled on a one-to-one basis, rather than in committee, it will allow for considerable scope for satisfying the multiple interests that converge on a form.

Finally, before-and-after data on a form's performance can be extremely important in persuading people to continue allowing you to improve their forms. But to succeed, you have to insist on measurement at both ends of the process. If you tell people that you have improved their forms but you have no evidence to prove it, what does 'improvement' mean?

### 11.6.3   Forms as instruments of social control

It is impossible to consider forms in any depth without acknowledging that they are instruments of social control. Forms constitute one of the major unobtrusive methods by which bureaucratic societies exercise control over citizens and consumers.

Issues of social control have been much debated in our western culture. In recent times that debate has focused on the role cultural artefacts play in social control. And it has been argued that we are defined as subjects in and through the dominant discourses in our society. We are, as it were, already inscribed in the texts we read.

Cultural critics have pointed to the objects of popular culture, literature and art as the coercive apparatus of the state and big business capitalism. But this has always struck me as odd. In comparison with the coercive power of forms, popular culture and the arts seem the most resistible of artefacts. I can switch off the television, refuse to open a book, and never visit the art gallery, but I cannot turn away from the car insurance form, the income tax form, or the census. The consequences of not watching television are trivial compared to the consequences of not having car insurance. The sensation of being inscribed in a text of somebody else's making is not very strong when it comes to television, yet the feeling is all too real and palpable when completing a form.

Perhaps one of the clearest symptoms of the power exercised by forms is the fact that they are objects of nervous humour. I have yet to see a newspaper article on forms, or be interviewed by a reporter about them, without some weak joke being made or implied. Yet forms are very unfunny things.

I suggest that we need a cultural critique of the form. What type of subject do our bureaucracies construct in the forms we have to fill in? Can forms in our type of society ever be artefacts that we associate with dignity and respect for ordinary people, as Miller suggests they should be? These are, of course, not questions about forms *per se*, but about the whole nature of the relationship between citizen and state, business and consumers. As we help our large organizations improve the quality of their forms, we need to ask ourselves continually whether we are handmaidens to a system that helps us or coerces us. Do we reveal the hand that cares or disguise the fist that controls?

## REFERENCES

BARNARD, P., WRIGHT, P. and WILCOX, P. (1979) Effects of response instructions and question style on the ease of completing forms. *Journal of Occupational Psychology* **52**, 209–226.

CUTTS, M. and MAHER, C. (1981) Simplifying DHSS forms and letters. *Information Design Journal* **2**, 28–32.

FELKER, D. B. (1980) Instructional research. In: FELKER, D. B. (Ed.), *Document Design: A Review of the Relevant Research*, Technical Report 75002–4/80. Washington, DC: American Institutes for Research.

FISHER, P. and SLESS, D. (1990) Information design methods and productivity in the insurance industry. *Information Design Journal* **6**, 108–29.

FOSTER, J. J. (1990) Standardising public information symbols: proposals for a simpler procedure. *Information Design Journal* **6**, 161–168.

FROHLICH, D. M. (1986) On the organisation of form-filling behaviour. *Information Design Journal* **5**, 43–59.

HOLLAND, V. M. and REDISH, J. C. (1981) 'Strategies for using forms and other public documents', paper presented at Georgetown University Round Table on Languages and Linguistics, Document Design Centre, American Institutes for Research.

JONES, C. J. (1980) *Design Methods: Seeds of Human Futures.* London: Wiley.

LENEHAN, LYNTON and BLOOM (1985) *Market Testing of Two Draft Designs for a New Tax Form 'S'*, a qualitative/quantitative report prepared for the Australian Taxation Office, Canberra.

MILLER, R. (1984) Transaction structures and format in form design. In: ZWAGA, H. and EASTERBY, R. (Eds), *Information Design*, pp. 529–544. Chichester: John Wiley & Sons.

MOREHEAD, A. and SLESS, D. (1988) *Integrating Instructions with Australian Taxation Office Forms: Final Report.* Canberra: Communication Research Institute of Australia.

NIELSEN, J. and LEVY, J. (1994) Measuring usability: preference vs. performance. *Communications of the ACM* **37**, 66–75.

PENMAN, R. (1990) *New Car Insurance Proposal Form: Rationale and Evidence.* Report to: NRMA Insurance Ltd, Canberra: Communication Research Institute of Australia.

PENMAN, R. (1993) Conversation is the common theme: understanding talk and text. *Australian Journal of Communication* **20**, 30–43.

ROBERTS, P. D. (1988) *Plain English: A User's Guide.* London: Penguin Books.

ROSE, A. M. (1981) Problems in public documents. *Information Design Journal* **2**, 179–196.

SHNEIDERMAN, B. (1987) *Designing the User Interface: Strategies for Effective Human–Computer Interaction.* Reading: Addison-Wesley Publishing Co.

SIEGEL, A. (1979) Fighting business gobbledygook . . . How to say it in plain English. *Management Review* **68**.

SINGLETON, W. T. (1989) *The Mind at Work.* Cambridge: Cambridge University Press.

SLESS, D. (1979) Image design and modification: an experimental project in transforming. *Information Design Journal* **1**, 74–80.

SLESS, D. (1981) *Learning and Visual Communication.* London: Croom Helm.

SLESS, D. (1985a) *Form Evaluation: Some Simple Methods.* Canberra: Information Co-ordination Branch, Department of Sport Recreation and Tourism.

SLESS, D. (1985b) Informing information designers. *Icographic* **6**, 2–3.

SLESS, D. (1986) *In Search of Semiotics.* London: Croom Helm.

SLESS, D. (1988) Forms of control. *Australian Journal of Communication* **14**, 57–69.

SLESS, D. (1992) What is information design? In: PENMAN, R. and SLESS, D. (Eds), *Designing Information for People*, pp. 1–16, Canberra: Communication Research Press.

WALLER, R. (1984) Designing a government form: a case study. *Information Design Journal* **4**, 36–57.

WESTPAC BANKING CORPORATION (1987) 'Legalese – no breeze', *Changes*, May, p. 5.

WRIGHT, P. (1979) The quality control of document design. *Information Design Journal* **1**, 33–42.

WRIGHT, P. (1984) Informed design for forms. In: ZWAGA, H. and EASTERBY, R. (Eds), *Information Design*, pp. 545–577. Chichester: John Wiley and Sons.

WRIGHT, P. and BARNARD, P. (1975) Just fill out this form – a review for designers. *Applied Ergonomics* **6**, 213–220.

# CHAPTER TWELVE

# Forms usability and new technology: a real-world challenge

JANICE LEONG

## 12.1 INTRODUCTION

Designers have a well-earned reputation for being primarily concerned with the ephemeral or expressive qualities of graphic products. They often do not look beyond a client's brief or they are simply self-expressive.

Information designers start at the other end by trying to understand the needs of the users of graphic products and the way they use these products. We believe that serving the best interests of the user will also serve the best interests of the client. As such, testing graphic products with users as test persons (diagnostic or user testing) plays an important role in developing and confirming design solutions. However, introducing and conducting testing in the 'real world' can be a challenge in itself. In this chapter, this will be demonstrated in two case studies.

## 12.2 CASE STUDY 1: INTRODUCING INFORMATION DESIGN AND DIAGNOSTIC TESTING

The first case study describes how the introduction of new processing systems can present an opportunity to take a fresh look at the design of a company's graphic products and to introduce the information design approach. High volume laser printing was being introduced by an investment bank to update and integrate its various programming and printing systems. This would allow easier, efficient production of letters and statements with improved print quality.

The bank's Marketing team took this as an opportunity to rewrite their standard letters and to use their corporate typefaces on system-generated documents. They were advised by the laser printing systems supplier to consult with us on the information design of their documents because of our experience with developing graphic products for laser printing.

### 12.2.1   Information design is different to graphic design

When confronted with the proposed working method, the client realized that information design was quite different to graphic design. Many times they wondered why we wanted to know so much about their process and the document 'conversation' they had with their customer. The design results showed this difference even further. The client was pleasantly surprised to find that their information could be more useful and informative and look good as well.

The first product to be implemented was an investment product for retirees. The project scope was limited to six key documents with particular focus on the annual statement. Existing documents were reviewed and information obtained from the Client Services team and the Marketing team. Review of the documents found:

- different types of information scattered over the page;
- instructions buried within marketing prose;
- amounts expressed in abstract units relevant to the dealer, not the customer;
- unexplained variations between investment amounts and totals on statements.

Any group of customers receiving statements will include people ranging from those who are interested in a summary to those who are meticulous accounters. Retirees have the time and motivation to be very interested in both. The 'unexplained variations' were especially vexing for these customers because their investment was the superannuation on which they were to retire. Customers were often alarmed when they had invested $10 000 but received a statement which showed a balance closer to $8000!

Based on our experience we thought the best design would clearly identify the document as a statement (customers needed to identify it as an important document to keep). It would also group the document and customer references and instructions in a block on the right-hand side (this makes it easy to find documents in a file and places reference details close to the enquiries number). Also, it would first show a summary of the total investment value and then show details of transactions, including fees and taxes (Figures 12.1 and 12.2).

### 12.2.2   Diagnostic testing

Several options were developed, which were reviewed with the client. Although the client respected our opinion and advice, from their experience they thought the summary should come last and they were reluctant to show fees and taxes.

In all correspondence please
quote Investor Number    C021

| Date | Transaction | Amount $ | Number of Units | Units now Held | Value of Investment $ |
|------|------------|----------|-----------------|----------------|----------------------|
| **DEPOSIT UNITS** | | | | | |
| 01JUL90 | Opening Balance | | | 0.00 | 0.00 |
| 06JUN91 | Deposit | 10,525.99 | 5,195.45 | 5,195.45 | |
| 30JUN91 | Closing Balance | | | 5,195.45 | 10,593.52 |
| **INVESTMENT UNITS** | | | | | |
| 01JUL90 | Opening Balance | | | 0.00 | 0.00 |
| 06JUN91 | Deposit       * | 16,213.66 | 5,491.50 | 5,491.50 | |
| 30JUN91 | Closing Balance | | | 5,491.50 | 15,472.30 |

TOTAL VALUE OF YOUR INVESTMENT IN THE BT LUMP SUM FUND
AS AT 30 JUNE 1991 IS:                                 $25,065.83

\* An initial service fee          may have been
deducted from the amount you invested

**Figure 12.1**  Statement before redesign (only part of the form is shown).

This 'stalemate' of opinion led us to recommend diagnostic testing of the design with customers and investment advisers. The client was reluctant as their experience of testing with graphic designers and advertising groups was expensive, time-consuming market survey groups. However, after the method and benefits of diagnostic testing had been clarified, the client consented to have as much testing done as allowed by the budget and schedule.

Diagnostic testing can be used *during* the design process as well as to *confirm* a solution. It focuses on revealing how a product is *actually* used by the user, which can be very different from a user explaining how they *would* use the product.

Testing is conducted through interviews with individuals or very small groups, so it can be easily scheduled. Whereas one user can reveal much about a proposed design, a sample of four to six users is better, although the number will depend on the project and resources. Usually, it is recommended to interview users before, during and after developing design solutions. In the case study presented here, however, the client did not consent to this kind of testing as part of the development process, so it was necessary to find a very time-efficient testing method.

### 12.2.3  Testing method

Interviews were arranged with a typical customer and two investment advisers. Three options were tested in each interview. From our staff, one person was nominated to conduct the interview while another person noted comments and observed the behaviour of the interviewee. The client also attended and a tape recording was made for later reference.

The subject was asked to look at the statement and read aloud starting from the top to the bottom, speaking out any thoughts and questions that came to mind. This method made it possible to discover what customers are interested in looking for on a statement, when and where they might expect to find information, and finally,

Mr Michael Jones
Address line 1
Address line 2
Address line 3

**investor number**
**C12345678**

**Lump Sum Fund**
**1992 Annual Statement**

**Please keep this statement**

## Summary of your investment at 30 June 1992

|  |  | investment value | redemption price | number of units |
|---|---|---|---|---|
| **30 Jun 92** | Investment Units | $ 44 000.00 | 2.000 | 22 000.00 |
|  | Deposit Units | $ 8 945.00 | 1.000 | 8945.00 |
|  | Capital Stable Units | $ 32 000.00 | 2.000 | 16 000.00 |
|  | **total investment value \*** | **$ 84 945 .00** |  |  |
|  | preserved amount of total\*\* | $ 20 000.00 |  |  |

## Details of your transactions from 1 July 1991 to 30 June 1992

| date | transaction | transaction amount | unit price | transaction units |
|---|---|---|---|---|
| **11 Jan 92** | additional investment | $ 10 000.00 |  |  |
|  | less contributions tax | -$ 200.00 |  |  |
|  | **amount invested in units** | **$ 8 000.00** |  |  |
|  | Investment Units | $ 4 000.00 | 2.000 | 2 000.00 |
|  | Deposit Units | $ 2 000.00 | 1.000 | 2 000.00 |
|  | Capital Stable Units | $ 2 000.00 | 1.500 | 3 000.00 |
| **28 May 92** | **switch from Deposit** | **-$ 2 000.00** | 1.000 | - 2 000.00 |
|  | switch to Capital Stable | $ 2 000.00 | 1.500 | 3 000.00 |
| **11 Jun 92** | **redemption** | **-$ 4 055.00** |  |  |
|  | less lump sum tax | -$ 55.00 |  |  |
|  | amount received | $ 4 000.00 |  |  |
|  | Deposit Units | -$1 055.00 | 1.000 | -1 055.00 |
|  | Property Units | -$ 3000.00 | 1.500 | -4 000.00 |

**Figure 12.2**  The redesigned statement brings the summary to the top and emphasizes the items that customers are looking for, the title and the total investment value (only part of the form is shown).

what features of the design and language are either clear or confusing. Afterwards questions were asked about the subjects' understanding of certain words and where they might seek more information; any comments about other services or experiences they had with the bank were captured.

### 12.2.4   Testing results

Overall, there was a good reaction to the statements. Providing more information was useful but this also made them complex. It was important to show the summary first as an overview. Itemizing of fees and taxes was very welcome – one adviser said it was very important to disclosure and showed the bank's integrity. On first reading, transactions and dollar values were more important in organizing the data. However, unit investment details were needed later when considering changes to the investment.

### 12.2.5 Follow-up testing and implementation

The client found this type of testing simple and manageable. After the design was further developed, one more interview was conducted to check the design. Lack of time prevented further testing.

Working from our specifications and sample documents, the client decided to implement the statement, although they insisted on the option with the summary following the details. However, a year after the project, they modified the statement to show the summary first.

Interestingly, the Systems team which set up the statements were glad that the Marketing team tested the design – a design that worked well for customers also meant fewer programming revisions later.

## 12.3 CASE STUDY 2: FORM DESIGN AND ICR TECHNOLOGY

### 12.3.1 Working to tight business schedules

During the first redesign project the bank's forms were improved significantly by applying general information design and forms design principles, such as considering the different types of form users (individuals, joint applicants, companies), placing instructions at the point where they apply, providing prompts and tickbox options where appropriate, shortening line lengths for text such as the declaration, and allowing enough space for an answer, signature, etc.

The bank had a hectic and overlapping product schedule. There were a number of investment products, each of which 'rolled over' or 'renewed' every six or 12 months at various times of the year. Each rollover provided the client with an opportunity to change the form.

However, when ICR (intelligent character reading) technology was introduced by the bank to improve speed and accuracy of its information processing, the tight schedule was a set-back. There were many unknowns about the technical requirements and there was not enough time in six months to understand, test and implement new forms.

### 12.3.2 Design led by 'techno-designers'

Early decisions and the implementation of ICR were carried out by the Systems team, largely based on advice from tenderers of the equipment.

Each tenderer made available their 'forms design' guidelines. However, these guidelines consisted of tight specifications of what was required on forms for the equipment to operate accurately. For example, skew marks are required to calibrate the scanning of the page when the paper is not fed squarely into the scanner. The Systems team, following these guidelines, specified that there should be two large target marks at the top of each page. Later, when we questioned this with the

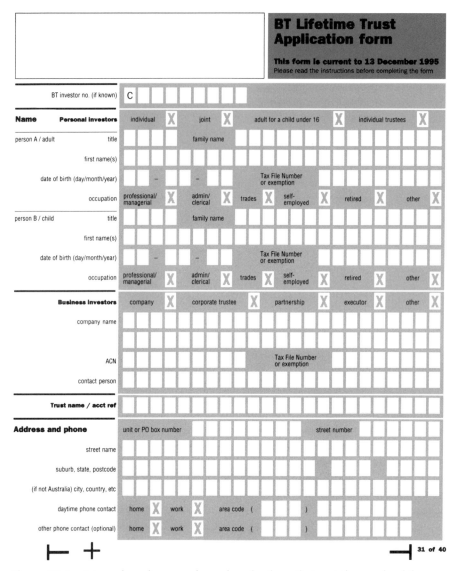

**Figure 12.3** A team-based approach produced a form that met the needs of the bank. However, it attracted sharp comments from the users. The redesign shown here produced a less daunting form that was tested by the bank with advisers and customers. At the bottom of the form two marks are included to calibrate the scanning of the page.

'techno-designer' we found that they only required a set of two perpendicular marks on opposite sides of the page. Although the marks needed to be quite large, we managed to design two marks that were more discreet while still meeting the technical requirements. Furthermore, the marks were put at the bottom of the page with other processing information (Figure 12.3).

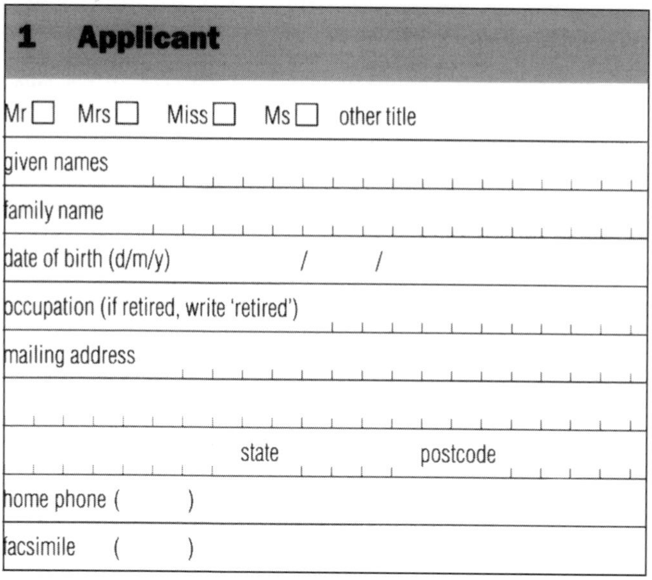
1 Applicant

Mr ☐ Mrs ☐ Miss ☐ Ms ☐ other title

given names

family name

date of birth (d/m/y) / /

occupation (if retired, write 'retired')

mailing address

state postcode

home phone ( )

facsimile ( )

**Figure 12.4** When ICR scanning of forms was first introduced, the Systems team requested the use of comb marks (detail of form).

Before the ICR system was investigated and implemented, the Systems team demanded introduction of comb marks to start 'training' customers to print clear, separate characters (Figure 12.4). The client from marketing was alarmed at what the customer response might be to this style of form, but did not know about other technically compatible and usable solutions. We presented her with Patricia Wright's well-known research (Barnard and Wright, 1976) about character separators and advised that white boxes in a colour field would be a functionally and visually better option. We both agreed on the importance of testing of the 'white box' form to see whether customers could complete the forms and to see what their reaction to the boxes might be. A researcher was consulted about the method to be used, and about how the questioning might be structured to measure the response. The form was tested with a small sample of customers. Although the customers found boxes 'rigid' and 'daunting' they were able to complete the form fairly easily when they tried. They said that they would accept the change if it meant faster processing of their investment transactions.

### 12.3.3 Design led by stakeholders

The Marketing team, concerned about the impact on the customer of changing to ICR, decided to set up a project outside the rollover schedule to develop a definitive 'model' form. It was important to have all relevant groups in the bank directly involved in the design of the new form and to conduct more extensive customer testing. The group included representatives from marketing, client services, information systems, administration, the legal department, and design.

Early meetings established the needs and wants of each of the stakeholders. In many cases, it was found that a simple 'want' by one team underestimated the effort required to implement it. Based on this shared understanding, the stakeholders negotiated the basic form requirements.

A form was developed that met the requirements of the group. However, we also wanted to test this new approach with customers. We felt there was too much emphasis on structuring the form based on how it was processed and feared that customers would be confused about the proposed division of the form for existing and new customers. Several interviews confirmed these difficulties. However, it became urgent to implement the form. Control of the project moved away from the user-oriented Marketing team to the technically-oriented Systems team and ICR equipment suppliers. After one more design iteration the form was implemented.

One user's letter described the form as, '. . . a form for the back-room boys . . .' not for customers. The expanded length of the form and the unfamiliar 'field' structure of questions prompted much negative response from investment advisers. One adviser was also concerned that he had to complete forms for his clients and that this practice might be illegal!

### 12.3.4  Redesign led by customer testing

While this form lived in the market-place for six months, the Marketing team took the lead again to redesign the form from a customer viewpoint. Customer testing was seen as a necessity.

As a way for the bank to reduce cost and share expertise we developed the testing materials and briefed the client about how to conduct the testing. This helped 'demystify' the process of diagnostic testing for the client.

The new form was tested with five customers. The comments were used to revise the form. The revised form was then tested with two advisers. The form was revised and tested again with one investor and one adviser. The final design (Figure 12.3) was a compromise but it also incorporated many of the needs of the Systems team. More importantly though, customers were able to complete the form with reasonable accuracy and ease.

### 12.4  SUMMARY

The information design approach stresses the point that in the design process of graphic products the usability and usefulness to the end user should be the first matter of importance. This emphasis is different to that of many graphic designers ('expressive') and techno-designers ('technical'). Diagnostic testing is an important means of testing design options and collecting information about the usability of graphic products.

Designers and researchers need to find ways of communicating the importance of diagnostic user testing to clients, particularly when new technology is introduced. Clients often use the following reasons to avoid user testing:

- the client *knows* the user and the context well enough;
- the designer *should* know what works ('experts');
- user testing is costly and time consuming;
- researchers are not interested in 'business' solutions.

In our experience, though, clients are prepared to rethink these arguments if designers and researchers are willing to look for flexible and affordable ways to conduct diagnostic testing. We have found co-operation with researchers in information design projects fruitful, not just in setting up diagnostic tests, but also to:

- advise us about user behaviour;
- help us to set design criteria and testing them;
- develop methods for the client to conduct testing and monitoring;
- help interpret research and testing conducted by other parties;
- offer expert opinion at different stages of a design.

#### REFERENCE

BARNARD, P. and WRIGHT, P. (1976) The effects of spaced character formats on the production and legibility of hand-written names. *Ergonomics* **19**, 81–92.

# CHAPTER THIRTEEN

# Artefacts of conversations: bills and organizations

DAVID ROGERS

## 13.1 BILLS AS CONVERSATIONS

In several studies substantial groundwork has already been laid for understanding bills and other public graphics as conversations (Holland and Reddish, 1981; Frohlich, 1986; Keller-Cohen *et al.,* 1990; Sless, 1992).

The basis of the conversational metaphor applied to bills in this chapter is discussed in detail elsewhere in this volume by MacKenzie-Taylor (Chapter 14) and Sless (Chapter 11). This chapter gives a glimpse of the type of analysis and design that is possible when applying this metaphor to the design of bills.

## 13.2 THE CONTEXT OF USE

Conversations are always located in settings or contexts – social, spatial and temporal – which provide the frame for meaning and action (Penman, 1992). Bill recipients develop their own understandings within their own specific contexts. Hence, from what superficially can appear to be simple, unproblematic documents, multiple possible meanings and actions can be generated.

When we engage in conversations, we are continually checking and negotiating the context with our conversational partners with an immediacy we cannot ignore. But when we write, the static form of print often beguiles us into a comfortable complacency. Unfortunately, it is the nature of text – its graphic or static form compared to other modes of communication – that often leads to the neglect of context (Ong, 1982). But it is only within a momentary context that we can attribute a specific meaning to an action, for the passage of time reveals retrospective and emerging contexts that constantly revise our interpretations. What are commonly taken as empirical 'instances', 'objects' or 'artefacts' of communication inadequately represent the communication process; instead, communication relies on a weaving of interdependent and continuously modifiable interpretations (Gergen, 1982).

When an organization issues a bill, it is performing one act in a series of acts that combine to form an ongoing conversation between a consumer and itself. Within this conversation, a negotiated narrative evolves, with events developing and unfolding over time. Whereas bills cannot encompass all of this narrative, they do act as a substructure, much like chapters of a story. The main plot is constructed from a set of primary 'events', including how much is owing, the date payment is due, and methods for paying. None of these events are objects of understanding *per se*. Rather, understanding requires considering the nature of the events, their placements and interrelationships.

In addition to the basic plot, subplots add secondary events. These include: reconciling previous accounts and payments, itemizing all the services consumed, negotiating legal obligations and rights, promoting different services, and instructing customers on how to manage better their use of the services provided.

For the information designer, the key challenge is to script all events by observing customers interpreting bills and then modifying the designs to reflect better temporal conventions, so the bill reader can interpret the elements coherently.

Figures 13.1 and 13.2 are electricity bills before and after redesign, showing the top portion without the payment slips. They show how the context of meaning, narrative and the conversational model have been used in bill design.

Research on the old bill showed that the context of use for electricity bills is similar to that of other utility bills. Few people seem to read them fully. Utility bills are usually taken from their envelopes, interrogated to see how much is owing, then set aside pending payment. However, a minority of customers closely examine their bills. Thus the bill has at least two primary audiences: those who only want to know what they owe, and when and how they should pay, and those who want to see every detail of their consumption and charges. For each audience, quite different information is needed.

When examining a bill, most customers expect to be able to read the following 'events' in the following order: who is sending the bill, how much do they owe, when do they have to pay by, and how do they pay. This is the implicit temporal convention for many bills. The plot in the bill in Figure 13.1 is confused by the proximity of many unrelated events, and several secondary events are given an unnecessarily strong typographic treatment (e.g. the digits for the account inquiries number). The revised bill in Figure 13.2 has a more systematic structure; its use of typographic voices greatly assists the plot, limiting doubts about the amount owing, the payment date, and available payment methods.

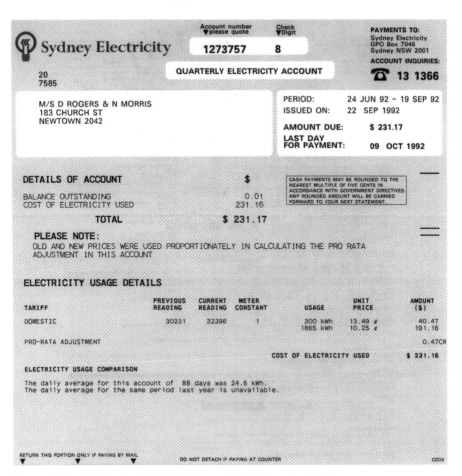

**Figure 13.1**   Original electricity bill used by Sydney Electricity.

### 13.3   HIERARCHICAL STRUCTURE AND ACCESS

Just as time and space help to contextualize and develop meanings, so we can use the hierarchical structure of a bill to help readers contextualize and develop meanings within given moments (Penman, 1993).

The prevailing convention of a hierarchical structure for a document is deductive, going from the general to the specific (though occasionally it is appropriate to use an inductive structure, going from the specific to the general). With a deductive structure, the upper levels in the hierarchy should be at a higher level of abstraction than those below, with each subsequent level subordinate to and encompassed by the preceding. When this is the case, the higher levels provide the contextual frame for the subordinate information and thus contribute to understanding. However, if this pattern is broken, the downward movement is disrupted and confusion may occur.

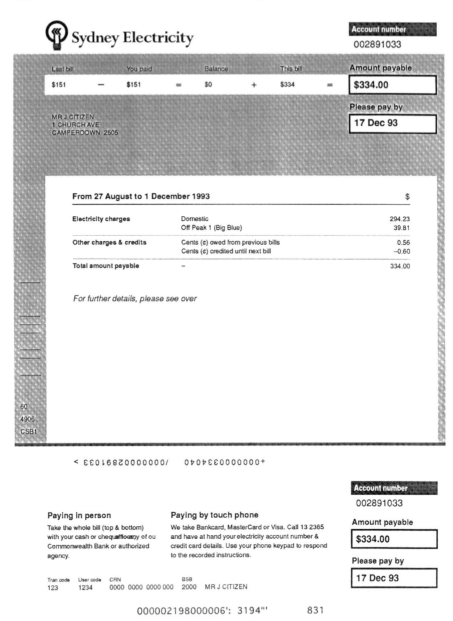

**Figure 13.2**   Revised version of the Sydney Electricity bill.

In personal conversations, we use a number of devices to negotiate constantly our position within an incomplete and fluid hierarchical structure. But with conversations-in-print, the hierarchical structure is not as fluid. As information designers, we are in charge of constructing hierarchy, and to do so successfully we must be attentive to readers' expectations. Explicit devices need to be employed to inform readers of shifts in hierarchy. Progression through a hierarchy can be presented typographically, with the most abstract encompassing layer being given the strongest visual priority. However, if the logic of the hierarchy is inadequate, typographic cues cannot be applied successfully.

Further, there is not always a well-defined beginning or ending to conversations. Participants in conversations, depending on their context and purpose, may enter at specific points, temporarily withdraw after they have acquired what they originally sought, then participate again at a later stage.

Likewise, when we read texts, we do not always read from the beginning to the end, especially if the text is anything other than a novel. Instead, we regularly read in a fractured manner, asking specific questions of the text depending on our specific purpose. As a consequence, we tend to use different access and search strategies according to our needs.

Whereas accessing and searching are minor issues for most single-sided bills, they are increasingly critical for lengthy itemized accounts that can carry over onto multiple pages. In such cases, it is important that there are adequate mechanisms to allow us to 'dip in and out' of the text – to ask specific questions and readily obtain the answers – much as we do in our many conversational enquiries.

The front and reverse sides of the bill (without the bottom payment slip) in Figures 13.3a and 13.3b illustrate the issues of hierarchical structure and access. Some problems arise here that do not generally arise with utility bills. With insurance, customers need to understand their legal rights and obligations. Insurance is based on the principle of utmost good faith; if customers fail in this regard they may not be covered when they make a claim. However, customers often treat insurance bills as utility bills, going straight to the amount they must pay and attending to little else.

With the design in Figures 13.3a and 13.3b we have 'negotiated' between what the customer wants to know and what the company believes they need to know. The structure of the document is similar to Figure 13.2 in that the page is divided into a top portion and a bottom payment slip. However, with the renewal notice, we have further divided the page vertically, providing a column for legal and other messages, plus a framed 'certificate' that details information specific to the customer. The design follows several conventions, including a deductive progression, reading gravity (a convention of ordering page content from top left to bottom right), and page order, from the top left-hand text on the front page informing customers of their legal duty, to specific information on the reverse page.

The accessibility of items is enhanced by statements and questions set slightly to the left of the main text in the 'certificate' section. These statements and questions also form a guiding narrative. In these ways, this design – which was developed within a dialogue created by our testing procedures – continues and enhances the conversation between customers and the insurance company.

## 13.4 MATTERS OF STYLE AND SUBSTANCE

Meaning is generated not only from the substance of an expression but also from its manner of delivery. Style and substance – or form and content – are inseparable aspects of the process by which meaning is formed.

ACN 004 208 084

# RACV INSURANCE Pty Ltd
## Motor Vehicle Insurance Renewal Certificate

Your current insurance policy ends on the **30 November 1992** at 4pm. To make sure your policy continues please pay for your renewal before that date. You have a legal duty to make sure that all the details on this certificate are correct. Please make any changes in the box below. If you want to talk about your insurance with us please ring the Car Owner's Hotline:

Melbourne  790 2000
Country  008 33 5566

There is important information on the back of this certificate—please turn over

Mr J.P. and Mrs L.M. Citizen-Smith

| Policy Number | Membership Number | Vehicle Reg. Number |
|---|---|---|
| 1234567 | 615398 | AWY 753 |

*You are insured for*

Comprehensive vehicle cover with Aussie Assist

*Excess you must pay with this policy*

- If you or someone else aged 25 or over is the driver, there is no excess
- If the driver is aged 22–24, the excess is $300
- If the driver is under 22, the excess is $600

*Rating 1—Maximum No Claim Bonus*

Because of your continued claim-free insurance record, you no longer need to pay to protect your Rating 1 this year—you are protected free. You can have one at-fault accident this year and still keep Rating 1.

*Amount to pay for 12 months cover to 30 November 1993*

| | |
|---|---|
| Basic premium | $375 |
| Removal of basic excess | $50 |
| **Total with Rating 1 protection free** | **$425** |

*Amount to pay for 6 months cover only to 30 May 1993*

| | |
|---|---|
| **Total with Rating 1 protection free** | **$228** |

---

RACV Motor Vehicle Insurance
Renewal Payment Slip

| Policy Number | Membership Number |
|---|---|
| 1234567 | 615398 |

Mr J.P. and Mrs L.M.Citizen-Smith
Wildwood
Morgans Mill Road
Lower Heidelberg 3333

*Please pay by*   |  30 November 1992

*You are paying for*
12 months insurance  ☐
6 months insurance  ☐
Removal of basic excess  ☐

*Please write any changes here*

*Total amount you are paying*  | $ |

*Please turn over for how to pay*

(a)

It is important that we have the correct details. If anything is wrong
you may not be covered properly or you may be paying the wrong amount.
Please write any changes in the box on the front page or ring us before you pay.

| | |
|---|---|
| Here is what we have on our current records. Is it right? | • Your vehicle is insured for Personal use<br>• You still have a loan on your car with Second Hand Harry |
| Have any of these things happened in the past year? If yes, please tell us immediately | • Have you changed your address?<br>• Has your vehicle been modified?<br>• Have you, or any regular driver of your vehicle,<br>    had physical or mental problems that affect driving?<br>    had an accident or driving offence? |
| The policy conditions have changed | You can now claim one broken windscreen a year without having to pay excess. |
| The amount you are asked to pay for insurance may change | • If you lodge a claim for damage or loss occurring before 30 November 1992, we may increase the amount you have to pay to renew this policy and the amount of the excess shown on this certificate<br>• If you only pay for 6 months insurance, the amount for the next 6 months may be different. |
| If you are late paying | • After 30 November 1992, you are not covered until we receive the amount owing. Your cover starts on the day we receive your payment.<br>• And if you do not pay by 30 January 1993, you will have to complete a new proposal form and have your vehicle inspected by us. |

*Any RACV branch, road service depot or agency which effects a contract of insurance does so as an agent of RACV Insurance Pty Ltd and not as your agent.*

## How to pay

| | |
|---|---|
| *By mail* | Send this tear-off payment slip with<br>• your cheque made payable to RACV Insurance,<br>• or your credit card details, to:<br>**550 Princes Highway, Noble Park VIC 3174** |
| *By phone* | Ring 03 790 2000 with your credit card details |
| *In person* | Take the whole certificate and your cash, cheque or credit card to your nearest RACV branch office |

| Bankcard | MasterCard | Visa | Expiry date |
|---|---|---|---|
| ☐ | ☐ | ☐ | / |

Credit card number

Signature | Amount paid
$

(b)

**Figure 13.3** Revised RACV Insurance renewal notice: (a) front page; (b) back page.

**Corporate Card**
**Statement of Account**

It's *The* Business Card.

**Enquiries**

J. P. CITIZEN
A BIG COMPANY PTY LTD
Corporate ID 123456
Period 2/3 to 3/4
Issued 6 April 1992

Sydney 886 2444
(ah) 886 0688
Elsewhere 008 221 659
(ah) 008 222000
GPO Box 4477 Sydney 2001

**Membership no.**

3760 123456 78901

| Previous balance | Payments & credits | Subtotal | New charges | Total due |
|---|---|---|---|---|
| $1431.57 | − $1481.57 | = $50.00cr | + $1132.68 | = $1082.68 |

*Please pay total immediately*

**PAYMENTS & CREDITS**                                                                      $

12/3   PAYMENT BY J. P. CITIZEN − 3760 123456 78901                          1,331.57  cr

14/3   ITEM CREDITED TO J. P. CITIZEN − 3760 123456 78901                    150.00  cr
       DAVID JONES, CHATSWOOD NSW
       BILL NO.: 62165887
       SMALL APPLIANCE

       SUBTOTAL                                                              1,481.57  cr

**J.P. CITIZEN** − 3760 123456 78901

5/3    CARDPHONE BROADWAY QLD                                                5.20
       LOCATION: P.O. SURFERS PARADISE QLD
       DATE/TIME: 10/01/92 16.43
       NO. CALLED: 02 517 462
       CARDPHONE NO.: 94597001

*...continued overleaf*

---

**Please do
not fold
or staple**

6 April 1992

**Paying by cheque** (other methods overleaf)

1. Make it out to *American Express International*
2. Write your Memebrship number &
   name on the back of the cheque
3. Put the cheque & this slip in
   the return envelope.

MR J. P. CITIZEN
A BIG COMPANY PTY LTD
1/2 LEAFY STREET
SUNNYDALE VIC 3004

Membership no.

3760 123456 78901

**Total due**

$1082. 68

*Please pay total immediately*

AMERICAN EXPRESS INT. INC.
GPO BOX 4477
SYDNEY NSW
AUSTRALIA 2001

**Figure 13.4**   Prototype charge card statement.

As a rule, when we engage in conversations we speak in a manner that befits the setting. But when we develop bills or other public documents, we do not have the same immediacy to regulate the appropriate presentation. We must rely on experience and evaluation processes to approximate the interaction of conversation.

What is appropriate in one billing context is not appropriate in another. Different styles can be seen in each illustration in this paper. In Figure 13.2 the style is predominantly utilitarian, suiting the context of electricity supply – embellishments might imply that the organization was extravagant and wasteful. With the design shown in Figures 13.3a and 13.3b we aimed to develop a style to reinforce the legal significance of the document and to set the organization apart as a quality company. We sought a similar quality 'feel' in Figure 13.4, but in this case the legal requirements were significantly fewer, and many of the design cues, such as colour and the fugitive background, were picked up from existing company materials. With all these designs, the appropriateness of the styles was confirmed by successive rounds of customer testing.

### 13.5 MANAGING MEANINGS

When we engage in conversations, we continually use all manner of devices to check and negotiate meanings constantly. These devices are so well embedded in our manner of talk, they occur seemingly automatically.

This continual monitoring and renegotiation of meaning is not so automatic with written texts. Indeed, putting language in a written, tangible form often makes us believe the words are permanent and the meanings non-negotiable. Unfortunately, neither is the case, for readers can interpret texts in different ways. In document design, we can manage meaning by using the diagnostic iterative testing procedures discussed by Sless (Chapter 11) and MacKenzie-Taylor (Chapter 14). In this way, readers can more usefully engage in a 'conversation' with the organization. Such conversations can be continued by systematically monitoring and reviewing the effectiveness of designs after they have been implemented. Since most billing contexts are unstable, ongoing changes to their design are usually required to maintain efficiency.

The value of testing cannot be stressed enough. It is only by engaging readers in the design process – by extending conversational principles to what we do – that genuinely effective bills and other public graphics can be developed and maintained.

### 13.6 CONCLUSION

By re-expressing many familiar design principles using a conversational model, I have demonstrated how we can build on the ground-breaking work of Frohlich and others. The conversational approach to information design offers many benefits, not only to the actual design of bills and other public documents or graphics, but also to the way we manage the design process and monitor the continuing effectiveness of our designs after they have been implemented.

## ACKNOWLEDGEMENTS

I wish to thank all of my colleagues who contributed to this chapter, especially Robyn Penman and David Sless. This chapter was made possible by the many organizations who have supported the Institute's research into billing systems.

## REFERENCES

FROHLICH, D. (1986) On the organisation of form-filling behaviour. *Information Design Journal* **5**, 43–59.

GERGEN, K. (1982) *Toward Transformation in Social Knowledge*. New York: Springer.

HOLLAND, V. M. and REDDISH, J. C. (1981) Strategies for understanding forms and other public documents. *Document Design Project, Technical Report No. 13*. American Institutes for Research.

KELLER-COHEN, D., MEADER, B. I. and MANN, D. W. (1990) Redesigning a telephone bill. *Information Design Journal* **6**, 45–66.

ONG, W. (1982) *Orality and Literacy: Technologising of the Word*. London: Methuen.

PENMAN, R. (1992) Good theory and good practice: an argument in progress. *Communication Theory* **2**, 234–250.

PENMAN, R. (1993) 'Conversation is the common theme: understanding talk and text', paper presented to the International Communication Association Conference, Washington DC, May 1993.

SLESS, D. (1992) Designing the Telecom bill. In: PENMAN, R. and SLESS, D. (Eds), *Designing Information for People*, pp. 77–97. Canberra: Communication Research Press.

PART FIVE

# Tables and Graphs

# CHAPTER FOURTEEN

# Developing design through dialogue: transport tables and graphs

MAUREEN MACKENZIE-TAYLOR

## 14.1 THE CONVERSATIONAL APPROACH

Researchers in document development and design are increasingly rejecting conventional wisdom about the nature of meaning and the role of documents. Penman (1992, 1994) has argued that the value which our western civilization places on the written document is both problematic and constraining. In our contemporary western society written texts are taken to be the hallmark of what distinguishes us from preliterate, and by implication, less advanced societies. With this emphasis has come an unwarranted elevation, and often reification, of written text. Written documents have taken on a life of their own. This is exemplified in such common expressions as 'the book says . . .'.

Text has become animate: it is seen to do things to people as if they are an active agent. As a consequence we have developed a very peculiar conception of the role of the human reader: the text–reader relation is seen as a one-way process in which the text, or table, or graph, transmits its meaning to the reader. It is the text that contains the meaning, the text tells us what to do and we, the readers, have little or no say in it. The ideas or meanings are in the words written. It follows from this view that all the designers have to do to make the meaning 'clear' is just fix up the words of a graphic display.

This assumption is simple and seemingly obvious but it is also constraining and problematic. Reddy (1979) has documented the pervasiveness of this simplistic 'conduit' view of communication – where meaning is sent from text to reader – and both he and Ong (1982) have described the inappropriateness of it. A printed document does exist as a tangible independent object, but the 'message' is not contained there simply to be taken out by the reader. Meaning only becomes a reality when a person *engages* with the printed words – meaning is brought into being by the interaction between the reader and the document. As Sless (1986; see also Chapter 11) argues, the basic unit of analysis in this framework is the relationship between the document and the reader; not the document alone. Communication is a complex, uncertain process, and one should think about documents as if they are part of a conversation. During their development and design, documents are treated as the tangible part of a conversation between an organization and its members, customers, or citizens. And just as there are 'good' and 'bad' conversations, there are also good and bad documents.

For most of us, a bad conversation is one in which, amongst other things, one of the participants:

- keeps on talking, *ad nauseam*;
- talks about things only of interest to him or her and not the other participants;
- takes no account of the other participant.

This suggests that a good conversation is one in which both participants are equally involved in the interaction, take account of each other, and have some overlapping frameworks of interest. In document research and development work, the aim is to design documents that reflect those features that are known to be characteristic of good conversations. Three important features (see also Rogers, Chapter 13) that are particularly relevant to good document design are:

- to design for the needs of the users, in terms of how they will use the documents in their own context;
- to design for action, so that the document's presentation facilitates the users' understanding and helps them to act;
- testing of prototypes of the documents to establish efficiency and effectiveness in use.

In everyday conversations there are always opportunities to ask questions and request clarification as the conversation proceeds. With documents this process is equally important. One should ensure that the conversational principles built into documents are appropriate for users by testing prototype documents in a situation that approximates the actual context of use. This kind of research methodology helps designers better understand users' needs and helps point out problems users might experience when using the document in the actual context, and the conditions that give rise to the problems. Testing user performance in this way also provides information about whether a particular design solution is likely to work effectively in the given context, i.e., whether it will meet the specifications.

To illustrate this approach, i.e., thinking about documents as if they are part of a conversation, and integrating the testing of documents in the document development process, a document design project in which this approach was used will be discussed in the remainder of this chapter.

## 14.2   UNDERSTANDING USERS AND EXPLORING DESIGN POSSIBILITIES

The State Department of Transport in Queensland, Australia, wanted a timetable format that would be easy for people to use and that could be applied across all public transport systems, i.e., one format that could be used by people using the various bus and train transport services. This project offered a challenge to the conversational approach. Could the approach developed for textual documents be as appropriate for visual graphic displays? Theoretically the answer was yes. Whether it is the written word or a graphic display, the meaning generation process is the same: the reader must still interact with the graphic display to generate meaning in the actual context of use.

The first phase in this project was to investigate systematically the users' needs and the context of use. Parallel to this investigation the design possibilities were explored. Only if the users' needs are fully understood and design possibilities are critically examined, is it possible to match needs and contexts of use with the most appropriate design features.

The various topics of investigation in this first step in the project were:

- an exploration of transport providers and users – to identify different kinds of users and understand their needs;
- discussions with transport providers and users on how, when, and why time-tables are obtained and used;
- discussions with users about structural analyses of existing timetables – to determine what information needs to be provided for adequate use of the system and what can be left out;
- what current aspects of data presentation are most helpful to users, and what aspects of current timetable formats are creating problems in data access;
- historical investigations – to explore the way other information designers have dealt with the problems of presenting timetable data, with emphasis on uncovering any effective principles of presentation revealed in the historical precedents;
- literature search – to build on the proven effectiveness (or ineffectiveness) of current timetable presentation options;
- technological investigations – to identify the current systems of data storage and production to ensure appropriateness of the proposed solution.

In the next sections, these different topics of investigation will be discussed in more detail.

### 14.2.1   Context of use and structural analysis of existing timetables

The approach to investigate user needs and contexts of use approximates the approach of a cultural anthropologist entering a new culture. We are foreigners trying to understand what the 'locals' do, how they understand things, and in what context they need to understand things. But unlike the anthropologist the interest is in the minutiae of everyday interactions with documents.

In the first phase of the project, bus-stops and train stations were observed, as well as how, when and under what conditions people referred to timetables. People were interviewed as they were using timetables, and questions they wanted to be answered by the timetable were recorded. The staff who supply timetable information were asked how, when and by whom this information was requested. Researchers travelled on the bus and train systems in Brisbane (the state capital of Queensland) and noted the information available (or unavailable, as often appeared to be the case). Also a range of timetables was collected from the various transport operators in Brisbane.

The initial exploration of the context of use and a structural analysis of current timetables in the Brisbane area revealed a number of problems within the wider context of the state transport system and also with the details of current timetable design. A timetable, no matter how well designed and tested, is only part of the answer to a 'legible' transport system (Bartram, 1984). For people to make full use of a timetable they need to be able to relate the information on it to other route-planning and in-transit information (Bartram, 1984). The visual information on the timetable must be consistent with and continually reinforce the data provided at each other point in the system such as at depots, stations, bus-stops, and on and inside buses and trains. The explorations in Brisbane showed that there was no coherent overall transport information system. Various timetable 'genres' were used by different transport operators; there were inconsistencies of information both within and across operators and transport types.

The 'legibility' of the total system was outside the scope of this project. But the fact that it is not a coherent system remains part of the context of use that had to be considered. Within this context of use one flexible timetable format had to be developed which would accommodate the complexities and service differences between all routes and carriers. If all carriers were to adopt the same timetable format, with consistent graphic devices, icons and colour coding, travellers would not need to learn to read many different timetable formats to complete one journey. It would be easier for users if they would only have to get familiar with one time-table format that would be applied across the entire state transport system.

From the user's point of view, a timetable is normally read with an action-orientated purpose – to organize travel from point A to point B at a particular time. It is read with the user's own familiar practice in mind. Penman (1993) has argued that users understand documents better if the document is structured in ways that match the users' familiar practice – if users are to make sure of timetable information, they must be able to apply it in real life by turning it into action. This means that the new designs would need familiar words and structures, and clear and legible typography. They would also need to be eminently portable – pocket-sized and functional in any situation, whether users are standing in an overcrowded train or at a windy bus-stop.

The current 'genre' for timetables presents data numerically, with the sequence of location stops as the vertical dimension, and the times of journeys across the horizontal axis. Yet research to assess people's ability to understand such timetables indicates that people have great difficulty understanding information presented in tabular form as a two-dimensional matrix (Wright and Fox, 1970; Bartram, 1984; Horne *et al.*, 1986), nor do they like using them (Bartram, 1984). As Bartram points out, the practice of running route stops down the vertical dimension is contrary both to our reading pattern, which is left to right, and to the fact that people visualize motion in terms of left to right. Yet throughout the world, timetable information continues to be presented in this form, even though everyday experience confirms the research findings that such timetables are notoriously difficult for the average passenger to understand (Bartram, 1980; Kinross, 1991).

The question was: what is the best way to arrange timetable data, which need to record both time and space, in such a way that it helps people understand how to act?

### 14.2.2   Historical precedents

Study of historical graphic designs and tables and charts revealed potential solutions that could be useful for the project. Many of these solutions became unfashionable and/or unfeasible because of technical limitations introduced as printing developed as a commercial technology. For instance, before the invention of moveable lead type and letterpress printing there was no necessity to separate text and image. Therefore there were graphic alternatives to representing complex two-dimensional data as a matrix of numbers. Figure 14.1 shows one of the oldest examples of spatial movement plotted across time. It is from an early manuscript, *circa* tenth century.

In the eighteenth century, William Playfair, a political economist, used the medium of copper engraving for his statistical graphs and linear charts (Figure 14.2). Playfair realized that numerical information could also be represented more graphically by using lines. His insights led him away from the alphanumeric presentation of data in tables to the exploration of graphic formats that allow the 'mind of the eye' to make sense of the data.

Playfair engraved a background grid of fine lines to indicate time, on top of which he plotted the economic data as heavier lines and blocks of colour, thus revealing the visual shape of the data, inviting comparison and improving memory retention of the facts. '. . . as much information may be obtained in five minutes as would require whole days to imprint on the memory . . . by a table of figures . . .' (Playfair, 1801, pp. xi–xii; cited in Biderman, 1990).

Other historical information designers also worked with this linear form to solve timetabling problems. Charles Ybry, a French engineer, increased the explanatory power of Playfair's time–series graphs by showing data moving over space as well as through time. He patented his graphic schedule for transport systems in 1846,

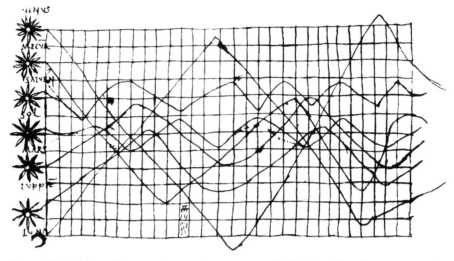

**Figure 14.1**   Monastic text, circa tenth century, probably the oldest known example of movements plotted across time (from Funkhouser, 1936).

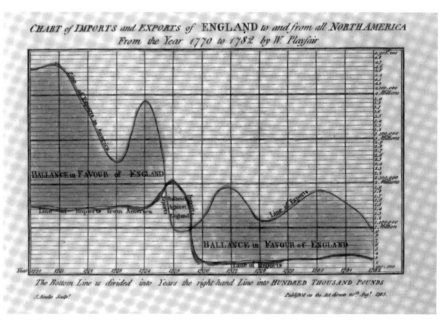

**Figure 14.2**   Playfair's chart of imports and exports (*Commercial and Political Atlas*, 1786).

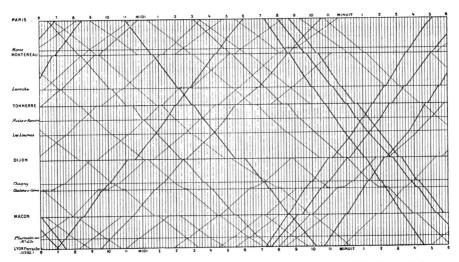

**Figure 14.3** Marey's schedule for train services, Paris to Lyons, 1888 (from Tufte, 1983, p. 115).

and his ideas were used by Marey in 1888 to schedule French railway services (Figure 14.3).

### 14.2.3 Technological considerations

Developments in printing technology during the nineteenth century meant that Ybry's hope for his visual schedule to be used by the general public was never realized. As copper engraving was replaced with letterpress, text could no longer be integrated readily with image, and non-alphanumeric depiction became 'an expensive off-line nuisance' (Biderman, 1980, p. 235). The use of graphs and grids became both economically inappropriate and unfashionable. The norms of visual language are mediated and limited by available technology. In the 1950s and 1960s the exponents of the Modern Movement and the New Typography stripped away every detail they thought was surplus to requirement – ornament, grid lines, even the serifs on letters. As recently as 1983, Tufte still argued that grid lines were 'chartjunk' – clutter that 'carries' no information. However, this view is now changing again, and some have come to realize that there are serious problems with the classification of grid lines as 'chartjunk'. It implies, as Kinross (1991) points out, a curious separation of the data from the data carrier, which falsely implies that presentation has no bearing on meaning.

In the 1990s the technology became available to reintroduce background grid lines without any accompanying technological limitations or commercial disadvantages. With photographic and digital computer generated graphics, and with multi-colour presses resident in even the smallest printer's premises, linear timetables can be produced cost-effectively with greater sophistication than either Playfair's or Marey's originals. Alphanumeric and linear means of representing data are resident in the same software systems. It is now possible to generate graphic rather than

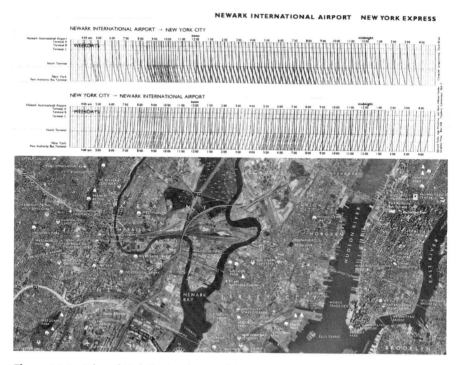

**Figure 14.4**   Edward Tufte's visual timetables for the New Jersey Transit
Department, 1990.

numeric artwork directly from the original database where timetable schedules are
prepared. Today's technology allows us to improve on the historical precedents by
creating a hierarchy of visual effects to match the ordering of content. If the background grid lines are muted, by printing in a soft grey, their visual treatment reflects
their subservience to the data, enabling faster and more accurate data readings than
was possible in Marey's day.

The first to have exploited the combination of Ybry's graphic schedule with
current technology in the design of a visual timetable is Edward Tufte. Moving
beyond his previous ideas of 'chartjunk', Tufte produced superbly crafted timetables for the New Jersey Transit Department (Figure 14.4), setting a precedent for
bringing quality into life's mundane details. Discussing his 'data-rich' timetables in
his recent book, *Envisioning Information*, Tufte comments:

> Hourly, daily, and weekly rhythms of the buses are clearly revealed, as well as details
> of each journey. During rush hours, lines densely crowd into spaghetti – but then
> service is so frequent that the jumble of lines informs the rider simply to show up, for
> there will be virtually no wait for whatever bus it is that arrives. The grey grid is set
> at ten-minute intervals in order to ease the visual interpolation of the times of arrival.
> The aerial photograph unveils the area mostly at the level of house resolution . . . so
> much richer than the typical schematic diagram of bus routes . . . Indeed, the reaction
> of those living in the area is to explore the photograph, personalizing the data, seeking
> to discover their own residence, school or workplace . . .        (Tufte, 1990, p. 108)

## 14.3   TOWARDS A FUNCTIONAL DESIGN RESOLUTION

Tufte's 'string timetables' are extremely elegant and sophisticated pieces of design, and are fine examples of the tradition of thought initiated by William Morris and the Arts and Craft Movement. Central in this tradition is that information design at its best should appeal to people's finer sensibilities as well as be functional (Sless, 1992; MacKenzie, 1993). Although Tufte's development of the tradition of the linear timetable is inspiring, it can be questioned whether Tufte's timetables really meet user needs.

Tufte's timetables still follow the established genre, with the times running along the horizontal axis and the route locations along the vertical axis. They do not take into account Bartram's (1984) significant finding that the practice of running route stops along the vertical dimension is contrary both to people's reading pattern and to the way people seem to visualize motion in terms of left to right. Bartram's research showed that his 'reflected timetable format' improved both scanning time and accuracy. In keeping with the understanding that documents can be best under- stood if they reflect people's familiar practice of transport use, it was considered important to develop and test a reflected or rotated linear timetable. So the first design decision was to adopt Bartram's (1984) rotated format, with the route travel- ling left to right horizontally and the times indicated vertically.

The initial exploration into user needs had also highlighted the importance of providing route information. Tufte's (1990) linear timetables present only departure and arrival times with some midway timing points. Detailed route information is provided on the accompanying detailed aerial photograph overlaid with a colour- coded route map. Tufte's solution has been severely criticized, for reproducing up- to-date aerial maps of a whole transport region is not economically viable, and the folded maps present problems for passengers handling such cumbersome timetables (Kinross, 1991, p. 225). The idea for this project was to achieve a more economic solution which would also better help users act.

The second design decision was to introduce a simple graphic stick map along the horizontal axis which names *all* stops along a particular route in chronological sequence. This would keep valuable route information with the equally important timing information, within a pocket-sized format, and avoid the expense and im- practicality of Tufte's aerial maps. The stick map would also make it possible to introduce additional information, in the form of visual icons, providing the user with an overview of where other services within the overall transport system con- nect with the local service, and with local information such as the location of park- and-ride facilities (Figure 14.5).

Thirdly, with users' needs at the forefront, it was decided to introduce wording and structures that parallel everyday ways of doing things. The 12-hour clock was used and not the 24-hour clock, because users found the latter to be more difficult to use; the words 'morning', 'afternoon' and 'evening' were used instead of the Latin abbreviations, a.m. and p.m., which are frequently misunderstood. Confusing abbreviations for types of services were replaced with simple graphic icons, such as arrows for express trains. Though Dewar's research (Chapter 23) shows that icons

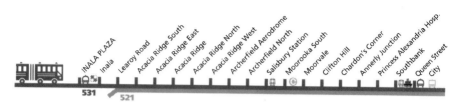

**Figure 14.5**  A detail of the prototypes, showing the horizontal stick route map with additional route information.

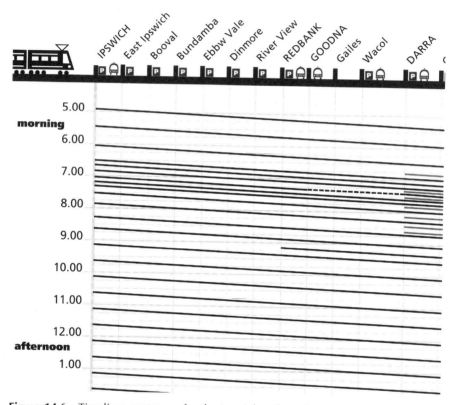

**Figure 14.6**   Timelines prototype for the Ipswich rail service.

may pose problems of their own, testing of prototypes showed broad acceptance of these particular icons. Furthermore, any content users did not need was removed from the timetables.

At this point in the design resolution a further choice had to be made: to present the timetable information numerically (as a table) or visually (as a graph). The historical precedents of Playfair, Ybry, Marey and Tufte argued for presenting the timing data with a visual line, rather than a series of numbers. Yet conventional precedents of timetables in use argued for numerical, tabular, presentation. It was decided to develop two prototypes – the Timelines (Figure 14.6) and the Enhanced numeric (Figure 14.7) – and subject both to user testing.

| | IPSWICH | East Ipswich | Booval | Bundamba | Ebbw Vale | Dinmore | River View | REDBANK | GOODNA | Gailes | Wacol | DARRA | Oxley |
|---|---|---|---|---|---|---|---|---|---|---|---|---|---|
| **morning** | 458 | 502 | 504 | 506 | 508 | 510 | 512 | 516 | 518 | 520 | 524 | 527 | 529 |
| | 529 | 531 | 533 | 535 | 537 | 539 | 541 | 543 | 547 | 549 | 551 | 555 | 558 |
| | 603 | 605 | 607 | 609 | 611 | 613 | 615 | 617 | 621 | 623 | 625 | 629 | 632 |
| | | | | | | | | | | | | 647 | 650 |
| | 634 | 636 | 638 | 640 | 642 | 644 | 646 | 648 | 655 | 654 | 656 | 700 | 703 |
| | 642 | 644 | 646 | 648 | 650 | 652 | 654 | 656 | 700 | 702 | 704 | 708 | 711 |
| | 649 | 651 | 653 | 655 | 657 | 659 | 701 | 703 | 707 | 709 | 711 | 715 | 718 |
| | | | | | | | | | | | | 721 | 724 |
| | 702 | 704 | 706 | 708 | 710 | 712 | 714 | 716 | 720 | ➡ | ➡ | 727 | 730 |
| | | | | | | | | | | | | 732 | 735 |
| | 712 | 714 | 716 | 718 | 720 | 722 | 724 | 726 | 730 | 732 | 734 | 738 | 741 |
| | 717 | 719 | 721 | 723 | 725 | 727 | 729 | 731 | 735 | 737 | 739 | 743 | 746 |

**Figure 14.7**  Enhanced numeric prototype for a train service on the Ipswich line.

The Timelines prototype uses a graphic solution; similar to the configural graphic displays described by Hurts (Chapter 15), but of a greater complexity. The dataline was colour-coded for the service it represents, thus allowing travellers detailed access to an additional level of route information – the frequency and pattern of services along a particular route over a particular time period. Some preliminary research with users indicated that the majority of people think in time units of quarter and half hours rather than in 10-minute units as proposed by Tufte. In keeping with the premise to work within normal behaviour patterns, the muted greyed background timing grid was printed in quarter hourly divisions, with thicker lines to denote each hour.

With the Enhanced numeric timetable, the colon generally used between the hours and minutes figures was removed; the space thus gained was then used to increase the size of the hour figure in relation to the minute figure, to improve legibility. Also more white space was introduced between the horizontal lines of figures so that people could track efficiently, following standards developed for the presentation of statistical tabular information (MacKenzie, 1992).

The Timelines prototype has an advantage over the Enhanced numeric, because of the potential to show at a glance, in a way alphanumeric tables never can, the overall picture of the number of buses/trains that pass a particular stop throughout the day. Instead of an endless repetition of numbers, as in a numeric timetable, the

Timelines design shows a clear contrast between the frequency of regular daytime or evening services and rush-hour peaks. The patterns of the service and any irregularities become evident, while service frequency can be seen as a clear and memorable 15-minute, half-hourly or hourly interval. However true this line of reasoning might be, the most significant part of design development – user testing – needed to validate or disprove these assumptions.

## 14.4   USER TESTING

### 14.4.1   The principles

User testing should be a critical and integral part of an iterative design process. The users are included as participants in the design process to predict the likely performance of documents in use.

Prototype documents are subjected to diagnostic user testing in face-to-face interviews. Users are asked to use the prototype document in a situation that approximates the actual context of use. Users are asked to undertake tasks they normally would perform when using the document. Records are made of their actions in performing these tasks, their speed and accuracy in performing the tasks, and their comments about the document. Observing the interaction between user and prototype allows one to see patterns of behaviour and thus understand *why* a particular form of presentation is problematic or not. Problems users have with the document are discussed with them, of course emphasizing that it is the document at fault, not them. The procedure highlights misunderstandings and inappropriate user behaviour. The observations and data collected are used to formulate alternative design solutions.

This approach to testing falls broadly within the category of formative or process research discussed by Adams (Chapter 1), and by Nijhuis and Boersema, who describe in detail the use of this iterative approach to design of testing, modification, testing again (Chapter 2). It is essential that the testing method should be strongly task-orientated: people should be asked to do things with the document – not to just demonstrate comprehension. Furthermore, the testing should be diagnostically oriented: the tasks should be used to analyse problems with the documents; this is what Adams calls 'process testing' as opposed to 'outcome testing'.

The power of the iterative testing method comes from its use in a repeated process of testing and modification. Based on the test results the document is modified to minimize user misunderstanding and confusion. A problem with a document is considered to have been eliminated when the behavioural symptoms associated with that problem disappear in subsequent tests. Repeated experience has shown that conclusions from such testing are robust in practice. With diagnostic testing it is not necessary to use large numbers of respondents (Virzi, 1992; see also Adams, Chapter 1). The intent is to identify major problems and minimize or resolve them.

### 14.4.2   Testing the prototype timetables

In the case of the timetables for the State Department of Transport in Queensland the commission was for a single round of testing only. This is a common practical constraint. Nevertheless, one extensive round of testing can give many insights for design development and can give an indication as to how far the designs are from a useful solution.

The testing was expected to confirm the problems in existing timetables (which had been diagnosed in the first phase of the project) and to indicate where these conditions had been successfully dealt with in the Enhanced numeric and Timelines prototypes. The testing was also expected to indicate how the prototypes would have to be changed to improve user performance further, and to highlight any unacceptable side-effects of the proposed solutions.

Usability data were collected from 52 respondents over a period of two days at two inner-city locations. The participants were from many ethnic backgrounds: Australian, European, Asian, Aboriginal and Pacific Islanders. The majority were regular users of public transport (65 per cent), and the rest were casual users. Of the respondents, 67 per cent were adults, 12 per cent were youths, and 21 per cent were senior citizens. Use of English was problematic for 13 per cent, and 11 per cent of respondents were tourists with no local knowledge.

Three different means of presenting timetable data were compared:

- Standard – the existing alphanumeric Queensland Rail timetable for the Ipswich line. It provided a baseline for comparative assessment.
- Enhanced numeric – the alphanumeric prototype timetable for the Ipswich Rail line (Figure 14.7). It was included to assess the effects on performance of the many graphic changes which were applied in both prototypes; however, compared to the Timelines prototype, arrival and departure information were presented in a more traditional, i.e., numeric fashion.
- Timelines – the linear graphic timetable prototype for the Ipswich Rail line (Figure 14.6). It has the same rotated format as the Enhanced numeric, and the same graphic devices to clarify route and interchange information. The numeric timing points, however, are replaced with linear representation.

First each respondent saw the three alternative timetables briefly, and was then handed one particular version and given some familiarization time. Next, respondents were asked to perform a number of tasks (without help or instruction from the interviewers).

The tasks used were based on the initial research establishing the different ways people use timetables. The tasks were designed to test respondents' ability to identify key elements on the timetable, and to allow observation of the ease or difficulty with which respondents could locate correct times, distinguish between the different scheduling periods and recognize frequency patterns (MacKenzie et al., 1993).

Two performance measures were used: accuracy of interpretation (correct or incorrect answer) and ease of access (timed in number of seconds until the correct answer was given). In addition, respondents' comments and suggestions were documented.

Based on earlier experience with the interpretation of diagnostic quantitative data, a 30 per cent failure rate was defined as an unacceptable level of performance. That is to say, if 30 per cent or more of the sample failed to respond correctly to a particular task, the results indicate that the timetable has a major problem in need of repair.

## 14.5    WHAT THE TESTING SHOWED: NUMERIC OR GRAPHIC

The full results of the test are published in MacKenzie and Howell (1993). A summary of the results will be presented here.

The Standard timetable posed considerable problems to users in accessing and acting on information. On average, respondents could not complete eight of the 11 performance-based tasks with this timetable. This confirms the previous research of Bartram with this type of time-table (1984).

The Enhanced numeric and Timelines performed significantly better than the Standard. Although respondents were unfamiliar with the Timelines, they quickly overcame their initial response of alienation, and performed most of the table look-up tasks more quickly and efficiently than those respondents using the Enhanced numeric timetables.

The test performance of the respondents suggests that a number of components of presentation contributed to the significant improvements in the performance of our prototypes over the standard genre: use of the 12-hour clock, use of the rotated format, use of common language terms, the increased legibility of figures on the Enhanced numeric and the use of simple graphic icons instead of abbreviated words (MacKenzie and Howell, 1993).

We found that the Timelines approach had its potential value, as well as its very real limitations. In the next section both aspects – benefits and limitations – of the Timelines approach will be discussed.

### 14.5.1    Potential value – the issue of patterns

Analysis of the test results showed that the Timelines approach can be read in a different way to numeric timetables, allowing users to generate new understandings of the services provided. Two of the tasks were designed to test whether people could use the arrival and departure time information to identify a pattern of the regularity and frequency of train services throughout the day. It became apparent during testing that most respondents had not thought about extracting this kind of information from timetables before: 'A regular pattern? I had no idea the trains were like this . . .'.

Respondents using the Standard and Enhanced numeric both failed to see clearly when regularity patterns changed. By contrast, respondents using the Timelines prototype reacted positively when they discovered the possibility to read easily the changing frequency of service throughout the day. Commuters commented on the value of this level of understanding; for example, it made it easier to plan a journey to coincide with a range of peak hour services and it was also easier to note a possible range of times for working late before they would need to bring the car.

People using the Timelines format became actively involved in constructing new meanings and considering new actions in ways they could not do with the numeric timetables.

### 14.5.2  Limitations – the issue of precision

Although the visual presentation of the Timelines triumphed over the alphanumeric presentation when the task was to recognize the pattern of services, the testing diagnosed a serious side-effect in the Timelines design – a lack of precision. Using the Timelines 72 per cent of the respondents could not specify the departure times with a greater accuracy than five minutes, indicating that, for the majority of respondents, the Timelines design has a precision range of five minutes. This lack of minute-by-minute precision proved to be inadequate for 56 per cent of users:

> 'I don't like it at all. It's not accurate enough . . . I'd have to check on the phone . . .'
> 'I wouldn't want to miss my train by 2 mm!'

Others (44 per cent), were unconcerned about the lack of precision:

> 'This is a significant improvement. Speaking as an old man it would be a tremendous help to old people. You can see things at a glance – you're not disadvantaged by failing eyesight, and I always get there a bit early anyway . . .'
> 'It's less jumbled. I don't need all the times on it because that just gets confusing with all the different columns of times of trains . . .'

These findings highlight a critical point about the design of tables and graphs: no one style or solution is appropriate for all users, or all tasks that are likely to be carried out. User testing of the Timelines highlights how documents are open to the generation of different meanings. Documents do not have concrete, immediate messages. The meaning of a document arises as people use it. Different people created different interpretations depending on the actions they wanted to perform. Users who wanted accurate times (56 per cent of the sample) found the Timelines lacked precision. But nearly 50 per cent of the respondents found that the graphic voice Timelines spoke more directly to them.

### 14.6  MANAGING MEANINGS

Timetables are read for very specific purposes by specific readers with specific needs. When reading a timetable people rarely need to go from beginning to end. Instead, they enter at a specific point and leave when they have found the information they need. The Standard timetable provides very little in the way of access features. It is a voice which is not easily understood by the majority of users; it also uses a bad conversational style.

The Enhanced numeric and Timelines prototypes introduced a more graphic voice which focused travellers' attention, to allow users to enter the timetable at a place relevant to them. For example, in both prototypes the route and direction of travel were emphasized, with the train/bus icon on the left, and the arrangement of the stops running from left to right. The route travels with reading gravity, left to right. It is a better match with people's expected reading pattern than the current genre of timetables which has the stops running vertically, and thus better supports the traveller to identify the particular departure and arrival points.

This investigation highlights that there is no one strategy for searching or accessing that suits all users and tasks. One conclusion is that information needs to be presented in different ways to different people, because different people have different needs.

The research has been encouraging, showing that the introduction of the graphic voice in timetable design development does address particular access problems of the standard genre of timetables. By introducing wording and structures (the rotated format) which are closer to people's normal everyday way of doing things, performance across the range of tasks tested improved. The two timetable prototypes, with their more visually oriented presentation, provide people with a broader understanding of individual routes and open up an understanding of the overarching system of route and service connections.

Unfortunately, it was outside the scope of the commission to take up the challenge to explore how to integrate both prototypes, combining the advantages of the numeric and visual information presentation and balancing the limitations; not for design reasons, but for another factor critical to the design of any dialogue. In every research and design project there are many voices that need to be considered. In this project, because of the nature of the contract with the State Transport Department, it was not possible to listen directly to the voices of the urban and local transport providers, or to take sufficient account of their interests. As they were left out of the dialogue, they understandably did not feel any ownership towards the new timetables, and rejected the Department's proposal for integration.

David Sless (Chapter 11) has discussed at length the challenge information designers face in dealing with the organizational and broader political contexts. He also stresses that information design needs to encompass more than a process for design development. Work in information design is entangled in an organizational and political web. If designers are to implement the designs they develop, their very real challenge is to position themselves so they can manage the weaving of that web.

## REFERENCES

BARTRAM, D. (1980) Comprehending spatial information: the relative efficiency of different methods of presenting information about bus routes. *Journal of Applied Psychology* **65**, 103–110.

BARTRAM, D. (1984) The presentation of information about bus services. In: EASTERBY, R. and ZWAGA, H. (Eds), *Information Design*, pp. 299–319. Chichester: Wiley.

BIDERMAN, A. D. (1980) The graph as a victim of adverse discrimination and segregation. *Information Design Journal* **1**, 232–241.

BIDERMAN, A. D. (1990) The Playfair enigma: the development of the schematic representation of statistics. *Information Design Journal* **6**, 3–25.

FUNKHOUSER, H. G. (1936) A note on a tenth century graph. *Osiris* **1**, 260–262.

HORNE, M., ROBERTS, J. and ROSE, D. (1986) Getting there: an assessment of London Transport's endeavour to improve bus passenger information literature for central London, 1979–1985, Parts 1 and 2. *Information Design Journal* **5**, 3–27, 87–110.

KINROSS, R. (1991) Richness against flatness: Edward Tufte's 'Envisioning Information'. *Information Design Journal* **6**, 221–228.

MACKENZIE, M. A. (1992) New design standards for ABS Publications: a case study. *Australian Journal of Communication* **19**, 43–70.

MACKENZIE, M. A. (1993) Appearance and performance. *Communication News* **6**, 1–3.

MACKENZIE, M. A. and HOWELL, K. (1993) Timetables: a user view. *Papers of the Australasian Transport Research Forum, 1993*, Vol. 18, Part 2, 563–586.

MACKENZIE, M. A., ROGERS, D., SHULMAN, A. and HOWELL, K. (1993) 'Timetable concept testing', Report for Queensland Department of Transport. Canberra: Communication Research Institute of Australia.

ONG, W. (1982) *Orality and Literacy: Technologising of the World.* London: Methuen.

PENMAN, R. (1992) Plain English: wrong solution to an important problem. *Australian Journal of Communication* **19**, 1–18.

PENMAN, R. (1993) Conversation is the common theme: understanding talk and text. *Australian Journal of Communication* **20**, 30–43.

PENMAN, R. (1994) 'Beyond plain English', Paper presented at a one-day seminar. Canberra: Communication Research Institute of Australia.

REDDY, M. (1979) The conduit metaphor – a case of frame conflict in our language about language. In: ORTNEY, A. (Ed.), *Metaphor and Thought.* Cambridge: Cambridge University Press.

SLESS, D. (1986) *In Search of Semiotics.* London: Croom Helm.

SLESS, D. (1992) What is information design? In: PENMAN, R. and SLESS, D. (Eds), *Designing Information for People: Proceedings from the Symposium.* Canberra: Communication Research Press.

TUFTE, E. R. (1983) *The Visual Display of Quantitative Information.* Cheshire, CT: Graphic Press.

TUFTE, E. R. (1990) *Envisioning Information.* Cheshire, CT: Graphic Press.

WRIGHT, P. and FOX, K. (1970) Presenting information in tables. *Applied Ergonomics*, **1**, 239–242.

# CHAPTER FIFTEEN

# Configurality in statistical graphs

KAREL HURTS

## 15.1  INTRODUCTION

Perhaps the most salient feature of statistical graphs is their ability to show 'patterns' (or 'figures') in the individual data values plotted. These patterns are easily detected by the human eye and are therefore often used for 'exploratory data analysis' (Tukey, 1977). Moreover, these patterns are easily remembered. Indeed, data patterns are more easily remembered than the individual elements they are composed of.

A second salient feature of statistical graphs is their providing a 'spatial analogue' of quantitative values. That is, quantities are expressed in spatial magnitudes. In fact, one of the first comprehensive theories of graph reading and comprehension, Cleveland's basic task model (Cleveland and McGill, 1984), consists of an ordering of types of analogical coding (which they called 'specifiers'), such as length, angle and area, in terms of their relative effectiveness for reading off and comparing numeric values.

Although patterns and the spatial analogue are distinct notions, the combination of the two in a single graph provides an additional advantage. Indeed, patterns are often used to make numerical estimates and these estimates are in turn based on the spatial analogue. For example, if the data values plotted in a bar graph reveal an increasing (or decreasing) trend, going from the first to the last value, the size of the increment (or decrement) can be estimated by inspecting the imaginary line connecting the values and assessing the size of its slope with respect to the x-axis (of course, this line may actually be drawn, as well). Comparing the slopes of two (or more) lines displayed in the same graph is even easier.

Despite the evidence for the importance of patterns in the use of graphs, still little is known about the precise conditions under which patterns are useful. In fact, not even the definition of 'pattern' is always clear and consistent. This chapter therefore attempts to provide a general framework for understanding the role patterns play in determining the effectiveness of statistical graphs; in particular, the framework addresses how these patterns relate to graph-related, data-related and task-related factors. Such a framework not only has theoretical value, but can also be of practical use, because it can help us predict the relative effectiveness of a new type of graph, given a description of the above mentioned factors. Examples of such practical use will be discussed in Section 15.4.

## 15.2  BACKGROUND

Data displays in which a (geometric) pattern arises from the individual data values are usually called 'configural'. Many studies have shown configural displays to be easier to use than non-configural displays (also called 'separable' displays, usually in the form of bar graphs) on so-called integrated tasks; these are tasks that require the consideration of several data values simultaneously (Carswell and Wickens, 1987; Wickens and Andre, 1990).

However, there are several problems with this traditional notion of configurality (for a review of these criticisms, see Bennett and Flach, 1992). Studies have shown, for example, that it is more important for configural displays to contain 'emergent features' than merely to consist of a closed, geometric figure. In other words, they must contain higher-level information which arises from the combination of lower-level data in some form and which is easily perceived (Pomerantz, 1986). An example would be the bar graph revealing a trend, which was mentioned in the previous section. Most graphs are configural in this sense, although they can differ in the amount and type of configurality they exhibit. Another problem is that not even emergent features may be beneficial for task performance if they do not map into important domain constraints that must be considered during task execution (Bennett et al., 1993).

To this list of problems two other problems may be added, revealed by my own research. The first is that under some circumstances configural displays have either no effects or even detrimental effects when the information in the display has to be recalled from memory – that is, if the display is blocked from view at the time questions about the display have to be answered, also called 'retrospective' processing (Hurts, 1995). Secondly, configural displays have mostly been studied in 'dynamic' task environments, that is, environments in which the display changes continuously, sometimes as a result of actions taken by the user. A typical example of such a display is the polar plot display used in process control systems: a polygon with, for example, eight spokes. The standard regular display represents normal process conditions. A distortion in the shape of the polygon indicates a disturbance in the process. In contrast, statistical graphs as used in newspapers and journals are 'static'. Examples of how retrospective processing and static graphs may influence performance and how they may interact with configurality will be given in the next two sections.

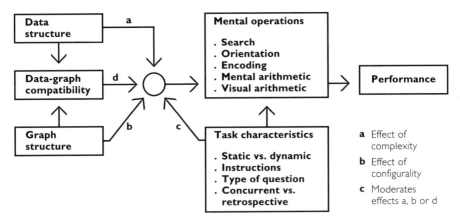

**Figure 15.1** Framework for relating graph-related factors, task-related factors and performance on tasks requiring graphical perception and comprehension.

## 15.3 CONFIGURALITY AND TASK-RELATED PROCESSING

In this section a framework will be proposed to relate configurality to other factors that can be assumed to influence graph effectiveness in various tasks using static graphs. The emphasis in this framework will be on data set structure, graph structure, tasks, and mental processing. Only static graphs will be considered in order not to complicate the discussion.

Figure 15.1 shows a schematic model of this framework. At the centre of this model are basic 'mental operations' required for graph reading and comprehension. These are: orientation, search (for specific variables or combinations of variables), encoding (of the numeric value of variables), mental arithmetic (making computations using the numbers found in the encoding step), and visual arithmetic (making computations only using the spatial analogue). Not all operations are required for every task. The last four of these operations are distinguished by Gillan and Lewis (1994). 'Orientation' is added as an operation separate from 'search', the distinction between the two being what the user does *before* he or she has read the question to be answered (orientation) and what he or she does *after* he or she has read the question or performed the task (search). Although not much is known yet about how these operations are affected by various tasks and various graph characteristics, it seems that most mental behaviour during graph reading and comprehension can be described in terms of (a subset of) these operations. Examples of graph-related and task-related factors and the role they play in tasks requiring graphical perception and comprehension will be given below.

As stated above, static tasks differ from dynamic tasks in a number of ways. In addition to the obvious differences, three more subtle differences should be mentioned. Firstly, the amount of preparation for the task to be performed is usually greater for dynamic tasks. Secondly, the complexity of the data structure underlying the display is likely to be of greater influence in static tasks. Finally, the degree of fit between data structure and graph structure (data–graph compatibility) is likely to have a greater effect in static tasks. The terms 'data structure complexity', 'graph structure' and 'data–graph compatibility' will be explained below.

'Data structure complexity' is loosely defined in terms of the number of dimensions necessary to describe a data set: the more dimensions, the more complex the structure (other plausible defining characteristics will, for the sake of simplicity, not be discussed here). 'Graph structure' is loosely defined in terms of the graph syntax (see also Warren, Chapter 16): the rules that should be followed in order to be able to read (and understand) the data values plotted. Finally, 'data–graph compatibility' refers to the fit (in a psychological sense) between the data structure and the graph structure: the greater the fit, the easier it is to use the graph.

Not much is known yet about the effects of data structure and data–graph compatibility and how these factors differentiate between static and dynamic tasks. However, in the next section examples will be given of their potential importance during the performance of static tasks.

The relationship between configurality, data structure complexity, and data–graph compatibility can be explained as follows. In order to display graphically data coming from a certain data structure (data set), a graph structure must be chosen. This graph structure is always limited in the types of emergent features it can display. Depending on the task to be performed (see below), the user either will or will not be able to use these emergent features. But at the same time, performance will be influenced directly (regardless of the type of emergent features) by data structure complexity and data–graph compatibility. In general, one would expect performance to be better for less complex data structures and more compatible data and graph structures (arrows a and d in Figure 15.1).

As mentioned above, configural displays have usually been found to be superior to non-configural displays on so-called 'integrated' tasks. These tasks are usually contrasted with so-called 'focused' tasks, where the user only has to read or remember individual data values. As shown by Bennett *et al.* (1993) configural displays are not necessarily more difficult to use for focused tasks than non-configural displays, because lower-level data can be made more salient perceptually by using a variety of layout techniques. However, in general it is fair to say that configural graphs lend themselves better for integrated tasks, provided that the emergent feature(s) have a straightforward mapping into the type of information that needs to be integrated.

Finally, a word about the distinction between 'concurrent' (display-based) and 'retrospective' (memory-based) processing. Not surprisingly, the memory image of a graph turns out to have different characteristics than the physical image of the same graph that is available for inspection. For example, single numeric values are not remembered as well as general patterns in the data. Surprisingly, however, there are indications that retrospective processing sometimes renders configural displays less effective than non-configural displays, whereas the opposite finding is usually observed under concurrent conditions (Hurts, 1995). Much depends, however, on the precise procedures and instructions used for the retrospective task (see also Bennett and Flach, 1992).

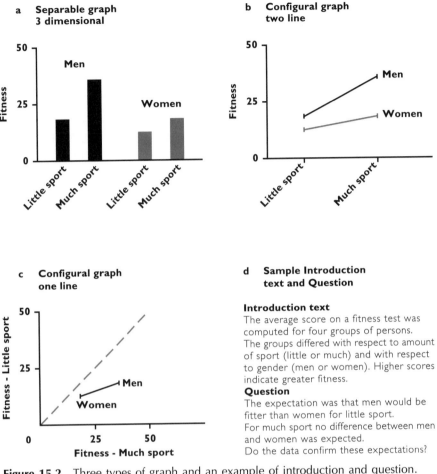

**Figure 15.2**  Three types of graph and an example of introduction and question.

## 15.4   EXAMPLES OF HOW TO USE THE FRAMEWORK

Figure 15.2 shows some examples of graphs. In an experiment, the presentation of every graph was preceded by an introductory text describing the background of the data to be seen (Figure 15.2d). When the subject indicated that he or she had read the story, one of the graphs (Figures 15.2a, 15.2b, 15.2c) would be displayed. After the graph had been inspected and memorized, a question would appear. An example is shown in Figure 15.2d. To answer the questions correctly, all data values had to be taken into account (integrated task). The story and the graph would either both disappear after inspection or both would remain available for inspection, the probability of each event being p = 0.50. Dependent variables were time needed to answer the question and correctness of the answer. In addition, the time needed to read the story and inspect the graph were recorded.

All figures shown in Figure 15.2 are based on four data values taken from a three-dimensional (trivariate) data set. The bar graph of Figure 15.2a is a separable graph, because it hardly has any task-relevant emergent features. The line graphs of Figures 15.2b and 15.2c are configural graphs and have (virtually) identical emergent features (i.e., the angle formed by the two lines shown at their actual or imagined point of intersection) that help answer the questions. However, Figure 15.2b has more compatible data and graph structures than Figure 15.2c.

The results for 12 subjects (within-subjects design) show that the separable graph was inferior to the two-line configural graph (Figure 15.2b) with respect to *concurrent* processing (both story and graph present), but superior to the same graph under *retrospective* processing conditions (both story and graph absent). This result shows the importance of configurality under concurrent conditions and the problems that may arise with configural graphs if the memory for the graph is tested. Performance was worse for the one-line configural graph (Figure 15.2c) than for the two-line configural graph under both processing conditions, showing the negative effect on performance of low data–graph compatibility.

Finally, another example of the effect of data–graph compatibility is demonstrated by the comparison between the separable graph of Figure 15.2a and the same graph presented as showing a two-dimensional (bivariate) instead of a three-dimensional (trivariate) data set. The last type of graph was basically formed by using the *x*-axis for showing the values of a single, continuous (independent) variable, for example 'Amount of study' (in order to prepare for an exam), consisting of four values: 10, 20, 30 and 40 hours. The question for this graph type might be: 'Determine if the average grade for an exam (dependent variable) increases from 10 hours to 20 hours of study by the same amount as from 30 hours to 40 hours of study'. Notice that this question requires subjects to make the same kind of judgement as in Figure 15.1a, although its physical appearance is quite different.

The results for this comparison show that questions about the two-dimensional separable graph were answered better under retrospective conditions and faster under concurrent conditions than those about the three-dimensional separable graph. The trivariate separable graphs were also inspected during a longer time before the question was presented than the same graphs interpreted as showing a bivariate data set. These results show the negative effect of low data-graph compatibility on performance. (Admittedly, the results mentioned may also be due to the data structure of the trivariate data set being different from the one of the bivariate data set, even though the same data values were contained in both data sets). (For more details, see Hurts, 1996)

## 15.5   CONCLUSIONS

In this chapter configurality is considered a graph-related determinant of graph effectiveness that has to be distinguished from task-related, data-related and other graph-related determinants, with which it interacts. Although the interaction between configurality and specific task features has already been investigated previously, the framework described in this chapter attempts to elaborate on, and provide a more principled basis to this work. Examples were shown of how specific graph types and their relative effectiveness, as determined in psychological experiments, may be described in terms of this framework. However, the precise nature of the relationships between the characteristics mentioned and graph effectiveness remains an issue for research.

## REFERENCES

BENNETT, K. B. and FLACH, J. M. (1992) Graphical displays: implications for divided attention, focused attention, and problem solving. *Human Factors* **34**, 513–533.

BENNETT, K. B., TOMS, M. L. and WOODS, D. D. (1993) Emergent features and graphical elements: designing more effective configural displays. *Human Factors* **35**, 71–97.

CARSWELL, C. M. and WICKENS, C. D. (1987) Information integration and the object display: an interaction of task demands and display superiority. *Ergonomics* **30**, 511–528.

CLEVELAND, W. S. and McGILL, R. (1984) Graphical perception: theory, experimentation, and application to the development of graphic methods. *Journal of the American Statistical Association* **70**, 531–554.

GILLAN, D. J. and LEWIS, R. (1994) A componential model of human interaction with graphs: 1. Linear regression modeling. *Human Factors* **36**, 419–440.

HURTS, C. M. M. (1995) The effect of configural and separable graphs on memory-based integrated task performance. In: HASAN, H. and NICASTRI, C. (Eds), *HCI: A Light into the Future, OZCHI'95 Proceedings*, pp. 122–128. Downer, Australia: CHISIG/ Ergonomics Society of Australia.

HURTS, C. M. M. (1996) The effect of configural graphs on concurrent and retrospective performance. In: *Proceedings of the 40th Annual Meeting of the Human Factors and Ergonomics Society*, pp. 1160–1164. Santa Monica, CA: Human Factors and Ergonomics Society.

POMERANTZ, J. R. (1986) Visual form perception: an overview. In: NUSBAUM, H. C. and SCHWAB, E. C. (Eds), *Pattern Recognition by Humans and Machines: Vol. 2, Visual Perception*, pp. 1–30. Orlando, FL: Academic.

TUKEY, J. W. (1977) *Exploratory Data Analysis*. Reading, MA: Addison-Wesley.

WICKENS, C. D. and ANDRE, A. D. (1990) Proximity compatibility and information display: effects of color, space, and objectness on information integration. *Human Factors* **32**, 61–78.

# CHAPTER SIXTEEN

# Prolegomena for a theory of table design

THOMAS L. WARREN

## 16.1 INTRODUCTION

When writers make rhetorical decisions about textual elements, they frequently consider the reader, the 'rules' found in style manuals, and research so they can adapt their text to fit the reader's ability to process it and their need for information. When writers decide to design a table, however, this concern for the way readers process the information is outweighed by the 'rules' of the style manuals because the research on tables is neither plentiful nor well known.

Table designers must know how readers process information because readers are constantly confronted with tables of all kinds in their daily lives. To move from point to point, they need to read transportation schedules; to complete numerous forms, they need to consult data tables; and to learn what is missing, they consult tables that arrange what is known so as to highlight that which is unknown.

It is surprising how little research is actually done on designing tables – as early as 1970, Wright and Fox lamented the lack of research into table design. American technical writing textbooks offer advice on how to construct tables as do style manuals and countless articles, but that advice is based primarily on tradition – what has worked in the past rather than research. This approach, therefore, points to questions unanswered by either the research or the guidelines.

## 16.2 PUBLISHED LITERATURE

The published literature on designing tables falls into two major categories: advice found in textbooks on technical writing (which I will not cover); and advice to be inferred from research (which I will only briefly mention). The first category is by far the largest, but there is an increasing amount of material for designers in the second.

### 16.2.1   Research literature

Most of the advice based on research was offered before 1990, with principle advice coming from Manning (1989), Dragga and Gong (1989), Guthrie (1988), Hartley (1985), Bartram (1984), Gross (1983), Ehrenberg (1977), Wright (1977, 1980, 1982), Wright and Barnard (1975), Wright and Reid (1973), Enrick (1972) and Wright and Fox (1970), to name but a few.

Most recently, however, some research has appeared that promises to shift the 'advice' away from the mechanics of preparing a table to the response the user will have. Guthrie *et al.* (1993) build on previous work done by them together and individually to report on how people cognitively read and understand several graphic forms (including tables). They argue that reading visuals and reading text are somewhat similar activities.

Guthrie (1988) developed a five-stage model for how people process visuals such as schedules: goal formation, category selection, information extraction, integration, and recycling. When readers have a specific informational need (such as determining when a plane or train leaves), this need becomes a goal and the object of the search. They then examine the various categories of information in the table for those appropriate to satisfy the goal. Should readers have encountered a similar or the same table before, the search time and discrimination of categories are much more efficient. Note that the model works for discovering information that will lead to both direct action (such as catching a train or plane) and indirect action (such as filling in an income tax form). It does not cover tables found in articles or reports, or tables used to identify missing information.

Guthrie *et al.* (1993) also speculate about how local search strategies differ from global strategies. The local search strategy occurs when the reader looks for a specific piece of information – such as when does the train/plane leave – and category selection becomes the most important element (see Guthrie, 1988; Guthrie and Mosenthal, 1987). Integration also plays an important role in local searches (Guthrie *et al.*, 1991). Global search strategies determine the holistic, generalized information a visual contains. A table may show an increase in particular sales over time, and the reader would have to infer the trend, whereas with a line graph, the overall impression of the line gives the reader a global meaning for the data. Interestingly enough, Wainer (1992) argues that through rounding and judicious use of white space, general impressions of trends are possible from tables. People use tables, therefore, more for local searches than for global searches. So the textbook advice that the reader should use a graph if the purpose is to show trends (or some other global expression) and not a table is supported by this research.

## 16.2.2 Design considerations

How then, can the table designer arrange the data? The designer cannot allow the context to be completely controlled by the reader. Readers have particular contexts and demand answers (data) based on those contexts with a minimum of extraneous information. But the extraneous information for one reader becomes the relevant information for another. That is the designer's problem for any type of table. As Nelms (1981) points out, the table must be self-indexing – that is, it must solve the problem of pertinent and extraneous information for all readers by allowing each to access the needed information with as little confusion as possible.

But how is the designer to do that? The tools the designer has with which to create the table are essentially the tools used to design text or another type of visual: white space, typeface and enhancement, rules and borders, colour and (or) grey scale, etc. There is a significant difference, however, for the designer of a table. Normally, cost prohibits using the design elements fully because of the half-life of most tables (for example, railway timetables are sometimes valid for only 30 days) and their cost prohibits expensive design alternatives such as colour.

Designers must also be aware of the approaches readers will use. For example, will they skim the whole table to get a general idea of what the table contains, where it contains it, and how it is organized? Do readers casually approach tables the same way they would approach text – for example, a newspaper or magazine (see also Wright and Reid, 1973; Wright, 1980)? Will they scan the table for specific information – matching the appropriate row and column based on the head words? Or will the reader search more deeply, trying to understand all the information. In all cases, the communication function of the table becomes extremely important to the designer.

## 16.3 ELEMENTS TO CONSIDER: SEMANTICS, SYNTAX, PRAGMATICS OF VISUALS

The important point about using tables for readers is selecting the right piece of information. Thus, designers must understand the meaning of the categories (semantic level), the way the columns work together to generate meaning (syntactical meaning), and the context out of which the need for information comes (the pragmatics of the situation).

## 16.3.1 Semantics

Tables are a form of symbolic visual because they rely on alphanumeric symbols for their meaning. Whether the table supports an assertion in a report or an article, or provides a reference, or identifies missing information, the semantic elements are essentially the same. For example, a value of '3.5' contains semantic meaning at both a literal and a figurative level. The '3.5' has a specific value and has a meaning relative to, among others, '3.0' and '4.0'. Even the design elements of rules and borders could play an important role as do the other symbols such as monetary signs, units of measurement, mathematical signs and words. A second part of meaning comes from syntax.

### 16.3.2    Syntax

The table's syntax associates the individual datum one with the other. Just as the syntax of a sentence provides meaning that is greater than the sum of its parts, so too does one find that the meaning of the sum of the various data reflects something greater than the sum of the parts. Tables, for example, rely on the cognitive processing of sequence similar to that used in processing a sentence. Gross (1983) argues that in a table the reader will generate syntactical units based on the columns and rows. Wright and Fox (1970) hint at the importance of syntax when they observe that the designer can place data such that the reader searches along rows in implicit tables (full data), rather than explicit tables (selected data) (see also Wright, 1980). In a decision table, where, for example, a worker decides about retiring and drawing a pension, the series of units are of an if . . . then . . . type. The relationship between cells is linear, beginning with the information in the first column head. The user looks in Column 1 that shows, for example, years of service, and then reads across to another column, showing salary upon retirement, to find the monthly pension.

Furthermore, reading a table is like reading text in the sense that the reader develops sentences by taking data from the table and adding appropriate structural words (i.e., verbs). So, the complexity of tables can involve the number of columns and the other modifications such as units of measure. One key piece of research that is missing is whether or not readers can compare data more effectively when presented horizontally or vertically.

As we know from rhetorical studies of prose, semantic and syntactic meaning are only two sources of meaning. The third, pragmatics, requires much more consideration by the table designer.

### 16.3.3    Pragmatics

Pragmatics refers to meaning associated with data through context (immediate or previous and what the reader brings to the table). Does the reader have a generalization that fits the data together? Most psychologists agree that readers bring a context or schema to the text when they are looking for specific information. These schema set patterns that focus the readers' attention and evolve as the readers search for particular information as well as when they approach the text more casually.

Readers bring knowledge of two types: knowledge of and knowledge how. They may already know something about the subject and that may be highly specific or general. They may also have simple or complex search strategies available. If the table is the right one, the reader searches the table proper, presumably again reading from top to bottom in Column1 to find the relevant category and then horizontally to find the relevant data. Except for a study published by Wright (1980), not much evidence appears to confirm this assumption (but see Warren, 1997).

## 16.4  CONCLUSION

The purpose in this chapter has been to introduce some issues associated with designing tables. These issues have included how those who prepare/design tables learn the principles and what the research has told us about how readers use tables. A theory of table design must consider both elements in addition to what tradition has passed along through the textbooks and guidelines. Currently, guidelines focus attention on the variables the designer has at hand and say little about how readers read and use tables. The principles seem to be that 'here are the design elements and, by the way, they help readers understand the table', rather than 'help the reader understand the table by using these design elements'.

Likewise, the designer must consider that tables appear in at least three contexts: to provide reference materials, including schedules, tax tables, and standard statistical values; to support assertions made in articles and reports; and to show visually where new information is needed. In all three cases, the reader turns to a table for specific information. Tables are an integral part of communicating in societies that rely on acquiring and dispensing information to their citizens, so their effectiveness needs to be of as much concern as is the effectiveness of the prose.

## REFERENCES

BARTRAM, D. (1984) The presentation of information about bus services. In: EASTERBY, R. and ZWAGA, H. (Eds), *Information Design*, pp. 299–319. Chichester: John Wiley & Sons.

DRAGGA, S. and GONG, G. (1989) *Editing: The Rhetoric of Design*. Amityville, NY: Baywood.

EHRENBERG, A. S. C. (1977) Rudiments of numeracy. *Journal of the Royal Statistical Society* **140**, 227–297.

ENRICK, N. L. (1972) *Effective Graphic Communication*. Princeton: Auerbach.

GROSS, A. G. (1983) Primer of tables and figures. *Journal of Technical Writing and Communication* **13**, 35–55.

GUTHRIE, J. T. (1988) Locating information in documents: examination of a cognitive model. *Reading Research Quarterly* **23**, 178–199.

GUTHRIE, J. T. and MOSENTHAL, P. (1987) Literacy as multidimensional: locating information and reading comprehension. *Educational Psychologist* **22**, 279–297.

GUTHRIE, J. T., BRITTEN, T. and BARKER, K. G. (1991) *Effects of Document and Strategy Type on Cognitive Components on Search*. Boston: American Educational Research Association Convention.

GUTHRIE, J. T., WEBER, S. and KIMMERLY, N. (1993) Searching documents: cognitive processes and deficits in understanding graphs, tables, and illustrations. *Contemporary Educational Psychology* **18**, 186–221.

HARTLEY, J. (1985) *Designing Instructional Text* (2nd ed.). London: Kogan Page.

MANNING, A. D. (1989) The semantics of technical graphics. *Journal of Technical Writing and Communication* **19**, 31–51.

NELMS, H. (1981) *Thinking with a Pencil.* Berkeley, CA: Ten Speed.

WAINER, H. (1992) Understanding graphs and tables. *Educational Research* **21**, 14–23.

WARREN, T. L. (1997) Graphic information: how do readers put the pieces together? *The Editorial Eye* **20**, 1–3.

WRIGHT, P. (1977) Decision making as a factor in the ease of using numerical tables. *Ergonomics* **20**, 91–96.

WRIGHT, P. (1980) The comprehension of tabulated information: some similarities between reading prose and reading tables. *NSPI Journal* **19**, 25–29.

WRIGHT, P. (1982) A user-oriented approach to the design of tables and flowcharts. In: JONASSEN, D. H. (Ed.), *The Technology of Text: Principles for Structuring, Designing, and Displaying Text*, 2, pp. 317–340. Englewood Cliffs, NJ: Educational Technology Publications.

WRIGHT, P. and BARNARD, P. (1975) Effects of 'more than' and 'less than' decisions on the use of numerical tables. *Journal of Applied Psychology* **60**, 606–611.

WRIGHT, P. and FOX, K. (1970) Presenting information in tables. *Applied Ergonomics* **1**, 234–242.

WRIGHT, P. and REID, F. (1973) Written information: some alternatives to prose for expressing the outcomes of complex contingencies. *Journal of Applied Psychology* **57**, 160–166.

# PART SIX

# Maps and Plans

# CHAPTER SEVENTEEN

# Maps as public graphics: about science and craft, curiosity and passion

PAUL MIJKSENAAR

## 17.1 MAPS FOR EVERYDAY USE

There is a large variety of maps for everyday use. Well-known examples are: city maps, public transport maps, road maps, maps in travel guides, recreational maps and maps in directories. Most people are likely to associate the word 'map' with atlases and topographic maps, impressive panoramic maps, or very specialist maps such as those of the ocean floor. Here, however, the main theme will be the maps people use for activities in their daily lives. An example of this kind of map is the one shown in Plate 17.1 showing a map for tourists in Amsterdam.

### 17.1.1 Attractiveness and functionality

People who use maps for very mundane reasons may also have a passion for maps. The reason for this often encountered passion has little or nothing to do with their practical use. It is the aesthetic pleasure which prevails. The practical use in this case only serves the user as an excuse for unrestrained buying behaviour that for some will result in extensive collection building. Maps can bring this about, because the map designer, while preserving functionality, can add much aesthetic quality to a map. This does not necessarily make maps any better but they do become much more attractive. It can be argued that this attractiveness in itself forms a functional aspect in the case of public graphics, at least according to the

AIDA formula (mentioned as part of the sales method in the car trade): Attention, Interest, Desire, Action.

A product that does not catch the attention and as a consequence fails to arouse interest, will not be put to use. Visual attractiveness is an important factor leading to attention. Although catching attention, or conspicuity, should not be confused with visual quality, it is sometimes difficult to make a distinction between the two. There are forms of visual chaos that draw attention and offer visual quality, but not quite in the way the makers intended. However, when done properly, visual quality adds something extra to the sum of the parts: parts that in themselves are often of slight significance but as a whole produce a new pattern, not unlike a quilt. Wallpaper and textile pattern designers are well aware of this phenomenon, precisely because they work the other way around. They aim at a total effect but they constrain themselves to the form and order of the detail. Cartographers also make use of this effect when applying patterns to represent areas such as parks, swamps, forests, dunes and cemeteries.

### 17.1.2  Designing useful maps

Originally, making maps consisted mainly of first gathering the precious geographic data and then applying expertise to visualize these data. In visualizing the data, important choices had to be made. The most important of these was how to represent the originally spatial, spheroidal information on a flat surface (e.g. Gardner, 1975). Up to today cartographers have been struggling to find the ideal projection method. Plate 17.2 shows one of the options. The choice of projection method should match the task or priorities of the intended user of the map. To navigate reliably at sea one needs to plot measurable courses. A car driver is mainly interested in driving times and routes. In skiing areas the main point is to decide on the attractiveness of the different runs.

Unique are the maps of public transport systems. In public transport maps there is a strong need for schematization to represent adequately the accumulation of data in the centre of a city. Around 1932, Henry Beck, in his much acclaimed scheme for the London Underground, 'stretched' the metropolitan area and strongly compressed the rest of London. (See Garland (1994) for a detailed account of the development of the London Underground map.)

In cartography, inventiveness and professional skill play an important role. Mathematical training is indispensable for calculating the often complicated projections. Maps have been made for thousands of years and one can therefore surmise that by trial and error, much insight has been acquired into the way people use maps. Cartography is a craft that only recently been substantiated by objective knowledge.

A parallel can be found in typography where contemporary legibility research seems to confirm what has been common knowledge to typographers for ages. This does not imply that guidelines based on behavioural research cannot be useful. They should be used, however, in a well-considered way; otherwise the resulting design can be a complete failure. In an investigation performed by an ergonomist and a graphic designer, the rules obtained in ergonomics research had been rigidly applied in a layout. This layout resulted in such a degree of visual exaggeration that to any typographer it was blatantly obvious that something was wrong. On the other hand, typographers, too, manage to produce designs that make the hair of every true scientist stand on end because it is evident that these designs will never serve their purpose. In my opinion these things happen because many designers are unable or unwilling to distinguish between personal creative expression and objective rules. Aside from the actual lack of familiarity of designers with the results of scientific research, for which they can hardly be blamed due to the relative obscurity of many scientific reports, too many designers presume that innovative creativity is more important than practical use. Consequently, it is no wonder that this leads to creativity prevailing over the usability of the information contents of a design.

An example of a design where creativity took precedence over usability was the map of the New York subway system designed in 1978 by the New York graphic designer Massimo Vignelli (Plate 17.3). This map replaced the existing, rather traditional, topographic map. Seen from a distance on the wall of a subway station, the new map looked wonderful: colourful, smooth, and well-organized. However much this prize-winning design was acclaimed among fellow designers, it had to be replaced after massive protests from the subway passengers. In their eyes Vignelli had overstepped the limits of acceptable distortion of the representation of the shape of the city. No one recognized the map as one of the city they knew so well. The map that replaced it in 1980 (Plate 17.4) was much closer to the old one but it unmistakably showed the hand of John Taurenac, a masterly map-maker. Much to the users' satisfaction, the street pattern, one of the main keys to reality on the surface level, was shown again in a light grey that left the smooth and beautiful pattern of the curved subway lines undisturbed. What makes today's New York subway map so attractive is that it clearly shows one of the most important characteristics of maps, namely the clear presence of the unpredictable and unyielding reality showing through in the design.

## 17.2 FUNCTIONALITY AND AESTHETICS IN MAP DESIGN

The purpose of many of the maps designed for everyday use is to help us find our way in an environment we do not know. It still remains to be seen, however, whether maps allow us to find the way to our destination better than a clear route description. Most people prefer a route description indicating, for instance, the nearest bus-stop or mentioning the major streets ('near the market'), than consulting a map. Yet maps, although taking up more space, offer much more information on spatial relations, to the extent that more routes (there and back) can be given at the same time. A map allows one to explore the environment.

Especially for those who provide routeing information, for example at an information desk, a map is an efficient and versatile aid to performance of their task. Maps function relatively independently of text. The text on a map can be limited to the names of a few streets and buildings and sometimes road numbers for the motorist.

This makes maps easily adaptable for use by an international public. A map can be indispensable as is the case in Tokyo where street names do not exist. A map is a must to describe the location of a shop or an office (Plate 17.5).

### 17.2.1    Information layers in maps

What makes maps special as information presenting artefacts is that they usually combine several information layers. The users can 'browse' through the information of all layers at random, guided only by their curiosity, provided that they have sufficient understanding of the semantics, syntax and lexicon of that specific map. Examples of these layers are: streets and roads, buildings and land use, public buildings, public transport, routes and attractions.

The fact that these layers do not overlap is mostly a result of their topographic arrangement: where there is water there can be no buildings, where there is a road there cannot be a railway and where there is a hotel there cannot be a town hall. The main task of the map designer is to give these layers sufficient distinction within a harmonious whole. Through the years, a set of more or less agreed-upon image conventions have arisen for many of these information layers, or categories. It is striking that with colours map-makers have always tried to maintain a natural association: blue for water, green for forests and brown for mountains. The use of different shades of a colour to denote height differences is however less natural: light green for lowland and dark green for very low lying land!

From time to time new insights break through, causing major changes. A striking example is the new Rand McNally atlas (Plate 17.6) the colours of which have been adjusted to match those of the satellite pictures which have become familiar to many of us. As a trend, we find that over the years the variety in colours has become less extreme; the colours have become softer with a pastel quality and blend more smoothly with each other. This trend in the choice of colours certainly enhances the legibility of text on a map.

### 17.2.2    The influence of map-making techniques on map design

The technique of map-making – drawing, reprography and printing – has also influenced the designing of maps. Some 30 years ago it was already possible to print a map in six or more colours. But this demanded an extraordinary accuracy, achieved through high-quality craftsmanship, to make each colour match exactly with the others. The procedure required a separate drawing for each colour, and separate printing plates had to be prepared after which, for each colour in turn, the paper had to be fed into the printing press, or series of connecting printing units. For a long time, producing maps in this way was too costly for mass-produced maps for everyday use. For the cheap map used by the man in the street only a few colours were used, usually black with one supporting colour.

With the arrival of the Apple computer and the advanced matching graphic software, such as the drawing program Freehand, it became possible for designers to see almost every conceivable colour directly on their own colour screens and to select them for use on a map by simply pressing a button. The coloured map could be automatically specified by the computer and printed as ready-to-use litho films using comparatively simple equipment. Colour printing has now also become possible for daily newspapers. The American newspaper *USA-Today* achieved pioneering results with maps showing an elaborate and detailed use of colour.

As mentioned above, the choice of colours for maps had become restrained. This changed drastically with the introduction of advanced computer applications. After colour printing became simple, people rushed to produce maps in bold colours somewhat in the way that Technicolor took Hollywood by surprise. Of course, there were objections from the dwindling designers élite, raised in the best of Bauhaus traditions, who had hardly recovered from the transition from black-and-white to colour television. As is usual with the introduction of innovative developments, the scales tipped. History, however, teaches us that after a while a 'natural' balance will be found again. The demand for colour, however, cannot be expected to return to its level from before the time when colour printing became simple. Costs are not any longer limiting the use of colour and, more importantly, people love colour! When asked what the function was of the excessive use of colour in his very successful Access travel guides, Saul Wurman replied: 'Colour sells.'

### 17.2.3 Functionality and aesthetic preference

The aim of designers and researchers is not to define the ideal map but to define the limiting conditions of functionality. Research suggests that the use of different types of letters has an effect on functionality. However, types of letters, which are *distinguishing variables* (to be discriminated from *hierarchic variables* such as positioning, size, contrast, etc.) do exert an enormous attraction not only on designers, but also on non-professionals. The first thing many people do after installing their new printer is to use as many different letter types and letter sizes in their documents as possible.

Ergonomics guidelines tell us that the legibility and/or readability of printed words is affected differently by *serif* and *sanserif* letters, and that people can at the very most identify eight colours and only a few shades of each colour by name, whereas considerably more colour differences can be distinguished when compared simultaneously. Obviously, the behaviour of users of a design artefact is different when they serve as subjects in an investigation where objective usability is the main criterion to when they are standing as consumers in a shop where 'quantity' is the main attraction and where subjective preferences play a leading role.

Related to the preferences of users is the designers' concept of 'visual quality', which is just as difficult to grasp. Probably because up to now we have hardly succeeded in selecting objective criteria for visual quality, we, in the designers' world, tend to ignore the need to find these objective criteria and like to believe that visual quality is something that evades objective measurement. For the sake of convenience it is supposed that designers as craftsmen automatically add aesthetic quality as extra value to a product. Fortunately, this often is the case because most educational institutes for the visual arts are concerned with precisely this intangible aspect and after many years of experience manage to teach their students how to master aesthetic problems. An aspect that seems to get far less attention in design education is the usability of a product. This applies even more to the relation between functionality and beauty, which is hardly ever part of the curriculum.

### 17.2.4   Models or standard solutions for design problems

Aesthetic quality is certainly related to visual quality but there are differences. Visual quality is the result of knowledge of and craftsmanship in applying all available graphic means as effectively and in as balanced a way as possible. But that in itself is no guarantee of aesthetic quality. And although a good design distinguishes itself from a bad one by the extra value added to the sum of its parts, it is worthwhile having a closer look at some of those separate parts.

One of the ways to come to terms in our daily lives with the confusing world we live in is to approach things systematically, to make diagrams and models. Sometimes we are successful in doing so, and sometimes we are not. In designing too we have to schematize and standardize, otherwise our products would become too expensive, or there would be a different solution for each product which would not contribute to the identification and mutual coherence as a series. But here also there will always be problems which remain unsolved.

An example of a failure to find a universal model is the already mentioned map of the London Underground. At first sight it looks more like a diagram than a map. The number of angles used to map the colour-coded lines has been strictly limited, with a small number of symbols per type of stop and interchange station. Anything unimportant has been left out. The only slightly realistic element in the map is the river Thames. This is an example of the clever use of a landmark that helps the user to interpret this diagram. To all appearances it seemed that Beck had found a system/model for the ideal representation of an urban railway network. However, Beck was the first to deny that a universal principle was at work here. In his view the design was the result of many years of redesigning, adding, and especially omitting: the result of this was an almost organic diagram that fitted London exactly. However, attracted by its success the Paris Metro officials commissioned Beck to design a similar diagram for Paris. The story goes that Beck did spend a few days in Paris before returning the commission because he had come to the conclusion that his solution for London would not work for Paris.

To this day, the London map is used by designers of public transport maps as an example when designing a network map. Maps of Los Angeles' freeways, of German cities with an S- or U-Bahn, of Tokyo's underground, and of Amsterdam's metro system (Plate 17.7) were designed in the London style. It should be noted, however, that these system maps are designed only in a comparable style, and that the system (the set of design rules) used is not the same as the one used by Beck for the London system map.

During a design exercise with Beck's map at the Faculty of Industrial Design Engineering in Delft, students analysed the difficulties passengers had in using the map when they had to change lines more than twice. An example of those problems has to do with two stations which according to the Underground map are 45 minutes apart (as a rule one can assume that the travelling time between stations is three minutes). In fact, these two stations are within a five-minute walking distance from each other. There are evidently cases where the system map is misleading when planning a trip. The reason for this is that Beck's map is only intended to show functional relationships. It has no intention to show geographically correct relationships. There are, however, elements in the design of the map suggesting a certain degree of geographically correct representation. As a consequence, passengers tend to use the functional and diagrammatical system map as a map also showing geographic relationships. In fact, to plan a trip properly a traveller also needs a street map.

An alternative map developed by the Delft students (Plate 17.8) combined the best of the two representations. In the metropolitan area all lines are represented topographically correct so that important above-ground landmarks such as parks, main streets and museums could be added. In this way a trip can be planned more efficiently, and alternative ways of transport, such as walking, can be considered. Outside the metropolitan area the lines are represented even more schematically than in the original diagram because here only the linear or functional relationship between the lines is important.

### 17.2.5  A design problem: orientation information in maps

An important item in maps for daily use, such as a city map, is the requirement to provide for the need of users to orient themselves on the maps ('Where are we?'). Usually, important buildings or other landmarks are used to assist in this orientation task. From a designer's point of view it is a problem how to depict this orientation information in such a way that it can easily be used as an aid and at the same time fits in a coherent way into the 'map image'.

An approach often used to incorporate orientation information in maps such as city maps is based on the familiarity of landmarks or of the recognizability of other conspicuous items in the environment. A design solution is the consistent application of the 'erect' (three-dimensional) representation of such objects while the rest of the map remains 'flat'; consistent because the objects are oriented in the same direction as the map and, just like the rest of the map, are seen from above though not perpendicular. Only the vertical scale is violated by strong exaggeration. A way to avoid this exaggeration is demonstrated on a beautiful map of Washington (Plate 17.9). The designer has tried here to keep the vertical exaggeration as flat as possible by the sophisticated use of cast shadows; thus, the buildings are represented as flat as possible. In spite of all good intentions this approach is still not ideal for the users because they will almost never know what the object they are searching for looks like from above. To recognize a building, they usually need to see the façade of it. This is only the case when the building is oriented towards the viewer.

Other, more unorthodox map-makers think it is sufficient to 'paste' a picture on the spot on the map where the building is supposed to be. A disadvantage of this solution is that large parts of the map become covered. One step further is the combination of near correct three-dimensional projections and flat frontal views. This, too, is a compromise between more or less accurate cartographic principles and providing for the needs of the public. Panoramic overviews are without exception very impressive but they mainly serve as souvenirs and wall decorations or have an educational purpose. As a navigational aid they are of little use.

What these examples demonstrate is the conflict between the map designer's intentions and the user's needs. On the one hand there is the designer with his unambiguous and sound principles based on logical reasoning and a systematic way of working, and on the other hand there are the users who use the carefully selected and depicted information in a map in every way they think fit. It is exactly here that the help of a human behaviour specialist will be useful. The researcher, just like the user, is not primarily interested in the aesthetics of the map and the reasons for depicting information in one way and not in another. In the design phase, a researcher is interested in the requirements a map should meet to be useful as an aid in performing a certain task. In the evaluation phase a researcher is interested in the reasons why people have difficulties in using the map. The crucial question is: are people making design-related errors or task-related errors? In this cooperative approach to map design, the designer should expect to be flexible and willing to think of unorthodox answers, while not losing sight of visual quality through clarity and good organization.

## 17.3  DESIGN ASPECTS AND USABILITY OF MAPS

### 17.3.1  Scale

It is a fallacy to think that maps are much easier to read than text. Reading maps, just as reading directions and graphics, requires a certain level of knowledge and training. The different ways of depicting information on maps belong to the set of map conventions, and most of them have to be learned. It is a well-known fact that scale and the use of symbols cause most of the problems when reading maps. What would be an easy way to indicate the scale of a map? This is a crucial question because maps can have very different scales. An interesting way to get the idea of scale across is to combine the scale of the map with a grid in such a way that for instance one side of a grid square equals a 15-minute walk.

### 17.3.2  Representation of factual data

Reliability and the correct representation of the conditions as they really are, is the most important requirement a map should meet. Does the map show the correct number of side roads, the accessibility of streets, or changes in the type of road? Michelin is an excellent example of how to guarantee the reliability of the information: all year round a small army of inspectors are busy driving around France spotting and reporting changes. Reliability as correctness of representation is also related to convenience or usability. It is very convenient to be able to see on city plans where the entrance to a public building is situated. For orientation on the road it is important to know whether crossings (e.g. with a railway) are at the same level or at different levels.

When representing the data, map-makers always have to find a balance between keeping the map as factual as possible and making the necessary simplifications which we call 'generalization'. Sometimes exaggeration is necessary at the cost of a realistic representation. On a map with a scale of 1:1 000 000, the factual width of a normal road would be drawn on the map as a line not much wider than 0.0002 mm, whereas the actual lines on the map indicate a road of 20 km wide. Every map user understands that the width of a road, a railway, or a river bears no relation to their factual width. On the other hand it is also possible that a small difference has to be exaggerated, because it is important to show this detail. If at a road junction two roads are not an exact continuation of one another but actually have an offset of tens of metres, this information should be shown in some way on a map if it is a road-map. The argument that this discontinuity cannot be shown because of the scale of the map is not relevant given the navigation task of the intended user of the map. In their care and effort for a systematic and logical approach to the design of a map, many map-makers forget all too easily that a map is a tool that should support the performance of a specific task, in this case selecting the correct route to a destination.

### 17.3.3  Symbols

Preferably, symbols must be explained on the map itself, not at the rear or tucked away at the back of a guide. The red Michelin hotel guide solves this problem by printing a key to the most important symbols on a bookmark. Another good solution is a fold-out, for instance as part of the cover. This is a handy solution but comparatively costly. International standardization of map symbols would be advantageous not so much for the purpose of comprehension (the legend of the map is always at hand) but because it contributes to the reuse of previously acquired knowledge. Many map-makers already use identical or similar symbols. However, this is not the work of official standardization but rather a result of internationalization of the map-makers' world. Initiatives in this field can be noticed in several lines of business. For instance, in The Netherlands research is being conducted into the possibility of standardizing public transport maps. This would greatly increase the usefulness of maps of cities which one visits only occasionally.

The compactness of symbols makes them particularly suitable for use on maps. Their feasibility is bound by the same rules as for symbols in stations, airports, on operating panels, etc. Dewar (Chapter 23) and Brugger (Chapter 24) discuss various procedures to test the comprehensibility of symbols. Because symbols can never be fully self-explanatory, possibilities should be offered to trace the meaning in the key to the symbols. For the representation of symbols extremely small, separately drawn, even more stylized versions are needed. The standardization sheet ISO 7001 (ISO, 1979) has already allowed for this.

A special category of symbols in maps are pattern symbols. These patterns symbols are composed of simple or geometrical elements, often in combination with colour, to indicate the nature of the land use. Because the effective use of maps is strongly influenced by the familiarity with the applied symbols, special attention should be paid to this by the publisher. A nice example of how to increase the familiarity of symbols is a kind of card game published by the Swiss Cartographical Authority where each symbol is exemplified by a photograph.

### 17.3.4   Handling maps

Maps have a natural tendency to be large and therefore difficult to handle. Ideally, one would like to see the whole map at a single glance. Because this is hardly ever possible, map-makers have come up with many, often very intricate solutions to compensate for this problem. An obvious solution is to divide the map into a series of smaller maps which are then made into a booklet. A disadvantage of this solution is that in such a booklet the coherence between the different sections of the map is lost. This loss of coherence causes problems when reading from one map section to another elsewhere in the book. Many different reference systems are used on the edges of the maps to keep the user oriented when going from one section to another.

Another solution, which has been used by Falkland Publishers for years, is a very ingenious way of folding the map. In this folding system the map is folded and partly cut into sections in such a way that the user can page from left to right as well as up and down through these sections. The required sections can be unfolded. It is also possible to open the entire map although it is not recommended to do this in a car or in the open with a strong wind blowing. The chances of refolding the entire map in the original order are negligible.

More effective and easy to use are ways of folding based on the Origami principle. Here, a map can be opened and closed with one movement of the hand. Up to now the application of this method has been limited to small format maps but the Japanese designer Miura invented an Origami technique which is applicable to larger formats.

### 17.4   MAPS AND WAYFINDING

Before maps, or rather plans, can be used as a part of the signposting system in buildings they should ideally meet two conditions: they should be displayed in an (almost) horizontal position, and their orientation should match the real world. Left on the plan should be to the left in reality, and right on the plan should be to the right. A drawback of plans complying with these requirements is that, because of this horizontal position, they are not very conspicuous and can be overlooked easily. Another disadvantage is that they take up a lot of floor space. Therefore the majority of the plans in shopping malls, railway stations and airports are vertically positioned. However, such maps are more useful for general orientation than for signposting. Insurmountable problems arise with plans in shopping malls, museums, etc. where the plans of several floors are presented next to each other or stacked sandwich style. One cannot expect more than a mere impression of what each floor has to offer. Of course, it is possible to include a key such as the names of the wings or the passages which can subsequently be found through the normal signing. O'Neill (Chapter 18) presents a detailed overview of the requirements usable plans should meet.

It has been established before that using a plan as a part of signing is chiefly a way of meeting the demands of the user who wants to get a general impression of a new and unknown environment. If such a map can also be taken along as a hand-held map it can be an aid in wayfinding. The question was raised at Amsterdam Airport whether a plan of the station building had to be projected straight from above or at a slight angle, like 'a bird's-eye view'. Interviews with passengers gave the impression that the second option would increase the recognizability of the environment. The acceptance of this bird's-eye view approach would have as a consequence that separate plans would have to be drawn for arriving and departing passengers depending on the point of view. In public waiting lounges different maps might be found, from different points of view. All these different maps would certainly cause confusion. It was decided to draw the plan at a backward angle without vanishing points so that the building elements at the back of the map would be represented just as large. This would also facilitate the drawing of future up-dates. In the plan only those elements which were expected to support orientation, such as façades, entrances, staircases, conveyor belts, and prominent works of art, were represented three-dimensionally.

The application of modern computer techniques in the development of maps allows the integration of maps, photographs, drawings and text in every conceivable colour. A beautiful but not very practical example of such integration is the loose-leaf guide to the Tokyo metro. Each section of the guide deals with one station. Panoramic views of the surrounding area and the station are combined with maps of the underground situation and cross-sections of platforms. All this is supplemented with details such as markings on the map that indicate where two political murder attempts took place.

## 17.5   NEW MEDIA

New technologies create new opportunities for the easy use of maps. The CD-ROM on which hundreds of maps and matching data can be stored and which can be 'played' on compact and affordable navigation equipment, symbolically retrieves the dusty map from the glove compartment. In these car navigation systems, the maps are projected on an LCD or CRT screen and always correspond with the actual travelling direction. A fixed cursor indicates the current position. Warnings are issued when the driver accidentally attempts to turn into a closed road, and in the case of detours alternative itineraries are selected within seconds. An advantage of these new maps is that the map image, the way the map is presented, can be chosen in such a way that it increases the usability of the map. When showing a route, road connections and route characteristics can be stressed. Because the navigation system indicates the correct route and direction, traditional details can be omitted. This creates space for data on nearby facilities, e.g. restaurants, hotels, shops, which are shown at request. One of the navigation systems, the Global Positioning System (GPS), now even allows the use of ordinary paper maps. Initially intended for military purposes only, this technique is now available for the consumer market.

Regular printed maps are also 'handed out' by electronic information booths such as are placed at an increasing rate in office complexes and along the access roads of industrial estates, airports, and even towns. By means of a built-in printer the itinerary is reproduced on a pre-printed map and provided with supplementary data, such as addresses, phone numbers and business hours. Comparable systems have found their way to owners of personal computers to map out travel routes, railway connections, etc.

Typical for the new electronic applications is the option to introduce layers of information. With maps produced in this way each category of information is stored in a separate layer. There are applications that allow a user to select from more than a hundred of these layers. At the user's command layers can be 'turned on or off', so that many thematic maps can be derived from one basic map. It is also possible to design maps adapted to different levels of knowledge (for use in schools, for adults, or for experts) or maps to support different kinds of tasks (very detailed for everyday use and simplified for general planning). Another option is to design maps for the visually handicapped: large letters, bright colours, etc. We are no longer limited to the colours, symbols, and types of lines which we selected earlier, because with every application they can be redefined.

However, the most important development is that an increasing number of geographical databases can be linked up with graphic design equipment. This means that the data can be generated from the basic map, and that the role of the designer is limited to graphic designing. An impressive example of such semi-automatic map production is the map material for the preliminary policy-making paper on the proposed construction of the 'Betuwelijn', a railway line for freight trains only, connecting the Rotterdam harbour with the German industrial region just across the eastern border of The Netherlands. At relatively little expense a large number of maps were produced, covering various aspects of this railway line.

With these new, advanced developments map designers should shift their attention from the actual map-making to what is now seen as the preliminary work in which all the visual ingredients have to be selected in such a way that they will harmonize in the final product. One can expect that the map design of the future will be restricted to designing the legend from which every map required can be generated by means of statistical and graphic software.

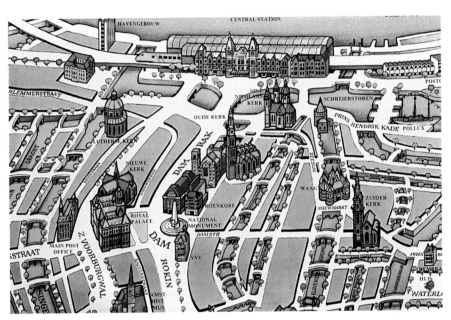

**Plate 17.1**   Tourist map of Amsterdam, designed by Oogappel Design. Only the buildings of interest are shown in elevation on a bird's-eye view map.

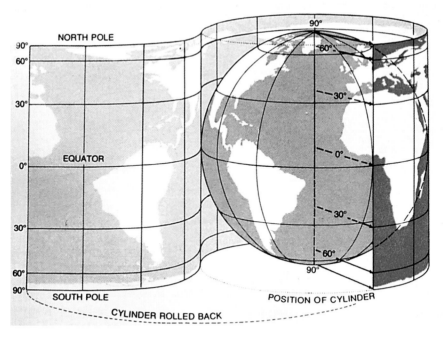

**Plate 17.2** Cylindrical projection of the globe on a flat surface (from Gardner, 1975, p. 121).

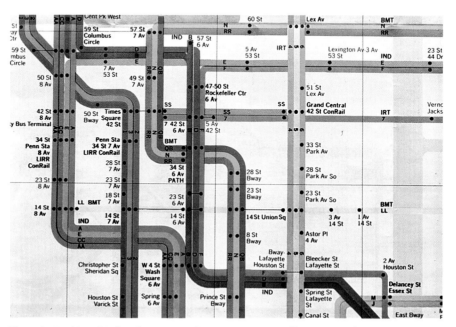

**Plate 17.3** New York subway map by Massimo Vignelli (New York City Transport Authority, 1978). The structure of Manhattan is barely distinguishable.

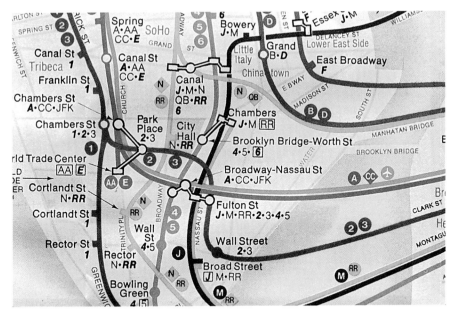

**Plate 17.4** A revised map of the New York subway, designed by John Taurenac in 1979 (New York City Transport Authority, 1979). Compared with the map of Plate 17.3, the subway lines are represented topographically more correctly, and the street pattern is clearly recognizable.

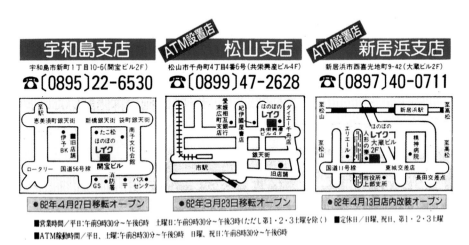

**Plate 17.5** Wayfinding maps in an advertisement of a chain of department stores in Tokyo.

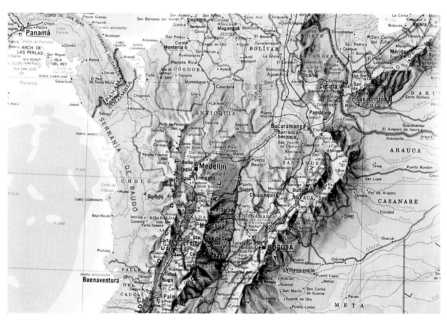

**Plate 17.6** Satellite surveys changed the ideas about the use of colours, as reflected in an atlas by Rand McNally (*The International Atlas*, Rand McNally & Company).

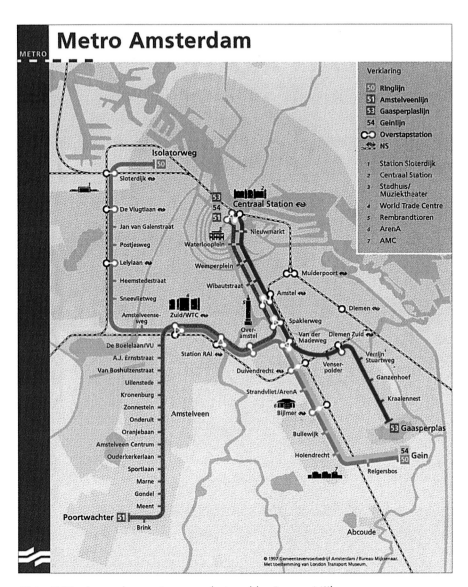

**Plate 17.7** Amsterdam metro map, designed by Bureau Mijksenaar (Gemeentevervoerbedrijf Amsterdam, 1997). It is a topographically correct map with Beck-like station symbols and line colours.

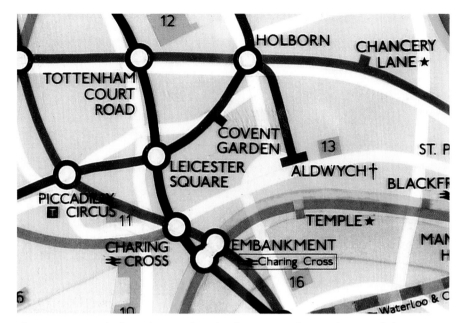

**Plate 17.8** Detail of a redesign of Beck's famous London Underground diagram by the Visual Information Design Group at Delft University of Technology. The redesigned map shows, correctly, that Aldwych station (now closed) is within a five-minute walking distance from Temple station. Beck's map suggests that the two stations are 45 minutes apart (by train).

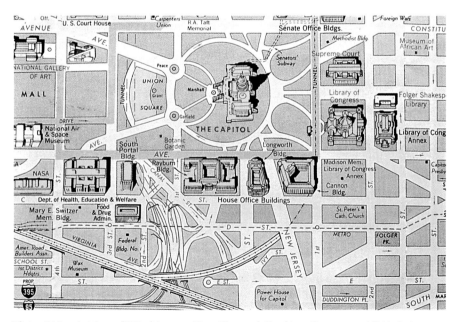

**Plate 17.9** A Map of Washington City (General Drafting Company, USA). It is an exemplary combination of a flat map and a three-dimensional representation of buildings, bridges and fly-overs.

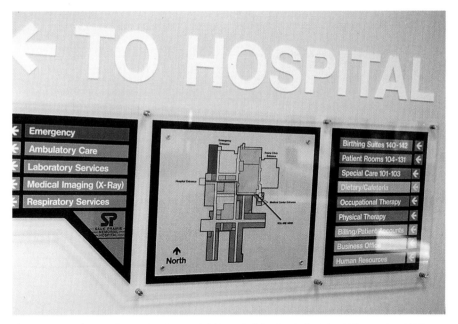

**Plate 18.1** The Sauk Prairie Memorial Hospital in Sauk Prairie, Wisconsin, USA (new design).

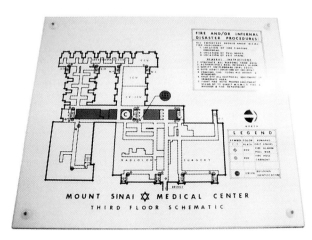

**Plate 18.2** The Sauk Prairie Memorial Hospital in Sauk Prairie, Wisconsin, USA (old design).

## 17.6  THE FUTURE OF MAPS

Maps, like no other medium, provide an insight into spatial relations. For other types of information their usefulness is limited: maps lack the possibility to reproduce exact data, unless these are added in a numeric form, as with a table; they cannot show causal relationships like a graph or a diagram; they lack the veracity of a photograph or illustration and always need a description or explanation. In infographics, pictures with additional information, we see the use of maps restricted to their specific possibilities; together with many other visual means maps can tell a story in images.

The proper combination of maps and other visual means is a difficult information design problem. Therefore, there is a strong need to make an inventory of relevant cognitive, ergonomic, graphic and conceptual criteria. This may seem only a matter of compiling the findings of literature searches, but it has proved to be a rather unsuccessful approach. It appears that, at present, these criteria are very incomplete. New knowledge has to be acquired to fill the many gaps.

It is expected that new ways of using maps will only be induced by technical progress in the field of electronic data processing. To steer this technology push in the right direction, more research into the requirements and abilities of the individual user is required. This development will force map-makers to integrate the right data sources with the right means of data transmission.

Love for maps and map-phobia: the former is even more outrageous than the latter. Maps do not fail to fascinate. If you are prepared to invest some effort beforehand, a map can be an efficient, dependable and practical travel companion, and for those who know how to appreciate a map, it can be a graphic treasure.

### REFERENCES

GARDNER, M. (1975) Mathematical games. On map projections (with special reference to some inspired ones). *Scientific American* **233**, 120–125.

GARLAND, K. (1994) *Mr Beck's Underground Map*. Harrow Weald, Middlesex: Capital Transport.

ISO (1979) *Public-information Symbols: Index, Survey, and Compilation of the Single Sheets, ISO 7001*. Geneva: International Organization for Standardization.

# CHAPTER EIGHTEEN

# Theory and research in design of 'You Are Here' maps

MICHAEL J. O'NEILL

## 18.1 INTRODUCTION

Within buildings and other large-scale environments, 'You Are Here' (YAH) maps are often used to provide orientation information, and guide wayfinding. In this chapter our understanding of spatial cognitive processes, informational cues provided by the built environment, and wayfinding behaviour will be related to the design and application of YAH maps. Other issues such as facility type, and user group characteristics and capabilities, are also considered. The YAH map can be the focal point for a wayfinding information system that integrates orientation information from a variety of sources.

The chapter begins with a discussion of the costs associated with facilities in which wayfinding is a problem. A model of the wayfinding task is then described, including a brief overview of cognitive processes involved in creating and using a mental map of the environment. The architectural features (including signage) typically used as wayfinding cues are discussed. Next an overview is presented of the research on signage and YAH maps as they relate to actual wayfinding behaviour. Following this section, other issues pertinent to development of effective YAH maps are discussed, including: purpose of the visit to the building, informational needs of the users, and capabilities and limitations of users. Next, a summary of design criteria for the development of effective YAH maps is presented. These general criteria draw from sections presented earlier in this chapter, including: theory on how people develop and use cognitive representations of the environment, physical design features that can be used as wayfinding cues, the research on signage and wayfinding behaviour, and user intentions and characteristics. Finally, two examples of recently implemented wayfinding systems using YAH maps are presented to highlight the use of the criteria presented in the chapter.

### 18.1.1 The wayfinding problem

Lynch (1960) thought that design characteristics could affect the 'legibility' of a city. Lynch defined legibility as 'the ease with which its [the city's] parts can be recognized and can be organized into a coherent pattern'. At the building scale, legibility has been defined as 'the degree to which a building facilitates the ability of users to find their way within it' (Weisman, 1981). This definition of legibility implies that there is a link between the characteristics of the physical environment, and subsequent wayfinding behaviour.

The legibility of the architectural environment is an important design issue that influences the ease of wayfinding for many people. Evans (1982, p. 94) notes that the illegibility of a setting may induce stress by producing confusion and a feeling of incompetence. He suggests that legibility should be 'considered a criterion for useable habitats' for all users. Passini's opinion (1980) is that ease of wayfinding should become an active design criterion because of the costs of illegible design in lost time and efficiency. Weisman (1987) suggests that the degree of architectural legibility can affect the degree of activity, sense of control, and safety in emergency situations for the institutionalized elderly.

Numerous studies have discussed the importance of being able to find one's way through the built environment (Evans, 1980; Garling and Evans, 1991). These studies have found that when people have problems with wayfinding, there are costs in terms of time, money and public safety (Reizenstein et al., 1986; Weisman, 1987). There are also indirect human costs, such as stress resulting from disorientation in complex buildings (Evans et al., 1984). The very function of a building is impeded if wayfinding within it is a difficult task (Garling and Lindberg, 1984). For instance, a post-occupancy evaluation of an office building in New Zealand revealed that half of the sample of users had so much difficulty with wayfinding in the building that they required assistance from the staff (Beaumont et al., 1984). In a hospital setting at the University of Michigan, the result of a study showed that in a one-week period, 70 per cent of the staff had given directions to visitors, indicating the degree to which wayfinding was a problem there (Carpman et al., 1984).

Clearly, wayfinding problems occur in a variety of built settings and for many types of building users. The most common approach to solving wayfinding problems is to apply signage, or to redesign existing signs. The vast majority of these efforts are only partially successful, or outright failures. There are several reasons why wayfinding problems continue to plague both new and old buildings. Firstly, there is a lack of understanding about the cognitive processes that people employ to understand and use environmental information to solve wayfinding problems. Secondly, there is a lack of understanding about the environmental cues that people employ to orient and find their way within buildings. Finally, there is an inability to integrate knowledge about the cognitive processes involved in orientation and wayfinding, and the role of environmental cues in these processes, into the design of signage (especially 'You Are Here' maps). In addition, signage design and application rarely considers the viewpoint that signage is just one part of a wayfinding system – the building (including its unique features and layout), and the user him/ herself are the other two components of that system.

## 18.2   THE WAYFINDING MODEL

A wayfinding task is typically composed of a number of smaller problem solving tasks that culminate in finding the destination. Especially in large and complex settings, finding the destination does not occur in one step. Rather, wayfinding consists of starting from a known point and attempting to reach an intermediate subgoal. At this intermediate subgoal the user reorients him/herself and decides which direction to take to the next subgoal, until the task is complete.

Some type of decision-making process takes place at each choice point in the environment. Physical landmarks play a role in orientation during the wayfinding process. A variety of architectural features can act as landmarks at decision points. Larger scale landmarks can aid in the identification of 'regions' within a building. For example, a region could be the area in a shopping mall where the restaurants are grouped. Regardless of the scale of the environment, the wayfinding process is composed of perceptual input from physical features within the built environment and the cognitive processes by which we structure and use this information to find our way.

### 18.2.1   The cognitive map

The physical characteristics of the environment that we use as cues to find our way through the environment are stored in a mental representation of some type (Golledge, 1991). The psychological structure responsible for storing and retrieving spatial information about the environment is often referred to as the *cognitive map* (Tolman, 1948; Kaplan and Kaplan, 1982). The accuracy of the information in the cognitive map can influence wayfinding performance (O'Neill, 1991a, 1991b).

The cognitive map can store 'route' and 'survey' representations (Tolman, 1948). Route representations contain knowledge about individual places and the way they are connected through experience; the 'travelability' between places (Kuipers, 1983). This is known as 'topological' knowledge. Survey representations contain knowledge about metrical relations, such as the distance and direction of places in relation to each other. Developmental evidence suggests that people first learn routes, and over time develop more holistic survey representations of space (Hart and Moore, 1973). Thus, a basic element for successful wayfinding is knowledge of the connections between places, since this information is necessary for selecting successful routes from start to destination, even if one does not know how far away or in what direction the destination lies (O'Neill, 1991a).

## 18.2.2   Environmental features

People rely on various forms of environmental information to find their way through buildings. Five types of environmental features are used to aid orientation during wayfinding, including: landmarks, plan configuration, visual access, architectural differentiation; and signage (Lynch, 1960; Weisman, 1981). Landmarks serve as important physical cues to memory about individual locations within a building. Plan configuration is the overall form of the building's floor plan layout. The complexity of a plan has a powerful impact on wayfinding performance (O'Neill, 1992). Visual access involves the ability to see ahead to other useful landmarks or cues within, or outside, the building. Architectural differentiation is a design characteristic in which different areas within a building are visually distinct from each other (such as through the use of colour, different types of carpeting, ceiling heights, etc.). Signage is a form of environmental information that is common to almost every building with many new or infrequent visitors.

Signage, including 'You Are Here' (YAH) maps and directional symbols are typically employed to compensate for the complex floor plan layouts of settings such as underground railways (subways), hospitals, large governmental facilities, and even parks and other large outdoor areas. These are environments in which wayfinding is a chronic problem. Three types of information are commonly presented to assist wayfinding: identification (room numbers, business or department names), directional (arrows, text directions and graphic symbols), and layout (including 'You Are Here' maps and floor plans) (Passini, 1980; O'Neill, 1991c).

### 18.3   RESEARCH ON YAH MAPS AND SIGNAGE

Best (1970) found that signage placed at decision points in buildings improved wayfinding performance. Corlett *et al.* (1972) simplified existing signs within a university building and moved them to corridor intersections (decision points), and found that people took significantly less time to find their destinations after those changes. Wener and Kaminoff (1983) developed informational and directional signage for a visitors' reception area in a correctional facility. Signs (in two languages) placed at the entrance of the facility gave textual information on services available. A sign placed in the lobby area used directional arrows and text and symbols to direct visitors to various locations. Self-report measures taken from visitors showed that perceived length of wait, crowding and anger were significantly reduced for visitors after the introduction of the signs. There was also a significant reduction in observed wayfinding errors by visitors after the new signage was installed.

Garling *et al.* (1983) found that people with restricted visual access to their destination within a building learned the layout significantly more slowly than people with visual access. However, when given access to a map of the floor plan, the group with low visual access learned as quickly as people having visual access. The use of floor plan maps in this study parallels the application of schematized floor plans, such as 'You Are Here' maps in buildings. The findings suggest that the format and type of information contained within 'You Are Here' maps may assist building users in overcoming the negative effects of buildings designed with poor visual access.

Levine (1982) and Levine et al. (1984) proposed two fundamental principles for the design of 'You Are Here' maps: structure matching and orientation. Structure matching has to do with relating the shape or layout of the drawing of the floor plan to the shape of the actual building or area it represents. A minimum amount of graphic information is required so the viewer can understand the correspondence between the drawing and the real world. The orientation of this structure is also critical to the usefulness of the map to the viewer. The map should be oriented in such a way that the features displayed by the map are logically aligned with the view seen from a position in front of the sign. Levine et al. (1984) found that the proper structure and orientation of 'You Are Here' maps was related to improvements in wayfinding performance.

Research also suggests that a decrease in wayfinding performance can result if individual signs are poorly designed or the overall signage strategy is incorrect. In addition, user group characteristics may influence the degree to which signage is relied on for wayfinding guidance. Carpman et al. (1984) found that as the number of signs in a hospital hallway increased, wayfinding performance decreased. Seidel (1983) found that 76 per cent of people who had difficulty wayfinding in a large metropolitan airport had trouble understanding the signage, and 30 per cent of the sample felt there were too many signs. Weisman (1987) found that only 18 per cent of nursing home residents mentioned the use of signage as a strategy for wayfinding. The remaining 82 per cent mentioned using other architectural features as cues for orientation.

Beaumont et al. (1984) found that there was no significant difference in wayfinding performance between people who read a building directory sign and those who did not in a large governmental facility. The people they studied were more likely to employ strategies such as following others in hopes of locating their destination, or asking questions of other visitors. Their analysis of the signage system indicated that wayfinding problems were caused by poor signage location and redundant signs that confused visitors. They simplified the signs and relocated them to positions that were more usable to visitors (for instance, signs directly in front of elevators). The situational context can also influence how people use signs. In a review of almost 400 fires, Bryan (1982) found that in buildings with signage, less than 8 per cent of people fleeing fires reported relying on signage to find their way to exits.

O'Neill (1991c) examined the effects of three different signage conditions (no signage, textual signage or graphic signage) on actual wayfinding behaviour. The experiment took place within five different buildings varying from simple to complex in floor plan layout. Across all settings, the addition of signage resulted in a 13 per cent increase in rate of travel, a 50 per cent decrease in wrong turns, and a 62 per cent decrease in backtracking. Graphic signage produced the greatest rate of travel in all settings, but textual signage was the most effective in reducing wayfinding errors, such as wrong turns and backtracking. These results suggest that when time is not a constraint, textual signage is generally the most effective means of reducing major wayfinding errors, such as wrong turns. Perhaps textual signage produces the greatest accuracy because it provides the most explicit information to users. It probably takes longer to process textual information, hence the sacrifice in rate of travel with this type of signage. In this study, graphic symbols were less effective in terms of promoting wayfinding accuracy, but were better than no signage at all. Due to the focus of this study, it was not possible to determine whether the comprehensibility of the symbols was related to this outcome. In general however, the results suggest that graphic signage may be most appropriate for conditions in which rate of travel is the top priority and a high level of accuracy is less important.

Butler *et al.* (1993) examined different types of graphic and textual signage and concluded that wayfinding signs are more effective than 'You Are Here' maps for people with little prior knowledge of a building, perhaps because of the higher cognitive load imposed by maps. They suggested that people are more comfortable reading and simply following signs through a building.

## 18.4   USER GROUP AND SITUATIONAL CONSIDERATIONS

Before a signage system can be designed, a general analysis of the situational context and users' needs must be conducted. This analysis will help determine the requirements of the users. This information can be derived through meetings with client representatives to develop an understanding of the function of the facility and the purpose of visits.

### 18.4.1   Informational needs of the user group

The overall informational needs of the user group should be established. Is long-term learning desired over the course of repeated visits to the facility, or is the goal of the signage to provide immediate guidance to specific locations?

Where long-term learning is desired, the YAH map should be the primary source of wayfinding information, through representation of the building layout and important landmarks. This knowledge will permit the visitor to locate a variety of areas or places within the building due to broader understanding of the layout. In the case in which learning building layout is not important or desired, use of directional signage may be the most effective tactic.

In addition, the previous experience and knowledge of the building that the typical visitor possesses must be considered. Does the layout or function of the various areas within the building change regularly? Situations in which functions of areas within the building change often may require the construction of a YAH map using materials that allow labels to be easily changed, rather than creating an entire new map. Is security an issue? Do you want people to have detailed knowledge of all areas of the building? Such cases may dictate that the YAH map should be more schematic in nature, still showing major routes but omitting details of other areas.

## 18.4.2   The purpose of a typical visit

Consider the difference between a visit to a shopping mall and a visit to a hospital. The purposes of the visits are quite different in terms of stress experienced along with the visit, time pressures and outcomes of inaccurate wayfinding. Consumer spatial behaviour is influenced by variables such as needs, wants and social values (O'Neill and Jasper, 1992). Inaccurate wayfinding has few critical consequences for consumers.

Visitors to hospitals are often wayfinding under conditions of psychological stress, physical pain or time constraints, all of which serve to lower cognitive function temporarily (Reizenstein *et al.*, 1986). Hospital visits require a high degree of wayfinding accuracy.

## 18.4.3   User group characteristics and capabilities

The characteristics of a typical user, such as: age, language spoken, mobility, intellectual capability or physical disabilities should be considered when deciding on the placement, location and design of the YAH map. For instance, visual decrements associated with aged people may require larger lettering and high contrast backgrounds on YAH maps containing text.

### 18.5   DESIGN CRITERIA FOR YAH MAPS

In order to design effective YAH maps, several aspects of our wayfinding model need to be considered. An understanding of the process by which people create a cognitive map, and use that information, must be incorporated into YAH map design. An understanding of the wayfinding process is also important. The informational goals of the signage system, the purpose of a typical visit, and user group characteristics need to be understood. Most important is the understanding that signage, YAH maps and building design features form a system of information representation to the user, which need to be integrated into any potential solution. Each of these facets of the problem, as well as the wayfinding research described in the previous section, allow us to create a framework around which we can develop a number of key concepts leading to design criteria for YAH maps. Expense, time to develop the signage/map and life cycle of the signage system are additional important elements to consider.

These findings can be summarized to form research-based criteria for the development of YAH maps and signage. These criteria are summarized as follows:

1   People rely on a variety of architectural cues (such as atriums, elevators, variations in floor and wall colour, visual access to outside landmarks, plan configuration, etc.) to find their way through buildings. These architectural features form a system of landmarks. Design the YAH map in a way that incorporates those cues, when possible.

2   Orient YAH maps so they reflect the actual orientation of layout as seen from the location of the viewer. The map should be oriented so that 'forward is up'. If this is not done, then the user will have to mentally realign the map with the actual environment.

3   Information required for a correct decision must be close at hand. Place directional signage and YAH maps at decision points within the environment (such as corridor intersections, intersections of walkways). This will serve the dual purpose of placing the information where it is needed most (at a decision point), and the map or signage itself will become a landmark in the users' cognitive map of the building.

4   Use YAH maps within areas with restricted access to orientation landmarks (such as views to the outside from hallways, or short narrow hallways that block longer views to interior landmarks). The YAH maps will serve to supplement the missing orientation cues resulting from restricted visual access.

5   Relate the shape of the floor plan drawn in the YAH map to the actual shape of the building floor plan. This will reinforce learning of the facility layout, and make the YAH map easier to use.

6   Design directional signage to work as part of a system with the YAH map (for example, match colour of background, lettering size and type). This technique should allow you to reduce the number of signs used overall in the facility, which has been shown to enhance wayfinding effectiveness.

7   Locate YAH maps at main building entry points, mounted at locations that users can see and find easily.

8   YAH maps should combine graphics with minimal text to enhance the speed of wayfinding through the building, and maximize accuracy.

9   Employ YAH maps when time to destination is not a critical factor, because additional cognitive processing time is required to understand this type of information. Use YAH maps when the intent is to help users build a 'cognitive map', create a long-term understanding of building layout and function.

   Do not use YAH maps for 'one shot' or 'one location' visits. The best application for YAH maps is for recurring visitors who may need to learn multiple locations. If a YAH map is used in these situations, keep the layout simple and minimize the amount of information displayed. They may also be used within facilities such as hotels, if they are used in combination with signage for leading people out in emergencies.

10  People learn individual routes through buildings before they learn the overall layout. The YAH map should resemble a schematic of main corridor elements, as opposed to looking like an architectural floor plan.

11  Problems related to lack of comprehension of the information in YAH maps can cause stress and further disorientation. A YAH map that contains too much information cannot be understood effectively. There should be a balance between repeating information and overwhelming the viewer with information.

This is a critical point for YAH maps, which must present enough graphic information of the layout of the environment to cue and orient the user, but not too much detail, which can cause confusion. There are no prescribed measures for determining the level of complexity of a given YAH map, but if outside professional assistance is not within the realm of possibility, consider the 5-plus-or-minus-2 rule. The YAH map should not try to convey more than seven major pieces of information (floor plan shape, text about different building areas locations, YAH symbol, a colour coding scheme showing functional areas, etc.) and ideally around five information 'chunks'. An example of an overly complex YAH map is one in which multiple floors are displayed on the same map, often in different colours, with access points to different floors shown. Once the other necessary information is added to the map, the amount of information quickly becomes overwhelming. A quick comprehension test is to show a prototype map to a small test group of typical users. The average user should be able to identify their current location on the map, and explain how to get to a destination point (referring to the map) in less than one minute.

12   Design the 'You Are Here' marker within the YAH map to show the correct location and orientation of the user as they stand looking at the map. Failure to do this is the single most important mistake made when designing YAH maps. If possible, link the location of the 'You Are Here' marker to a distinct landmark in the environment.

13   Understand and work with the architectural context in which the signage will be placed. One way of accomplishing this is to refer to architectural elements in YAH maps and signage (atrium spaces, information desk, an area with plants, main elevator stack, etc.). Care must be taken to ensure that the symbol is selected to represent an architectural element on the map (such as the information desk) in a way that will quickly be recognized and understood by the users. A second approach to working with architectural context is to locate signage near major architectural cues (such as entrances). Additional reinforcement of this cue can then be provided by referring to the architectural cue in the YAH map.

14   People can understand YAH maps that are drawn in perspective view better than maps drawn in plan view. However, care must be taken to minimize the complexity of the perspective drawing. This type of approach often results in an overly complex YAH map (Guideline 11), and should be approached with some caution. In general, the traditional 'plan view' YAH map is preferable.

15   Do not use specialized terms, jargon or abbreviations within the YAH map. These may cause confusion and frustration for the user of the YAH map.

16   YAH maps should have built-in flexibility. Some facilities, such as hospitals and shopping malls, experience a great deal of change of location of functional areas, and thus reconfiguration of space. The physical construction of the YAH map and associated signage should be designed for ease of change to ensure that the YAH map is kept up to date with changes to the facility.

## 18.6   RECENT EXAMPLES OF YAH MAP IMPLEMENTATION

Hospital environments are often cited as a source of wayfinding problems for visitors. The Sauk Prairie Memorial Hospital (in Sauk Prairie, Wisconsin, USA) administration wanted to make their environment more user-friendly, and counter any new wayfinding problems that might develop as a result of a three-storey addition recently added to the facility. Their concerns centred around vertical circulation (related to the addition), and the potential for confusion because of the addition of two new main entrances, creating a total of four main entrances.

The design group that was retained to develop a wayfinding system that would address these needs, started by meeting with the administration to gather information about the intent of the facility as it relates to its users, the profile of the users, and other user characteristics. This consulting group then evaluated the existing wayfinding system, including: signage, floor plan layout, and architectural features that might be used for wayfinding. Through a questionnaire, a survey was conducted to assess problems and needs relating to wayfinding for staff and visitors. The design group then made recommendations to the administration, which included not only the design of the signage but also its placement, and they selected the signage vendor who would actually develop the signage.

Plate 18.1 shows a YAH map that was designed and installed as part of the solution for this facility. The development of this YAH map, and the associated signage, draws upon a number of the criteria described in this chapter. The numbers following in parentheses after descriptions of the signage refer to the criteria described in the previous section.

A system for wayfinding within the building was developed. The purpose of the system was to facilitate long-term learning of the hospital layout by staff and visitors (9). Interior design ideas relating to the creation of landmarks (such as graphics, interior colours, plants, creation of visually distinct areas) were developed. The consulting team recommended a simplification in corridor layout to enhance wayfinding, and to simplify grouping of departments. The intended effect of these changes was to enhance the imageability (Hunt, 1985) of the layout and permit users to form a cognitive map of the building more quickly (1). The YAH map is oriented as the user faces the map (left on the map is left in the actual building, right is right) (2). At important decision points such as corridor intersections, additional signage keyed to the YAH map enhances understanding of primary corridors and circulation routes in the building (3). The overall shape of the floor plan in the YAH map is identical to the plan of the building (5). Shape is simplified but scale is not distorted. The YAH map text, information, directions and colour match sign units throughout the facility, easing the identification of the appropriate signage by users as they engage in wayfinding tasks (6). The YAH maps are located at the two primary entrances (7), which also serve as important landmarks. The YAH map text is simple, and intended for users with low visual acuity and/or reading ability (8). To minimize cognitive processing required when reading the YAH map, text on the diagram of the map is minimized (8). Primary corridors are depicted without colour, to contrast with the areas on the YAH map that represent building departments (10). The YAH map is designed to be read by users that have limited time and understanding of buildings. Thus, only necessary information is displayed on the YAH map (11). The 'You Are Here' marker is placed to show the correct orientation and location of the users as they read the map (12). It is placed against a different colour background to increase contrast and readability. This YAH map is drawn in 'plan' view as opposed to 'perspective' view. This is acceptable in this case since the building is primarily a one-storey design (14). The YAH map uses colour to identify different functional areas within the building, helping the viewer to organize the space. The textual signage to the left and right of the YAH map (Plate 18.1) is colour keyed to the colours of the areas of the building shown on the YAH map. Thus, when the user enters the desired area, the associated signage in that area bears the colour coding used to depict that area on the YAH map (6). Directional signs are used in combination with the YAH map. Both wall units and overhead signs are used (6). All the components of the YAH map are modular, and can be easily removed and replaced with updated information, saving the time and expense of complete redrawing, redesign and reconstruction of a new YAH map every time there are changes in the facilities (18).

This wayfinding solution takes the systems approach in which a wayfinding system, drawing on all available visual cues, was designed. In this example, the YAH map is the focal point for a wayfinding information system that integrates orientation information from a variety of sources.

Plate 18.2 shows an older YAH map that is typical of earlier approaches to the design of YAH maps in large facilities. This map is placed to the side of an elevator bank, and thus is often not noticed by users who are disembarking from the elevator as they enter this area of the building (3, 7). The map is not oriented in the correct way so that the viewer must mentally rotate the map to attain the correct orientation (2). This YAH map effectively employs a schematic of an actual building floor plan. Main routes through a building are shown in simplified form. The YAH map shows the unique shape of the building exterior (see top of floor plan in map, Plate 18.1), which is architecturally different from other areas of the building. This display of information assists the viewer in orientation within a region of the building, and helps in forming a mental image of overall layout (1, 5). This YAH map has a great deal of text that is unrelated to the purpose of the sign, that is, to provide wayfinding information. The text is too small to be read by people with impaired vision (8, 11). The building area labels use abbreviations and jargon (16). The YAH map was not developed to work with signage, or other visual cues in other parts of the building (13). This YAH map is drawn on a single sheet, so that if layout of the building changes, or the function of areas changes, a complete redrawing of the map is required (17). All this tends to lead to inaccurate YAH maps since facilities rarely budget for major signage costs along with facilities redesign.

### 18.7 SUMMARY

The purpose of this chapter was to relate our understanding of spatial cognitive processes, informational cues provided by the built environment, and wayfinding behaviour, to the design and application of YAH maps. Other issues such as facility type, and user group characteristics and capabilities, were considered. It is argued that the YAH map can be the focal point of a wayfinding information system that integrates orientation information from a variety of sources. The criteria developed in this chapter draw upon our understanding of spatial cognition, the wayfinding task and the cues that people use to navigate through the environment. The design criteria are purposely kept at a general level so that they may be applicable to the widest range of built environments.

The case study described in this chapter demonstrates a theme discussed by Passini (Chapter 19), namely, that design for wayfinding needs to be integrated as part of the architectural design process. Passini notes the need for collaboration between architects and graphic designers for developing wayfinding systems. This chapter described one potential process for a close collaboration between architect, wayfinding consultant and signage designer. In this way, the implementation of a wayfinding system, incorporating all possible physical design elements, can best be realized.

## ACKNOWLEDGEMENTS

The author would like to thank Stephen Boelter of the Boelter Design Group (Verona, Wisconsin, USA) for generously sharing project information of Sauk Prairie Memorial Hospital, which is used to illustrate many of the criteria discussed in this chapter.

## REFERENCES

BEAUMONT, P., GRAY, J., MOORE, G. and ROBINS, B. (1984) Orientation and wayfinding in the Tauranga Departmental Building: a focused post-occupancy evaluation. In: DUERK, D. and CAMPBELL, D. (Eds), *Proceedings of the 15th Annual Conference of the Environmental Design Research Association*, pp. 77–91. San Luis Obispo, CA.

BEST, G. A. (1970) Direction-finding in large buildings. In: CANTER, D. (Ed.), *Architectural Psychology*. London: RIBA Publications.

BRYAN, J. (1982) *Implications for Codes and Behavior Models from the Analysis of Behavior Response Patterns in Fire Situations as Selected from the Project People and Project People II Study Programs*. College Park, MD: College of Engineering, University of Maryland.

BUTLER, D. L., ACQUINO, A. L., HISSONG, A. A. and SCOTT, P. (1993) Way finding by newcomers in a complex building. *Human Factors* **35**, 159–173.

CARPMAN, J. R., GRANT, M. A. and SIMONS, D. A. (1984) *No More Mazes: Research About Design for Way Finding in Hospitals*, Patient and Visitor Participation Project. Ann Arbor, MI: University of Michigan Hospitals.

CORLETT, E., MANENICA, I. and BISHOP, R. (1972) The design of direction finding systems in buildings. *Applied Ergonomics* **3**, 66–69.

EVANS, G. W. (1980) Environmental cognition. *Psychological Bulletin* **88**, 259–287.

EVANS, G. W. (Ed.) (1982) *Environmental Stress*. New York: Cambridge University Press.

EVANS, G. W., SKORPANICH, M. A., GARLING, T., BRYANT, K. and BRESOLIN, B. (1984) The effects of pathway configuration, landmarks and stress on environmental cognition. *Journal of Environmental Psychology* **4**, 323–335.

GARLING, T. and EVANS, G. (Eds) (1991) *Environment, Cognition, and Action: An Integrated Approach*. New York, NY: Oxford Press.

GARLING, T. and LINDBERG, E. (1984) Postoccupancy evaluation of spatial orientation and way finding. In: DUERK, D. and CAMPBELL, D. (Eds), *Proceedings of the 15th Annual Conference of the Environmental Design Research Association*. San Luis Obispo, CA.

GARLING, T., LINDBERG, E. and MANTYLA, T. (1983) Orientation in buildings: effects of familiarity, visual access, and orientation aids. *Journal of Applied Psychology* **68**, 177–186.

GOLLEDGE, R. G. (1991) Cognition of physical and built environments. In: GARLING, T. and EVANS, G. (Eds), *Environment, Cognition, and Action: An Integrated Approach*. New York, NY: Oxford Press.

HART, R. A. and MOORE, G. T. (1973) The development of spatial cognition: a review. In: DOWNS, R. and STEA, D. (Eds), *Image and Environment*, pp. 246–288. New York: Aldine.

HUNT, M. E. (1985) Enhancing a building's imageability. *Journal of Architectural Planning Research* **2**, 151–168.

KAPLAN, S. and KAPLAN, R. (1982) *Cognition and Environment: Functioning in an Uncertain World*. New York: Praeger (Ulrich's, Ann Arbor, 1989).

KUIPERS, B. J. (1983) The cognitive map: could it have been any other way? In: ACREDOLO, L. and PICK, H. (Eds), *Spatial Orientation: Research, Application, and Theory*. New York: Plenum.

LEVINE, M. (1982) You-are-here maps: psychological considerations. *Environment and Behavior* **14**, 221–237.

LEVINE, M., MARCHON, I. and HANLEY, G. (1984) The placement and misplacement of you-are-here maps. *Environment and Behavior* **16**, 139–157.

LYNCH, K. (1960) *The Image of the City*. Cambridge, MA: MIT Press.

O'NEILL, M. J. (1991a) Evaluation of a conceptual model of architectural legibility. *Environment and Behavior* **23**, 259–284.

O'NEILL, M. J. (1991b) A biologically based model of spatial cognition and way finding. *Journal of Environmental Psychology* **11**, 299–320.

O'NEILL, M. J. (1991c) Effects of signage and floor plan configuration on way finding accuracy. *Environment and Behavior* **23**, 553–574.

O'NEILL, M. J. (1992) Effects of familiarity and plan complexity on way finding in simulated buildings. *Journal of Environmental Psychology* **12**, 319–327.

O'NEILL, M. J. and JASPER, C. R. (1992) An evaluation of models of consumer behavior using the environment-behavior paradigm. *Environment and Behavior* **24**, 411–440.

PASSINI, R. E. (1980) Way finding: a conceptual framework. *Man-Environment Systems* **10**, 22–30.

REIZENSTEIN, M., CARPMAN, J., GRANT, M. and SIMMONS, D. (1986) *Design that Cares*. Chicago: American Hospital Publishing Inc.

SEIDEL, A. (1983) Way finding in public spaces: the Dallas-Fort Worth Airport. In: ARMEDEO, D., GRIFFIN, J. and POTTER, J. (Eds), *Proceedings of the 14th Annual Meeting of the Environmental Design Research Association*. Washington, DC.

TOLMAN, E. (1948) Cognitive maps in rats and men. *The Psychological Review* **55**, 189–208.

WEISMAN, G. D. (1981) Evaluating architectural legibility: way finding in the built environment. *Environment and Behavior* **13**, 189–204.

WEISMAN, G. D. (1987) Improving way-finding and architectural legibility in housing for the elderly. In: REGNIER, V. and PYNOOS, J. (Eds), *Housing the Aged: Design Directives and Policy Considerations*. New York: Elsevier.

WENER, R. and KAMINOFF, R. (1983) Improving environmental information: effects of signs on perceived crowding and behavior. *Environment and Behavior* **15**, 3–20.

# PART SEVEN

# Wayfinding Information

# CHAPTER NINETEEN

# Wayfinding: backbone of graphic support systems

ROMEDI PASSINI

## 19.1   INTRODUCTION

The circulation of people in buildings and cities was never a major issue in the eyes of architects and urban designers. The introduction of signage was, and often still is, a last minute thought and for many architects it represents a necessary evil, to be watched, so as not to 'disfigure' a building. Once sufficient circulation space was provided and signs were installed before opening day there was little more to worry about. Even if some settings, such as large hospitals, interconnected government buildings, and some transportation centres were known to be labyrinthine, it was taken for granted that circulation was no problem. People who had difficulties getting around were thought of as being deprived of a 'sense of orientation' and just had to blame themselves. It is only in recent years that the extent of circulation problems and disorientation, their nuisance and also their functional and financial costs are starting to be recognized.

The term circulation refers to a macro-view of people's movement in a setting which is not particularly suited for understanding problems of disorientation. The intention of the user is usually not to 'circulate' but to reach destinations. Even when going for a stroll, the person has a certain general destination in mind and eventually wants to return to home base. Reaching an unfamiliar place and even just taking a familiar route is in fact a highly complex interactive affair. If circulation refers to the macro-movement of people, 'wayfinding' and 'spatial orientation' relate to how users reach destinations and how they situate themselves in space. Wayfinding is the generic term most often used in today's literature to encompass the perceptual, cognitive and behavioural processes involved in reaching destinations.

Most people find that wayfinding difficulties and disorientation are highly stress-ful even in benign cases when the user of a setting is merely confused or delayed. Delays, of course, can also have more or less serious consequences and can even be life threatening in emergency situations. Transportation centres and airports in par-ticular can be stressful, and people appreciate when they are well designed with respect to wayfinding, a topic that is discussed by Kishnani with respect to Stansted Airport (Chapter 20).

Total disorientation and the sensation of being lost can be a frightening experi-ence and can lead to quite severe emotional reactions (Zimring, 1982; Carpman *et al.*, 1986). Some of these reactions, if rationally assessed, may well appear exagger-ated but they tend to signify more than just temporary spatial uncertainty. They evoke feelings of anxiety and insecurity; they affect self-esteem and judgement of competence. These reactions may well be linked to the evolution of mankind; in prehistory being lost could easily be a question of life and death. Even today, the word 'lost' has strong emotional connotations.

Given the emotional dimension of wayfinding, it is not surprising to find that people include wayfinding criteria when assessing the general quality of a setting. Buildings that cause wayfinding difficulties are certainly not considered design suc-cesses by the general population (Arthur and Passini, 1992). Even the perception of the quality of the services offered might be affected. Many organizations catering to the public have become aware that a poor judgement of wayfinding in the setting affects the way the organization itself is perceived (Carpman *et al.*, 1986). Today, one can find many examples advertising 'easy wayfinding' in hospital settings, commercial malls, museums and other large public settings, to convince the visitor of their user-friendliness.

Wayfinding quality of complex buildings also affects security in emergency evacuation. Without doing injustice to a complex field of study, it can be said that settings which operate well in normal conditions, especially if their floor layout is easily understood and if they offer clear alternatives of exiting, will also be safer in emergencies. The observation that people in emergency situations tend to use routes and exits they know (Canter, 1980; Sime, 1985) indicates that the often half-hidden, never-used emergency exits are not the answer to building safety.

Accessibility is also linked to wayfinding. Many people avoid settings in which they have had experiences of getting lost. Underground parking garages and certain shopping complexes are systematically avoided by some users for no other reasons than wayfinding difficulties. Venemans (Chapter 22) focuses on parking and shows how small design interventions can improve wayfinding and circulation.

The problem of accessibility is even more important for people with physical, sensory and cognitive dysfunction. Users of wheelchairs, if they have to use altern-ative access routes, often have to cope with more complex problems and less adequate information displays (Passini and Shiels, 1986). However, it is people with sensory dysfunction, blind people in particular, who will experience difficult-ies of getting around as being very stressful. This often amounts to psychological barriers to free access (Zimring and Templer, 1984; Passini and Shiels, 1986). The relation between wayfinding and cognitive dysfunction requires special solutions and is explored in the chapter on wayfinding and information processing in dementia (Passini *et al.*, Chapter 21).

## 19.2 WAYFINDING AND SPATIAL ORIENTATION

In the literature of psychology and environmental psychology, the notion of 'wayfinding' was preceded by 'spatial orientation' which referred to a person's ability mentally to imagine or represent a physical setting and to situate him or herself spatially within that representation.

The psychological concept for this mental representation is the 'cognitive map'. Planners tended to prefer the term 'image' (see for example Lynch, 1960). The earliest references to the importance of cognitive maps in spatial orientation were of a descriptive nature (Trowbridge, 1913; Griffin, 1948). Lord (1941), working from an educational perspective, was among the first authors to publish an empirical study of children's orientation abilities. However, it is probably Tolman (1948), who in a classic experiment with (the forever exploited) rats first demonstrated the importance of the cognitive map concept. The experiment showed that the animals learned to find destinations in a labyrinthine arrangement and that this learning could not be explained by the (then) popular stimulus–response model of the behaviourist school of thinking but required a cognitive model and, most importantly, a mapping ability.

The next major figure in this short historical review of spatial orientation research is Kevin Lynch (1960) who in cognitive mapping studies of American cities identified the physical elements people used in mentally constructing the image of their city. The five elements he identified (landmarks, paths, limits, nodes and districts) were assumed to be the components of a 'legible' and 'imageable' city and are still referred to in urban design.

In the early 1970s, researchers explored characteristics of cognitive maps and the various psychological, social, cultural and physical determinants. The existence of two fundamental types of cognitive map was probably among the most consequential results: the first type of map was structured on a linear, sequential basis in reference to the person moving through space – the egocentric map; the second type of map was structured on the basis of organizational characteristics of a setting without reference to the movement or position of the person – the coordinate or survey map (see for example Appleyard, 1970).

During the mid-1970s and early 1980s a certain paradigm shift occurred in the study of spatial orientation and related cognitive research. This shift was brought about by a methodological critique, in particular the difficulty of measuring spatial representation and of discerning the impact of the mode of expression, such as sketching, describing or modelling (Moore, 1979; Evans, 1980). Although most researchers argued that the subjects' output, most often a sketch map, was only a manifestation of a spatial representation and that the word mapping ought to be taken as a metaphor (Downs, 1981), sketches produced by subjects were often interpreted as being their cognitive map. The second argument leading to the paradigm shift was conceptual. It argued that a cognitive map was only a product of a cognitive mapping process that was likely to change and evolve, especially if people moved about in unfamiliar settings and that it was the process of cognitive mapping and not the product that needed to be studied (Downs and Stea, 1977). The third argument came from the anthropological literature and was probably the most important one. It showed that people getting around in monotonous environments like the snow fields of the north, the desert, and particularly the ocean (navigation in the South Sea) could not operate on the basis of a spatial representation (cognitive map) of an undifferentiated environment but had to rely on knowing what to do in order to reach destinations (Gladwin, 1970; Lewis, 1975).

The convergence of these arguments led to the notion of wayfinding which emphasized the processes involved in reaching destinations (Kaplan, 1976; Passini, 1977; Downs and Stea, 1977). The key processes can be modelled as being firstly, decision making and the development of a plan of action; secondly, decision execution, transforming decisions and the decision plan into physical behaviour; and thirdly, information processing comprising environmental perception and cognition, underlying both decision related processes. Wayfinding, in other words, can be seen as a problem solving process with a particularity: it operates in space and requires spatial information. The processing of information thus has to include representations of space, that is, cognitive mapping. For a similar conceptualization see Gärling et al. (1986).

Wayfinding, seen in terms of spatial problem solving, incorporates the previous definition of spatial orientation but it views a cognitive map as a source of information to be combined or partially replaced by other types of information necessary for making and executing decisions. The feeling of disorientation and being lost is, thus, the consequence of not having a cognitive map and of not having or not being able to develop a decision plan to get somewhere.

Cognitive mapping continued to be studied and in recent years has regained its popularity. Psychological research refining the concept of spatial cognition led to the distinction between propositional and analogue representations (Kosslyn et al., 1979) and the relation between verbal and spatial representations (Bryant et al., 1992). Environmental psychologists and planners explored relations between cognitive mapping ease and spatial characteristics such as floor plan configurations (Weisman, 1981; Peponis et al., 1990; O'Neill, 1991), angular and oblique routes (Montello, 1991), and the ability to integrate horizontal and vertical routes (Hanley and Levine, 1983; Montello and Pick, 1993). Other investigations concerned the link between cognitive maps, decision making and wayfinding ease (Gärling and Golledge, 1989; Rovine and Weisman, 1989).

An interesting parallel of disorientation studies is found in the field of neurology and neuropsychology (for a review see Benton, 1969; DeRenzi, 1982). The origin of this literature dates back over a century and comprises case-study reports of disorientation in brain-damaged patients. The studies show the importance and the function of basic spatio-cognitive processes. It is indeed in situations when a particular cognitive process is deficient or inoperative that its function with respect to wayfinding can be assessed. Among the most interesting cases is topographical amnesia, a condition which renders a patient incapable of mapping a route or a setting. Depending on the lesion, other cognitive abilities can remain relatively intact. Disorientation in cases of topographical amnesia is severe and the patient has to develop compensatory strategies in order to get around, such as remembering all of the wayfinding decisions along a path, in other words, memorizing a decision plan. Spatial amnesia shows the intricate relationship between cognitive mapping, decision making and decision execution.

A second major deficiency due to brain damage is topographical agnosia which manifests itself as an inability to recognize places and spatial features seen on previous occasions. A patient may typically describe a view in full detail but will not be able to recognize it if the view is presented at a later stage. Such patients are also severely disoriented; they cannot recognize 'familiar' paths. Compensatory strategies involve the coding of spatial information into verbal cues. Patients may code a typical characteristic of their home and when seeing the characteristics, infer that this is their home. Again we can see the ease and efficiency of spatial cognitive processes which in normal conditions we are blissfully unaware of.

Finally, a third major deficiency, unilateral attention, manifests itself by a rather bizarre condition in which, although the visuo-perceptual abilities are intact, only half of the visual field – usually the right half – has reality. The inexistence of the non-attended field is so total that the person is not even enticed to turn the head to find out. In terms of wayfinding, the person will typically be able to turn to the right but never to the left.

### 19.3    WAYFINDING DESIGN

Two major design interventions characterize wayfinding design: firstly, the spatial organization of functional entities and the ensuing planning of the circulation system which define the wayfinding problems users will have to solve; and secondly, environmental communication which provides the information the user needs to solve the problem. The necessity of considering wayfinding in both spatial organization and environmental communication is well illustrated in the Stansted Airport study by Kishnani (Chapter 20). The redesign of the underground parking garage presented by Venemans (Chapter 22), in contrast, shows the constraints of only being able to change an information system when the spatial cause of the problem is dominant.

Signs and graphic support systems in general are part of environmental communication. However, they cannot be seen independently of spatial organization and the circulation system. We shall, therefore, briefly review the key wayfinding issues in the architectural design of a setting and outline its relation to graphic supports.

### 19.4    SPATIAL ORGANIZATION AND THE CIRCULATION SYSTEM: THE ARCHITECTURAL CONCEPTION

The two notions, spatial organization and circulation system, are closely related. Spatial organization refers to the identification and arrangements of spatial units or zones, while the circulation system refers to its linkage.

### 19.4.1 Spatial organization

Complex settings are generally characterized by different functions located in identifiable spatial units. In a hospital, for example, one may find, among many other functional units, an out-patient unit, an in-patient unit, one unit that might be reserved for children, another for adults, and maybe yet another for the elderly. Within each unit one will also find sub-units grouped according to functions such as in the out-patient unit: a reception and admission unit, a general medical examination unit, a technical examinations unit comprising X-ray, scanning, etc. This first organization of multiple functions into units or zones is very important for wayfinding; it facilitates cognitive mapping of the setting and the formation of decision plans.

The organization of multiple functions into identifiable spatial units provides the person with the raw material to assemble a cognitive map, but it also expresses an order, usually a hierarchical order, to assemble the units into a coherent whole.

With respect to decision making, a person will typically decide to go to the hospital, then go to the out-patient section, then go to the reception, and so on. These spatial units, seen from the perspective of the wayfinding person, are destination zones. A complex setting, in which such ordering had not taken place, in which no destination zones were identifiable, or in which a number of identical destination zones existed, would be totally labyrinthine and no sign system, whatever its ingenuity, could make the setting work. Just imagine a large hospital in which all rooms had been distributed on a random basis!

Any planner and architect will design buildings by ordering spaces into units, but this order is not necessarily maintained. If a department requires more space, some of its facilities might be relocated in a different section of the building because, at that particular time, some space has become available. If space allocation on this basis becomes policy, as it most often is, the building is soon a wayfinding nightmare. Building managers, in our experience, often tend to be unaware of the real cause of wayfinding problems in their settings and will blame signage. The fact that, in such cases, the problems are rarely solved by introducing new signs should surprise nobody.

Similar problems of spatial organization occur in large uni-functional settings such as shopping malls. If there are no functional distinctions among the basic facilities, the whole setting may have a uniform repetitive character. There, the introduction of 'artificial' units through thematic decoration or architecturally distinctive areas can reduce the difficulties.

### 19.4.2  Circulation systems

Among various building typologies (see for example Ching, 1979) one might define a typology based on circulation systems. One might, thus, distinguish between circulation of, firstly, a linear order composed of paths; secondly, a centralized order composed of squares; thirdly, a mixed order (combining linear and centralized orders); and finally, an order of networks characterized by recurring relations between paths and/or squares.

One may be tempted to make a direct link between the type of circulation and the nature and the difficulty of wayfinding. It is easy to see, however, that no such direct link exists. A linear circulation might be among the easiest but it might also be totally confusing when arranged in a labyrinthine fashion. We believe that each system, if properly conceived and expressed, can be functional. The question is how these circulation systems can be designed to facilitate cognitive mapping. We must keep in mind that cognitive mapping is the mental act of organizing into a coherent ensemble that which is perceived in parts. The detection of an organization principle can provide the structuring rule.

We propose three basic organization principles. Settings can be organized according to a geometric form, a geometric law, or they can be arranged on a random basis. In identifying basic organization principles, one can try to find physical descriptors for the whole building. In terms of individual floor plans a number of measures have been explored: geometric configurations (Weisman, 1981), pattern line and sight connections based on Hillier's space syntax (Peponis *et al.*, 1990), and interconnection density referring to the number of links between places (O'Neill, 1991).

Settings which are organized according to a simple geometric form or Gestalt, as it is referred to in the psychological literature on perception, are most common in our architectural landscape. Forms, if they are simple such as an L-form, a T-form, etc., are easily retained. They are most effective organization principles. When buildings with relatively simple forms are linked together, as so often happens in institutional settings, the configuration becomes complex. The perception of the Gestalt, then, is often lost and the user will be incapable of identifying an underlying organization principle.

Settings can also be organized according to a geometric law. Facilities grouped around a central court, facilities arranged in a symmetrical order and arrangements based on rotations or hierarchical relations reflect the most common geometric laws found in architectural and urban design. Some of these, for example hierarchies, are more prevalent in large and complex settings. Buildings which are organized according to a geometric law, such as a symmetry, often also express a strong geometric form.

Settings may also lack organization and one might think that they do not lead to a cognitive map. Mapping studies have shown, however, that even paths following a random pattern (shoestring pattern) can be mapped if the user finds strong landmarks (Siegle and White, 1975). Landmarks can take on the function of anchor points. Information about the setting, the route, experiences, etc. are metaphorically attached to these anchor points. They become the structural foundation of a representation. Memories of events in a person's life tend to be similarly regrouped around major happenings.

If users are not able to perceive a geometric law, they may still be able to perceive a geometric form and if they are not able to perceive the form they may still be able to relate to some major landmarks, and operate as if the setting were organized on a chance basis. This points to the importance of expressing the organization principle and also of expressing landmark features that might be used if, for one reason or another, the principle is not understood by a person.

Understanding the organization principle in complex settings is difficult for many people, even if they use the setting regularly. Moeser (1988) showed that nurses who had worked for at least two years in a complex hospital, did not necessarily develop coordinate (survey) type maps. On the other hand, naive subjects able to consult floor plans, developed them more easily. Orientation maps are one of the few means to communicate the underlying organization principle of a setting. Although map reading is a learned skill (Thorndyke and Stansz, 1980), well-designed maps are generally appreciated and contribute to more satisfying user experiences (Carpman et al., 1986; Talbot et al., 1993).

An orientation map may also be used to complete or confirm a person's already established cognitive map. Sometimes, though, people live with two representations: one figurative, as obtained from an orientation map; one analogue, as obtained from direct experience with the setting (Gärling and Golledge, 1989). These two representations may complement each other; they may also contain conflicting information.

Graphic design can also contribute in helping users to make sense of a setting and, thus, facilitate cognitive mapping. The verbal reinforcement of destination zones, the emphasis given to anchor points, the communication of geometric forms or laws through maps, and the use of colour, texture, super graphics, etc., to indicate destination zones, major routes and landmarks, are all means to facilitate the understanding of the architectural characteristics of a setting.

Planning the circulation system, we have seen, has a major impact on wayfinding ease. It also bears directly on the graphic design of support systems which, as we shall outline in the next section, have to work within the constraints of the established circulation system.

## 19.5 ENVIRONMENTAL COMMUNICATION

The term 'environmental communication' is used purposefully to indicate the link between architectural and graphic information. Few would dispute the observation that wayfinding difficulties are often due to inadequate signage and graphic communication. People are much less aware that these difficulties are often also due to ambiguous architectural messages. The circulation system and its constituent units, that is, paths, squares, transition points and vertical circulation, are all important architectural features. They should not require support from signage. If properly articulated, there is no need for signs to an elevator, or a stair; there is no need for signs marking the location of an entrance or even an exit.

Often messages from architectural and graphic sources are poorly coordinated; sometimes they are even contradictory. It is quite common to find buildings in which a major entrance is clearly indicated by the architectural composition and entrance features, while signs show the user to the real entrance. Graphic communication, moreover, is often expected to compensate for architectural problems: signs may attempt to communicate the message that the entrance is on the other side of the building; the introduction of colour codes may attempt to structure amorphous spatial expression. Sometimes, people even expect graphics to create a spatial order where there is none. The results, however, are often disappointing. Graphic communication is important, but it also has limits: it cannot create architecture.

## 19.6 SIGNS AND GRAPHIC SUPPORT SYSTEMS

The development of graphic support systems, we have argued, has to be based on the spatial organization of a setting and its circulation system. It also has to be associated with architectural information, but most importantly it has to respect the behaviour of the wayfinding person. If wayfinding is defined as a spatial problem-solving process, graphic support systems have to provide the information necessary to solve the wayfinding problem, that is to make decisions and develop a decision plan for unfamiliar routes and to execute decisions on familiar routes.

In this respect, three major questions must be answered when conceiving a graphic support system: 'What information must be provided', 'Where should the information be', and 'Under which form should it be presented'. The 'What' question refers to the content of the message; the 'Where' question refers to the location of that message. Both are questions pertaining to decision making and decision execution in wayfinding. The form question concerns the actual design of the message in signs, maps and directories, and can be related to knowledge in environmental perception and cognition. We shall propose a short excursion into these fields in order to extract design ideas, both in the way of approaching the design of graphic support systems and in terms of specific suggestions.

### 19.6.1 Decision making – the content and location of wayfinding information

Decision making can be a very complex affair; the choice patterns between different types of residences, cars, or any other important consumer goods are not easy to predict. Decision making often includes a great deal of information, and the interplay of values and the trade-off that has to be made among considerations that are difficult to reconcile.

Decision making with respect to wayfinding, however, tends to be much simpler. The actual choice of alternative routes can involve various factors and complex interplay as a function of the person's priorities and time allocation (Säisä and Gärling, 1987; Allen et al., 1990); however, these types of decisions are not truly the concern of wayfinding design. All routes should provide adequate information. The information necessary for efficient wayfinding is less diversified, not as determined by personal values, and is not generally irreconcilable with other wayfinding information.

Having said that idiosyncratic considerations are less prevalent in wayfinding, different decision-making styles have nevertheless been observed. The most import-ant one refers to the amount of information the person considers necessary before making a choice (Wright, 1985). Some people will feel quite satisfied with min-imum information (just enough to go ahead) whereas others desire to be more thoroughly informed.

Not all decisions in wayfinding are of the same nature. Some types of decisions are based on cognitively more demanding operations than others. As outlined in our research on wayfinding in dementia in Chapter 21, the design of special wayfinding supports has to be based on an understanding of the decision-making abilities and limits of the user population.

It does not take much wayfinding experience to realize that many decisions have to be made when no, or only incomplete information is available. These exploratory decisions are usually aimed at finding information, or at trying to find the destina-tion directly by chance. The high prevalence of such decisions is often a sign of poor wayfinding design. Rather than being able to make wayfinding decisions on available information, people spend energy and time looking for it.

Up to this point we have focused on individual decisions. However, decisions are not made in isolation; they are linked and it is through their links that they become meaningful in a problem-solving situation. The task 'taking an elevator', for example, illustrates that a series of decisions executed in a prescribed order is required. 'Pressing a call-button', 'entering the cabin', 'pressing the destination floor number on the control board', 'checking the attained level', and 'getting out at the desired level' represent a kind of blueprint for the wayfinding task: 'taking an elevator'. In our jargon we call this blueprint a decision plan.

'Taking an elevator', however, is not a main wayfinding task. It is probably related to other decisions such as: 'to enter a building', or 'to find the location (address) of a destination', and once the indicated floor is reached by taking the elevator, it might be related to the decision 'to follow a corridor to the indicated door number'. All these decisions form a blueprint or decision plan to complete the original task of going to a given office. If one respects the logic between decisions, that is, if one links decisions according to an 'in-order-to relation' (in order to do A, I do B) one finds that wayfinding decisions are hierarchically structured. At the top of the structure is the original wayfinding task (expressed as a decision); at the bottom of the structure are the decisions leading directly to behavioural actions. In between are the 'higher-order decisions' which are subtasks when viewed from the bottom part of the hierarchy and part of a decision plan if viewed from the top of the hierarchy. For a detailed description of decision plans and the method for coding and structuring decisions see Passini (1984).

As shown by Lichtenstein and Brewer (1980), hierarchical structures of deci-sions underlay most purposeful cognitive endeavours. Investigations into problem solving pioneered by Newell and Simon (1972) underline the hierarchical function of decomposing complex problems into manageable subproblems. Inversely, hier-archical structures allow for the treatment of a subproblem while keeping in mind the general problem context.

Hierarchical structures are great mnemonic devices. They help in remembering decisions and information, which is particularly important when learning new routes. Non-driving passengers tend not to remember routes as well as drivers. Similarly, visitors who are shown around tend not to retrace their steps as well as when they had done the exploration on their own. Both the non-driving passenger and the accompanied visitor have engaged in wayfinding behaviours but they have not actually made the decisions and, thus, they have not structured them.

A decision plan indicates how a person has solved a wayfinding problem. If we accept that the purpose of graphic, and environmental communication in general, is to provide the information for decision making in wayfinding, we must conclude that the content of the messages on information displays should correspond to a person's wayfinding decisions. Following this line of reasoning, we can state that a graphic support system is an ensemble of information displays corresponding to a decision plan. The logic that links decisions into a plan is the same logic that links information displays into a system.

We cannot, however, conceive graphic support systems for individuals. Fortunately, one finds that people will develop quite similar decision plans for a given setting (Passini, 1984). After all, people faced with a wayfinding problem will develop their solution as a function of the available information and it stands to reason that the stronger the wayfinding support, the more similar the decision plans of the users.

Thus, it is suggested that graphic designers first identify the way users should arrive at the key destinations in a setting given the existing circulation system. Secondly, they should record it in the form of decision plans and then identify the information needed to make the necessary decisions. The procedure would be slightly different when designing a new setting in which graphic supports and architectural features can be conceived in parallel or when intervening in an existing setting where the architectural features are given, but the logic is the same in both cases.

If the content of required messages is given by the wayfinding decisions, then the decision points determine where the messages should be. We have ample evidence that signs are not seen just because they are there. They tend to be seen when they are needed.

### 19.6.2  Information processing – the form of wayfinding information

Graphic designers have a way of designing signs, maps and other wayfinding support systems that has evolved over many years; they have a design culture just as architects have a design culture. When it comes down to form and graphic design, I do not think that the aim of research is to change that culture profoundly. However, research can test design solutions, indicate new directions of development or fill in aspects that have not been of sufficient concern (see for example Zwaga and Boersema, 1983).

In our book, *Wayfinding: People, Signs and Architecture*, Paul Arthur assembled, discussed, and made suggestions on the design of graphic information systems (Arthur and Passini, 1992). This analysis, based mainly on the design culture of the profession and his own long-time experience, provides an overview of the various components of graphic wayfinding design such as typographies, pictographic, cartographic, photographic, computer graphics, and others. He also provides specific information on letter-forms, letter-composition, legibility and distance, angular distortions, halation, illumination of signs, systems of floor numbering, use of symbols and colours, even the design of arrows. For other references see Carpman *et al.* (1986), McLendon (1982) and Wildbur (1989).

In this chapter I focus on a general aspect of wayfinding and information processing which profoundly affects the form and the design of sign systems: people's behaviour when faced with complexity. When locating directional signs, Boersema *et al.* (1989) found that exploration time and eye movements increased with the number of advertisements introduced in the visual field. Graphic support systems are usually required when settings are of a certain size. Most are in the realm of public domains, which implies a certain density of people and functions. In commercial settings competition to attract customers by visual and auditory means further adds to the sensation of complexity. People also are complex. While they find their way they may be absorbed in thoughts, they may be mentally preparing themselves for a meeting, they may be conversing with another person, and even be exposed to a certain amount of stress and apprehension. People clearly do not disregard their normal preoccupation just because they are finding their way.

Information processing has to function in a selective and directive way to be efficient. Environmental perception while moving is based on glancing, that is, short periods of resting the eyes on objects of interest. The average period of fixation is about two-tenths of a second (Adachi and Araki, 1989). Cognitive psychologists tell us that the information obtained in a glance is first stored in an iconic memory of short duration (Neisser, 1967). If the information is to be properly understood, it has to be transformed into a memory of longer duration. This transformation can only occur if the number of information units is small. Experiments in sign reading have shown that directional signs containing more than three to four destinations can no longer be perceived in a glance. People typically stop walking and start reading the sign in a sequential fashion just as they would read a text in a book. This reading not only takes much more time, but it is considered by the users to be a disruption in 'normal' information processing. Signs that appear to be too complicated may simply be ignored.

In situations in which more than three units of information have to be presented on a sign, the designer may want to choose more than one sign or group the information units into three-unit maximum packages on a single sign. People thus will be able to read more complex messages in two or more glances.

Directories to buildings such as offices, display a great number of addresses. People tend not to read directories 'in a glance' but explore according to a given order by alphabet or function. It is therefore not necessary to group the information in three-unit packages. The three-unit principle we propose applies to displays from which information is picked up while moving through the setting.

Finally, it is necessary to describe a second, related phenomenon of perception and complexity. In some settings, particularly in commercial malls, fairgrounds, and places of other dense public gathering, people tend not to be able to take in information although the information is available and the users need it for wayfinding. In such settings people complain that they are bombarded with too much information. Comments such as 'there is so much that one cannot see anything anymore', are typical. This condition, referred to in the literature as information overload, can be seen as a last-resort adaptation process to cut out additional input when the cognitive system is overloaded. This condition reduces information processing and as a consequence reduces wayfinding ease. Avoiding information overload is one of the most crucial aims of graphic wayfinding design (Dewar, 1973; Riemersma, 1979).

Relatively little research has been done on information overload; some criteria leading to these conditions can, however, be outlined. First, it should be noted that stimulation in itself rarely leads to an overload condition. When simply looking at a complex site, people can use their normal information processing mechanism to cope with great quantities of nominal information. The situation might be less comfortable if the stimulation is very intense, if lights are excessively bright and moving, if sounds are deafening, if smells are overpowering. But these situations are relatively rare. Overload is much more common when people have to seek information to accomplish a certain task in a context in which the information sought is drowned by competing messages. Information overload is further aggravated when the person is operating under stress, emotional tension or just fatigue. The example of airport design in the research by Kishnani (Chapter 20) is particularly relevant in this respect.

Complex, information-dense settings are here to stay and little can be done about the physical or psychological state of the users. We believe, however, that the design and the placement of graphic support systems can do much to attenuate conditions of information overload and that certain design principles are particularly important when complexity of settings is high and the physical, mental or psychological conditions of users are weak.

Again, we have to keep in mind the purposeful, information-seeking aspect of environmental perception and cognition. If the person knows what the information looks like he will have greater ease finding it, even in a sea of competing messages. Research on memory shows that recognition is much more efficient than recall (Shepard, 1967), and that images are particularly easy to recognize. We were also able to show that, even after having been exposed only once to an information display with a specific form, users were able to identify other wayfinding displays long before they could read the message (Passini, 1984). Consistency in the design of a sign casing, for example its colour or graphic expression, are major factors in facilitating the perception of a sign and, thus, reduce chances of creating conditions of information overload.

Not only is it important that people know what to look for, but also where to look for wayfinding information. Consistency in the placement of information is the second major principle of facilitating the perception of graphic supports and the second antidote to information overload. Carr (1973), in an early study on signs in cities, first proposed the creation of information bands exclusively reserved for public messages. We made the same recommendation in our book (Arthur and

Passini, 1992), but given the characteristics of indoor settings we proposed two information bands: one at a low height between 1.20 m and 1.60 m for close reading – accessible also for people in wheelchairs – and one between 2.20 m and 3.00 m for distance reading. The information band could be placed somewhere else depending on the nature and the physical features of the setting. What remains important, though, is to ensure consistency in its location.

In his airport study, Kishnani (Chapter 20) rightly insists on the importance of post-occupancy evaluation. The complex interplay of spatial features and different types of information, coupled with user behaviour and users' emotional and cognitive conditions (a recipe for information overload), make it difficult to foresee all the effects of wayfinding design. Certain post-occupancy adjustments might, in fact, always be necessary in a complex setting. If the setting has been designed according to wayfinding criteria, the required interventions might indeed be adjustments rather than redesign.

## 19.7  CONCLUSION

Throughout this chapter we have argued that if the spatial organization of a setting and the circulation system define the wayfinding problem the user will have to solve, environmental communication provides the information the user will need to solve the problem. This description of wayfinding design shows the inevitable link between the two interventions. Environmental communication cannot be seen independently of spatial organization and the circulation system. Environmental communication, furthermore, concerns not only graphic design but also architecture.

Design for wayfinding is part of the architectural profession, including urban planners and landscape architects as well as graphic designers, and it is time for a collaborative effort among the design disciplines. The practice of letting graphic designers install a few signs hours before opening day should be vigorously denounced. Both design disciplines should know about each other's function and procedures and both should know about their contribution to wayfinding design.

## REFERENCES

ADACHI, K. and ARAKI, K. (1989) 'Eye fixation behavior in senile elderly', paper presented at the World Congress of Gerontology, Osaka, Kansai University.

ALLEN, J., HENDLER, J. and TATE, A. (Eds) (1990) *Reading in Planning*. Mateo, CA: Kaufman.

APPLEYARD, D. (1970) Styles and methods of structuring a city. *Environment and Behavior* **2**, 100–118.

ARTHUR, P. and PASSINI, R. (1992) *Wayfinding, People, Signs and Architecture*. Toronto: McGraw-Hill Ryerson.

BENTON, A. L. (1969) Disorders of spatial orientation. In: WINKEL, P. J. and BRUYN, G. W. (Eds), *Disorders of Higher Nervous Activities*: *Handbook of Clinical Neurology*, pp. 212–228. Amsterdam: North-Holland.

BOERSEMA, T., ZWAGA, H. J. G. and ADAMS, A. S. (1989) Conspicuity in realistic scenes: an eye-movement measure. *Applied Ergonomics* **20**, 267–273.

BRYANT, D. L., TVERSKY, B. and FRANKLIN, N. (1992) Internal and external spatial frameworks for representing described scenes. *Journal of Memory and Language* **31**, 74–98.

CANTER, D. (1980) *Fires and Human Behavior.* Chichester, UK: John Wiley.

CARPMAN, J. R., GRANT, M. A. and SIMMONS, P. A. (1986) *Design that Cares.* Chicago: American Hospital Association.

CARR, S. (1973) *City Signs and Lights: A Policy Study.* Cambridge, MA: MIT Press.

CHING, F. (1979) *Architecture, Form, Space and Order.* New York: Van Nostrand Reinhold.

DeRENZI, E. (1982) *Disorders of Space Exploration and Cognition.* New York: Wiley.

DEWAR, R. E. (1973) *Psychological Factors in the Perception of Traffic Signs.* Road and Motor Vehicle Traffic Safety Branch, Department of Transport, Government of Canada.

DOWNS, R. (1981) Maps and mappings as metaphors for spatial representation. In: LIBEN, L. S. *et al.* (Eds), *Spatial Representatioin and Behavior Across the Life Span: Theory and Application*, pp. 143–166. NewYork: Academic Press.

DOWNS, R. and STEA, D. (1977) *Maps in Mind.* New York: Harper and Row.

EVANS, G. W. (1980) Environmental cognition. *Psychological Bulletin* **88**, 259–287.

GÄRLING, T. and GOLLEDGE, R. (1989) Environmental perception and cognition. In: ZUBE, E. H. and MOORE, G. T. (Eds), *Advances in Environment, Behavior and Design*, Vol. 2. New York: Plenum Press.

GÄRLING, T., BÖÖK, A. and LINDBERG, E. (1986) Spatial orientation and wayfinding in the designed environment. *Journal of Architectural and Planning Research* **3**, 55–64.

GLADWIN, T. (1970) *East is a Big Bird: Navigation and Logic in Puluwat Atoll.* Cambridge, MA: Harvard University Press.

GRIFFIN, P. (1948) Topological orientation. In: BORING, E. G. *et al.* (Eds), *Foundation of Psychology*, pp. 380–386. New York: Wiley.

HANLEY, G. L. and LEVINE, M. (1983) Spatial problem solving: the integration of independently learned cognitive maps. *Memory and Cognition* **11**, 415–422.

KAPLAN, S. (1976) Adaptation, structure and knowledge. In: MOORE, G. and GOLLEDGE, R. (Eds), *Environmental Knowing*, pp. 32–46. Stroudsburg, PA: Dowden, Hutchinson and Ross.

KOSSLYN, S. M., PINKER, S., SMITH, G. E. and SCHWARTZ, S. P. (1979) On the demystification of mental imagery. *Behavioral and Brain Sciences* **2**, 535–582.

LEWIS, D. (1975) *We, the Navigators: The Ancient Art of Landfinding in the Pacific.* Honolulu: University Press of Hawaii.

LICHTENSTEIN, E. H. and BREWER, W. F. (1980) Memory for goal directed events. *Cognitive Psychology* **12**, 412–445.

LORD, F. E. (1941) A study of spatial orientation in children. *Journal of Educational Research* **34**, 481–505.

LYNCH, K. (1960) *The Image of the City.* Cambridge, MA: MIT Press.

McLENDON, C. (1982) *Signage, Graphic Communications in the Built World.* New York: McGraw Hill.

MOESER, S. D. (1988) Cognitive mapping in a complex building. *Environment and Behavior* **20**, 21–49.

MONTELLO, D. R. (1991) Spatial orientation and the angularity of urban routes. *Environment and Behavior* **23**, 47–69.

MONTELLO, D. R. and PICK, H. L. (1993) Integrating knowledge of vertically aligned large-scale spaces. *Environment and Behavior* **25**, 457–484.

MOORE, G. (1979) Knowing about environmental knowing; the current state of theory and research in environmental cognition. *Environment and Behavior* **11**, 33–70.

NEISSER, U. (1967) *Cognitive Psychology*. Englewood Cliffs, NJ: Prentice-Hall.

NEWELL, A. and SIMON, H. A. (1972) *Human Problem Solving*. Englewood Cliffs, NJ: Prentice-Hall.

O'NEILL, M. (1991) Evaluation of a conceptual model of architectural legibility. *Environment and Behavior* **23**, 259–284.

PASSINI, R. (1977) 'Wayfinding: a study of spatial problem solving', PhD Dissertation, Pennsylvania State University.

PASSINI, R. (1984) *Wayfinding in Architecture*. New York: Van Nostrand Reinhold.

PASSINI, R. and SHIELS, G. (1986) *Wayfinding Performance Evaluation of Four Public Buildings*. Ottawa: Public Works Canada, Architectural and Engineering Services.

PEPONIS, J., ZIMRING, C. and CHOI, Y. K. (1990) Finding the building in wayfinding. *Environment and Behavior* **22**, 555–590.

RIEMERSMA, J. B. (1979) Perception in traffic. *Urban Ecology* **4**, 139–149.

ROVINE, M. and WEISMAN, G. D. (1989) Sketch-map variables as predictors of wayfinding performance. *Journal of Environmental Psychology* **9**, 217–232.

SÄISÄ, J. and GÄRLING, T. (1987) Sequential spatial choices in the large-scale environment. *Environment and Behavior* **19**, 614–635.

SHEPARD, R. N. (1967) Recognition memory for words, sentences and pictures. *Journal of Verbal Learning and Verbal Behavior* **6**, 156–163.

SIEGLE, A. W. and WHITE, S. H. (1975) The development of spatial representations of large scale environments. In: REESE, H. W. (Ed.), *Advances in Child Development and Behavior*, Vol. 10, pp. 9–55. New York: Academic Press.

SIME, J. (1985) Movement towards the familiar: person and place affiliation in a fire entrapment setting. *Environment and Behavior* **17**, 692–724.

TALBOT, J. F., KAPLAN, R. and KAPLAN, S. (1993) Factors that enhance effectiveness of visitor maps. *Environment and Behavior* **25**, 743–760.

THORNDYKE, P. W. and STANSZ, C. (1980) Individual differences in procedures for knowledge acquisition from maps. *Cognitive Psychology* **12**, 137–175.

TOLMAN, E. C. (1948) Cognitive maps in rats and men. *Psychological Review* **55**, 189–208.

TROWBRIDGE, C. C. (1913) On fundamental methods of orientation and imaginary maps. *Science* **38**, 888–897.

WEISMAN, J. (1981) Evaluating architectural legibility: way finding in the built environment. *Environment and Behavior* **13**, 189–204.

WILDBUR, P. (1989) *Information Graphics*. New York: Van Nostrand Reinhold.

WRIGHT, P. (1985) Decision variance. In: WRIGHT, G. (Ed.), *Behavioral Decision Making*. New York: Plenum Press.

ZIMRING, C. (1982) The built environment as a source of psychological stress: impacts of buildings and cities on satisfaction and behavior. In: EVANS, G. W. (Ed.), *Environmental Stress*. Cambridge, UK: Cambridge University Press.

ZIMRING, C. and TEMPLER, J. (1984) Wayfinding and orientation by the visually impaired. *Journal of Environmental Systems* **13**, 333–352.

ZWAGA, H. J. G. and BOERSEMA, T. (1983) Evaluation of a set of graphic symbols. *Applied Ergonomics* **14**, 43–54.

# CHAPTER TWENTY

# Evaluation of the wayfinding system at Stansted Airport

NIRMAL KISHNANI

## 20.1 INTRODUCTION – THE POST-OCCUPANCY PERSPECTIVE

The presence of a wayfinding designer in the early stages of a building's design has its advocates (Arthur and Passini, 1992) who argue that decisions at the conceptual level – spatial organization and architectural form – affect the legibility of the environment as a whole. What has been less forcefully articulated, though, is the role of the designer after the building's completion.

A post-occupancy evaluation is significant as a culmination point in the design process, partly because behaviour can rarely be sufficiently foreseen on the drawing board – especially behaviour that is a response to the interaction between space, signs and other information in different media, in multiple-user settings such as airports. Partly also, wayfinding is affected by factors beyond the designer's control, such as daily routines and operational imperatives. The influence of these factors becomes evident only after the building has attained a certain capacity of usage.

Post-occupancy adjustments, therefore, are a way to tie in information types and media, making them consistent with each other and with the cues which come from the way the building is managed.

## 20.2 WAYFINDING AND AIRPORTS

For most travellers there is inherent stress in flying that relates to the cost, complexity and uncertainty of modern air travel. Airport design in itself cannot compensate for all these concerns but it can alleviate some of the stress by clarifying choices and affirming decisions – in effect, making transparent what is to be done and where a user needs to be.

257

Wayfinding behaviour at airports, in general, is typified by heavy reliance on signposting. This is partly due to the specific nature of user paths and partly because many destinations along these paths (such as check-in counters and baggage claim carousels) tend to be identical in appearance. The effect of this dependency is that even when a destination is clearly visible, users can overlook it because it is inadequately signed. Other important aspects of wayfinding are considered below.

### 20.2.1   User segregation

Distinct user groups are separated by why they use the terminal building and what facilities they use – namely passengers, visitors and staff. It is possible to mark out zones and paths on the building plans according to user group access.

### 20.2.2   The time imperative

Departing passengers, who have a limited amount of time before their flight, move quickly through the terminal. Arriving passengers, however, with no apparent time constraints, move even more quickly.

### 20.2.3   The information grid

Airport users must navigate an information system relating to flight operations. Flight information televisions (FITV) and automatic flipboards (large display panels showing flight schedules) tell people where to go and when to be there; boarding passes identify passengers to their flight, and the public announcement is a form of acoustic signing. The clarity of these sources and manner in which information is mutually reinforced is vital to the legibility of the environment.

### 20.3   A FRAMEWORK FOR EVALUATION

Given the difficulty of reviewing the separate effect of each information source in a setting where information is derived from different, yet interrelated, media sources, the study looked at the composite effect of information on behaviour (Kishnani, 1992).

The routes of international arriving and departing passengers were marked out on the building plan as a series of user paths. Signs and information sources at choice nodes along this path were then evaluated against how effectively decisions were made. The evaluation was based largely on behavioural observations of passengers moving through the nodes. This was supplemented with a user survey and informal discussions with airport staff.

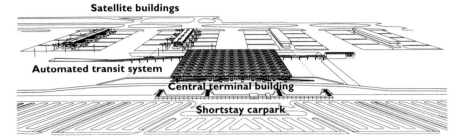

**Figure 20.1** Stansted terminal and satellite buildings.

## 20.4 STANSTED AIRPORT

The airport complex consists of a two-storey central terminal building that is connected to several satellites by an 'automated people transit system' (a driverless shuttle) that moves on a trackway. The satellites are three storeys high, consisting mostly of circulation spaces and waiting areas from which passengers board or into which they disembark aircraft via airbridges (Figure 20.1).

The main terminal hall is distinguished by a unique structural system in which 36 steel 'trees' hold the roof aloft. This space has glass walls on four sides, forming a transparent box within which all arrival and departure facilities are located. The roof hovers 15 metres above eye level in such a way that the four sides of the glass box are visible from most points in the building.

The architect had envisaged a direct line-of-sight through the central terminal building, so that departing passengers would have a view of their waiting aircraft (Figure 20.2). This objective is inevitably compromised by the accommodation needs of an airport building which impede the view at eye level (toilets, shops, offices, etc.) All such facilities, however, are controlled in appearance and height. This aesthetic control is carried through in all aspects of the terminal design. Air-conditioning outlets, flight information TVs, lights and signs are localized within modular pods at the base of the structural trees (Figure 20.3).

Unlike most other airports, no signs have been suspended from the ceiling. The signposting is kept to a minimum. It consists of several large wall-mounted graphics (for toilets, restaurants, etc.); non-lighted lettering on white background and lighted yellow directional signs.

## 20.5 STANSTED STUDY — THE USER SURVEY

The study began with a survey aimed at determining opinions about:

- ease of wayfinding;
- effectiveness of signage;
- effectiveness of the flight information system.

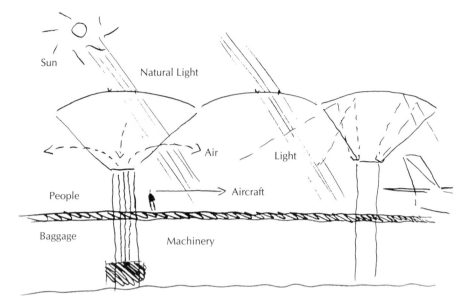

**Figure 20.2** Architect's conceptual sketch of movement through the main hall.

**Figure 20.3** Typical 'tree-pod' with clock and fire-fighting equipment.

**Table 20.1**  Summary of the results of the user survey (sample size: 60)

| Scale | General ease of wayfinding | Effectiveness of signage | Effectiveness of flight information |
|---|---|---|---|
| 1 | 0 | 0 | 0 |
| 2 | 0 | 0 | 4 |
| 3 | 2 | 2 | 5 |
| 4 | 5 | 5 | 5 |
| 5 | 11 | 10 | 7 |
| 6 | 16 | 25 | 16 |
| 7 | 26 | 18 | 23 |
| Mean response | 6.0 | 5.9 | 5.6 |

To measure ease of wayfinding, respondents were asked to rate the airport on a seven-point scale ranging from 1 (very difficult) to 7 (very easy). Effectiveness of signage and the flight information system were each measured against a separate seven-point scale where 1 was very ineffective and 7 was very effective.

The survey was carried out at several locations where the respondents in the sample represented a mix of user groups (departures, well-wishers, greeters, etc.), each differing in the objective and extent of its encounters with the building. They were also asked how often they had been to airports in general and to Stansted in particular. This would establish the effect of familiarity. Other variables were also noted – namely age, gender, nationality and purpose of travel (in the case of passengers). The results are summarized in Table 20.1.

Analysis of the ratings showed that no one user variable had a significant relationship to the respondent's evaluation of wayfinding. The sole exception to this was the respondent's 'frequency of visits to other airports'. If respondents visited other airports more than once a year, they were likely to rate Stansted higher.

Wayfinding at Stansted is generally highly rated (mean response 6.0) along with the signage system (mean response 5.9). The rating of the flight information system is lower (mean response 5.6), mainly because glare – from the high level of natural light in the building – makes it difficult to read some of the screens. Also, there are no complementary flight information flipboards so that waiting visitors have to periodically walk up to an FITV screen to check on flight updates.

## 20.6  BEHAVIOURAL OBSERVATIONS ALONG USER PATHS

### 20.6.1  Departure route

Visitors arrive at the airport by road or rail. The train station is below the main hall; the car park is situated adjacent to the terminal building. From either, the departing

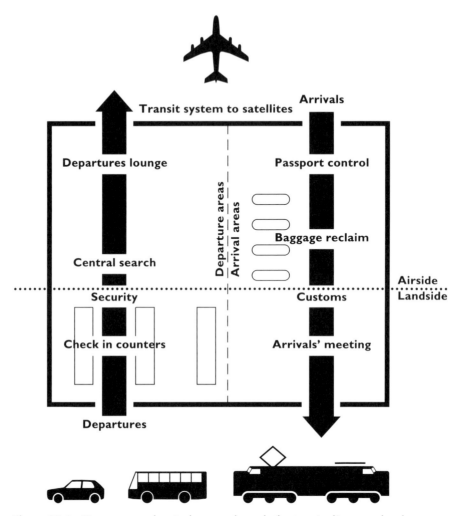

**Figure 20.4**   Departure and arrival routes through the terminal's upper level.

passenger ascends via escalators or lifts to the departures half of the public concourse (Figure 20.4).

    After check-in passengers pass through a screened central search area into airside,
where they can wait in the departure lounge with its duty-free shops and restaurants. The automated people transit system starts from here. This shuttle takes 90
seconds to get from terminal to satellite, initially moving along an elevated track
before descending into a concrete tunnel that ends at a station in the basement of
the satellite building. The passengers then ascend to the top floor, via lifts or
escalators, to the departure gates where they wait. When the flight is ready to be
boarded passengers are led down one level, through airbridges and into the aircraft.

## 20.6.2  Arrival route

Although arriving and departing passengers share the same airbridge access to the aircraft, segregation of the two user groups (for security reasons) makes it necessary for the latter to wait at the top floor of the satellite building while arriving passengers disembark into the middle level. Upon entering the satellite, arriving passengers move through the arrivals corridor from which they descend to the transit station in the basement. This station is a mirror image of the one used by departures. The shuttle has, after dropping off the departing passengers, looped over to the arrivals side.

The shuttle takes the arriving passengers to the main terminal building (Figure 20.3) where they pass through passport control counters, a baggage reclaim hall, and customs check area. When they emerge from these airside areas, they are met by greeters in the arrivals half of the public concourse. From here, the passengers leave the complex via the car parks or train station at the level below.

The Stansted observations can be grouped according to several determinants of wayfinding behaviour. The first of these is familiarity. In the case of airports, many first-time visitors bring to bear their experience and expectations of airports in general. There exists a kind of mental map of the building type in terms of the sequencing of events and the appearance of certain elements (e.g. information counters). The automated transit system linking terminal and satellite at Stansted is, as such, a relatively uncommon element in airport planning that many passengers – especially those who travel infrequently – find difficult to understand. The shuttle is the single most frequent cause of wayfinding difficulties and for passengers' questions, and seems to affect both arriving and departing passengers equally.

The second determinant is group behaviour. Often, passengers emerging from the confines of aircraft or trains arriving at Stansted move with some kind of herd instinct. There is a shared group objective (e.g. find baggage reclaim), which makes it acceptable for some to be led by others. This sometimes makes up for deficiencies in the signage; at other times entire groups are led astray. For instance, at the train station below the main hall there are no signs to inform visitors that they may use either escalators or lifts to go up. Most take their cue from those ahead of them – sometimes struggling onto escalators with heavy luggage. Similarly, groups of passengers disembarking from the aircraft into the arrivals corridor move with relative ease towards the transit station below. Passengers who are alone however, attest to the deficiency of the signage in the uncertainty of their movements and some backtracking.

The third determinant is response to space. The influence of spatial logic had been observed by Peponis et al. (1990) in the context of a health care facility. The most conspicuous example of this influence at Stansted occurs in the public concourse, where arrivals emerging from the customs check area sometimes overlooked designated exit doors (to the train station/car park below) and moved unwittingly into the departures half of the concourse – drawn by the shaft of space that cuts across the width of the building.

Most of the wayfinding problems at Stansted could be redressed by the addition or removal of signs. Some signs need to be made more visible, either by increasing size or adjusting contrast with context. In some cases, the information presented collectively by a group of signs needs to be better prioritized.

The biggest challenge, however, lies in improving the relationship between information types. The cognitive problem with the transit system, for instance, could be tackled on several fronts: the transit station at the departure lounge could be made more visible by making it stand out architecturally against its glass wall context; passengers could be informed at check-in counters of the need to board the shuttle with, say, a reminder on their boarding passes; signs could be placed throughout the departure lounge reminding passengers that they should allow some time for the shuttle trip to their gates; FITVs could prompt passengers who check departure times to board the shuttle; and finally the term 'automated people transit system' could be switched to something more accessible, say 'terminal shuttle' or 'passenger train'.

## 20.7   EVALUATION

Wayfinding design at Stansted began with the architectural concept. The transparency of the building and a single-level, straight-line circulation are elementary wayfinding principles that were also the architect's early design intentions (Pawley, 1991). His guiding hand over the appearance of all elements, including signage (Fletcher, 1993), has created a unified visual field where space and form are easily read. The placement of signs and FITVs at the structural tree pods gives the system a logic that is transparent and easily accessible.

The strategy of creating line-of-sight, from point-of-entry to destination, works best for departing passengers who seem propelled by a sense (if not a view) of airside. The arrivals' objective is less literal because the main terminal building cannot be seen from their point-of-entry (the satellite building). It is disconcerting for some to have to descend to the basement station – with no views out – where they must wait for the transit shuttle.

The transit system is, in fact, the weak link in the spatial sequencing of both arrival and departure routes. This unfamiliarity is compounded by a lack of signs informing the passengers of where they are heading. The visual link between inside and outside – so fervently sustained in the main terminal building – is lost in these subterranean spaces.

Much of these (and other) ambiguities could have been redressed with signposting if not for a certain dogmatism. The architecture, it is asserted, must have its own 'logic' (Fletcher, 1993), and this logic, presumably, is apparent to all. Conspicuous by their absence are directories showing location of airport amenities and 'You Are Here' plans. Even where signs are present, they are visually low-key for reasons of aesthetic restraint. Given the high proportion of first-time users in airports – and their reluctance to search out available options leisurely – this degree of understatedness in the presentation of information is clearly problematic.

Significantly though, Stansted Airport is highly regarded by its users. According to the user survey, the number of times visitors have been to Stansted apparently does not relate to their evaluation. Whilst this seems counter-intuitive – i.e., increased familiarity should improve evaluation – it could mean that most visitors peak in their wayfinding confidence during the first visit.

Stansted regularly tops the list of seven airports run by the British Airport Authority (BAA) in an in-house user survey, possibly due to its relative lack of congestion as compared with its London rivals (Churchill, 1994). This may also explain results of the 'ease-of-wayfinding' survey in which the passengers' evaluations of Stansted improve with the frequency of their visits to other airports.

The study also illustrates that wayfinding design is not simply a matter of where to position signs. It begins with the operational logic of the building's functions and extends into the realms of architecture and interior design. Post-occupancy adjustments to public graphics designs – even elegant ones such as at Stansted – are not an admission of design failure. Rather they constitute the final and necessary step in any system's implementation.

## REFERENCES

ARTHUR, P. and PASSINI, R. (1992) *Wayfinding – People, Signs and Architecture*. Toronto: McGraw-Hill Ryerson.

CHURCHILL, D. (1994) Stansted Airport. *The Times*, 16 June 1994, 18–21.

FLETCHER, A. (1993) Signs at Stansted. *Domus Dossier/Airports* Issue 1, 92–95.

KISHNANI, N. (1992) 'Wayfinding in architecture, an evaluation of wayfinding perception and behaviour at Stansted Airport', Unpublished MSc Thesis, University of Surrey.

PAWLEY, M. (1991) The London Stansted Airport by Foster Associates. *Casabella*, June 1991, 4–19.

PEPONIS, J., ZIMRING, C. and YOON KYUNG CHOI (1990) Finding the building in wayfinding. *Environment and Behaviour* **22**, 555–590.

# CHAPTER TWENTY-ONE

# Wayfinding and information processing in dementia

ROMEDI PASSINI, YVES JOANETTE, CONSTANT RAINVILLE and
NICOLAS MARCHAND

## 21.1 DEMENTIA AND WAYFINDING

Dementia of the Alzheimer type (DAT), the clinical condition corresponding to Alzheimer's disease, is a disorder of the central nervous system occurring in middle or late life. It progressively affects cognitive functions, such as memory, attention, judgement and reasoning (Cambier *et al.*, 1982; Rosen, 1982). All intellectual abilities weaken over time but not necessarily at the same rate (Ripich and Terrel, 1988; Joanette *et al.*, 1992).

Disorientation is among the first symptoms of DAT. According to Reisberg *et al.* (1982), orientation difficulties in the earliest stages (to Stage 3) impact on unfamiliar journeys at the macro-scale. At Stage 4, which corresponds to a light to moderate deterioration of intellectual abilities, patients start experiencing difficulties on a local scale, but are still mobile in familiar places. During Stage 5, patients need help with their daily activities and autonomous mobility is further reduced. At Stage 6 deterioration is severe and the person loses purposeful mobility.

The general aim of our study was to understand better the wayfinding abilities of moderate DAT patients and to use this understanding to suggest design interventions of both graphic and architectural nature (for complementary aspects of design for dementia see Cohen and Weisman, 1988).

The conceptual framework of the study is wayfinding, which encompasses the cognitive abilities necessary for purposeful mobility. Defined in terms of spatial problem solving, it is composed of three interrelated processes:

- decision making and the development of plans of action;
- decision executing – transforming plans into behaviour at the right place and time;
- information processing which sustains the two decision processes (Passini, 1984).

## 21.2  OBJECTIVES OF THE STUDY

The first objective was to identify the type of decisions DAT patients were able to make and those beyond their scope. It was hypothesized that decisions based on explicit environmental information were still possible whereas decisions requiring memory (including cognitive maps) and inferences no longer corresponded to their abilities.

The second objective was to identify their ability to plan wayfinding solutions, that is, to establish an interrelated sequence of decisions aimed at solving a wayfinding problem. The hypothesis was that DAT patients would have difficulties developing overall solutions to complex wayfinding problems.

The third objective was to identify general difficulties in information processing in the context of a typical hospital setting.

## 21.3  METHOD

### 21.3.1  The sample

The experimental sample consisted of 14 DAT patients who corresponded to Stage 4 or 5 of the Reisberg global deterioration scale described above. Their age varied between 64 and 75 years. A control group of 28 healthy seniors was matched in terms of age, sex and education.

### 21.3.2  Task and data gathering

Subjects had to reach the dental clinic in a Montreal hospital (Côte-des-Neiges) from the closest bus-stop. Once the destination was reached, they had to return to the bus-stop by the same route.

Subjects were asked to verbalize everything that went through their mind on the way to their destination. An accompanying observer assured full verbalization. The conversation was taped and transcribed into the wayfinding protocol. Coding rules were used to identify decisions and the relation between decisions (Passini, 1984). All protocols were coded by two analysts on an independent basis.

### 21.3.3  The setting and the route

The chosen hospital caters for the elderly and DAT patients. The route corresponding to the task is shown in Figure 21.1.

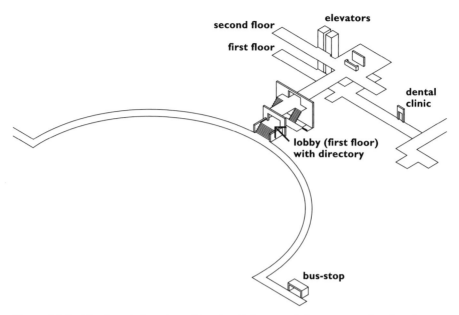

**Figure 21.1**   The hospital setting, Côte-des-Neiges, and the route to the dental clinic.

The subjects had to enter the hospital by the main entrance. In the lobby they had to obtain the 'address' of the dental clinic from a directory. From the lobby they had to reach the ground floor, but could only do so by going up to the second floor and descending by an elevator. Once on the ground floor, a directional sign led to the dental clinic.

This rather complex task confronted the subjects with a diversity of decisions and a need to plan. If the subject was lost, the observer intervened by providing the appropriate decision.

### 21.4   RESULTS

### 21.4.1   General performance profile

The trip leading from the bus-stop to the dental clinic was completed without the help of the observer by 21 of the 28 subjects from the control group. The performance in the DAT group was much poorer. Not a single subject was able to complete the task without help.

The differences between the two groups were even more important for the return trip. Twenty-four subjects in the control group made it without help. No DAT patient completed the task without help.

**Table 21.1** Distribution of decision types for the original trip

| Group | Type A | | | | | Type B | | | | | Total |
|---|---|---|---|---|---|---|---|---|---|---|---|
| | A1 | A2 | A3 | A4 | Total A | B1 | B2 | B3 | B4 | Total B | |
| DAT | 122 | 44 | 1 | 33 | 200 | 122 | 70 | 65 | 82 | 339 | 539 |
| % | 22.63 | 8.16 | 0.20 | 6.12 | **37.11** | 22.63 | 12.99 | 12.06 | 15.21 | **62.89** | 100 |
| Control | 241 | 89 | 4 | 133 | 467 | 0 | 9 | 176 | 327 | 512 | 979 |
| % | 24.62 | 9.09 | 0.40 | 13.59 | **47.70** | 0.00 | 0.92 | 17.98 | 33.40 | **52.30** | 100 |
| t test | NS | NS | – | * | | * | * | NS | * | | |

* Significant difference between the two groups; NS, no significant difference; – not tested, insufficient data.

**Table 21.2** Distribution of decision types for the return trip

| Group | Type A | | | | | Type B | | | | | Total |
|---|---|---|---|---|---|---|---|---|---|---|---|
| | A1 | A2 | A3 | A4 | Total A | B1 | B2 | B3 | B4 | Total B | |
| DAT | 76 | 17 | 26 | 9 | 128 | 63 | 37 | 15 | 7 | 122 | 250 |
| % | 30.40 | 6.80 | 10.40 | 3.60 | **51.2** | 22.30 | 13.10 | 5.30 | 2.50 | **48.8** | 100 |
| Control | 121 | 102 | 195 | 26 | 444 | 0 | 9 | 27 | 22 | 58 | 502 |
| % | 24.10 | 20.32 | 38.85 | 5.18 | **88.45** | 0.00 | 1.79 | 5.38 | 4.38 | **11.55** | 100 |
| t test | NS | * | * | NS | | * | * | NS | NS | | |

* Significant difference between the two groups; NS, no significant difference.

## 21.4.2 Analysis of decision types

In order to be able to identify the decisions DAT patients were able to make, a decision typology was introduced. This typology classifies decisions according to two wayfinding conditions:

- when information is available (A decisions);
- when no relevant information is available (B decisions).

For each condition four types of decisions were identified.

*A decisions:*

- A1: individual decisions based on simple, explicit information.
- A2: set of decisions based on simple, explicit information leading to routine sets of behaviours.
- A3: decisions based on memory and cognitive maps.
- A4: decisions based on inferences.

*B decisions:*

- B1: exploring without explicit aim.
- B2: exploring in order to find (perceive directly) the destination.
- B3: exploring in order to find any useful information.
- B4: exploring in order to find specific information.

The data for the original trip (Table 21.1) were subjected to a multivariate test (Hotelling's $t^2$). The overall difference between the two groups was significant at $p < 0.0000$. A Student's $t$ test was then applied to compare individual variables.

The comparison between the two groups for A decisions showed no marked differences with the exception of A4 (inference based) which were prevalent in the control group. A3 decisions (memory based), although more common in the control group, were too few to be taken into consideration. Patients could cope quite well with A1 decisions (based on explicit information) and to a certain extent A2 decisions (routine sets).

A remarkable result is the distribution of B decisions. B1 decisions (walking without explicit aim), which were only found in DAT, accounted for almost a quarter of all decisions made. Similarly, B2 (finding the destination directly) was predominant in the DAT group. B4 (finding specific information) decisions were made by both groups but significantly more so by the control group.

On the return trip, a major shift from the exploratory B to A decisions occurred for the control group. Of all decisions 88.45 per cent were of the A type and more than a third (38.85 per cent) of all decisions were A3 (memory based). In contrast, the distribution for the DAT group remained unchanged. The Hotelling test analysing the overall difference between the two groups was again significant at $p < 0.0000$. The Student's $t$ test between pairs of variables showed significant differences for A2, A3 and B2. B1, again, was only made by DAT patients (see Table 21.2). B1 and B2 remained unchanged.

### 21.4.3   Solving wayfinding problems

Decision plans were identified by coding the protocols and establishing the hierarchical 'in order' relations between decisions.

The results, in summary, point to the difficulty of DAT patients to plan a route. Only two of 14 patients were able to develop an overall plan to go from the bus-stop to the dental clinic. This compares with 26 of the 28 control subjects. Similarly, no DAT patient was able to develop the plan to go to the ground floor from the entrance lobby via the second floor. Of the control subjects 23 could develop such a plan.

On the other hand, almost every DAT patient (13 of 14) was able to complete the task going from the bus-stop to the entrance lobby of the hospital. These decisions (A1 type), based on simple, explicit architectural information, were related in a sequential fashion, requiring no overall plan. The task of finding the destination on the ground floor, again did not require complex planning. Of the 14 DAT patients 12 developed appropriate solutions.

### 21.4.4   Observations on information processing

DAT patients' difficulty in obtaining information was evident throughout the study. Often they were unable to distinguish relevant from irrelevant information. Situations occurred when patients were systematically reading signs and directories and everything they could find on their way. This non-discriminatory reading was not only useless but exhausting and patients typically lost sight of the reason for their search.

Most patients had problems decoding symbols and abbreviations on graphic displays. The spatial disposition of messages on signs also led to confusion. Signs were not understood because the arrow was too far away from the destination name, while independent messages were associated and interpreted as one because of close proximity.

Finally, instances were noted when inappropriate behaviour was triggered by strong stimuli. Patients, seeing a doorbell (for night use) at the hospital, spontaneously decided to ring. On more than one occasion, the elevator doors opened as patients were following a corridor. They entered the elevator although they had never consciously decided to do so.

### 21.5   IMPLICATIONS FOR DESIGN

The experiment suggests that patients with moderate DAT are still able to find their way under certain facilitating conditions. Graphic and architectural support systems should allow for an essentially sequential style of wayfinding, leading patients from one decision point to the next, thus reducing the need to generate complex plans. The articulation of entrances to buildings, of entrances to identifiable zones within buildings, of horizontal and vertical circulation, and of landmarks, would seem to be particularly important in this respect.

The non-discriminatory reading of information by DAT patients was among the most confusing interferences in the wayfinding process. Cluttering information on circulation routes should therefore be tidied up.

DAT patients tended to have difficulties retracing their steps. The task was treated as if it were a new problem. This means that information for return trips, usually not required by the average user, must be provided for.

Wandering, a common behaviour of DAT patients, requires special design considerations (Cohen and Weisman, 1988). The observed tendency of stimulus-bound behaviour points to the danger of messages, like fire exit signs, leading them to choose undesirable routes.

Much research is still needed in order to understand better wayfinding in dementia of the Alzheimer type. The design suggestions made in this chapter are of a generic order. If they are incorporated in a design, they should be tested by post-occupancy evaluation. Both fundamental and post-occupancy research are necessary to develop appropriate health care settings in which patients are secure and as mobile and autonomous as their condition permits.

## REFERENCES

CAMBIER, J., MASSON, M. and DEHEN, H. (1982) *Neurologie*. Paris: Masson.

COHEN, U. and WEISMAN, G. D. (1988) *Environments for People with Dementia: Design Guide*. Milwaukee: University of Wisconsin-Milwaukee, Center for Architecture and Urban Planning Research.

JOANETTE, Y., SKA, B., POISSANT, A. and BÉLAND, R. (1992) Neuropsychological aspects of Alzheimer's disease: evidence of inter- and intra-functions heterogeneity. In: BOLLER, F., FORETTE, F., KHACHATURIAN, Z., PONCET, M. and CHRISTEN, Y. (Eds), *Heterogeneity of Alzheimer's Disease*. New York: Springer.

PASSINI, R. (1984) *Wayfinding in Architecture*. New York: Van Nostrand Reinhold.

REISBERG, B., FERRIS, S. and CROOK, T. (1982) Signs, symptoms and course of age-associated cognitive decline, Alzheimer's disease: a report of progress. In: CORKIN, S. *et al.* (Eds), *Aging*. New York: Raven Press.

RIPICH, D. N. and TERREL, B. Y. (1988) Patterns of discourse cohesion and coherence in Alzheimer's disease. *Journal of Speech and Hearing Disorders* **53**, 8–15.

ROSEN, W. G. (1982) Evolution of cognitive decline in dementia. In: CORKIN, S. *et al.* (Eds), *Alzheimer's Disease: A Report of Progress*, pp. 183–188. NewYork: Raven Press.

# CHAPTER TWENTY-TWO

# Redesign of a car park: the application of wayfinding principles

PIET J. VENEMANS

## 22.1 INTRODUCTION

In the wayfinding literature the aim generally is to increase the body of tested knowledge about wayfinding behaviour in relation to the built environment. The main quality criterion for this research is the validity of the results. In design situations an additional quality criterion is whether the results will be applicable given the requirements and the restrictions of the situation at hand. The results should also be *productive*, that is, useful for analysis and for translation into proposals for realizable design interventions.

Passini *et al.* (Chapter 21) classify design interventions as:

- *spatial characteristics of the environment*, which define the wayfinding problem to be solved by the visitor, including the spatial organization of destinations, as well as the circulation system, the routes to, from, and between the destinations;

- *environmental communication*, to provide the information necessary for the wayfinding problem solving, including both sign systems and architectural means to enable recognition of the route elements and the destinations searched for.

These design intervention groups are reflected in the general criteria I have formulated previously to classify the building characteristics found in the literature as relevant for wayfinding (Venemans *et al.*, 1993; Venemans, 1994).

These criteria and the relevant building characteristics can be used as a base for proposals in building design to realize the above mentioned design interventions. For example, the design decisions concerning the circulation system and the location of destinations should provide sight lines to the most important destinations. This will result in what has been defined by Weisman (1979) as 'perceptual access'. For these sight lines to be effective, the visitor should be able to recognize the destination, an aspect of environmental communication affected by subsequent design decisions.

## 22.2   RESTRICTED POSSIBILITIES FOR REDESIGN OF EXISTING SITUATIONS

In situations which are to be designed from scratch, the realization of design interventions for wayfinding is a question of considering them in time. For example, for the circulation system the main decisions are taken in the early stages of the design process (Venemans *et al.*, 1994). This is different for redesign of existing situations. When a built situation causes complaints about wayfinding and orientation, redesign possibilities are restricted, e.g. by the supporting structure of the building (Janssen and Venemans, 1983), and redesign, if at all possible, will be rather expensive (Bol, 1993).

Although one of the main design issues defining the wayfinding problem to be solved concerns the circulation system, generally, in an existing building it is difficult to change this system, even when it has proved to be a major cause of wayfinding difficulties. In a car park, adaptation of the circulation system is much simpler, especially when the layout is indicated by painted lines on the floor surface. Such a redesign of a car park layout is described below.

## 22.3   CASE: AN OFFICE CAR PARK CAUSING COMPLAINTS

In a new office building complex with a car park in the basement of the building (Figure 22.1), about half of the parking area was intended for visitors (the paths in the visitors' zone were painted blue); the remainder was reserved for employees, each having a designated space (paths in the employee zone were painted medium grey). This zoning was indicated by a coloured sign along the entrance path. The entrance to the office reception hall was located at the visitor parking area.

From the start complaints arose about this car park, from both visitors and employees. The employees mainly complained about finding their reserved parking space occupied by a visitor's car. After parking their car, visitors found it difficult to find the entrance to the office building, and after their visit they found it difficult to locate their car. In spite of continuing discussions, the facility management did not find a workable solution which could be realized within reasonable time constraints and at reasonable cost. A proposal to add some 30 signs was rejected as being only a partial solution, and there would also be the risk of creating information overload. Mounting an extra automated barrier, a rather expensive solution, would not be effective either.

sign at the wall:

| visitors | employees |
|----------|-----------|
| blue zone ↑ | grey zone ↑ |

(white text (white text
on blue) on grey)

exit sign:
to (name shopping
centre)

exit barrier at start
of exit slope

paths painted grey

exit sign:
to (name shopping
centre)

paths painted grey

paths painted blue >¦< paths painted grey

(grey)

(grey)

(grey)

(blue)

(blue)

office
entrance

0   5   10m

**Figure 22.1**  Car park – floor plan of old situation.

### 22.3.1   Analysis of the situation

To analyse the situation the wayfinding criteria mentioned in Section 22.1 were used to test their productiveness.

When arriving in the car park, the visitor's wayfinding task concentrated on two goals:

- finding a place to park the car;
- finding the entrance to the office building.

In the same way, the wayfinding goals at the end of the visit could be summarized as:

- locating the car;
- finding the exit of the car park.

Only with regard to the last goal there appeared to be no problems; the other wayfinding goals were closely related to the problems mentioned before.

Interviews with visitors who were observed parking in the employee zone showed that they did not understand the meaning of the blue and grey destination zones. This is the kind of problem reported for signs when the information presented is not supported by the perceived environment (Arthur, 1988). As no other blue colour was visible in the environment, the coloured sign was interpreted as a one-way sign. Hence, the visitor would park the car at the first suitable empty parking space which was available, often an employee parking space.

Sight lines to the office entrance were restricted by the many columns and obstacles in the car park. The entrance was not visible from the path towards the visitor area. For the visitor leaving the building, it was difficult to locate his or her car, as the sight lines to the parking area were also interrupted. Moreover, in the visitor area a suitable identification system for the parking spaces was lacking, and the small space numbers in the employee area, if noticed at all, did not reflect the location of a specific parking space.

Although no complaints were registered about car damage due to parking and backing-out manoeuvres, the battered surface of the concrete columns between adjacent parking spaces indicated a direct relation. As shown in Figure 22.1, the boundary line separating two parking spaces was sometimes drawn towards the centre of the column, suggesting more manoeuvring space than there was actually available. This was not a wayfinding problem in the strict sense, but it certainly affected the circulation system.

### 22.3.2   Redesign: towards a workable solution for the reported problems

For redesign, the main question was whether a workable solution could be found which kept adaptation of built elements to a minimum to limit the costs in terms of time and money. Starting from the analysis, a realizable solution was developed (Figure 22.2) without relocating columns or the office entrance, based on the

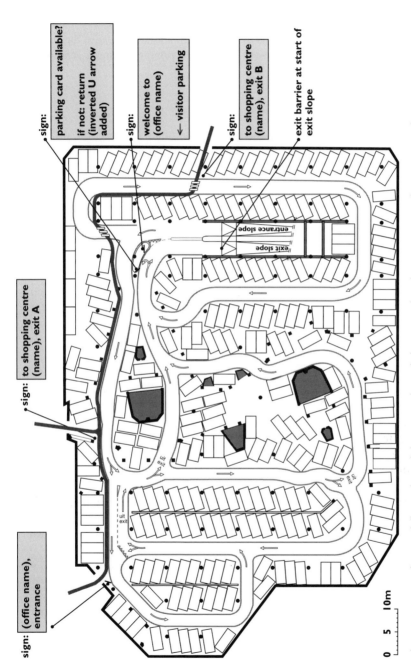

**sign:** parking card available?
if not: return (inverted **U** arrow added)

**sign:** welcome to (office name)

← visitor parking

**sign:** to shopping centre (name), exit B

exit barrier at start of exit slope

**sign:** to shopping centre (name), exit A

**sign:** (office name), entrance

exit slope

entrance slope

uit exit

uit exit

uit exit

0  5  10m

**Figure 22.2** Redesigned floor plan of the car park (path letters and parking space numbers are not shown).

considerations described below. Although no facilities were provided to test its effectiveness, it was expected that the redesigned car park would diminish the problems mentioned, because the recommendations were based on a careful and systematic analysis of the conditions in the car park and also because the solutions for the problems were based on sound and proven principles aimed at improving the environmental interpretation.

### Locating and recognizing the office entrance

To enhance early recognition of the location of the office entrance, the path to the visitor area had to provide visual access to the office entrance as soon as possible after the visitor arrived in the car park. Making the former exit path the direct connection from the entrance slope to the visitor parking area, would make the office entrance visible almost from the first turn in the car park.

In addition, the illumination level of the office entrance had to be increased and a large sign mounted displaying the office name and the word 'Entrance'.

### Indicating the visitor parking area

To inform the visitors about the distinction between visitor and employee parking zones a decision point was created at the end of the entrance slope. This indicated the visitor destination zone, before the visitor arrived at the employee parking area.

### Legible path layout with main and secondary paths

Because of the restricted lines of sight, one path had to present itself as the *main* path for pedestrians going from their car to the office entrance and vice versa. This path should connect with the office entrance as well as the exits to be used on Saturdays for visitors to a nearby shopping centre. The secondary paths had to originate from the main path and run mainly parallel to one another. The new path to the office entrance was best suited to function as the main path – also because all visitors driving to the visitor area would have to see this path. To indicate that this main path also served as the main footpath, a 50-cm-wide strip with the outlines of a walking figure at regular intervals was painted along the main path in a different colour. This strip ran parallel to the car entrance path and up to the second exit to the shopping mall at the employee zone (Figure 22.2).

The new entrance path was only in some places wide enough for two-way traffic. Therefore, a separate car exit path was needed which had to run on the other side of a large building element. As a consequence the ideal solution, i.e., connecting all secondary paths directly with the main footpath, could not be realized.

### Address code to identify the parking space location

Each space had to be given an identifying address code to indicate its location. For this the paths were labelled with lower case letters starting at the office entrance, and for each path, the spaces themselves were numbered, with the letter label of the path as a prefix, starting from the main path, like the odd–even numbering of houses along a street. When visible in front of the parked cars, these space location numbers also reflected the wanted 'sense of sequence, direction and distance' (Weisman, 1979).

## Other requirements

Additional considerations for redesign were a better perceptual guidance of parking manoeuvres (e.g. parking space boundary lines indicating the actual space available, and more conspicuous painting of the columns), spaces suitable for wheelchair users and traffic safety criteria. Furthermore, it had to be possible for a visitor in search of an empty space to recirculate through the car park. Also, a connection near the end of the exit path to the entrance path was needed, as well as a sign providing a timely reminder that a valid parking card was needed to pass the exit barrier.

## 22.4   CONCLUSION

The general criteria mentioned in the introduction proved to be productive in diagnosing the reported problems in the car park and arriving at suggestions for a workable solution to these problems.

The main design intervention was to express the visitor destination zone as a well-indicated decision point, visually related to the office entrance. This was a major change of the circulation system, made possible however without changing the built elements of the car park. The path layout could be changed using paint as a form of signing graphics. The parking space numbers, traffic arrows, and 'Exit' indications are painted on the floor, too. Only a few signs had to be mounted (but with better legibility than the old ones) to support the new layout, together with an increased illumination level of the office entrance itself.

However, a still better solution could have been realized when it had been possible to choose better locations for the entrance, the exits, and the sloping entrance/ exit paths, in order to limit the consequences of the restricted sight lines given the obstacles and the large number of columns. In the design stage of the whole building, the location of the obstacles and columns, too, could have been chosen weighing the mentioned criteria against the other architectural criteria, to prevent situations in which serious orientation and wayfinding problems would arise.

In the analysis some relevant aspects showed up about which the wayfinding literature is not very clear. One aspect is recirculation. This can be interpreted as an aspect of making the environment less sensitive to wayfinding errors ('error-tolerant design'). Another aspect is whether in the decision plan of the visitor, some subplans and the goals associated with them, run in parallel and hence will interact with each other. The available literature treats decision plans mainly as sequential, starting a new subtask after the previous one is finished.

## ACKNOWLEDGEMENTS

The author wishes to thank M. Hovens and G. Okhuijsen for their help with the traffic aspects of the car park redesign.

## REFERENCES

ARTHUR, P. (1988) *Orientation and Wayfinding in Public Buildings, an Overview*. Ottawa: Public Works Canada, Architectural and Engineering Services.

BOL, J. (1993) In 't Kanaalcentrum weten ze nu de weg [In the Channel Centre people can now find their way around; in Dutch]. *Gebouwbeheer* **4**, 28–32.

JANSSEN, F. J. and VENEMANS, P. J. (1983) Herziene indeling van een bouwlaag vanuit routing [Redesigned circulation on a building floor; in Dutch]. In: *Proceedings Ergonomie en het Ziekenhuis*, Rotterdam, 3 December 1983, p. 3, Amsterdam: Nederlandse Vereniging voor Ergonomie.

VENEMANS, P. J. (1994) Wayfinding and orientation, sign systems and buildings. In: ZWAGA, H. J. G., BOERSEMA, T. and HOONHOUT, H. C. M. (Eds), *Proceedings of Public Graphics*, pp. 21.1–21.12. Utrecht: Stichting Public Graphics Research.

VENEMANS, P. J., DARU, R. and VAN WAGENBERG, A. F. (1993) Buildings and wayfinding: a framework for guidelines. In: FELDMAN, R. M., HARDIE, G. and SAILE, D. G. (Eds), *Power by Design, Proceedings of EDRA24*, pp. 233–240. Oklahoma City: EDRA.

VENEMANS, P. J., DARU, R. and VAN WAGENBERG, A. F. (1994) 'Orientation in and around large buildings: guidelines and architects', paper presented at the 2nd DDSS (2nd International Symposium, Design and Decision Support Systems in Architecture and Urban Planning), Vaals, August.

WEISMAN, G. D. (1979) *Way-finding in the Built Environment: A Study in Architectural Legibility*. Ann Arbor: University Microfilms International.

# PART EIGHT

# Graphic Symbols

# CHAPTER TWENTY-THREE

# Design and evaluation of public information symbols

ROBERT DEWAR

## 23.1 INTRODUCTION

One of the oldest forms of visual communication among people involves the use of pictorial representation. The terms 'symbol', 'pictograph', 'pictogram', 'icon' and 'glyph' all refer to commonly used pictorials. These terms will be used to mean more or less the same thing in the present chapter (although their strictly correct usage may be different from that used here). The term 'icon', for example, is widely used in computer applications. A symbol is essentially a picture or visual representation which depicts one or some of the features of the referent (real-world object or concept) it represents.

With the increase in international travel and trade, there is a growing need to communicate with people who do not understand the language of the country they are in. Perhaps the best examples of this are signs in international airports and information on dashboards of cars. In both of these cases the intent is to provide information accurately and quickly without using words. The use of symbols is one of the most popular ways of trying to meet these requirements. There is no shortage of examples of these devices, as they appear in our daily environments and on the products we use. They can be found in a great variety of forms in handbooks and catalogues (e.g. Dreyfuss, 1972; Modley, 1976).

Compared to word messages, symbols have a number of advantages. They can be identified at a greater distance and more rapidly, can be identified more accurately when seen at a glance (Dewar and Ells, 1974), and can be seen better under adverse viewing conditions (Ells and Dewar, 1979); they can be understood by people who do not read the language of the country in which they are used; and they can be detected more readily than can word signs (Jacobs *et al.*, 1975). Another advantage of pictorials is their compactness – they can represent information in a spatially condensed form. In addition, pictorial information has the advantage that it can be multi-dimensional, incorporating such features as colour, shape and size, as well as combinations of these, into the basic symbol message.

Symbols first appeared as paintings or carvings on caves and stone walls as early as 50 000 BC, with the first depiction of humans dating back about 11 000 years. As used today, symbols can be divided into five main categories: industrial and occupational (in the workplace); representing methods (machines, instructions); management of public places (transportation, museums, hospitals); knowledge; and particular activities (sports). Here, the use of these devices, their current problems, development and evaluation are examined, and symbol design guidelines are recommended.

## 23.2   CRITERIA FOR EFFECTIVE SYMBOLS

Several criteria must be met for a symbol to be effective. Initially, it must command attention or be easily detected by the person who needs the information. It must be legible at the appropriate distance and must often be legible when seen for a very brief time (e.g. a highway sign) or under adverse viewing conditions (e.g. low illumination, glare). In some situations, such as on the roadway, the information must also be quickly identified, as drivers often have only a second or two to interpret and respond to the message. The symbol must be clearly understood and the action to be taken in response to the message should be immediately obvious.

These various criteria can be in conflict and their relative importance has never been established. In an attempt to determine the relative weightings that ought to be attributed to the main criteria for traffic sign symbols, Dewar (1988a) solicited the views of sign experts and traffic engineers in four countries (Australia, Canada, New Zealand and the USA). Although there were some national differences, there was widespread agreement that comprehension was most important, followed by conspicuity, reaction time and legibility distance (the last two being similar in importance). Learnability was rated lowest. Not only are these various criteria never all measured in one study, but there is no effort to assign relative weights to them when more than a single measure is used in conducting an overall assessment (Mackett-Stout and Dewar, 1981).

It is essential that symbols are designed while keeping in mind the information system into which they will be placed. This is especially the case when introducing new ones. They must be distinguishable from others in the system (e.g. cleaning instructions on clothing, hazard warnings on trucks, computer icons), so as not to be confused. When one considers the plethora of icons for use with computers it is understandable that confusions will arise. A book devoted specifically to computer icons (Horton, 1994) comes with a disk containing 500 such icons.

The specific criteria for individual symbols or sets of symbols depend on their application. Legibility distance is essential in the case of traffic signs and many building signs, but not for symbols on maps or consumer products. The potential users of the information must also be taken into account. In addition to these task-specific criteria, factors affecting the performance of potential users must be considered, such as the effects of increasing age and low intelligence on the comprehension of symbols.

### 23.3  PHILOSOPHY AND THEORY OF SYMBOL DESIGN

### 23.3.1  A model of the relation between signal, sign and referent

Familant and Detwailer (1993) have proposed a way of looking at symbols and their referents as follows (Figure 23.1). According to them information becomes encoded as a 'signal' which can be interpreted if the signal is mapped to a 'referent' in the real world. The signal's features depend on the medium of communication. The spoken word 'house' has acoustical features, whereas a picture of a house has visual features. A 'sign' is the relationship between the signal and its referent, and it succeeds in communicating if a user can unambiguously refer to the sign's referent. Signs can be 'iconic' or 'symbolic'. In the case of the former, the two sets of features (those in the signal and the referent) intersect. For example, the dustbin used as a computer icon to represent 'erase a file' represents the features related to getting rid of something. Symbolic sign relations involve no similarities (except by accident) between the signal and the referent. The relationship is arbitrary, as would be the case with the symbol for 'radioactive'.

**Figure 23.1**  The sign, signal, referent relationship (Familant and Detwailer, 1993).

### 23.3.2  Classifications of symbols

Familant and Detwailer (1993) have presented a summary and critique of several taxonomic systems for classifying icons. To some degree these overlap, with different terminology used to indicate the same things. The important categories appear to be: arbitrary/abstract vs. pictorial/concrete, analogous, and exemplars. Classification can also be in terms of their form, function, referent or referent mappings. A classification system using a higher level of analysis based on a referent mapping approach has been proposed by Rogers (1989). She suggests that icons can fall into the following categories: form, which includes resemblance, or use of an analogous image (e.g. the 'falling rocks' road sign symbol); exemplar, or use of a typical example for a class of objects (e.g. a book to represent 'library'); symbolic, where an image represents a higher level of abstraction than the image itself (e.g. cracked wine glass to show 'fragility'); and arbitrary, or the use of an image that has no relationship to the referent (e.g. the symbol for 'biohazard'). Other classification systems include: image-related, referring to real objects by resemblance (pictograph);

concept-related, referring to a perceptual concept, rather than real objects (abstract); and arbitrary, with no resemblance or relation to the object or concept.

Using their model of the relationship between signal, sign and referent, Familant and Detwailer indicate that the mapping between a signal and its referent can be either part–part or part–whole. In the part–part mapping both the pictograph and its referent share some, but not all, features. An example is the previously mentioned computer icon (dustbin) for indicating 'erase file', where the icon is a metal container sharing some of the features (used to get rid of things) that the referent has. In a part–whole relation the pictographs's features are a proper subset of the referent's feature set. Reference to a part would indicate the whole. A part–whole relationship would be exemplified by a picture of a golf club and ball to represent 'golf course'. Using their feature mapping approach in this way Familant and Detwailer developed an elaborate classification for icons.

### 23.3.3   Understanding symbols

It is important to examine the psychological processes involved in recognizing and understanding pictographs. Interpretation of concrete symbols can recruit resources involved in interpreting the real world. Abstract ones invoke referents only at the conceptual level, whereas concrete ones invoke specific objects or exemplars. Cultural experience and context can play a role in the understanding of symbols. Changes in the form of objects over time are also important. For example, traffic signs in many parts of the world depict a railway train with an old-fashioned steam engine, whereas most trains now are diesel/electric and do not have a distinctive shape with a smoke stack. Therefore, the old-fashioned train may be more distinctive visually, even though it is out of date.

There are a variety of approaches to the presentation of information using symbols. A warning message can indicate either the nature of the hazard or its consequences. For example, a curved arrow on a traffic sign shows the nature of the roadway alignment ahead, whereas a symbol showing a car out of control illustrates the consequences of a wet road surface.

The object and message referred to by a symbol will determine its ease of design and probably also its effectiveness. Important here are the type of information and its 'psychological attributes' (Rogers, 1989). In computer applications, for example, certain abstract concepts are difficult to convey in pictorial form. Abstract concepts can be more readily represented by icons if they have a high degree of imageability and association with concepts used within the specific system (e.g. computer commands, hazardous materials, laundry instructions). The computer command 'go to the bottom of the text' is easier to represent in icon form than a command such as 'save', which is much more difficult to depict.

Kolers (1969) points out that writing systems are made up of elements (smallest interpretable units) and compounds (their combination). In alphabets, letters are elements and words are compounds, but letters can be considered compounds of lines, bars, loops, etc. There are different levels of analysis. An element in picture writing is 'any whole picture whose decomposition creates uninterpretable parts for the relevant level of analysis' (Kolers, 1969, p. 356).

Unlike verbal language, the construction of visual compounds has not been based on rules. We do not fully understand why people interpret a combination of image elements in a certain way. In the early development of icons for computers a number of them looked like, and represented, certain office functions – papers, folders, filing cabinets, mail boxes. For these icons the functions were directly analogous to some physical object in an office. However, the number of messages that could be represented easily was small. Many computer operations (e.g. compiling operations) just do not have pictorial representations. It became necessary to design icons that did not look like any object, and even letters and words became 'icons'.

An interesting psychological, almost philosophical, question arises in connection with the choice of image for some types of symbol messages. For example, should drivers be told what they can (or must) do, or what they cannot do on the road? The difference is illustrated in turn restriction messages. 'No right turn' can be indicated by a right arrow and a red ring with a diagonal slash or with left and straight arrows inside a green ring. The latter, permissive, version was (and to some extent still is) used in Canada, whereas the prohibitive version of such messages is widely used in many parts of the world. Work by Dewar and Swanson (1972) on glance legibility suggested the merits of the permissive symbol for turn restrictions, but their results could have been a function of the fact that they used Canadian drivers, who were more familiar with the permissive version at the time. The main point against the prohibitive approach is that the slash obscures the message (Dewar, 1976). A potential problem with the permissive design is that the message is indirect and the viewer must infer what is not allowed. This version of the turn restriction symbol, for example, does not specifically indicate that one cannot turn right. In spite of these observations, at this stage in the development of traffic sign symbols it may be that the prohibitive restriction symbol is best, in view of its widespread use throughout the world.

### 23.4  PROBLEMS WITH SYMBOLS

In spite of the advantages of symbols, there are still a number of problems associated with their design and use. Many are too small to be seen from a distance, even at reading distance (e.g. on maps and brochures), or they have very small or unnecessary detail. Some are very similar to others, leading not only to confusion between symbol images, but also to misunderstanding of the messages. Part of the problem may be due to a lack of syntactic and semantic rules equivalent to those of verbal language. Whatever the cause, the main difficulty with graphic symbols is that their meanings are not always obvious to the user. This is a serious problem, because one of the primary reasons for the widespread use of symbols is the need to communicate with people who do not read the language of the country in which these symbols are used. It is often mistakenly assumed that they will convey the intended information to people of all languages.

It may seem obvious how you would draw a picture to represent 'chair' or 'phone', but chairs and phones come in many shapes. A knife and fork may seem appropriate to depict 'restaurant', but would not be for those who had only eaten with chopsticks. Many objects differ not only by style, but among cultures and over time within a culture. Modern phones are a good example. It is often adequate, or preferable, to present a caricature or drawing that is not a copy of the object. A caricature that emphasizes certain features of an object is often even easier to recognize than a photograph of that same object.

Cross-cultural differences can be seen from the results of the work of Olmstead (Chapter 25). She found substantial differences across two cultural groups (American and Chinese) with respect to understanding of symbols for health care facilities. Using as a criterion the estimated comprehensibility of 87 per cent, as suggested by Zwaga (1989), 11 of the 41 symbols tested met this criterion for the American group, and eight for the Chinese group. However, three symbols understood by the Chinese were different from those understood by the American group.

Early International Organization for Standardization (ISO) evaluations of public information symbols also showed differences across countries for some symbols. An example is an effort by the ISO to develop a symbol to indicate 'police' by using a hat worn by police. The problem was that the hat varies throughout the world and not everybody can be expected to be familiar with the hats worn by police in different countries. There is a need to have as much uniformity as possible across different information systems (e.g. from one computer manufacturer or automobile manufacturer to another).

## 23.5   STANDARDIZATION OF SYMBOL DESIGN AND USE

It would seem obvious that uniformity of both the design and implementation of symbols is desirable. However, uniformity is generally lacking in both of these areas. There are, of course, clear and often rigid design standards for certain applications. Most jurisdictions, for example, have manuals of uniform traffic signs, with symbol designs, dimensions, colours, etc. specified in detail. However, the belief that there is a set of 'international' traffic sign symbols is a myth. A widely used system exists in Europe, but even there each country has a few unique ones, and the European system is certainly not used world-wide. Efforts by the ISO have led to some internationally accepted symbols, but the world is still filled with a variety of designs for everything from toilets to car rental. An examination of any catalogue of symbols (e.g. Dreyfuss, 1972; Modley, 1976) illustrates the great variety of symbol designs in use for specific messages. A few of the variations on health care symbols and public information symbols can be found in the chapters by Brugger (Chapter 24) and Olmstead (Chapter 25). Not only do symbol designs vary geographically, but also within the same countries and cities across different applications. Note the different ways of depicting an airplane in airports and on road signs, or the variety of versions of the message for toilets on maps and building signs.

The other area where standardization is lacking, or where there are simply no standards, is the determination of acceptable levels of understanding, legibility distance, etc. The standards for comprehension vary from 67 per cent (ISO) to 85 per cent (American National Standards Institute). The acceptable level of comprehension depends in part on the nature of the message and the consequences of failing to understand it. Surely it is more important to understand a symbol indicating 'radioactive' than one meaning 'no littering'. Likewise, standards for legibility distance would be quite different for a road sign symbol indicating 'do not enter' than one for 'campground'.

### 23.6  METHODS FOR EVALUATING SYMBOLS

A great variety of techniques has been employed for the evaluation of symbols (see Mackett-Stout and Dewar (1981) for a general review and critique of methodology). Methods can be divided into field and laboratory procedures. Assessment may also be based on subjective methods such as clarity ratings, preference ranking and 'expert opinion'. In the traffic engineering community it is not unusual to see decisions about national standards being made by majority vote in a meeting of 30 or so 'experts', when the main 'data' are the experiences of a single jurisdiction, or the personal opinions of those who cast the votes. Many important decisions have been made on the basis of little or no objective evidence.

### 23.6.1  Comprehensibility and the ISO test procedure

One of the few well-established evaluation procedures is the one used by the ISO to assess public information symbols. Brugger (Chapter 24) provides an account of this approach. Brugger compared the comprehension test (the standard ISO procedure – write out the symbol's meaning) with three measures for the preselection of symbols prior to full comprehension testing – appropriateness rating, a three-class rating procedure, and Zwaga's (1989) comprehension estimation procedure, described below. Brugger's findings showed that the comprehension estimation method is most effective.

The ultimate index of the adequacy of a symbol is how clearly and quickly the message is understood by the persons for whom it is intended. However, it is often too costly to conduct field evaluations of symbols. A more efficient and much less expensive approach is to evaluate them in the laboratory. Psychological and psychophysical methods such as reaction time, glance legibility, legibility distance, comprehension, preference ratings and signal detection have been employed to gauge the effectiveness of symbols. Laboratory techniques have the advantage of economy of time and money. However, it is essential to ensure that these methods are properly validated against real-world measures of the effectiveness of the symbols in context. Unfortunately, there has been a tendency to accept these methods without properly validating them against appropriate criterion measures.

The ease of understanding is the most important single index of a symbol's effectiveness. One of the best ways to measure this is to show subjects a photo or slide of the sign (preferably in context) and have them write in an answer booklet the symbol's meaning. Data reduction is time-consuming, but the extra effort pays off in terms of a wealth of information about people's confusions and the types of errors they make, and may assist in the redesign process. Although multiple-choice methods are more efficient, it is often difficult to select appropriate wrong responses and to minimize the effects of guessing.

Zwaga (1989) used a novel approach wherein subjects estimated the understandability of information symbols intended to convey destinations in a hospital (e.g. X-ray, surgery). The subjects' task was simply to estimate what percentage of the population they thought would understand the meaning of the symbol. Subjects were told the meaning of the symbol prior to making their estimates. In order to compare these data with comprehension data, another sample of subjects were shown the symbols (one of the four or five versions of each of 22 messages) and asked to indicate their meanings. Correlations between estimated and actual comprehension levels were high, ranging from 0.63 to 0.93 across the sets of symbols.

In his study Zwaga demonstrated that use of the comprehension estimation procedure could be used to eliminate the need for further testing of the really bad and very good symbols. Using the ISO acceptance criterion of 67 per cent comprehension, he suggested that the comprehensibility of symbols with an estimation score falling within an 'uncertainty range' of 20 per cent around the 67 per cent ISO standard (i.e., between 47 per cent and 87 per cent) should be verified in a comprehension test. The range of 20 per cent above and below the 67 per cent criterion was based on the standard error of measurement when calculating the correlation between the two sets of scores (estimation scores and comprehension scores). The use of this procedure was found to be highly reliable, resulting in no false accepts and only one false reject out of the 104 symbols examined. Compared to the ranking test, the estimation test has a number of advantages. The most important of these is that it improves the efficiency of the evaluation of a set of symbols significantly because the very bad as well as the very good versions of the same message do not have to be tested any further for comprehension.

### 23.6.2  An index of symbol effectiveness

A major shortcoming of much of the research on symbols is its reliance on a single measure of effectiveness. As mentioned above, there are several criteria for the efficacy of a symbol, which implies that more than one measure is required for a proper evaluation. The need for an approach involving a number of measures is obvious (Mackett-Stout and Dewar, 1981). One of the few studies to use and combine a number of measures was that of Roberts et al. (1977), who examined both symbol and text versions of 19 traffic sign messages. Most messages had one text and four symbol versions. Five measures were used – understanding time (the time required to indicate a sign's meaning), comprehension, certainty (how confident the subject was of his/her understanding of the sign's meaning), preference (rank ordering of the symbols used to convey a specific message) and identification time (minimum exposure time at which subjects could accurately identify all elements of the symbol).

The authors derived an 'efficiency index' for each symbol version of each message – what they called the 'relative goodness of performance' of that symbol. For each individual symbol the Z-score for each variable was calculated 'based on the position of its mean relative to the overall distribution of means for that particular variable across *all* signs'. The efficiency index for a specific symbol was the sum of the Z-scores for the five variables. It was assumed that each variable contributed an equal weight to the overall index, a widespread assumption that has never been properly examined.

Mackett-Stout and Dewar (1981), in a study of public information symbols, modified the method of calculating the Z-scores for the efficiency index, basing it on the data from each version of each message, rather than on means for the particular variable across all signs. They argue that the Roberts *et al.* procedure could result in a low value of the index, even though a particular version of a message was the best of the ones being tested. The adequacy of a symbol ought to be measured relative to other symbols representing that same message, otherwise the measure of performance is dependent on the evaluation context (the total set of symbols being tested).

### 23.6.3 Analysis of meaning

Designers may have difficulty knowing whether a candidate symbol is appropriate for use until it has been tested for comprehension. One technique that has been used to gauge the comprehension of symbol elements is the semantic differential. This consists of a series of carefully selected bipolar adjectives (e.g. beautiful–ugly; simple–complex; strong–weak). Dewar and Ells (1979) showed that ratings on this scale correlate well with comprehension measured by having subjects write out the meanings of traffic sign symbols. Caron *et al.* (1980) used this approach to gauge the 'psychological meaning' of public information symbols, as well as individual elements of these symbols and their contribution to the meaning of the symbol. Using discriminant analysis and classification analysis with semantic differential ratings, they were able to determine how well the meanings of symbols and the meanings of individual symbol components were comprehended. For example, the match between the word 'telephone' and the phone handset was much better than that between the word and the phone cradle, and even better than the match with the two combined (Figure 23.2).

### 23.6.4 The effects of context and familiarity on comprehension

Most of the research on comprehension of symbols is done in laboratory or classroom settings using visual material that does not convey any information about the

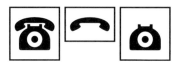

**Figure 23.2** Symbol and its components for the message 'telephone' (Caron *et al.*, 1980).

context in which the symbol might appear. Vukelich and Whitaker (1993) examined the importance of context in symbol comprehension by providing subjects with full context (a two-sentence description of the setting in which the symbol might be seen), partial context (a two-word description of the context), or no context information. An example of a full context for the 'lost and found' symbol would be the following: 'You are walking in an international airport. This symbol is located on a sign extending from the wall overhead'.

Comprehension for the 20 symbols used was highest with the full context verbal description. Familiarity with the symbols also enhanced their comprehension. In general, the levels of understanding were low, even with full context provided (35 per cent and 68 per cent, respectively, for low and high familiar symbols). Other studies (e.g. Cahill, 1975, 1976) have also demonstrated that providing a context when showing symbols tends to increase comprehension levels. Familiarity with traffic sign symbols was found by Dewar *et al.* (1994) to correlate with their comprehension, in the case of two-thirds of the 85 symbols they evaluated.

## 23.7  SPECIFIC APPLICATIONS

The design, application and evaluation of symbols will be illustrated with selected examples of research on two topics – traffic signs and Olympic Games pictographs.

### 23.7.1  Traffic signs

Although a great deal of research has been done on symbols for traffic signs, only one study has been selected for detailed examination, as it is one of the few to use several measures on a large number of symbols. A study on traffic sign symbols by Dewar *et al.* (1994) examined the effectiveness of all symbol signs in the US 'Manual on Uniform Traffic Control Devices' (MUTCD), with emphasis on older drivers. The authors also developed and tested alternative symbol signs that could alleviate the difficulties of some problematic signs. Recommendations were made for design changes to many of the current symbols and symbol sign design guidelines were proposed.

The study was conducted in two phases and all experiments involved licensed drivers in three age groups: young (18–39), middle-aged (40–59), and older (60+). The first two studies in Phase I were a laboratory experiment on daytime legibility distance and a survey of driver comprehension of all 85 symbols in the MUTCD. A number of additional measures (legibility distance under night and night-with-glare conditions, glance legibility, reaction time and conspicuity) were then made on a set of 18 of these symbols. In Phase II, seven of the 18 symbols were modified and seven were redesigned, based on the findings in Phase I. In addition, five novel symbols were designed, using an image-processing reiterative filter/redesign approach. Digitized images of each sign were reiteratively redesigned and filtered through a sequence of low-pass filters to optimize the lowest cut-off level at which all critical details were preserved. These signs were evaluated on measures of comprehension, and legibility distance under day, night and night-with-glare conditions.

The comprehension survey indicated that 16 of the 85 symbols were very well understood (95 per cent or more correct) and that ten were understood by fewer than 40 per cent of drivers. The older drivers had poorer understanding than did those in the two other age groups on 39 per cent of the symbols examined. In the daytime legibility study, mean legibility distances on every sign were lower for the older drivers than for their young and middle-aged counterparts.

Compared to the young drivers, under night and night-with-glare conditions, legibility distances were lower for older drivers for all but one sign. The night legibility distances corresponded very closely to those of the daytime legibility study ($r = 0.965$). Under the night-with-glare condition older drivers identified symbols at shorter distances than did the young drivers for all but two signs, and compared to the middle-aged drivers, the older drivers had shorter legibility distances for all but five signs.

Modifications and redesigns to the selected symbols (including two new designs for one of the messages) resulted in no change for seven symbols, better understanding of three, and poorer understanding of four. Understanding of the five novel symbols was at the same level as that of the redesigned symbols. Comprehension levels were consistently lower for older drivers. Mean daytime legibility distances were inversely related to driver age. Compared to the legibility of their standard versions, the legibility of six of the seven modified signs and five of seven redesigned signs was increased. In the evaluation of night legibility older drivers performed poorer than did the youngest age group on all but one sign and poorer than the middle-aged group on eight of the 19 signs. Under night-with-glare conditions performance of the older drivers was poorer than that of the young drivers on all signs, and below that of the middle-aged drivers on all but two signs. Glare systematically reduced legibility of the signs only for the old drivers. More details on the method used in designing and revising symbols can be found in the following sections, and Chapters 24 and 25.

## 23.7.2  Olympic Games pictographs

Among the most interesting and ever-changing applications of symbols are those used for the Olympic Games. There has been a constant introduction of newly designed symbols to represent athletic events, and in some cases the development

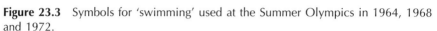

**Figure 23.3** Symbols for 'swimming' used at the Summer Olympics in 1964, 1968 and 1972.

of new sets of symbols for public information as well. The reason that a new set of symbols is developed by each host country is that those developed by previous hosts are under copyright to be used exclusively by that country. This has been the case since the initial use of such symbols in the 1948 Summer Games in London, with the exception of the Montreal Games in 1976, where the host country bought from the previous hosts (Munich) the right to use theirs. The great variation in design can be seen in the three symbols for 'swimming' used in different Summer Olympics (Figure 23.3).

If the objective of symbols is to communicate consistently, one wonders why organizers go to the effort and expense of new designs for *each* Games (every four years, for both Summer and Winter Games). Perhaps it has to do with national pride. Surely it would make sense to develop a uniform set of symbols for the events and have them used on a continuing basis, introducing new ones as needed for new events.

One discouraging factor about the development of new Olympic Games symbols is the apparent lack of objective data supporting their effectiveness. One would hope that at least comprehension and legibility had been objectively measured before their adoption, but such is not usually the case. Their scrutiny and approval by a national committee is a more typical approach. Such was the case for the 1980 Moscow Summer Games when the entire set of symbols was developed in about six months and their adoption was based on approval by the relevant committee (Firsikov, 1994). For these games also a set of 244 original pictographs for public information was developed, which was divided into eight categories. The system was so inclusive that there were separate pictographs for a great variety of foods (pancakes, dumplings, ravioli, sausages). These took the form of a waist-length picture of a chef holding a dish full of the specific food. One wonders how many of these were understood by the public.

Those who develop Olympic Games symbols seem confident that they are very effective. The following quotes reflect this confidence. The Moscow 1980 symbols were deemed to be 'a very clear picture, immediately recognizable from afar' (Firsikov, 1994). These symbols were also said to be 'perfectly comprehensible'. I am not aware of any symbol that is perfectly comprehensible, except perhaps to those who have designed it. This thinking is typical of designers of such information systems – what they create makes perfect sense to them, so therefore it should make sense to others. In a description of the 1964 Japanese Summer Games symbols, they were considered to be 'understood by everyone'. The inadequacy of

**Figure 23.4** Symbols for 'short track speed skating', 'ice hockey', 'bobsleigh' and 'luge' at the 1994 Winter Olympics.

many Olympic Games symbols has been demonstrated by Dewar (1988b), who found great variability in both the comprehension levels and the legibility distances among a set of eight messages from each of four Winter Olympics. Mean correct comprehension across the four sets of pictographs varied from 83.4 per cent (1980, Lake Placid) to 75 per cent (1984, Sarajevo), and average comprehension levels ranged from 44 per cent to 99 per cent. The average legibility distances varied somewhat across the four sets of symbols, but the range of average distances was very wide (by a factor of more than four).

A variety of approaches have been taken by those designing Olympic pictographs, from the part representing the whole in the London and Mexico Summer Games (e.g. an arm holding a ring to represent gymnastics; two arms interlocked for wrestling) to the use of very stylized images for the 1992 Barcelona Games and the 1998 Nagano Winter Games. Perhaps the most interesting and unusual approach has been the 1994 Lillehammer Winter Games for which the 4000-year-old petroglyph of a skier, discovered drawn on a rock in Norway, provided inspiration for their design. The symbols developed with this theme appear very primitive, as if drawn by a child, but may well be effective in terms of comprehension (Figure 23.4). Their very simplicity is their strong point.

### 23.8   GUIDELINES FOR GRAPHIC SYMBOLS

When considering the use of guidelines, a distinction should be made between those intended for determining image content of symbols and guidelines for the graphic requirements which make symbols legible, understandable, etc. However, the use of guidelines is not as straightforward as it might seem. Although they may provide general or even specific guidance for design, background knowledge is required to appreciate when and how to use a guideline for a specific application. As with all designs, they should be evaluated to determine whether the use of the guidelines has resulted in effective symbols.

### 23.8.1   Guidelines for the image content of symbols

It is essential in the initial stages of developing any symbol to standardize the image content description, as opposed to the image itself. This will permit slight variations in the graphic design of the image to allow for cultural differences, corporate identity requirements and changes in technology. It also permits some creativity on the part of the designer. However, basic design criteria for comprehension and legibility must still be met. All too often designers begin by creating visual images, with little thought to the appropriateness of their content.

Symbols must be meaningful, legible, learnable, memorable and used consistently, therefore users and designers should share a common 'visual vocabulary'. Some studies have suggested that symbols which emphasize distinguishing features are more easily recognized even than photographs (Kolers, 1969; Barthelemy *et al.* 1990). This may involve 'stylization' or the portrayal and exaggeration of the useful and essential elements of an object relevant to its identification.

In order to determine the effectiveness of combining design variables in the development of visual warnings for swimming pool slides Boersema and Zwaga (1989) examined comprehensibility of a number of versions of each of five messages. The designs incorporated a side, top and 2 1/2 dimensional views of the dangerous behaviours, with the message being either prohibitive (behaviour is forbidden), prohibitive and proactive (the safe way to use the slide into the pool is shown) or reactive (consequences of the hazardous behaviours are shown). The ISO procedure for appropriateness ranking was used to select ten symbols for evaluation of comprehension with children aged 7 to 17 years. The four with the highest percentage correct were all of the prohibitive type. The most difficult message to convey was a warning against stopping on the slide. No firm conclusions could be made about the best way to depict a message with a symbol, as it depended on the situation or the activity.

### 23.8.2   Guidelines for the graphic design of symbols

As outlined earlier, there are several criteria that should be met if a symbol is to be effective. The following guidelines are directed at these criteria as they relate to the graphic design of symbols.

#### Uniformity of design

Uniformity of design, both within and between symbol systems aids understanding, especially for new symbols. Where appropriate, symbols should be designed with content and form similar to those found to be effective in systems in other locations and applications.

#### Complexity and detail

No simple rules are available to help the designer of symbols to select an appropriate design style for the image. In general, symbols should be as visually simple as possible. Therefore, the basic design concept should involve an easily discriminated figure with few details. However, some small details may be necessary for adequate comprehension.

There are two types of details in symbols – those necessary for adequate visibility at a greater distance and those desirable for understanding of the message. The latter are likely to be more detailed and may be illegible at the distance from which the message must be identified, but they can be discriminated clearly at a closer distance. These are helpful in promoting understanding of the symbol's meaning. They have educational value but do not contribute to identifying the symbol at a distance. Care must be taken, however, to ensure that these small details do not interfere with the legibility of the details which are essential for identification of a symbol at a distance.

### Specific symbol elements

It is most appropriate to use silhouette (side) views of certain components such as vehicles, in cases where the front or end view is likely to have poor legibility distance or comprehension, or where there may be confusion among messages (e.g. 'bus-station', 'bus-stop'). A side view of vehicles typically contains distinctive features that enhance understanding (e.g. bonnet/boot of a car; cab of a truck).

### Discriminability

An important criterion for the effectiveness of a symbol within a set of others is the degree to which it differs from others in the set. Many symbols have only minor differences from others in their set. Geiselman *et al.* (1982) studied discriminability of symbols in an attempt to develop a human-factors-based criterion for selecting candidates for the US Army's conventional symbol set. They reasoned that one must first know the basis on which people make similarity judgements. The objective was to discover the attributes that determined perceived similarity and to construct and validate a formula for quantifying a symbol's perceived discriminability. Each of 20 symbols selected from the Army's standard symbology, FM 21–30, was defined in terms of primitive symbol attributes. The next step was to determine which attributes predict inter-symbol perceived similarity. Stepwise multiple regression was used in which similarity ratings were predicted on the basis of symbol attributes. An equation was developed for use by designers to estimate similarity among symbols in the set. This formula was then validated in a follow-up experiment.

Nine 'primitive attributes' were defined, e.g. number of straight lines, arcs or 90 degree angles. A second set of 'configural properties' (e.g. triangle or rectangle shape, solid or open circle) was constructed, based on how the primitive attributes combined to form more complex configurations. In the experiment subjects made similarity judgements (on a five-point scale) on all possible pairwise comparisons. Similarity ratings could be partially accounted for (25 per cent of the variance) by a combination of four primitive attributes – number of lines in the external shape, number of straight lines in the internal shape, number of alphanumeric elements, and number of arcs. For the configural attributes, 12 of the 20 predictors were significant sources of information about sameness ratings, accounting for 67 per cent of the variance. The 'discriminability index' for a symbol was based on the number of unique configural attributes of the symbol, the number of unique attributes of the symbols in the set to which it belongs, and the number of attributes it had in common with the others. Following calculation of this index for all symbols a second experiment was conducted to validate the formula. Those with higher discriminability were selected faster in a search task than were others. On the basis of this, the authors claim a 'reasonable degree of validity' for the discriminability index.

## Legibility

Legibility of symbols can be enhanced with the application of a few simple guidelines. The following are taken primarily from the recent work of Dewar *et al.* (1994).

- *Feature size*. Other things being equal, larger features are legible from greater distances than are small ones. A sign's 'critical' features should be as large as possible while remaining consistent with guidelines for ease of comprehension. Solid rather than outline figures are preferable.

- *Feature separation/gap size*. Contour interactions between elements of the same feature, or between adjacent features can make a feature unrecognizable. Separation from other features and from the border of a sign should be maximized.

- *Feature familiarity*. Because the legibility and comprehension of familiar forms is greater than that for unfamiliar ones, the use of pictorially realistic features is preferable to more abstract or stylized forms.

- *Contrast*. Maximizing the luminance and colour contrast between adjacent features and between a symbol and its background will enhance their legibility.

### 23.9 NEW DESIGN TECHNIQUES

### 23.9.1 Enhancing legibility through low-pass image filtering

As mentioned above, legibility of an unfamiliar symbol is often limited by the small size and/or contour interactions of one or more of its critical features. Because problems of size or contour interaction are exacerbated by low-pass computer or optical filtering (see below), the relative susceptibility of a sign's components to such effects can be used in assisting a designer to identify and remedy such problems. Kline and Fuchs (1993), for example, showed that the visibility distance of selected symbol signs could be increased by approximately 50 per cent when the features limiting their legibility were redesigned to enhance their resistance to strong optical blur. In their approach, video images of symbols are digitized into a computer and then filtered through a progressive series of low-pass filters to identify features and feature interactions most vulnerable to loss of small detail. Once identified, these are increased in size or separation to increase their resistance to filtering. This process can be repeated to achieve the lowest cut-off threshold for feature design or location. The maximum cut-off threshold of a symbol's critical feature(s) appears to be a powerful determinant of its legibility. Regardless of driver age, the correlation between low-pass cut-off threshold of symbols and their daytime legibility was found to be close to 0.90. This procedure, described in detail by Schieber *et al.* (1994) has also been shown to be a good predictor of legibility distance of traffic sign symbols.

### 23.9.2 A sequential-component approach to sign design and modification

In their conclusion to a large study of traffic sign symbol design, Dewar *et al.* (1994) recommend a sequential-component approach to symbol design to enhance both understanding and legibility. It should be noted that design features which contribute positively to one of these dimensions, may even detract from the other. The approach to design could be improved by use of a procedure in which features are added to the 'base design' for the symbol in discrete steps. This base design would consist of the minimum elements needed to present the symbol's message to naive viewers (i.e., the 'critical elements'). The elements that bring about the greatest increment to understanding would then be added one at a time until some predetermined threshold level of comprehension was reached. Once the minimal feature configuration for a symbol was established in this way, the legibility of the design elements would be optimized, perhaps utilizing the low-pass filtering process described above. Only after the sign's critical elements were determined and their legibility maximized would additional features that enhanced a symbol's comprehension be added. For example, if this approach were applied to a 'school bus-stop ahead' symbol, the base design might consist only of a large outline drawing of the back of a bus and an 'ahead arrow'. If this did not yield the acceptable level of comprehension, features that most increased understanding (e.g. rear doors, a student or students) could be added. The legibility of the symbol could then be maximized using a low-pass filter process. If desired, and its layout permitted, additional 'educational' elements could be added (e.g. 'flashing red lights', rear windows, books or a backpack) to increase the sign's legibility through the subsequent 'top-down' benefits of enhanced comprehension.

### 23.10 CONCLUSIONS

It is evident from this brief review of selected work on symbols that, in spite of their widespread and increasing use, there is much room for improvement in their design. Kolers has warned against overrating the usability of graphic symbols. He states: 'pictograms can never fully replace alphabetic languages nor are they a magic road to international communication' (Kolers, 1969, p. 360). They are restricted to identifying and locating objects and conveying instructions. One problem is that there is no basic vocabulary for symbols. Kolers suggests that what we need is not a dictionary of pictures, but knowledge of the kinds of information that different cultures have found useful to convey with pictures. We also need to know the cognitive processes underlying the interpretation of symbols. The mechanisms by which people make inferences and draw conclusions from symbols require study, and we need to know the 'syntax of picture writing', as well as how people code, interpret and use symbols.

With respect to the potential use of this method of visual communication, Kolers (1969, p. 355) concludes that 'it should be clear that the claims of "immediacy" and "directness" of understanding of pictograms, and especially the claims of "instant language" are drastically excessive'.

There is clearly a need to coordinate the efforts of graphic designers, as well as specialists in applied behavioural research (e.g. psychologists, vision specialists) to enhance the ultimate effectiveness of all types of symbols and to improve the quality of research on symbols.

## REFERENCES

BARTHELEMY, K. K., MAZAR, K. M. and REISING, J. M. (1990) Color coding and size enhancement of switch symbol critical features. In: *Proceedings of the Human Factors Society 34th Annual Meeting*, pp. 99–103. Santa Monica, CA: Human Factors Society.

BOERSEMA, T. and ZWAGA, H. J. G. (1989) Selecting comprehensible warning symbols for swimming pools. In: *Proceedings of the Human Factors Society 33rd Annual Meeting*, pp. 994–997. Santa Monica, CA: Human Factors Society.

CAHILL, M. (1975) Interpretability of graphic symbols as a function of context and experience factors. *Journal of Applied Psychology* **60**, 376–380.

CAHILL, M. (1976) Design features of graphic symbols varying in interpretability. *Perceptual and Motor Skills* **42**, 647–653.

CARON, J., JAMIESON, D. and DEWAR, R. E. (1980) Evaluating pictographs using semantic differential and classification techniques. *Ergonomics* **23**, 137–146.

DEWAR, R. E. (1976) The slash obscures the symbol on prohibitive traffic signs. *Human Factors* **18**, 253–258.

DEWAR, R. E. (1988a) Criteria for the design and evaluation of traffic sign symbols. *Transportation Research Record* **1160**, 1–6.

DEWAR, R. E. (1988b) Comprehension and legibility distance of Olympic Games pictographs. In: *Proceedings of the 10th Meeting of the International Ergonomics Association*, pp. 569–572, Sydney, Australia.

DEWAR, R. E. and ELLS, J. G. (1974) A comparison of three methods for evaluating traffic signs. *Transportation Research Record* **503**, 38–47.

DEWAR, R. E. and ELLS, J. G. (1979) The semantic differential as an index of traffic sign perception and comprehension. *Human Factors* **19**, 183–189.

DEWAR, R. E. and SWANSON, H. A. (1972) Recognition of traffic control signs. *Highway Research Record* **414**, 16–23.

DEWAR, R. E., KLINE, D. W., SCHIEBER, F. and SWANSON, H. A. (1994) *Symbol Signing Design for Older Drivers, Final Technical Report*. Washington, DC: Federal Highway Administration, Contract No. DTFW61-01-C-00018.

DREYFUSS, H. (1972) *Symbol Sourcebook*. New York: McGraw-Hill.

ELLS, J. G. and DEWAR, R. E. (1979) Rapid comprehension of verbal and symbolic traffic sign messages. *Human Factors* **21**, 161–168.

FAMILANT, M. E. and DETWAILER, M. C. (1993) Iconic reference: evolving perspectives and an organizing framework. *International Journal of Man-Machine Studies* **38**, 705–728.

FIRSIKOV, E. (1994) The Moscow 'Olympics-80' in pictograms. *Olympic Message* **34**, 20–27.

GEISELMAN, R. E., LANDEE, B. M. and CHRISTEN, F. G. (1982) Perceptual discriminability as a basis for selecting graphic symbols. *Human Factors* **24**, 329–337.

HORTON, W. (1994) *The Icon Book*. New York: John Wiley and Sons.

JACOBS, R. J., JOHNSTON, A. W. and COLE, B. L. (1975) The visibility of alphabetic and symbolic traffic signs. *Australian Road Research* **5**, 68–86.

KLINE, D. W. and FUCHS, P. (1993) The visibility of symbolic highway signs can be increased among drivers of all ages. *Human Factors* **35**, 25–34.

KOLERS, P. A. (1969) Some formal characteristics of pictograms. *American Scientist* **57**, 348–363.

MACKETT-STOUT, J. and DEWAR, R. E. (1981) Evaluation of symbolic public information signs. *Human Factors* **23**, 139–151.

MODLEY, R. (1976) *Handbook of Pictorial Symbols*. New York: Dover Publications, Inc.

ROBERTS, K. M., LAREAU, E. W. and WELCH, D. (1977) *Perceptual Factors and Meanings of Symbolic Information Elements*, Vol. 2. Washington, DC: Federal Highway Administration, Technical Report No. FHWA-RD-77-65.

ROGERS, Y. (1989) Icon design for the user interface. In: OBORNE, D. J. (Ed), *International Reviews of Ergonomics*, Vol. 2, pp. 129–154. New York: Taylor and Francis.

SCHIEBER, F., KLINE, D. W. and DEWAR, R. E. (1994) 'Optimizing symbol highway signs for older drivers', Paper presented at the 12th Congress of the International Ergonomics Association, Toronto, August 1994.

VUKELICH, M. and WHITAKER, L. A. (1993) The effects of context on the comprehension of graphic symbols. In: *Proceedings of the Human Factors and Ergonomics Society 37th Annual Meeting*, pp. 511–515. Santa Monica, CA: Human Factors and Ergonomics Society.

ZWAGA, H. J. (1989) Comprehensibility estimates of public information symbols: their validity and use. In: *Proceedings of the Human Factors Society 33rd Annual Meeting*, pp. 979–983. Santa Monica, CA: Human Factors Society.

# CHAPTER TWENTY-FOUR

# Public information symbols: a comparison of ISO testing procedures

CHRISTOF BRUGGER

## 24.1 INTRODUCTION

Technical Committee 145 of the International Organization for Standardization (ISO) has been working on improving the introduction of comprehensible public information symbols since the beginning of the 1970s. After reviewing world-wide research undertaken until this date, the working group concerned with testing procedures proposed a series of tests to be applied for evaluating symbols in order to base standardization of symbols on an objective and scientific approach (Easterby and Zwaga, 1974).

As a preliminary test to reduce the number of symbols to be used in further tests, a preference ranking test was proposed, even though ranking does not provide any information on absolute quality of a symbol, since it only shows the relative position within the set tested. In the next stage, the variants selected on the basis of preference ranking results were to be examined by asking respondents the meanings of these symbols. Parallel to testing comprehension, the same variants were supposed to be compared with a third test – the matching test – where the respondents have to indicate which symbol out of a set of symbols matches the function specified.

In a cross-cultural evaluation of these testing procedures (Easterby and Zwaga, 1976), the comprehension test as a paper–pencil method with symbols presented in random order in small booklets, was shown to be most effective by not only showing the degree of correct comprehension of the variants under test as a measure of quality, but also by providing additional information on the effects of misleading

**Table 24.1** Response categories for the evaluation of the comprehension test according to ISO 9186

| Category | Criterion |
| --- | --- |
| 1 | Correct understanding of the symbol is certain |
| 2 | Correct understanding of the symbol is likely |
| 3 | Correct understanding of the symbol is marginally likely |
| 4 | The response is opposite to the intended meaning |
| 5 | The response is wrong |
| 6 | The response given is 'Don't know' |
| 7 | No response is given |

visual elements, which hamper the correct interpretation of the symbol. The matching test did not yield sufficient information to justify the high demands on the field work resources.

Conclusions from this project brought about some modifications of the test procedures applied in the next large-scale study under the sponsorship of ISO in 1979–1980 (Easterby and Graydon, 1981a, 1981b). In this study with 36 referents, some with more than 40 variants, further limitations of the preference ranking test became obvious. Standard categories for evaluating the responses of the comprehension/recognition test were introduced to improve the evaluation of results from seven participating countries. Additional observations from a subsequent ISO study in five countries (Brugger, 1987) and local research in various countries finally led to the international standard, *ISO 9186: Procedures for the Development and Testing of Public Information Symbols* (ISO, 1989). The procedure prescribed by the standard is as follows. After detailed preparations which include the analysis of the given communication problem and the collection of alternative symbol designs three variants are selected for comprehension testing on the basis of appropriateness ranking tests conducted in at least two countries. Responses from subsequent comprehension/recognition testing in four or more countries are categorized by three independently working judges using the seven categories shown in Table 24.1. Only if a variant exceeds the acceptance criterion of 66 per cent responses in the categories 'certain' and 'likely' will it be used as a basis for the standard image content, which is a verbal description of the image of this variant.

In 1989 Zwaga recommended the use of a rating test. With five sets of a total of 109 hospital symbols he was able to show that estimation scores of comprehensibility were good predictors of comprehension scores. He also indicated that the efficiency of the ISO testing procedure could be improved by replacing the preference ranking test with this estimation test. Conforming to previous practice using the ranking test, for each referent only the three variants with the highest estimation scores were supposed to be included in the comprehension test. To avoid wrong decisions, Zwaga proposed the definition of an 'uncertainty range' around the ISO acceptance criterion, with dimensions derived from the standard error of estimates of the regression equations for the symbol sets tested. Variants exceeding the upper

limit of this uncertainty range were assumed to reach the ISO criterion of acceptance safely and could therefore be proposed for standardization without additional
comprehension testing. On the other hand, variants not reaching the lower limit of
this uncertainty range were expected to fail in the comprehension test anyway and
should not be tested either. Compared to the ranking test this procedure seemed to
be far more efficient.

In a detailed proposal for a new standard, Foster (1991) suggested the replacement of the ranking test by a rating procedure based on a three-point scale, but was
confronted with the necessity of defining numeric criteria for acceptance or rejection of symbols, something that is not reasonably possible without any previous
field research. The author also supported testing ease of learning, using a recall test
as an alternative to the comprehension test.

The aim of this latest set of experiments was to provide an objective basis for
deciding on the future preselection test in the ISO testing procedure. The appropriateness ranking according to the official ISO testing procedures, the appropriateness rating procedure proposed by Foster (1991) and the comprehensibility estimation
procedure according to Zwaga (1989) were compared with regard to their ability to
predict the results of the ISO comprehension test.

## 24.2  APPROPRIATENESS RANKING TEST

### Respondents

Fifty respondents (28 male and 22 female) ranging in age from 15 to 78 years, with
a mean age of 34 years, participated in this experiment. None of these respondents
took part in any other experiment of this series. This is also the case with the
respondents in the other tests. Data for this test and all of the following experiments
were collected in or in the vicinity of Vienna, Austria.

### Stimuli

All symbols of Figure 24.1 were used as stimuli. Each symbol was displayed in
black and white on an A7-sized card in centred position with a size of 30 mm ×
30 mm. For each referent an information card was prepared, showing the name of
the referent, its function, its field of application, and, if any, the excluded functions.

### Procedure

A respondent had to rank, successively, the symbol variants for each of the referents. For each referent the respondent received the corresponding information card
and a stack of cards, each of which depicted a variant symbol for the referent. The
respondent was asked to read the information card, to spread all the test cards on a
table, and to rank-order the variants according to their appropriateness for the
particular referent. The rank given to each variant was then recorded by the experi-
menter on a specific form.

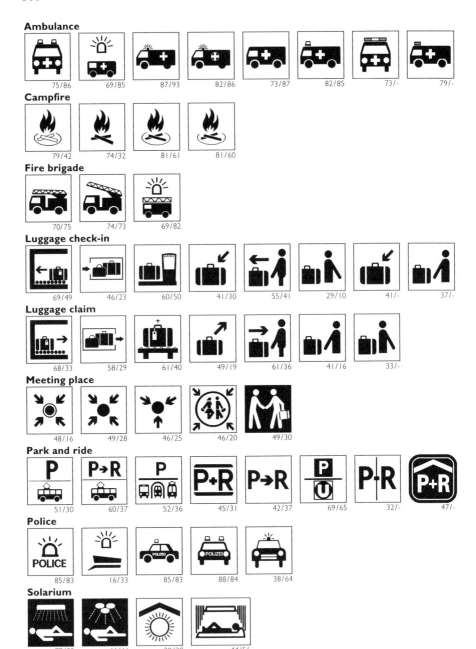

**Figure 24.1** Test symbol set and selected results. The first number below each symbol is the mean of the comprehensibility estimations. The second number is the comprehension score. The symbols in columns 7 and 8 were not subjected to a comprehension test.

## Scoring

The median ranking positions in accordance with ISO 9186 were determined for each symbol. To eliminate any possible bias introduced by the varying number of variants per referent, the median values for each referent were transformed into normalized values (100 is best, and 0 is worst).

## 24.3   APPROPRIATENESS CLASS ASSIGNMENT TEST

### Respondents

The average age of the 67 respondents was 32 years. There were 34 men and 33 women. Each completed the test individually.

### Stimuli

The stimuli were identical to the stimuli used in the appropriateness ranking test.

### Procedure

As in the appropriateness ranking test all cards for one referent were handed over in a stack with the information card on top. After reading the information card and inspecting all variants the respondent had to assign to each variant one of three classes of appropriateness: highly appropriate, slightly appropriate, or not appropriate.

### Scoring

According to the proposed method, the frequency of Class 1 assignments of a variant (highly appropriate) was used as a measure of its appropriateness.

## 24.4   COMPREHENSIBILITY ESTIMATION

### Respondents

Fifty-one respondents (22 men and 29 women) were recruited for the test. Their average age was 33 years.

### Stimuli

All symbols in Figure 24.1 were used as stimuli. For one referent all variants, each about 30 mm × 30 mm in black and white, were arranged in a circle on an A4-sized page with the referent, its function, and, if any, the excluded functions printed in the centre of the circle. The pages for all referents were collated into books using six different random orders. The instructions were printed on the front page.

*Procedure*

The respondents were instructed to read the information in the centre of each page
of the test book and to write next to each symbol an estimation of the percentage of
the Austrian population that, in their opinion, would understand its meaning.

*Scoring*

The mean estimation score was computed for each symbol.

## 24.5   COMPREHENSION TEST

*Respondents*

A total of 311 respondents (198 men and 113 women) took part in the test, 50 to 55
respondents for each of six symbol sets (see below). According to ISO recommendations respondents aged 15 to 30 years and above 50 years were overrepresented.

*Stimuli*

A maximum of six variants for one referent were used for comprehension testing.
Each variant was assigned to a different test set. For each test set black and white
copies of the symbols with a size of 30 mm × 30 mm were made on A7-sized pages,
one symbol per page. Pages for each set were collated in a number of different
random orders into test booklets. The first page was a title sheet also used for re-
gistering age and sex of the respondent. The second page was the instruction sheet
and the third page showed an example.

*Procedure*

Each respondent was handed a booklet and instructed to write below each symbol
his or her interpretation of the meaning. No information about context of use was
given. A respondent completed only one test booklet. Because a test booklet only
held one symbol variant for a referent, a respondent never had to give the meaning
for more than one symbol variant for a specific referent.

*Scoring*

As specified by ISO 9186 each answer was assigned to one of seven possible
categories (Table 24.1) by three independently working judges. In the cases where
the judges did not agree on one single category, the category assigned by the
majority of the judges was chosen. According to the standard's new proposal to
determine the comprehension score, in this study the comprehension score is derived from the percentages of responses in Categories 1 to 3, assigning Category 1
a weight of 1.0, Category 2 a weight of 0.75 and Category 3 a weight of 0.5. The

possible range of comprehension scores therefore lies between 0 for completely misunderstood or incomprehensible symbols, and 100 for perfectly comprehensible symbols.

## 24.6    RESULTS AND DISCUSSION

In many cases the ranking data were not distributed normally and parametric tests could not be used. The ranking results for each referent were subjected to Friedman tests and subsequently to Wilcoxon signed-ranks tests. Although significant differences ($p < 0.01$) were found within all sets, there was, overall, a sufficient degree of consistency of rankings. The wide range as well as the even distribution of the comprehension scores provided a suitable base for a validation study. The only drawback was related to a part of the responses for 'luggage claim', as there is some ambiguity in the corresponding German wording. Therefore, the judges were less certain and less consistent when classifying these responses.

In each of the three preselection tests respondents were told the meaning of the symbols. The differences between these tests are therefore primarily based on the kind of judgement required from the respondents. The product–moment correlations between these tests, based on the scores of all 52 symbols of this study, are always highly significant. This supports the view that the tasks the respondents had to perform are highly similar. The relation between the two rating tasks seems to be closer ($r = 0.82$) than the relation between the rating tasks and the ranking task ($r = 0.49$ and $0.70$).

Because the primary reason to conduct this study was to examine the validity of the preselection tests in predicting comprehension scores based on the standard ISO test, correlations between comprehension scores for 45 public information symbols and corresponding data of the preselection methods under examination were computed. While appropriateness ranking scores showed only minimal correlations with comprehension scores ($0.21$), correlations of the rating scores with comprehension scores were highly significant with $r = 0.51$ for appropriateness class assignment means and $r = 0.76$ for comprehensibility estimation scores.

The plan to revise ISO 9186 as presented by Foster (1991) would only result in a minor improvement. Using the Appropriate Class Assignment test and the proposed method of omitting comprehension testing for all variants with more than 65 per cent of assignments to Category 1 (highly appropriate) would have resulted in a reduction of the symbols to be tested by a number of five, while falsely accepting three symbols not meeting the ISO comprehension criterion of 66 per cent (see Table 24.2). Based on the present data this criterion would have to be raised to 75 per cent assignments to Category 1 to prevent accepting inadequate variants, reducing the number of symbols included in the comprehension test by only one as compared to the ranking procedure.

The use of only three categories is probably the main cause of the low validity of this test. This sometimes led to strange or inconsistent ratings. Apparently the use of only three categories did not sufficiently take into account the fact that

**Table 24.2** Effects of various preselection methods on the extent of ISO comprehension testing based on a set of nine referents with a total of 45 symbols

| | Preselection method | | |
| --- | --- | --- | --- |
| | Ranking | Class assignment | Estimation (mean) |
| Symbols to test | 27 | 22 | 17 |
| Symbols to keep | 10 | 13 | 10 |
| Referents to test | 9 | 9 | 6 |
| Referents to keep | 4 | 6 | 4 |
| False rejects or accepts | 0 | 3 | 0 |

respondents want to differentiate between ratings even within a set of well comprehensible symbol variants. In such a set of symbols variants, they still assigned Categories 2 and 3 to some of them in order to highlight the differences between these variants.

Data based on the comprehensibility estimation procedure proposed by Zwaga (1989) showed the highest correlations with comprehension scores. These correlations are close to the results reported by Mackett-Stout and Dewar (1981) as well as Zwaga (1989).

Using Zwaga's approach to select a test criterion, the uncertainty range – based on the standard error of estimates of the regression equation – could be set to 16 above and below the ISO criterion of 66 per cent. Considering this range 17 symbols would be included for comprehension testing, compared to 27 based on the traditional ISO ranking procedure, correctly rejecting four variants and accepting six without testing. Out of this set of 45 symbols not one would be falsely rejected or accepted.

### 24.7 CONCLUSIONS

As Zwaga (1989) already noted and as has been confirmed in this study, replacing the ranking procedure by the comprehensibility estimation will considerably improve the efficiency of the ISO testing procedure. With the Appropriateness Class Assignment method proposed by Foster (1991) too much of the information available from the respondents is lost without any additional benefit. ISO has therefore decided that this test will not be a part of the future standard testing procedure and to use the Comprehensibility Estimation test instead.

### ACKNOWLEDGEMENTS

Parts of this work were supported by the Austrian Standards Institute.

## REFERENCES

BRUGGER, CH. (1987) *Evaluation of Public Information Symbols; ISO 1986 Test Series: Comprehension/Recognition Test, ISO TC 145/SC 1*, Document No. 167, Vienna.

EASTERBY, R. S. and GRAYDON, I. R. (1981a) *Evaluation of Public Information Symbols, ISO Tests: 1979/80 Series, Part I: Appropriateness Ranking Tests, AP Report 99*, Department of Applied Psychology. Birmingham: University of Aston.

EASTERBY, R. S. and GRAYDON, I. R. (1981b) *Evaluation of Public Information Symbols, ISO Tests: 1979/80 Series, Part II: Comprehension/Recognition Tests, AP Report 100*, Department of Applied Psychology. Birmingham: University of Aston.

EASTERBY, R. S. and ZWAGA, H. J. G. (1974) *The Evaluation of Public Information Symbols, AP Note 50*, Department of Applied Psychology. Birmingham: University of Aston.

EASTERBY, R. S. and ZWAGA, H. J. G. (1976) *Evaluation of Public Information Symbols; ISO Tests: 1975 Series, AP Report 60*, Department of Applied Psychology. Birmingham: University of Aston.

FOSTER, J. (1991) *Proposed Revised Method for Testing Public Information Symbols, ISO/TC 145/SC 1*, Document No. 220, Manchester.

ISO (1989) *Procedures for the Development and Testing of Public Information Symbols, ISO 9186*. Geneva: International Organization for Standardization.

MACKETT-STOUT, J. and DEWAR, R. (1981) Evaluation of symbolic public information signs. *Human Factors* **23**, 139–151.

ZWAGA, H. J. G. (1989) Comprehensibility estimates of public information symbols; their validity and use. In: *Proceedings of the Human Factors Annual Conference 1989*, pp. 979–983. Santa Monica, CA: Human Factors Society.

# CHAPTER TWENTY-FIVE

# The usability of symbols for health care facilities: the effects of culture, gender and age

WENDY T. OLMSTEAD

## 25.1 INTRODUCTION

A variety of public information symbols have been developed to support wayfinding in hospitals and health care facilities. For the most part the development and application of these symbols has taken place with a good deal of unfounded presumptions about their comprehensibility. In only a few instances was the usability of the symbols evaluated objectively.

As with any form of information presentation, signs should present a message clearly. Incorrectly interpreted signs can cause disorientation, frustration and stress (Weisman, 1981). There are several factors which may explain the misinterpretation of signs, such as the use of technical jargon, unusual graphic images, stress of the user and cultural differences between sender and receiver. Carpman *et al.* (1984) found that the occurrence of wayfinding difficulties was rated as the first of 15 causes of stress by patients and visitors of a hospital. The same authors also emphasize the point that the information presented on signs in hospitals has to take into account the background of a diverse audience: patients, visitors, medical staff and service personnel. The majority of sign users, however, are patients and visitors. A further complication is that for many, English is their second language. Therefore, the need for language independent routing information is great. To accommodate this need symbols are introduced on signs instead of text to facilitate wayfinding.

A wide variety of mostly pictorial symbols for similar or identical referents have been designed and are in use on hospital signs throughout the world (e.g. Dreyfuss,

1975). Whether patients and visitors correctly understand the meaning of all these symbols has rarely been examined. The objective of the study reported here has been to determine the usability (understandability) of information symbols intended for patients and visitors of hospitals, especially in relation to cultural, gender and age differences.

There is certainly a need for objective evaluation of these kind of symbols. Only a limited amount of research has been published on the comprehensibility of information symbols for health care facilities; only two relevant publications were located. Troedson (1979) conducted a matching test with 35 symbols (for an overview and description of the different test methods see Dewar, Chapter 23). Troedson found negligible effects of gender, age, country of origin (language) and professional training. Zwaga (1989), while defining a substitute for the ISO appropriateness ranking procedure (ISO, 1989), compared the estimated comprehensibility of hospital symbols with their comprehension level as measured by the ISO comprehension test. No data were reported on the effects of gender or age.

As a measure of the comprehensibility of symbols it was decided to use Zwaga's comprehensibility estimate in this study (see Section 25.2). This estimate is the median value of all estimates given to a symbol by the respondents in a sample. Zwaga's validation results show that a symbol with an estimation score of 87 per cent will meet the acceptance criterion in the ISO comprehension test of 66 per cent correct interpretations. Subsequent validation studies have confirmed this finding (Brugger, Chapter 24; Zwaga *et al.*, 1991). The measure seems particularly suited for this study, because it is easy, reliable and not costly to use. There is no need for large numbers of respondents, the test material is simple to make, and the processing of the data is quick and does not require special training.

## 25.2   METHOD OF INVESTIGATION

The set of symbols used in this study consisted of a selection of 41 symbols for seven referents (five to six symbols per referent) used on hospital signs (see Figure 25.1).

Comprehensibility estimates were determined to predict the understandability of the symbols. To determine this estimate for a symbol, the respondents in a sample are asked to estimate the percentage of the population they expect will understand the symbol. The median value of the estimated percentages is the comprehensibility estimate of the symbol. As mentioned in Section 25.1, other research has shown that symbols with an estimate of 87 per cent or higher would meet the comprehensibility score of 66 per cent defined in the ISO standard for public information symbols (ISO, 1989) for acceptable symbols.

Data were collected from adult patients and visitors of a medical facility in a large metropolitan area in the United States and in the People's Republic of China. The two samples comprised respectively 45 and 72 respondents. Table 25.1 presents an overview of the demographics of the samples.

| Referent | Function | Symbol variants |
|----------|----------|-----------------|
| Admissions | To check in | |
| Emergency room | To get immediate help | |
| Information | To ask questions | |
| Outpatient services | Treatment not requiring overnight stay | |
| Patient rooms | Where patients stay | |
| Pharmacy | To get medicine | |
| Waiting room | Where you wait | |

**Figure 25.1** Overview of the referents, a description of their function and the symbol variants used.

**Table 25.1** Demographics of the two samples

| | 18–24 years | | 25–64 years | | 65+ years | | |
|--------|------|--------|------|--------|------|--------|-------|
| Sample | Male | Female | Male | Female | Male | Female | Total |
| USA | 8 | 7 | 7 | 8 | 9 | 6 | 45 |
| China | 15 | 13 | 21 | 11 | 7 | 5 | 72 |

Only descriptive or simple non-parametric statistics were used to analyse the data. For this analysis a meaningful symbol is defined as a symbol with a median estimate of 87 per cent or higher. The data were analysed in four ways to answer the following questions.

- Which of the 41 symbols are acceptable for users of health care facilities, i.e., have a median comprehensibility estimate of 87 per cent or higher?
- Is there a gender effect?
- Is there an age effect?
- Are there differences between the estimates of the two samples?

**Table 25.2** Overview of the number of symbols meeting the acceptance criterion. The results are specified per age group, gender and over the whole sample

| | Age group | | | Gender | | |
|---|---|---|---|---|---|---|
| Sample | 18–24 | 25–64 | 65+ | Male | Female | Overall |
| USA | 9 | 13 | 4 | 4 | 14 | 11 |
| China | 9 | 9 | 5 | 6 | 10 | 8 |

### 25.3   RESULTS

### 25.3.1   Results of the American sample

The data show (Table 25.2) that 11 of the 41 symbols can be accepted as sufficiently meaningful; their median estimate is 87 per cent or higher. For one of the referents (Outpatient services) none of the symbols is acceptable. For each of three referents (Admissions, Emergency, Information) there is one acceptable symbol, for one referent (Patient rooms) there are two acceptable symbols, and for two referents (Pharmacy, Waiting room) there are three acceptable symbols. Overall, this means that acceptable symbols are available for six of the seven referents.

There is a clear gender difference in the results. Males rated only four of the symbols acceptable and females 14 ($\chi^2 = 5.76$, $p < 0.02$).

There is a significant effect of age on the estimation scores of the symbols ($\chi^2 = 5.93$, $p < 0.05$). The senior group (65 and older) and the middle group (25–64) clearly differ; the number of acceptable symbols is respectively four and 13. Perhaps the youngest group (18–24) with nine acceptable symbols, does worse than the middle group, and is better than the senior group, but the differences are not as distinct here as the difference between the senior and the middle group.

### 25.3.2   Results of the Chinese sample

The data show that eight of the 41symbols reach the acceptance criterion. There are no acceptable symbols for two of the seven referents (Outpatient services, Waiting room). There is one acceptable symbol for three of the referents (Admissions, Information, Pharmacy). There are two symbols for the referent 'Emergency room' and three symbols for 'Patient rooms'. Overall, there are acceptable symbols for five of the seven referents.

The males and females rate respectively six and ten symbols as acceptable. Statistically this difference is not significant, although there is a trend comparable to the results of the American sample. There are no significant differences ($\chi^2 = 1.71$) between the number of acceptable symbols for each of the three age groups (for the young, middle, and old group respectively, nine, nine, and five symbols). However, just as in the American sample, the senior group has the lowest score.

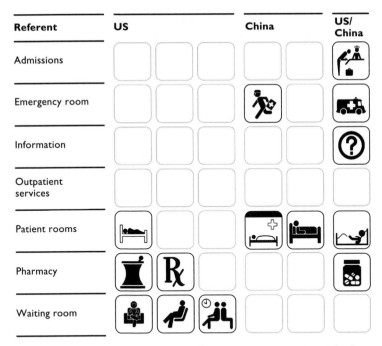

**Figure 25.2** The symbol variants meeting the acceptance criterion. The last column shows the symbols meeting the acceptance criterion in both samples.

### 25.3.3 Comparing the two samples

The results of the two samples show that five symbols for five referents meet the acceptance criterion in both samples (see Figure 25.2). There is no statistically significant difference between the samples with regard to the effects of gender and age on the number of acceptable symbols. The total number of acceptable symbols (11 versus eight) does not differ between the samples. Although not significant, the level of performance of the Chinese sample is, on the whole, below that of the American sample.

### 25.4 GENERAL CONCLUSIONS

The result, considering both cultures, that only five of the 41 symbols evaluated meet the acceptance criterion, certainly shows that the meaning of most of these public information symbols is not self-evident.

The results with regard to the effect of age indicate that the symbols are less well suited for the elderly than for younger age groups. Perhaps this is due to the increased use of pictoral representations in recent years. The higher performance of women in both samples might be related to the higher frequency with which women, compared to men, visit hospitals as primary caretakers of children and the elderly.

In general, the differences between the results of the two culturally different samples are small. The low number of acceptable symbols, providing only symbols for five of the seven referents, clearly shows that the meaning of most symbols is not self-evident. Evaluation of proposed public information symbols is clearly necessary.

## REFERENCES

CARPMAN, J. R, GRANT, M. A. and SIMMONS, D. A. (1984) *No More Mazes, Research about Design for Wayfinding in Hospitals*. Ann Arbor: University of Michigan.

DREYFUSS, H. (1975) *Symbol Sourcebook* (6th ed.). New York: McGraw-Hill.

ISO (1989) *Procedures for the Development and Testing of Public Information Symbols, ISO 9186*. Geneva: International Organization for Standardization.

TROEDSON, S. (1979) *Report on Test of Symbols for Signposting in Health Care Establishments*, Spri. Drn. Reg. No. 561/A72, Stockholm.

WEISMAN, G. D. (1981) Way-finding in the built environment. *Environment and Behavior* **13**, 189–204.

ZWAGA, H. J. G. (1989) Comprehensibility estimates of public information symbols: their validity and use. In: *Proceedings of the Human Factors Society 33rd Annual Meeting*, pp. 979–983. Santa Monica, CA: Human Factors Society.

ZWAGA, H. J. G., HOONHOUT, H. C. M. and VAN GEMERDEN, B. (1991) The systematic development of a set of pictographic symbols for warnings and product information. In: LOVESEY, E. J. (Ed.), *Contemporary Ergonomics 1991*, pp. 233–238. London: Taylor & Francis.

# Index